Official Autodesk Training Guide

Learning
Autodesk® Maya®
2009

Foundation

PUBLISHED BY: AUTODESK, INC.
111 MCLNNIS PARKWAY
SAN RAFAEL, CA 94903, USA

Acknowledgements

Art Direction
Michiel Schriever

Sr. Graphic Designer
Luke Pauw

Cover Image
Delgo is a production of Fathom Studios LP.
© Copyright 2008 Electric Eye Entertainment Corp. All rights reserved.

Copy Editor
Erica Fyvie

Technical Editor
Alan Harris

Video Producer
Peter Verboom

Project Manager
Lenni Rodrigues

Special thanks go out to:
Roark Andrade, Mariann Barsolo, Carmela Bourassa, Eugene Evon, Julie Fauteux, John Gross, Tonya Holder, Tim Wong, Laura Nixon, Richard Lane, Danielle Lamothe, Cory Mogk, Mary Ruijs, Carla Sharkey, Michael Stamler, Claire Tacon, Dave Lajoie, and Chris Vienneau.

This book would not have been possible without the support of Fathom Studios. We would like to extend a special thank you to Warren Grubb.

Primary Author

Marc-André Guindon | NeoReel

Marc-André Guindon is the founder of NeoReel Inc. (*www.NeoReel.com*), a Montreal-based production facility. He is an Autodesk® Maya® Master and an advanced user of Autodesk® MotionBuilder® software. Marc-André and NeoReel have partnered with Autodesk Inc. on several projects, including the Learning Maya series from version 6.0 to present. NeoReel was also the driving force behind the Maya Techniques™ DVDs, such as *How to Integrate Quadrupeds into a Production Pipeline* and *Maya and Alias MotionBuilder®*.

www.NeoReel.com

Marc-André has established complex pipelines and developed numerous plug-ins and tools, such as *Animation Layers for Maya* and *Visual MEL Studio*, for a variety of projects in both the film and game industries. His latest film projects include pre-visualization on *The Day the Earth Stood Still* (20th Century Fox), *G-Force* (Walt Disney Productions), *Journey 3D* (Walden Media), as well as visual effects for *Unearthed* (Ambush Entertainment), and *XXX: State of the Union* (Revolution Studios) among others. He also served in the game industry to integrate motion capture for *Prey* (2K Games) for the Xbox 360™, *Arena Football*™ (EA Sports) and the *Outlaw Game Series: Outlaw Volleyball*™, *Outlaw Golf*™, and *Outlaw Tennis*™ (Hypnotix).

Marc-André continues to seek challenges for himself, NeoReel, and his talented crew.

About *Delgo*

Fathom Studios founder, Marc F. Adler, has always had passion for filmmaking. Growing up, he and his cousin dreamed of forming "Farfelian Films," taking the title from their mothers' maiden name. "When my cousin lost a battle to cancer in 2000," Adler says, "I realized life's too short to wait to pursue your dreams." With fellow friend and co-director, Jason Maurer, they worked outside the Hollywood studio system to develop and produce an animated feature. Created using Autodesk® Maya® software, *Delgo* is already generating buzz and touring the world's most prestigious animation festivals.

Fathom Studios began as an offshoot of the successful interactive agency, Macquarium Intelligent Communications, which has been generating computer animations for clients since 1991. Although gearing up for *Delgo* was an ambitious undertaking, Adler explains that it wasn't such a big leap from prior work at Macquarium. "Ultimately, the two companies work together where Macquarium creates pixels for the computer screen and PDAs while Fathom creates pixels for the silver screen and television."

Featuring a talented cast that includes Academy-Award® winner Anne Bancroft, best actress winner for her role in *The Miracle Worker* (1962), and Jennifer Love Hewitt, *Delgo* is film for all ages about two very different cultures coming together and embracing each other for who they are. Influenced by fantasy adventure films such as *The Dark Crystal*, *Indiana Jones* and *The Neverending Story*, *Delgo* creates an immersive world for the audience. To develop the vibrant color palette, art directors Mark A.W. Jackson and Jang Chol Lee studied coral reefs and tropical fish as well as painters such as Roger Dean.

While the team was excited about the scope for imagination that the world of Jhamora provided, Adler admits it also presented certain challenges. "Designing a believable fantasy world is both an art and a science; particular attention was given to all facets of concept development to ensure that the world, while fantastical, was grounded in logic." Animation director, Warren Grubb agrees that it was difficult to gauge how test audiences would respond. "If you're making a palm tree, you know if it looks like a palm tree. We had this creature early on called 'the floating bunny' that could bound really lightly as though it was on the moon, due to internally generated gas, like a puffer fish with helium. People thought it was animated incorrectly because they weren't expecting a rabbit to do that and it made it hard for them to suspend their disbelief."

Since one of the people of Jhamora can fly, designers had to invent a realistic wing, eventually deciding on a hybrid of part-dragonfly, part-fairy. While the intricate wings of the Nohrin race provide visual interest, they were a challenge to animate and render, especially in crowds. "One of the biggest difficulties was getting them to Motion Blur well," Grubb says. "Especially in crowds, you couldn't just flap them on ones or twos, you had to flap them on sub-frames to get the motion to look correct." To create a more fluid motion, animators created a secondary motion Maya Embeded Language (MEL) script, which was much faster than animating by hand.

This ability to customize the software using MEL was one of the features that initially drew Fathom Studios to Maya. "The whole toolset is great," Grubb says, "but the real reason why we went with Maya is the ability to get in there and modify just about anything you want. Anytime we ran into a technical hurdle we could code around it." Technical director John Lytle concurs. "I don't think there was a problem we couldn't resolve using MEL and a couple of other scripting hacks here and there. We never felt backed into a corner we couldn't get out of—that was key for this film."

This attention to detail paid off in the action scenes in the film—in particular, a swordfight between two of the flying characters, played by Val Kilmer and Malcom McDowell. "It really feels like a throw-back Western style fight," Lytle says. "But it's got guys swordfighting, flying through the clouds and bouncing off rocks. It's a really beautiful sequence."

Many *Delgo* enthusiasts have already had a sneak peak at these scenes. Unlike most films, where audiences must wait for trailers to be released, work-in-progress animation files have been available on the *Delgo* website since 2001. There, fans can visit the Digital Dailies, an online message board where the studio's artists submit and comment on animation in production.

Although they were published online early on, the Digital Dailies first emerged as an in-house file management system. Since many of the staff work on flextime, it was important for project files to be externally accessible. To accommodate this, Lytle developed a web-based tracking system that was integrated into Maya software. "When the shot was done and ready for review," Lytle says, "the animator just hit a MEL button and it would run a script that would update a database. The directors could then talk about what they liked."

In many ways, making these files public took courage. "It offers a glimpse into the process of computer animation," Adler says, "the good and the bad, the mistakes and the triumphs." Although the team was excited to go public, there were concerns that it would give away too much of the story. "I never saw it that way," Grubb explains, "because I figured if someone was dedicated enough to learn the story from the dailies, they were going to go to the film anyway." In the end, their faith paid off, generating interest from schools as well as individuals. "It's definitely something we'd consider doing again."

Fathom Studios currently has five projects in the pipeline, including a four-minute test short. Just as the company has been expanding, Maya software has continued to evolve, a fact that Fathom Studios appreciates. "Autodesk keeps adding new features that keep us coming back," Grubbs says. "Things like the muscle system and Geometry Caching are exciting additions we're looking forward to using on upcoming projects." Lytle agrees, "It's kind of funny, some of the things we wrote a script for during *Delgo* are now part of the whole package."

Although independently producing a film of this caliber required patience, dedication and, as Adler puts it, "every resource possible," the greatest factor in the film's success may have been the team's passion for the project. "Anyone who worked on *Delgo* had to really love what they were doing," Grubb says. "It's a very challenging industry—you really do have to spend a lot of time and invest a lot of emotional energy in the job. At the end of the day, however, I always feel lucky to be working as an artist."

Table of Contents

Introduction

Autodesk® Maya® software is a character animation and visual effects system designed for professional artists. Built on a procedural architecture called the Dependency Graph, Maya software offers incredible power and flexibility for generating digital images of animated characters and scenes.

This tutorial book gives you hands-on experience with Maya software as you complete a series of project-based lessons. In the projects found in this book, you will model, animate, texture map, add visual effects, and render.

How to use this book

How you use *Learning Autodesk Maya 2009 | Foundation* will depend on your experience with computer graphics and 3D animation. This book moves at a fast pace and is designed to help you develop your 3D skills. If this is your first experience with 3D software, it is suggested that you read through each lesson and watch the accompanying demo files on DVD, which may help clarify the steps for you before you begin to work through the tutorial projects. If you are already familiar with Maya software or another 3D package, you might choose to look through the book's index to focus on those areas you would like to improve.

Updates to this book

In an effort to ensure your continued success with the lessons in this book, please visit our Web site for the latest updates available: *www.autodesk.com/learningtools-updates*

Windows and Macintosh

This book is written to cover Windows and Macintosh platforms. Graphics and text have been modified where applicable. You may notice that your screen varies slightly from the illustrations, depending on the platform you are using.

Things to watch for

Window focus may differ. For example, if you are on Windows, you have to click on the panel with your middle mouse button to make it active.

To select multiple attributes in Windows, use the **Ctrl** key. On Macintosh, use the **Command** key. To modify pivot position in Windows, use the **Insert** key. On Macintosh, use the **Home** key.

Autodesk packaging

This book can be used with either **Autodesk® Maya® Complete 2009**, **Autodesk® Maya® Unlimited 2009**, or the corresponding version of **Autodesk® Maya® Personal Learning Edition**, as the lessons included here focus on functionality shared among all three software packages.

As a bonus feature, this hands-on book will also introduce you to compositing in Autodesk® Toxik.

Learning Autodesk Maya 2009 DVD-ROM

The *Learning Autodesk Maya 2009* DVD-ROM contains several resources to accelerate your learning experience including:

- Learning Maya support files
- Instructor-led videos to guide you through the projects in the book
- Excerpt from the Fathom Studio Inc. feature film *Delgo*
- A link to a trial version of Autodesk Toxik software
- Autodesk Maya reference guides

Installing support files

Before beginning the lessons in this book, you will need to install the lesson support files. Copy the project directories found in the *support_files* folder on the DVD disc to the *Maya\projects* directory on your computer. Launch Maya software and set the project by going to **File** → **Project** → **Set...** and selecting the appropriate project.

Windows: *C:\Documents and Settings\username\My Documents\maya\projects*

Macintosh: *Macintosh HD:Users:username:Documents:maya:projects*

Understanding Maya

To understand Autodesk® Maya® software, it helps to understand how it works at a conceptual level. This introduction is designed to give you the story about Maya software. In other words, the focus of this introduction will be on how different Maya concepts are woven together to create an integrated workspace.

While this book teaches you how to model, animate and render, these concepts are taught with a particular focus on how the underlying architecture in Maya software supports the creation of animated sequences.

You will soon learn that Maya architecture can be explained by a single line—nodes with attributes that are connected. As you work through the book, the meaning of this statement will become clearer and you will learn to appreciate how the Maya interface lets you focus on the act of creation, while giving you access to the power inherent in the underlying architecture.

The user interface (UI)

The Maya user interface (UI) includes a number of tools, editors and controls. You can access these using the main menus or special context-sensitive marking menus. You can also use *shelves* to store important icons or hotkeys to speed up workflow. Maya software is designed to let you configure the UI as you see fit.

To work with objects, you can enter values using coordinate entry or you can use more interactive 3D manipulators. Manipulator handles let you edit your objects with a simple **click+drag**.

The Maya UI supports multiple levels of *undo* and *redo* and includes a drag-and-drop paradigm for accessing many parts of the workspace.

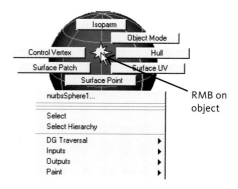

Marking menu

Working in 3D

In Maya software, you will build and animate objects in three dimensions. These dimensions are defined by the cardinal axes that are labeled as X, Y and Z. These represent the length (X), height (Y) and depth (Z) of your scene. These axes are represented by colors—red for X, green for Y and blue for Z.

The Maya default has the Y-axis pointing up (also referred to as *Y-up*).

As you position, scale and rotate your objects, these three axes will serve as your main points of reference. The center of this coordinate system is called the origin and has a value of 0, 0, 0.

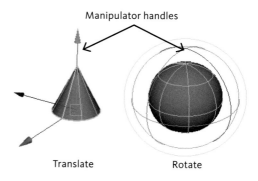

Maya manipulators

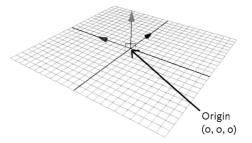

The cardinal axes

UV coordinate space

As you build surfaces in Maya software, they are created with their own coordinate space that is defined by U in one direction and V in another. You can use these coordinates when you are working with *curve-on-surface* objects or when you are positioning textures on a surface.

One corner of the surface acts as the origin of the system and all coordinates lie directly on the surface.

You can make surfaces *live* in order to work directly in the UV coordinate space. You will also encounter U and V attributes when you place textures onto surfaces.

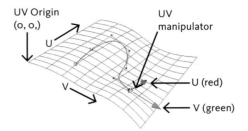

UV coordinates on a live surface

Views

In Maya software, you visualize your scenes using view panels that let you see into the 3D world.

Perspective views let you see your scene as if you were looking at it with your own eyes or through the lens of a camera.

Orthographic views are parallel to the scene and offer a more objective view. They focus on two axes at a time and are referred to as the *top*, *side*, and *front* views.

In many cases, you will require several views to help you define the proper location of your objects. An object's position that looks good in the top view may not make sense in a side view. Maya software lets you view multiple views at one time to help coordinate what you see.

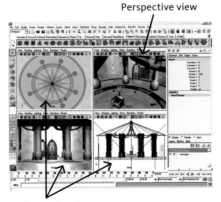

Orthographic and Perspective views

Cameras

To achieve a particular view, you look through a digital camera. An Orthographic camera defines the view using a parallel plane and a direction, while a Perspective camera uses an *eye point*, a *look at point* and a *focal length*.

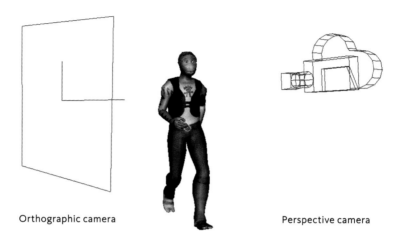

Orthographic camera   Perspective camera

Perspective and Orthographic cameras

Image planes

When you work with cameras, it is possible to attach special backdrop objects called *image planes* to the camera. An image plane can be placed onto the camera so that as the camera moves, the plane stays aligned.

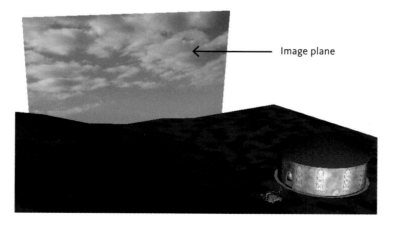

Image plane

Image plane attached to a camera

The image plane has several attributes that allow you to track and scale the image. These attributes can be animated to give the appearance that the plane is moving.

Image plane seen looking through the camera

The Dependency Graph

The Maya system architecture uses a procedural paradigm that lets you integrate traditional keyframe animation, inverse kinematics, dynamics and scripting into a node-based architecture that is called the **Dependency Graph**. As mentioned on the first page of this introduction, the Dependency Graph could be described as *nodes with attributes that are connected*. This node-based architecture gives Maya software its flexible procedural qualities.

Below is a diagram showing a primitive sphere's Dependency Graph. A procedural input node defines the shape of the sphere by connecting attributes on each node.

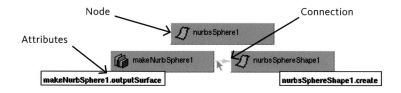

The Dependency Graph

> **Tip:** When multiple attributes are connected between two nodes, the connection is drawn with a thicker line. Hover your mouse cursor over the connection to see its content.

Nodes

Every element, whether it is a curve, surface, deformer, light, texture, expression, modeling operation or animation curve, is described by either a single node or a series of connected nodes.

A *node* is a generic object type. Different nodes are designed with specific attributes so that the node can accomplish a specific task. Nodes define all object types including geometry, shading and lighting.

Shown below are three typical node types as they appear on a primitive sphere:

Transform nodes contain positioning information for your objects. When you move, rotate or scale, this is the node you are affecting.

Shape nodes contain all the component information that represents the actual look of the sphere.

Input nodes represent options that drive the creation of your sphere's shape such as radius or endsweep.

The Maya UI presents these nodes to you in many ways. Below is an image of the Channel Box where you can edit and animate node attributes.

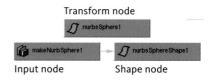

Node types on a sphere

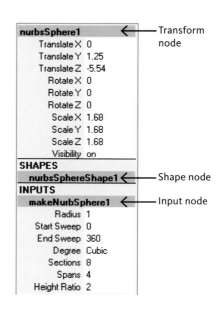

Channel Box

Attributes

Each node is defined by a series of attributes that relate to what the node is designed to accomplish. In the case of a transform node, *X Translate* is an attribute. In the case of a shader node, *Color Red* is an attribute. It is possible for you to assign values to the attributes. You can work with attributes in a number of UI windows including the *Attribute Editor*, the *Channel Box* and the *Spread Sheet Editor*.

Attribute Editor

One important feature is that you can animate virtually every attribute on any node. This helps give Maya software its animation power. You should note that attributes are also referred to as *channels*.

Connections

Nodes don't exist in isolation. A finished animation results when you begin making connections between attributes on different nodes. These connections are also known as *dependencies*. In modeling, these connections are sometimes referred to as *construction history*.

Most of these connections are created automatically by the Maya UI as a result of using commands or tools. If you desire, you can also build and edit these connections explicitly using the *Connection Editor*, by entering *MEL*™ (Maya Embedded Language) commands, or by writing MEL-based expressions.

Pivots

Transform nodes are all built with a special component known as the pivot point. Just like your arm pivots around your elbow, the pivot helps you rotate a transform node. By changing the location of the pivot point, you get different results.

Pivots are basically the stationary point from which you rotate or scale objects. When animating, you sometimes need to build hierarchies where one transform node rotates the object and a second transform node scales. Each node can have its own pivot location to help you get the effect you want.

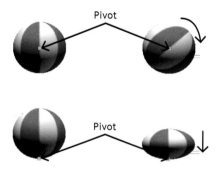

Rotation and scaling pivots

Hierarchies

When you are building scenes, you have learned that you can build dependency connections to link node attributes. When working with transform nodes or joint nodes, you can also build hierarchies, which create a different kind of relationship between your objects.

In a hierarchy, one transform node is *parented* to another. When Maya software works with these nodes, it looks first at the top node, or *root* node, then down the hierarchy. Therefore, motion from the upper nodes is transferred down into the lower nodes. In the diagram below, if the *group1* node is rotated, then the two lower nodes will rotate with it.
If the *nurbsCone* node is rotated, the upper nodes are not affected.

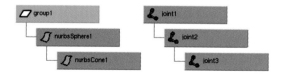

Object and joint hierarchy nodes

Joint hierarchies are used when you are building characters. When you create joints, the joint pivots act as limb joints while bones are drawn between them to help visualize the joint chain. By default, these hierarchies work just like object hierarchies. Rotating one node rotates all of the lower nodes at the same time.

You will learn more about joint hierarchies later in this introduction (see "Skeletons and Joints"), where you will also learn how *inverse kinematics* can reverse the flow of the hierarchy.

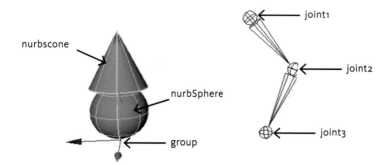

Object and joint hierarchies

MEL & Python scripting

MEL stands for Maya Embedded Language. In Maya software, every time you use a tool or open a window, you are using MEL. MEL can be used to execute simple commands, write expressions or build scripts that will extend Maya software's existing functionality. The Script Editor displays commands and feedback generated by scripts and tools. Simple MEL commands can be typed in the Command Line, while more complex MEL scripts can be typed in the Script Editor.

Python™ scripting is for programmers who would like to implement their tools using an alternate and popular scripting language. The implementation of Python scripting in Maya software provides the same access to native Maya commands as is provided through MEL. Note that only the built-in Maya commands are accessible through Python.

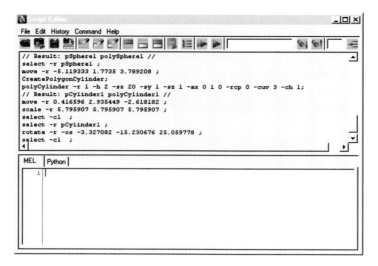

The Script Editor

Scripting is the perfect tool for technical directors who are looking to customize Maya software to suit the needs of a particular production environment. Animators can also use scripting to create simple macros that will help speed up more difficult or tedious workflows.

Animation

When you animate, you bring objects to life. There are several different ways in which you can animate your scenes and the characters who inhabit them.

Animation is generally measured using frames that mimic the frames you would find on a film reel. You can play these frames at different speeds to achieve an animated effect. By default, Maya software plays at 24 frames per second, or 24FPS.

Keyframe animation

The most familiar method of animating is called *keyframe animation*. Using this technique, you determine how you want the parts of your objects to look at a particular frame, then you save the important attributes as keys. After you set several keys, the animation can be played back with Maya software filling motion in-between the keys.

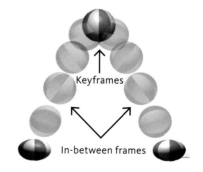

Keys and in-between frames

When keys are set on a particular attribute, the keyed values are stored in special nodes called *animation curve* nodes.

These curves are defined by the keys that map the value of the attribute against time. The following is an example of several animation curve nodes connected to a transformation node. One node is created for every attribute that is animated.

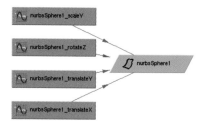

Dependency Graph showing curve nodes

Once you have a curve, you can begin to control the tangency at each key to tweak the motion in-between the main keys. You can make your objects speed up or slow down by editing the shape of these animation curves.

Generally, the slope of the graph curve tells you the speed of the motion. A steep slope in the curve means fast motion, while a flat curve equals no motion. Think of a skier going down a hill. Steep slopes increase speed while flatter sections slow things down.

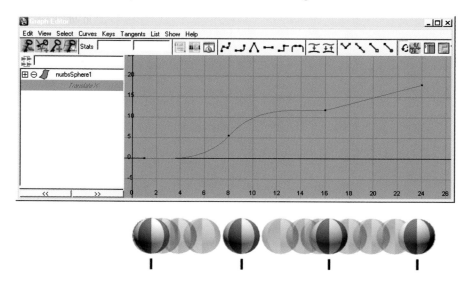

Graph Editor

Path animation

Path animation is already defined by its name. You can assign one or more objects so that they move along a path that has been drawn as a curve in 3D space. You can then use the shape of the curve and special path markers to edit and tweak the resulting motion.

Path animation

Non-linear animation

Non-linear animation is a way to layer and mix character animation sequences independently of time. You can layer and blend any type of keyed animation, including motion capture and path animation. This is accomplished through the Trax Editor.

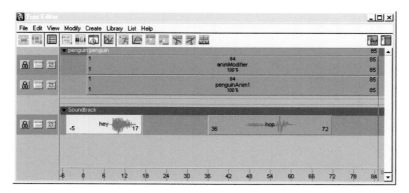

Trax Editor

Animation Layer Editor

The Animation Layer Editor lets you manipulate animation layers and change the way they blend together to create your result animation. Using this feature, you can modify a base animation easily. You can also isolate motions to specific layers, thus being able to modify the keyframed animation on its own.

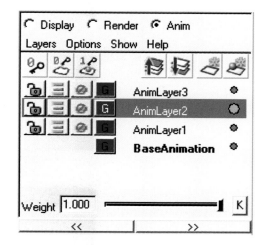

The Animation Layer Editor

Reactive animation

Reactive animation is a term used to describe animation in which one object's animation is based on the animation of another object.

An example of this technique would be moving gears when the rotation of one gear is linked to the rotation of other gears. You can set keys on the first gear and all the others will animate automatically. Later, when you want to edit or tweak the keys, only one object needs to be worked on and the others update reactively.

Diagram of animated gears

You can set up reactive animation using a number of tools including those outlined below:

Set Driven Key

This tool lets you interactively set up an attribute on one object to drive one or more attributes on another.

Expressions

Expressions are scripts that let you connect different attributes on different nodes.

Constraints

Constraints let you set-up an object to *point at*, *orient to*, or *look at* another object.

Connections

Attributes can be directly linked to another attribute using dependency node connections. You can create this kind of direct connection using the Connection Editor.

Dynamics

Another animation technique is *dynamics*. You can set up objects in your scene that animate based on physical effects such as collisions, gravity and wind. Different variables are *bounciness*, *friction* or *initial velocity*. When you play back the scene, you run a simulation to see how all the parts react to the variables.

This technique gives you natural motion that would be difficult to keyframe. You can use dynamics with rigid body objects, particles or soft body objects.

Rigid body objects are objects that don't deform. You can further edit the rigid body by setting it as either *active* or *passive*. Active bodies react to the dynamics, whereas passive bodies don't.

To simulate effects such as wind or gravity, you add *fields* to your dynamic objects.

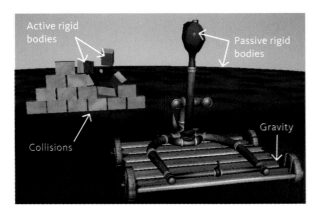

Rigid body simulation of catapult and wall colliding

Particles are tiny points that can be used to create effects such as smoke, fire or explosions. These points are emitted into the scene where they are also affected by the dynamic fields.

Particles

Soft bodies are surfaces that you deform during a simulation. To create a soft body, create an object and turn its points into particles. The particles react to the dynamic forces, which in turn deform the surface.

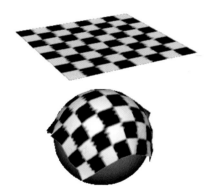

Soft bodies

Modeling

The objects you want to animate are usually built using either NURBS surfaces or polygonal meshes. Complementary to these two basic geometry types, subdivision surfaces (SubDs), mix the best features of both NURBS and polygons. Maya software offers you both of these geometry types so that you can choose the method best suited to your work.

NURBS curves

NURBS stands for *non-uniform rational b-spline* which is a technical term for a spline curve. By modeling with NURBS curves, you lay down control points and smooth geometry will be created using the points as guides.

Shown below is a typical NURBS curve with important parts labeled:

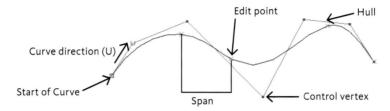

NURBS curve

These key components define important aspects of how a curve works. The flexibility and power of NURBS geometry comes from your ability to edit the shape of the geometry using these controls.

As your geometry becomes more complex, you may need more of these controls. For this reason, it is usually better to start out with simpler geometry so that you can more easily control the shape. If you need more complex geometry, then controls can be inserted later.

NURBS surfaces

Surfaces are defined using the same mathematics as curves, except now they're in two dimensions—U and V. You learned about this earlier when you learned about UV coordinate space.

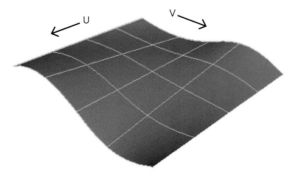

NURBS surface

Below are some of the component elements of a typical NURBS surface:

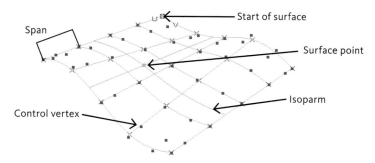

NURBS components

Complex shapes can be, in essence, sculpted using this surface type as you push and pull the controls to shape the surface.

Completed NURBS model

Polygons

Polygons are the most basic geometry type available. Whereas NURBS surfaces interpolate the shape of the geometry interactively, polygonal meshes draw the geometry directly to the control vertices.

Below are some of the components found on a polygonal mesh:

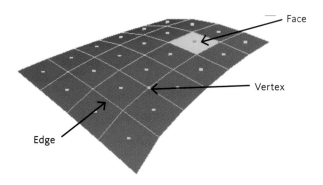

Polygon components

You can build up polymeshes by extruding, scaling and positioning polygonal facets to build shapes. You can then smooth the shape to get a more organic look for your model.

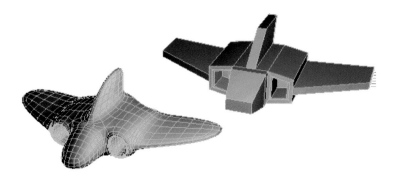

Polygonal model before and after smoothing

Construction history

When you create models, the various steps are recorded as dependency nodes that remain connected to your surface.

In the example below, a curve has been used to create a revolved surface. Maya software keeps the history by creating dependencies between the curve, a revolve node and the shape node. Edits made to the curve or the revolve node will update the final shape.

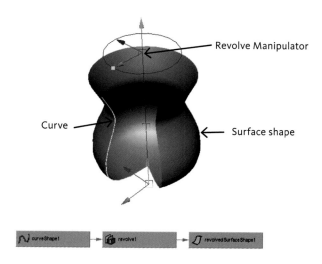

Revolve surface with dependencies

Many of these nodes come with special manipulators that make it easier to update the node attributes. In the case of the revolve, manipulators are available for the axis line and for the revolve's sweep angle.

It is possible to later delete history so that you are only working with the shape node. Don't forget though, that the dependency nodes have attributes that can be animated. Therefore, you lose some power if you delete history.

Deformations

Deformers are special object types that can be used to reshape other objects. By using deformers, you can model different shapes, or give animations more of a squash and stretch quality.

Deformers are a powerful Maya feature—they can even be layered for more subtle effects. You can also bind deformers into skeletons or affect them with soft body dynamics.

The following lists some basic deformer types available:

Lattices

Lattices are external frames that can be applied to your objects. If you then reshape the frame the object is deformed in response.

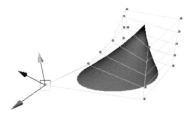

Lattice deformer

Sculpt objects

Sculpt objects lets you deform a surface by pushing it with the object. By animating the position of the sculpt object, you can achieve animated surface deformations.

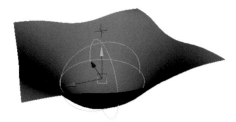

Sculpt object deformer

Clusters

Clusters are groups of CVs or lattice points that are built into a single set. The cluster is given its own pivot point and can be used to manipulate the clustered points. You can weight the CVs in a cluster for more control over a deformation.

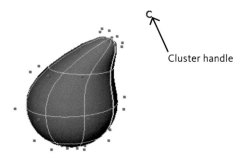

Cluster handle

Cluster deformer

Character animation

Character animation typically involves the animation of surfaces using skeleton joint chains and inverse kinematic handles to help drive the motion.

Skeletons and joints

As you have already learned, skeleton joint chains are actually hierarchies. A skeleton is made of joint nodes that are connected visually by bone icons. Binding geometry to these hierarchies lets you create surface deformations when the joints are rotated.

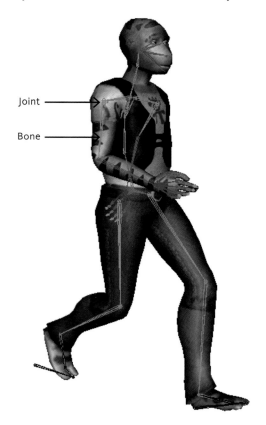

Joint

Bone

Joints and bones

Inverse kinematics

By default, joint hierarchies work like any other hierarchy—the rotation of one joint is transferred to the lower joint nodes. This is known as *forward kinematics*. While this method is powerful, it makes it hard to plant a character's feet or move a hand to control the arm.

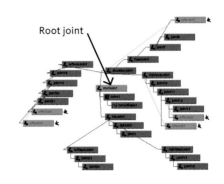

Root joint

Character joint hierarchy

Inverse kinematics lets you work with the hierarchy in the opposite direction. By placing an IK handle at the end of the joint chain, Maya software will solve all rotations within that joint chain. This is a lot quicker than animating every single joint in the hierarchy. There are three kinds of inverse kinematic solvers—the IK spline, the IK single chain, and the IK rotate plane.

Each of these solvers is designed to help you control the joint rotations with the use of an IK handle. As the IK handle is moved, the solver solves joint rotations that allow the end joint to properly move to the IK handle position.

The individual solvers have their own unique controls. Some of these are outlined below:

Single chain solver

The *single chain solver* provides a straightforward mechanism for posing and animating a chain.

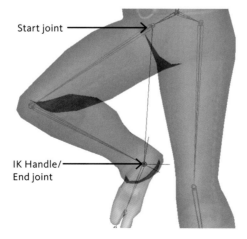

Start joint

IK Handle/
End joint

IK single chain solver

Rotate plane solver

The *rotate plane solver* gives you more control. With this solver, the plane that acts as the goal for all the joints can be moved by rotating the plane using a *twist attribute* or by moving the *pole vector handle*.

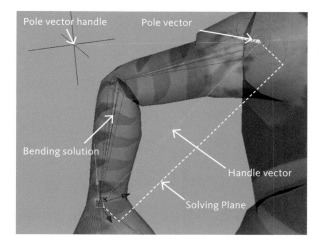

IK rotate plane solver

IK spline solver

The IK spline solver lets you control the chain using a spline curve. You can edit the CVs on the spline to influence the rotation of the joints in the chain.

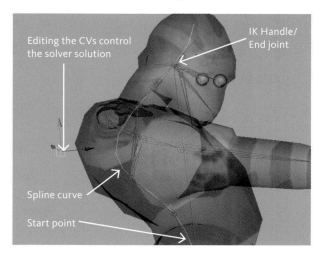

IK spline solver

Skinning your characters

Once you have a skeleton built, you can bind skin to the surfaces of your character so that they deform with the rotation of the joints. You can use either smooth skinning or rigid skinning. Smooth skinning uses weighted influences while rigid skinning does not.

Surface deformations

Flexors

In some cases, skinning a character does not yield realistic deformations in the character's joint areas. You can use flexors to add secondary level of deformations to help control the tucking and bulging of your character.

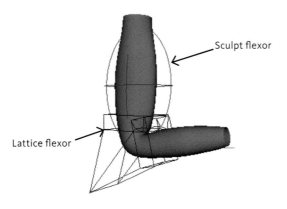

Flexors

Rendering

Once your characters are set up, you can apply color and texture, then render with realistic lighting.

Shading networks

Adding texture maps and other rendering nodes create shading networks. At the end of every shading network is a shading group node. This node has specific attributes such as displacement maps and mental ray for Maya ports, but more importantly, it contains a list of objects that are to be shaded by that network at render time. Without this node at the end of the network, the shader won't render.

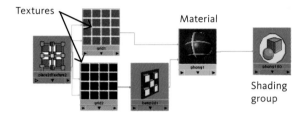

Shading group dependencies

You can think of a shading network as a bucket into which you place all the color, texture and material qualities that you want for your surface. Add a light or two and your effect is achieved.

Texture maps

To add detail to your shading groups, you can *texture map* different attributes. Some of these include bump, transparency and color.

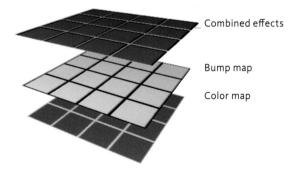

Texture map layers

Lighting

You can add light to your scenes using any number of lights. These lights let you add mood and atmosphere to a scene in much the same way as lighting is used by a photographer. You can preview your lights interactively as you model, or you can render to see the final effect.

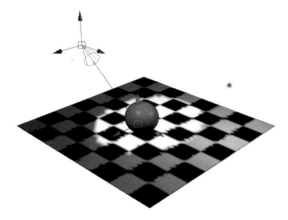

Light manipulator

Motion blur

When a real-life camera takes a shot of a moving object, the final image is often blurred. This *motion blur* adds to the animated look of a scene and can be simulated in Maya software. There are two types of motion blur—a 2 1/2 D solution and a 3D solution.

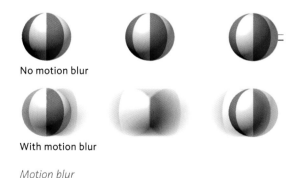

No motion blur

With motion blur

Motion blur

Hardware rendering

Hardware rendering uses the power of your graphics card to render an image. This is a quick way to render as the quality can be very good or it can be used to preview animations. You will need to use the hardware renderer to render most particle effects. These effects can be composited in later with software rendered images of your geometry.

Hardware rendering

A-buffer rendering

The Maya rendering architecture is a hybrid renderer. It uses an EAS (Exact Area Sampling) or A-buffer algorithm for primary visibility from the eye (camera), and then raytraces any secondary rays.

A-buffer rendering

Raytrace rendering

Raytracing lets you include reflections, refractions and raytrace shadows into your scenes. Only objects that have their raytrace options turned on will use this renderer. Raytracing is slower than the A-buffer algorithm and should only be used when necessary.

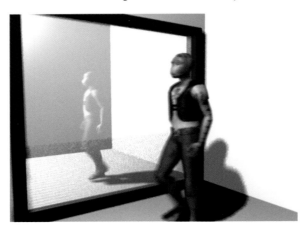

Raytrace rendering

Note: *Objects have raytracing turned On by default, but the renderer's raytracing is turned Off by default.*

How the renderer works

The Maya renderer works by looking through the camera at the scene. It then takes a section or tile and analyzes whether or not it can render that section. If it can, it will combine the information found in the shading group (geometry, lights and shading network) with the Render Settings information, and the whole tile is rendered.

As the renderer moves on to the next section, it again analyzes the situation. If it hits a tile where there is more information than it wants to handle at one time, it breaks down the tile into a smaller tile and renders.

When you use raytracing, each tile is first rendered with the A-buffer, then the renderer looks for items that require raytracing. If it finds any, it layers in the raytraced sections. When it finishes, you have your finished image, or if you are rendering an animation, a sequence of images.

Rendering of A-buffer tiles in progress

IPR

The Interactive Photorealistic Renderer gives you fast feedback for texturing and lighting updates without needing to re-render.

IPR rendering in progress

Conclusion

Now that you have a basic understanding of what Maya software is designed to do, it is time for you to start working with the system directly. The concepts outlined in this introduction will be clearer when you experience them firsthand.

Project 01

In Project One, you are going to learn the basics of object creation, along with the fundamentals of animation, shaders, and textures. This will give you the chance to explore the Maya workspace while building your scene.

You will start by creating a room similar to the throne room from the *Delgo* movie. You will then fill it with simple models in order to learn how to create, move, and modify objects. Then, you will explore the rudiments of hierarchies and animation by creating a simple door. After that, you will experiment with shaders and textures, which will allow you to render your scene.

These lessons offer you a good look at some of the key concepts and workflows that drive Autodesk® Maya® software. Once this project is finalized, you will have a better understanding of the Maya user interface and its various modules.

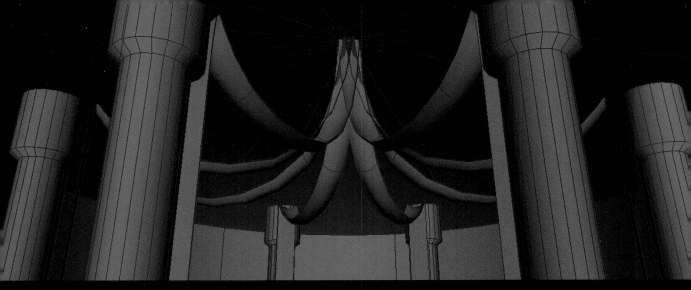

Primitives

This lesson teaches you how to build and transform primitives in 3D space in order to create a rudimentary environment, in which you will set-up some animation shown in this book. You will explore the Maya user interface (UI) as you learn how to build and develop your scene.

In this lesson, you will learn the following:

- How to set a new Maya project
- How to create primitive objects
- How to move objects in 3D space
- How to duplicate objects
- How to change the shape of objects
- How to delete polygonal faces
- How to use the Maya view tools
- How to change the display of your objects
- How to name your objects
- How to save your scene

Setting up Maya software

The first step is to install the Autodesk® Maya® software. Once that is done, you should copy the Learning Maya support files to your Maya *projects* directory. The support files are found in the *support_files* directory on the DVD-ROM included with this book.

In order to find your *projects* directory, you need to launch Maya software at least once so that it creates your user directory structure. Here is where the *projects* directory is typically located on your machine:

Windows: *Drive:\Documents and Settings\[username]\My Documents\maya\projects*

Mac OS X: *Users/[username]/Documents/maya/projects*

Note: *To avoid the Cannot Save Workspace error, ensure that the support files are not read-only after you copy them from the DVD-ROM.*

When Maya software is launched for the first time and you have other Maya versions installed, you will be asked if you want to copy your preferences or use the default preferences. In order to follow the course, you should be using default preferences. If you have been working with Maya software and have changed any of your user interface settings, you may want to delete or back-up your preferences in order to start with the default Maya configuration.

Creating a new project

Maya software uses a project directory to store and organize all of the files (scenes, images, materials, textures, etc.) related to a particular scene. When building a scene, you create and work with a variety of file types and formats. The project directory allows you to keep these different file types in their unique sub-directory locations within the project directory.

1   Launch Maya software

2   Set the project

To manage your files, you can set a project directory that contains sub-directories for different types of files that relate to your project.

- Go to the **File** menu and select **Project → Set...**

  A window opens that directs you to the Maya projects directory.

- **Open** the folder *support_files*.

- Click on the folder named *project1* to select it.

- Click on the **OK** button.

  This sets project1 as your current project.

- Go to the **File** menu and select **Project** → **Edit Current...**

  Make sure that the project directories are set-up as shown below. This ensures that Maya software is looking into the proper sub-directories when it opens up scene files.

Edit Project window

- Click the **Accept** button when done.

3 Make a new scene

- Select **File** → **New Scene**.

  This will create a new scene in the current directory when you save it.

Build the environment

Every scene you create in Maya software will most likely contain objects such as surfaces, deformers, skeleton joints, or particle emitters. For this scene, you will build a throne room, but first, you will need a large outdoor environment.

To start, you will build a ground plane surrounded by a large sky dome. These first objects will be a primitive polygonal plane and a primitive NURBS sphere. You can view the finished scene to get an idea of what you are about to create by opening the file called *o1-room_o1.ma*.

1 Launch Maya software

2 **Change menu sets**

There are five main menu sets in Maya software: *Animation, Polygons, Surfaces, Dynamics,* and *Rendering.* These menu sets are used to access related tool sets.

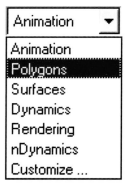

- From the drop-down menu at the left edge of the Status Line (Toolbar), select **Polygons**.

  As you change menu sets, the first six menu items and the Help menu item along the top of the viewport remain the same while the remaining menu items change to reflect the chosen menu set.

Menu set pop-up menu

3 **Create a polygonal plane**

A primitive plane will be used as a large ground plane on which you will build the house. It will be built using polygonal geometry. Throughout this lesson and in the next project, you will learn more about this geometry type.

- **Disable** the interactive creation mode of models (which is enabled by default), by selecting **Create → Polygon Primitives → Interactive Creation**.

- From the **Create** menu, select **Polygon Primitives → Plane**.

  A small plane is created at the origin.

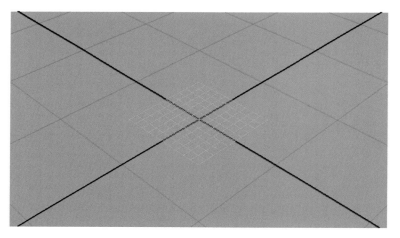

Perspective view of pPlane1

4 Change the plane's dimensions

The plane is a procedural model. This means that it is broken down into parts called *nodes*. One node contains its positioning information, one contains its shape information, and another contains input information that defines the plane's construction history using attributes such as width, height, and subdivisions. You can edit this Input node's attributes in the Channel Box in order to edit the plane's basic shape.

The Channel Box is found at the right side of the screen and lets you make changes to key attributes very easily.

> **Note:** *If your Channel Box is not along the right side of the screen, you can access it by selecting* **Display → UI Elements → Channel Box/Layer Editor.**

- From the Channel Box's **Inputs** section, click on *polyPlane1*.

  This will make several new attributes available for editing.

- Type **100** in the **Width** entry field and press the **Enter** key.

- Type **100** in the **Height** entry field and press the **Enter** key.

  Now the plane is very large in the Perspective view, but this is intended since you don't want to see any ground plane edges as you are working.

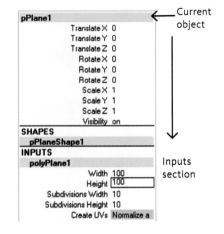

Channel Box

> **Note:** *Another method for increasing the size of the plane would be to scale it. In Maya, you can often achieve the same visual results using many different methods. Over time, you will begin to choose the techniques that best suit a particular situation.*

5 Rename the Plane node

You should rename the existing Transform node to make it easier to find later.

- Click on the *pPlane1* name at the top of the **Channel Box** to highlight it.

- **Type** the name *ground*, then press the **Enter** key.

Renaming the node in the Channel Box

6   **Create the sky**

You will now create another object to be used as a large sky dome.

- **Disable** the interactive creation mode of models by selecting **Create → NURBS Primitives → Interactive Creation**.
- Select **Create → NURBS Primitives → Sphere**

7   **Modify the sphere**

- With the *pSphere1* still selected, set the **Scale X, Y,** and **Z** in the **Channel Box** to **50**.

  The sphere should now be as big as the ground plane.

> **Note:**   *You can dolly out in the* **Perspective** *view to see the entire scene by holding the* **Alt** *key and* **click+dragging** *the* **RMB.**

- Click on the *makeNurbSphere1* node in the **Channel Box**.
- Set the following:

    End Sweep to **180**;

    Sections to **4**.

  By changing the sphere's input, the sphere automatically updates. The sphere is now half a sphere with fewer sections.

8   **Rotate the sphere**

- With the *pSphere1* still selected, set **Rotate X** and **Y** in the **Channel Box** to **-90 degrees**.

  Doing this rotates the sphere so it covers the ground plane. You now have a closed environment in which you will create the rest of the scene.

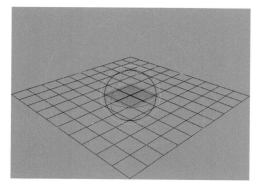

The ground plane with a sky dome

9   **Rename the sphere**

- Rename the *pSphere1* to *skydome*.

Viewing the scene

When you work in 3D space, it is important to see your work from different angles. The different view panels let you see your work from the front, top, side, and perspective views.

You can also use the view tools to change the views in order to reposition how you see your scene. In some cases, a view change is like panning a camera around a room, while in other cases a view change might be like rotating an object around in your hand to see all the sides. These view tools can be accessed using the **Alt** key in combination with various mouse buttons.

1   Edit the Perspective view

You can use the **Alt** key with your mouse buttons to tumble, track, and dolly in your Perspective view.

- Change your view using the following key combinations:

  Alt + LMB to tumble;

  Alt + MMB to track;

  Alt + LMB + MMB or **Alt + RMB** to dolly.

  You can also combine these with the **Ctrl** *key to create a bounding box dolly where the view adjusts based on a bounding box. This is useful when you want to dolly on a precise section of the view or quickly dolly out to get the general look of the scene.*

  Ctrl + Alt + LMB to box dolly.

  Click+drag from left to right to dolly in, and from right to left to dolly out.

  You can also undo and redo view changes using the following keys:

  To **undo** views use [;

  To **redo** views use] .

- Alter your Perspective window until it appears as shown below:

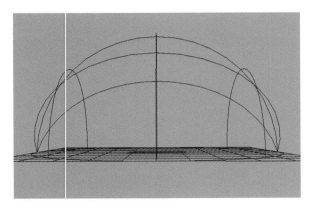

Changed Perspective view

2 **Four view panels**

By default, a single Perspective window is shown in the workspace. To see other views of the scene, you can change your panel layout.

- At the top of the Perspective view panel, go to the **Panels** menu and select **Saved Layouts → Four View**.

  You can now see the environment using three Orthographic views—top, side, and front—that show you the models from a projected view. You can also see them in a Perspective view that is more like the everyday 3D world. This multiple view setup is very useful when positioning objects in 3D space.

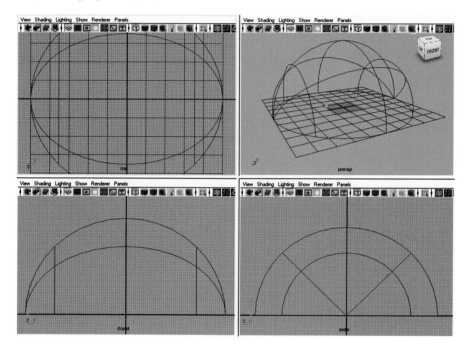

Four view panels

Tip: *Tapping the keyboard **spacebar** will switch from a single view panel to a four-view panel.*

3 Edit the view in the side view

Orthographic views use similar hotkeys, except that you cannot tumble by default in an Orthographic view.

- In the side view, change your view using the following key combinations:

  Alt + MMB to track;

  Alt + LMB + MMB or **Alt + RMB** to dolly.

- Keep working with the *Orthographic* views until they are set-up as shown:

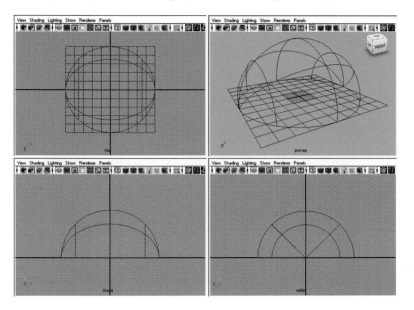

New Orthographic views

4 Frame Selected and Frame All

Another quick way to navigate in the different views is to use the **Frame Selected** or **Frame All** hotkeys for the active view.

- Select the *ground* plane.
- While in the *four-view* panels, move your mouse over a view.
- Press the **f** hotkey to frame the selected geometry in the view under your mouse.
- Press the **a** hotkey to frame everything visible in the view under your mouse cursor.
- Press the **Shift+a** hotkey to frame everything in all views at once.

Setting display options

The view panels let you interactively view your scene. By default, this means viewing your scene as a wireframe model. To better evaluate the form of your objects, you can activate hardware shading.

1   Turn on hardware shading

To help visualize your objects, you can use hardware shading to display a shaded view within any panel.

- From the Perspective view's **Shading** menu, select **Smooth Shade All**.

  This setting affects all of the objects within the current view panel.

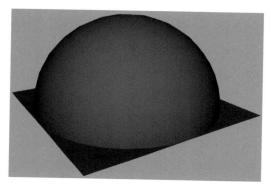

Smooth shaded view

Tip: *You can also turn on Smooth Shading by moving your cursor over the desired panel, clicking with your middle mouse button and pressing the 5 key. The 4 key can be used to return the panel to a wireframe view.*

2   Hide the grid

You can hide the world grid to simplify your view using one of two options:

- From the view panel's **Show** menu, select **Grid** to hide the grid for that view only.

  OR

- From the **Display** menu, deselect **Grid** to hide the grid for all views.

Moving inside the environment

In order to have the feeling of being inside the environment in the Perspective view, you need to move the Perspective camera inside the sky dome geometry. You will soon realize that even if you can see inside the sky dome, sometimes its geometry will appear in front of the camera while moving, thus hiding the interior. The following steps will prevent this from happening.

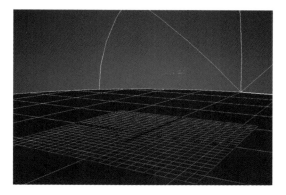

Perspective inside the environment

1 Change the sky's display

To simplify your scene interaction, there is a way of seeing inside the sky dome even when the camera is outside of it. To do so, you will have to change the way the geometry is displayed. The following actions are somewhat more advanced than what you will undertake in this project, but they will allow you to see inside the environment more easily.

- Select the *skydome*.

- Select **Window → Attribute Editor**.

  The Attribute Editor is similar to the Channel Box, but with many more accessible attributes.

- **Expand** the **Render Stats** section by clicking the small arrow button.

  This section controls how the models are displayed in the viewports and render time.

- **Disable** the **Double-Sided** attribute.

  This tells Maya to hide the sides of the geometry facing away from the camera.

- **Enable** the **Opposite** attribute.

  This tells Maya that you want the geometry to be displayed inside out.

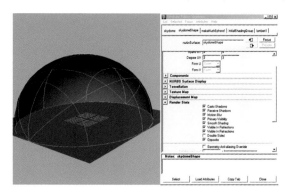

Seeing inside the environment

Create the room

Now that you have established a proper sky dome and ground plane, you will create the actual throne room. In this example, you will build the room from primitives.

1 **Create a polygonal cylinder**

Here, you will use the hotbox as an alternative method for accessing tools.

- Press and hold the **spacebar** anywhere over the interface to display the hotbox.

Hotbox access to menu items

- In the hotbox, select **Create** → **Polygon Primitives** → **Cylinder** → ❑.
- In the option window, set the **Normalize** option to **Off**.

  This option will make it easier for you to texture the floor later in the project.

- Click the **Create** button.

  A small cylinder is placed at the origin.

> **Tip:** You can access all functions in Maya using either the main menus or the hotbox. As you become more familiar with the hotbox, you can use the UI options found in the **Display** menu to turn off the panel menus and, therefore, reduce screen clutter.

2 **Rename the cylinder**

- Click on the *pCylinder1* node's name at the top of the **Channel Box** and type the name *floor*.

3 Scale the floor

You can now use the Scale Tool to resize the floor in the scene.

- Select the **Scale Tool** in the toolbox on the left of the interface, or press **r**.

 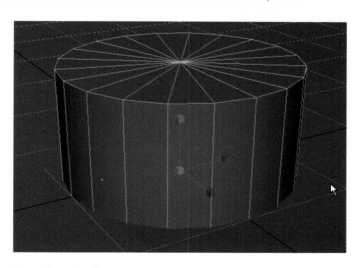

Toolbox   Manipulator handle

> **Tip:** The transform manipulator has three handles that let you constrain your motion along the X, Y, and Z-axes. These are labeled using red for the X-axis, green for the Y-axis, and blue for the Z-axis. The Y-axis points up by default, which means that Maya is "Y-up."

- **Click+drag** on the center manipulator handle to scale the floor along all axes to about **30 units**.

> **Note:** You will notice that as you are dragging the manipulators, the corresponding values are getting updated in the Channel Box.

- **Click+drag** on the green manipulator handle to scale down the floor along the Y-axis until the floor is just a little thicker than the ground plane.

  You will notice that the manipulator handle turns yellow to indicate that it is active.

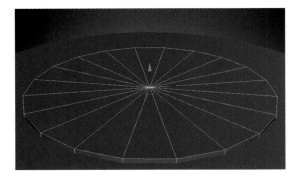

The floor geometry

> **Tip:** *Each cube at the end of the scale manipulator represents a different axis except for the central one which controls all three axes at the same time. You can also hold down **Ctrl** and **click+drag** on an axis to proportionally scale the two other **axes**.*

4 Create the wall

You will now use a NURBS cylinder to elevate the wall of the throne room.

- Select **Create → NURBS Primitives → Cylinder**.

- **Rename** the cylinder to *wall*.

- **Click+drag** on the center manipulator handle to scale the wall along all axes to about **28 units**.

- **Click+drag** on the green manipulator handle to scale down the wall along the Y-axis to about **10 units**.

- Select the **Move Tool** or press **w**, and then move the wall up on the Y-axis by about **10 units**.

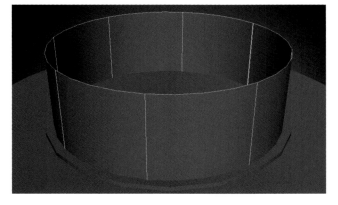

The wall geometry

5 Adjust NURBS smoothness

The display of NURBS surfaces in a viewport can be adjusted by increasing or decreasing its smoothness.

- Select the *wall*.
- From the main **Display** menu, select **NURBS**.
- Select any of the menu items between **Hull**, **Rough**, **Medium**, **Fine,** or **Custom NURBS Smoothness**.

  These settings will affect how selected NURBS objects are displayed in all view panels.

Tip: *A NURBS object can have its smoothness set differently in each viewport using the following hotkeys:*

      1—rough

      2—medium

      3—fine

6 Create columns

In order to create the large columns that will surround the throne room, you will use polygonal cylinders.

- Select **Create → Polygonal Primitives → Cylinder**.
- **Rename** the cylinder to *column*.
- **Click+drag** on the green manipulator handle to scale up the column along the Y-axis to about **10 units**.

Note: *Since you have been scaling everything so far from the origin, notice that your geometry is going through and underneath the ground plane.*

- Press the **w** hotkey to select the **Move Tool**.
- **Click+drag** on the green manipulator handle to move the column up on the Y-axis until the bottom of the column touches the top of the floor.
- With the *column* still selected, highlight the *polyCylinder2* node in the **Channel Box**.
- Set the following:

  Radius to **2**;

  Subdivisions Axis to **20**;

  Subdivisions Height to **5**;

  Subdivisions Caps to **1**.

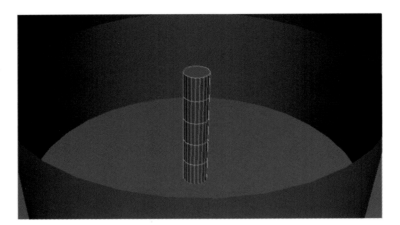

The column geometry

7   Repositioning the column

When moving an object in an Orthographic view, the move manipulator is limited to work in two axes. You can move an object in these two axes at once by dragging on the center of the manipulator or constraining the motion along a single axis using the handles.

- In the *top* view, **click+drag** on the square center of the move manipulator to move the *column* along both the X and Y-axes.

Note: *If you **click+drag** on the center of the manipulator in the Perspective view, you will notice that it doesn't move along any particular axis. It is actually moving along the camera's view plane.*

Tip: *Be sure to always refer to more than a single view to verify that the object is positioned properly.*

- Use the move manipulator to position the *column* in the background of the scene.

  By convention, a 3D scene is always facing at the positive Z-axis. This means that objects with greater Z-axis values will be closer to the foreground of the scene and objects with smaller Z-axis values will be further in the background.

Note: *You can refer to the view axis in the bottom left corner of the Perspective view to find the positive Z-axis.*

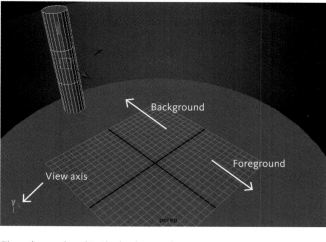

The column placed in the background

8 Change the shape of the column

At this time, the column is very round and could use some details. Now that you are familiar with transforming an object, you will learn how to modify the shape of an object.

- With the *column* selected, press the **f** hotkey to frame it in the view.
- In the Status Line located at the top of the interface, click the **Component Mode** button.

  *Working in this mode will display the components of the currently selected geometry. You can then select and transform the points defining a surface's shape. Polygon points are called **vertex/vertices** and NURBS points are called **control vertices** or **CVs**.*

The Component Mode button

- **Click+drag** around vertices in the viewport to select them.
- Select only the two rings of vertices in the middle of the column.

> **Tip:** When selecting components, hold down **Shift** to toggle the new selection, hold down **Ctrl** to deselect the new selection, and hold down **Ctrl+Shift** to add the new selection to the currently selected group of components.

- Select the **Scale Tool**, then hold down the **Ctrl** key, and **click+drag** on the Y-axis.

  Doing so will equally scale the vertices about the X and Z-axes.

- Let go of the **Ctrl** key, then **click+drag** on the Y-axis to make the central geometry as follows:

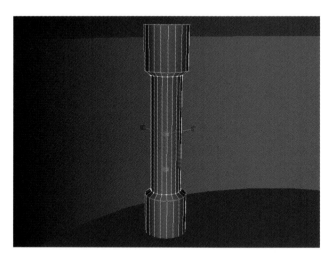

Shaped column

- Click on the **Object Mode** button in the **Status Line** to exit the Component mode.

Object mode

9 Make more columns

Instead of always starting from a default primitive object, you can duplicate an existing one, preserving its position and shape.

- Select your *column* and select **Edit → Duplicate**.

  When using the duplicate function, the new objects will be renamed to column1. Subsequent duplicates will be named column2, column3...

Tip: *You can use the **Ctrl+d** hotkey to duplicate the selected geometry without going into the menu each time.*

- **Duplicate** the columns **seven** times and place them all around the throne room from the *top* view.

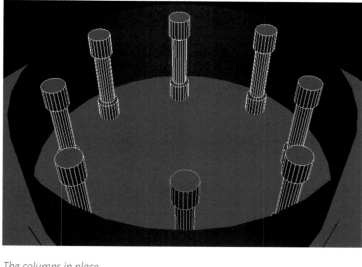

The columns in place

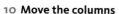

> **Tip:** If any pieces of geometry get in the way when you select and modify objects, you can temporarily hide them. To do so, select the geometry to hide, then select **Display → Hide → Hide Selection**. To show the last hidden objects, select **Display → Show → Show Last Hidden**. To show all hidden objects, select **Display → Show → All**.

10 Move the columns

In order to make it easier to select or move all the columns at once, you will now group them.

- Click on one *column* to select it, then hold down the **Shift** key and click the remaining columns one by one until they are selected.

- Press **Ctrl+g** to group them all together so you can move them all at once.

- **Rename** the group to *columns*.

- **Rotate** the new group to see the effect of grouping geometry.

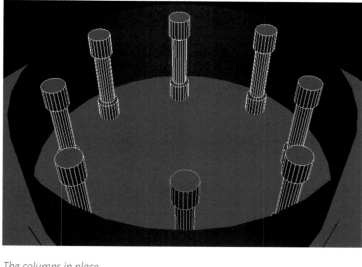

11 Save your work

- From the **File** menu, select **Save Scene As...**

- Enter the name *01-room_01.ma.*

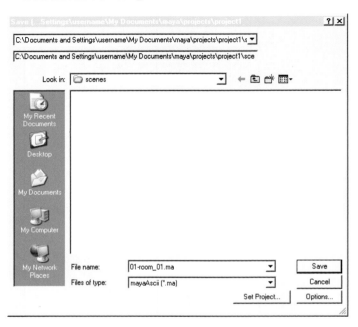

Windows Save As dialog box

- Click the **Save** button or press the **Enter** key.

More details

Now that you know how to place objects and interact with the Perspective view, you will add more details to the inner room by making a cathedral ceiling and adding decorative drapes coming down from it.

1 Create a roof

The last thing missing to complete the room is a roof.

- Select **Create → Polygon Primitives → Cone**.

- **Rename** the cone to *roof.*

- **Translate** the *roof* up on the Y-axis to about **25 units**.

- **Scale** the *roof* up on the Y-axis to about **6 units**.

- **Scale** up the *roof* in both the X and Z-axes by holding down the **Ctrl** key to about **30 units**.

2 Delete a polygonal face

If you move the Perspective camera inside the throne room, you will notice that the polygonal cone used to create the roof has a cap polygon covering its base. It would be nice to remove this face in order to get a cathedral ceiling.

- Select the *roof.*

- **RMB** on the *roof* to pop up its contextual radial menu, and select **Face**.

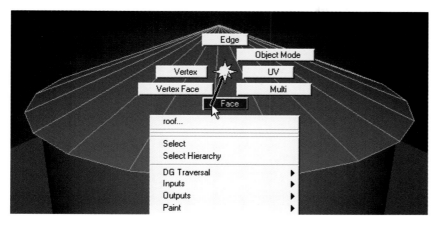

Polygon context menu

- Move the *Perspective* view to look at the ceiling from inside the room.

> **Tip:** *If you are having a hard time moving the perspective inside the room, you can use the same trick you used for the sky dome to have it not displayed as double-sided in the Attribute Editor.*

- Select the polygon by clicking on the **blue** square located in the center of the face.

  Notice that when you move your cursor over the face's center, the face turns red to specify the face that will be selected. Once selected, the face gets highlighted.

- Press the **Delete** key on your keyboard to delete the selected face.

- To exit the Component mode, **RMB** on the *roof* to pop up its contextual radial menu, and select **Object Mode**.

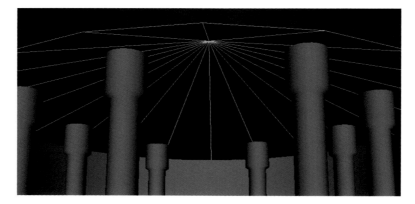

The cathedral ceiling

3   **Create a decorative drape**

Now that you are getting familiar with the Component mode, you will use this knowledge to create a decorative drape.

- Select **Create → NURBS Primitives → Plane**.
- **Rename** the plane to *drape*.
- In the **Channel Box**, highlight the *makeNurbPlane1* node and set **Patches V** to **4**.
- Set the following for the *drape* object:

   Rotate X to **90**;

   Scale X to **2**;

   Scale Z to **20**.

- **Move** the *drape* up so it interpenetrates with the center of the ceiling.

4   **Change the shape of the drape**

- Go into Component mode by pressing the **F8** hotkey.

   This is just another way of going into Component mode besides using the button in the Status Line or the contextual menu.

- From the *side* view, **click+drag** to select groups of CVs and tweak the shape of the drape as follows:

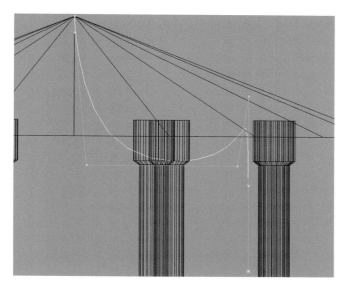

The shape of the drape

> **Tip:** *You might want to go into wireframe mode (hotkey 4), in order to select components more easily.*

- From the *Perspective* view, **RMB** on the drape and select **Hull**.

  Hulls define a continuous line of CVs. By selecting a hull, you can tweak the shape of several CVs at the same time.

- Click on the first hull along the length of the drape, then hold down the **Shift** key and select the opposite hull.

- Use the **Move Tool** to move the hulls up on their **Y-axis**.

  Doing so will give a nice dangling look to the drape.

5 Place the drape correctly

- Go back in **Object mode**.
- **Rotate** the *drape* so it is aligned with a *column*.
- **Tweak** the shape of the drape in Component mode as needed so the drape almost touches the column.

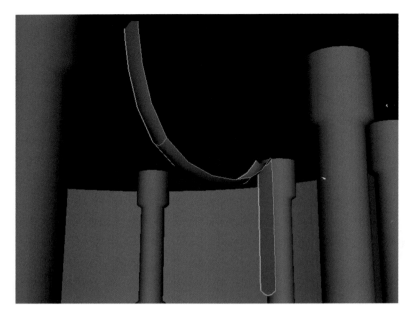

The final drape shape

6 Duplicate the drape

The Duplicate Tool has options that allow you to duplicate multiple copies of the same object, separated by a fixed translation or rotation value. For example, if you make one drape, you can make many other copies separated by 45 degrees, all in one easy step.

- With the *drape* selected, select **Edit → Duplicate Special → ❑**.
- Set the **Number of Copies** to **7**.

In order to determine the proper rotation axis, look at the view axis located at the bottom left corner of each view. If you want the copies to be created around the positive Y-axis, enter a value in the second field of the rotate vector. If you would like to create copies to be created along a translation axis, enter a value in the fields of the translate vector.

Axis letter points toward its positive values

- Set the second **Rotate** value to **45** and leave the others at **0**.
- Click the **Duplicate Special** button.

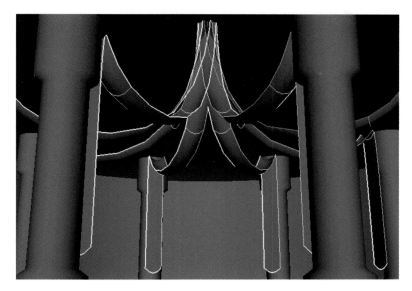

The duplicated drapes

- Select **Edit** → **Undo** or press **z** to undo the action and try again if the drape was not duplicated as expected.
- From the *top* view, make sure all the columns are properly placed behind each drape.

7 **Save your work**

- From the **File** menu, select **Save Scene As...**
- Enter the name *01-room_02.ma* and click the **Save** button.

  Make sure you save this file since you will be continuing with it in the next lesson.

> **Note:** *Throughout this book, you will be using the final saved file from one lesson as the start file for the next, unless specified otherwise. Save your work at the end of each lesson to make sure that you have the start file ready. Othewise, you can use the scene files from the support files.*

Conclusion

Congratulations! You have completed your first exercise using Maya software. You should now be able to easily navigate the different views and change the basic hardware display settings. You should also be confident in creating, duplicating, transforming, and renaming objects, along with using the translation, rotation, and scale manipulators. At this point you should also understand the difference between Component mode and Object mode. As well, be careful to save scene files.

In the next lesson, you will explore in greater depth how to model objects and details.

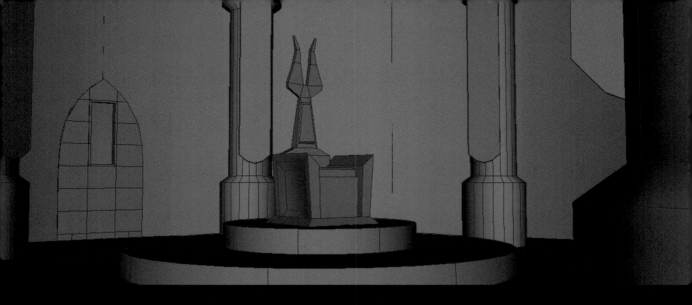

Adding Details

In this lesson, you will modify existing models to enhance the richness of the scene. You will first build steps using a special modeling technique called revolve. You will then create an opening in the wall for a door and then you will build the throne. This is a good time to experiment with basic modeling tools and concepts.

In this lesson, you will learn the following:

- How to open a scene
- How to draw and revolve a curve
- How to snap to grid
- How to project a curve onto a surface
- How to trim a surface
- How to extrude and move polygonal faces
- How to combine polygonal objects
- How to move the pivot of an object
- About construction history
- How to delete construction history

Working with a good file

Use the scene that you saved in the previous lesson or use the one provided in your *scenes* directory, *01-room_02.ma*.

1 Open a scene

There are several ways to open a scene in Autodesk® Maya® software. The following are three easy options:

- From the **File** menu, select **Open Scene**.

  OR

- Press **Ctrl+o**.

  OR

- Click on the **Open** button located in the top menu bar.

  File Open button

2 Find your scene

In the **File Open** dialog, if you cannot immediately locate *01-room_02.ma*, it might be because your project is not set correctly or that Maya did not direct you into the *scenes* directory.

- At the top of the dialog, if the path is not pointing to the project created in the last lesson, click the **Set Project...** button at the bottom of the window and browse to find the correct project directory. When you find it, click **OK**.

*When you open a scene, it should now automatically take you to your current project's scenes directory. If it doesn't, open the combo box located at the top of the dialog in Windows and near the bottom of the dialog in Mac OS X and select **Current scenes**.*

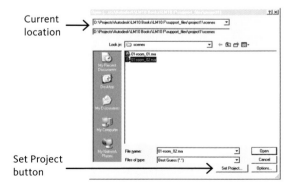

File Open dialog

- Select *01-room_02.ma* and click **Open**.

3 Save Scene As

Since you will be modifying this scene, it is a good idea to save this file under a new name right away. Doing so will allow you to keep a copy of the previous lesson in case you would like to start this lesson over.

- Select **File → Save Scene As...**.
- Type *02-addingDetails_01* in the **File name** field.
- Select *MayaASCII (*.ma)* in the **Files of type** field.

    Maya software can save its files in two different types of formats:

    Maya ASCII (.ma) saves your scene into a text file which is editable in a Text Editor. Though this format takes up more space on your drive, it is possible to review and modify its content without opening it in Maya. Experienced users find this very useful.

    Maya Binary (.mb) saves your scene into a binary file which is compiled into computer language. This format is faster to save and load, and takes up less space on your drive.

Stairs

In this exercise, you will use a different approach to create geometry that will introduce several new tools. Instead of starting from a primitive to create a set of stairs, you will draw a profile curve, which will then be revolved to create a round staircase.

1 Draw a curve

The first step for modeling the stairs is to draw a profile curve.

- Tap the **spacebar** to go into the *four-view* panel, and then tap it again with the mouse cursor placed over the *front* view.
- Select **Show → None** from the view's menu, then select **Show → NURBS Curves**.

    Doing so will clean the viewport so you can concentrate on your curve modeling.

- Select **Create → EP Curve Tool → ❑**.
- In the tool options, set **Curve** degree to **1 Linear**.

    By doing so, the curve will use linear interpolation between each point.

- Click the **Close** button.
- Hold down **x** to **Snap to Grid** and draw your first point on the thicker **Y-axis** grid line.

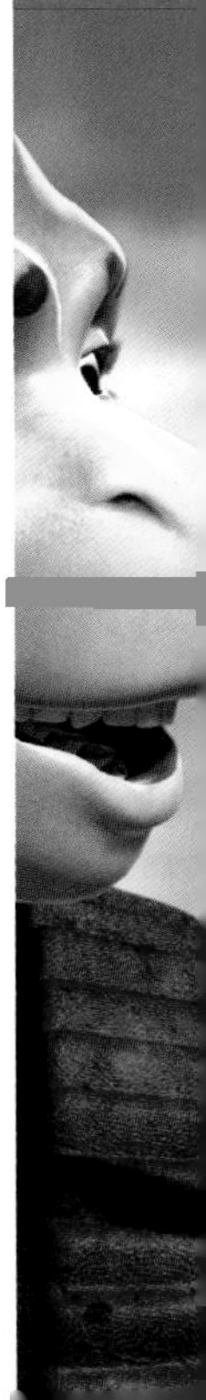

- Draw the following curve while still holding down the **x** hotkey:

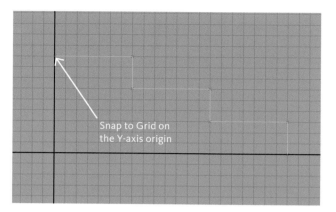

Snap to Grid on the Y-axis origin

The stairs' profile curve

 Tip: *You can press the Delete key to delete the last drawn curve point.*

- Hit **Enter** to complete the curve.
- Press **F11** to go into **Component mode** and fine-tune the curve's shape.
- Press **F8** to go into **Object mode**.

2   Revolve the stairs

- Go back into the *Perspective* view.
- Press **F4** to select the **Surfaces** menu set.
- With the profile curve selected, select **Surfaces → Revolve**.

The revolved stairs

- **Rename** the new geometry to *stairs*.

3 Construction history

Many tools in Maya create hidden nodes called construction history that are present in the scene. For instance, because of the construction history, you can still tweak the shape of the stairs by modifying the profile curve. Construction history nodes are also accessible through the Inputs section of the Channel Box. Changing nodes involved in the construction history will allow you to tweak action taken, without undoing and losing all of your work.

> **Note:** *Construction history will be discussed in greater depth in Lesson o6.*

- With the *stairs* selected, highlight the *revolve1* nodes in the **Inputs** section of the **Channel Box**.
- Try changing attribute values to see its effect on the geometry.
- Select the *profile* curve in the *front* view.
- Try to change the shape of the original curve to see its effect on the geometry.
- **Scale** down the original profile curve so the stairs have proper sizing in the room.

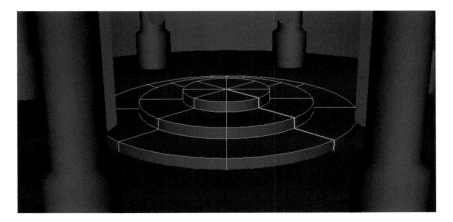

The scaled stairs

> **Note:** *Construction history can be very handy, but it can also lead to unexpected results, especially with object topology changes. You will see how to delete the construction history later in this lesson.*

Doors

You will now learn how to project a curve on a NURBS surface in order to trim it and create an opening that will accommodate a door.

1   Draw a door curve

- Select **Create → EP Curve Tool → ❑**.
- In the tool options, set **Curve** degree to **3 Cubic**.

  By doing so, the curve will use smooth interpolation between each point.

- Click the **Close** button.
- In the *front* view, draw a symmetrical curve centered on the **Y-axis** as follows:

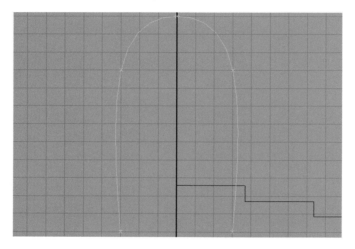

The door curve

- **Tweak** the positioning of the curve's CVs as desired by going into Component mode.

2   Close the curve

In order for the subsequent step to work, you need the door opening curve to be closed. This means that its start and end points need to be at the same location. One easy way of doing this automatically is by using the **Open/Close Curve Tool**.

- With your curve selected, select **Edit Curves → Open/Close Curve**.

The closed curve

3 Project the curve

Now you will project the curve on the wall surface, which will allow you to trim a hole.

- Still from the *front* view, select **Show** → **All**.
- Select the *wall* surface, then **Shift-select** the door curve.
- Select **Edit NURBS** → **Project Curve on Surface**.

  In the Perspective view, notice how the curve is projected on both sides of the wall surface.

> **Note:** *You can project a curve only on NURBS surfaces. When projecting a curve on a surface, the tool takes the active view to project the curve about.*

4 Trim a surface

Now that you have curves on the wall surface, you can trim it in order to create holes.

- Select the *wall* surface.
- Select **Edit NURBS** → **Trim Tool**.

  Doing so will change the display of the surface. You can pick directly in the viewport which sections of the surface you want to keep.

- Click in the viewport on the wall section.

  The section to keep will be highlighted with white lines while the sections to be discarded will be highlighted with hashed white lines.

Tip: *When you are not sure about the usage of a tool, it helps to look at the Help Line located at the very bottom of the Maya interface.*

- Press **Enter** to confirm your choice.

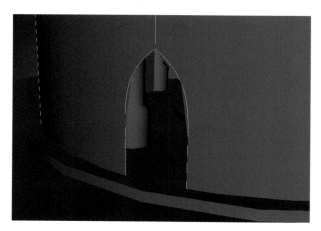

The door opening

Note: *Trimmed surfaces might not be displayed properly in the viewport but will render correctly. In order to see a better representation of the geometry in the viewport, select* **Display** → **NURBS** → **Custom Smoothness** → ❑ *and then increase the* **Shaded Surface div per span** *attribute.*

5 Create the door

Now that you have an opening for the door, you can create a door to go with it. There are several ways to create that kind of geometry, but the following will have you experiment with several tools.

- Select the original door curve located in the middle of the room.
- Select **Surfaces** → **Planar** → ❑.
- In the option window, set **Output geometry** to **Polygons** and **Type** to **Quads**.
- Click the **Planar Trim** button.

   Doing so will create a polygonal object from the door profile curve.

- Go back into Object mode and **rename** the new object to *door*.

6 Extrude polygonal faces

In this step, you will add thickness to the door since it is now totally flat. Extruding polygons is a very common action. To do an extrusion, you first need to pick polygonal face components, and then execute the tool.

- With the *door* selected, press the **f** hotkey to frame it in the view.
- With the *door* still selected, press the **F11** hotkey to go into Component mode with the polygonal faces enabled.

Tip: There are several hotkeys for going into Component and Object modes. The more you use Maya software, the better you will know the difference between these modes. The polygon-related hotkeys are listed here:

    F8 – Toggle between Object mode and the last Component mode
    F9 – Display vertices
    F10 – Display edges
    F11 – Display faces
    F12 – Display UVs

- **Click+drag** around the entire door to select all of its faces.
- Switch to the **Polygons** menu set by pressing **F3**.
- Toggle to **On** the **Edit Mesh → Keep Faces Together** option.

    This option will make sure that all the selected faces are extruded together.

Note: You will experiment more with the **Keep Faces Together** option in Lesson 07.

- Select **Edit Mesh → Extrude**.
- Press the **w** hotkey to select the **Move Tool**.
- **Translate** the new faces on the **Z-axis** to give thickness to the door.

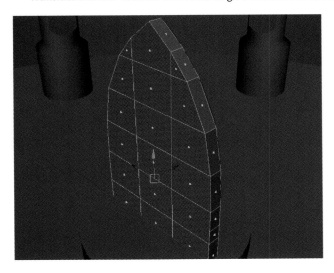

The door geometry

7 Extrude a window

- While in wireframe mode (**4** hotkey), select the appropriate faces to create a window in the door.

> **Tip:**   You can also **click+drag** *around face centers to select faces. Combine this action with the* **Shift** *key to toggle, the* **Ctrl** *key to deselect, or the* **Shift+Ctrl** *keys to add faces to the current selection.*

- Go back into shaded mode (**5** hotkey), and select **Edit Mesh** → **Extrude**.

  Notice a useful all-in-one manipulator displayed at the selection. This manipulator has all translation, rotation, and scale manipulators integrated.

  Single click on an arrow to display the translation manipulator.

  Single click on the outer circle to display the rotation manipulator.

  Single click on a square to display the scale manipulator.

  Toggle between local and global transformation by clicking on the round icon.

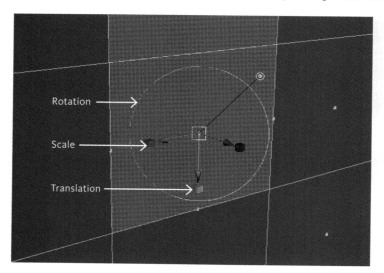

The all-in-one manipulator

- **Click+drag** the **blue** arrow manipulator to translate the face slightly outward to create a small border.
- Select **Edit Mesh** → **Extrude** again.

Tip: *You can invoke the last command used (Extrude) by pressing the **g** hotkey rather than always going back into the menus.*

- **LMB** on a square of the manipulator to enable its scale function.
- **LMB+drag** on the central square to scale down the extruded face.
- **LMB** on an arrow of the manipulator to use the translate function.

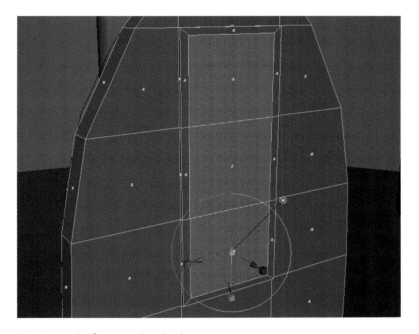

Manipulate the face to make a border

- Select **Edit Mesh** → **Extrude** again.
- **LMB** the round icon on the manipulator to change to global transformations.
- **Scale** down the faces on the **Z-axis** so the faces interpenetrate slightly.
- **Delete** the selected faces.

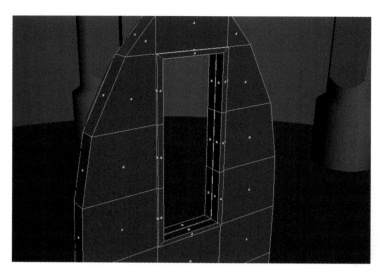

Door with a window opening

- Press **F8** to return to Object mode.

8 Place the door

- Select the *door* and translate it to one of the wall openings.
- **Duplicate** the *door* by pressing **Ctrl+d** and move it to the second door opening.

9 Save your scene

- **Save** your scene as *02-addingDetails_01.ma*.

Throne

Now that you have learned several ways of creating and modifying geometry, you should take some time to experiment and create a throne of your own. Following are some general guidelines, but feel free to experiment.

1 Create the seat

The seat of the throne can be quite simple and made of only polygonal cubes.

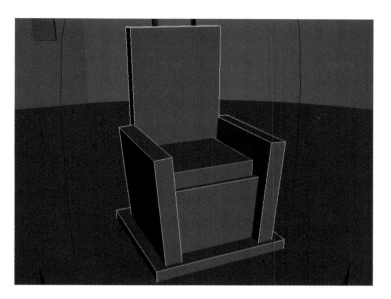

A throne made out only of cubes

2 Tweak the shape of the throne

You can now use the existing geometry to refine your throne. To do so, tweak the positioning of vertices and extrude faces at will.

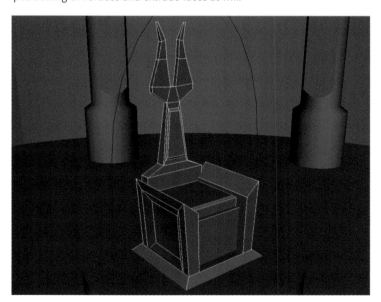

The modified throne

3   Combine polygonal objects

You might come across situations where you would like multiple polygonal objects to be treated as one single object. The **Combine** command will do that for you, so you will use it to combine the throne pieces together.

> **Note:** *Keep in mind that combined objects can no longer be individually moved. If individual objects need to move, group the objects instead.*

- Select all the throne pieces.
- Select **Mesh** → **Combine**.

  The throne is now combined into a single object.

- **Rename** the combined geometry to *throne*.

4   Center pivot

Notice that when objects are combined together, the pivot of the new object is placed at the center of the world. There are different ways of placing the object's pivot at a better location.

- With the *throne* selected, select the **Move Tool** by pressing **w**.
- Zoom out and notice where the object's pivot is located.
- Press the **Insert** key on your keyboard (**Home** on Macintosh).

  Doing so changes the current manipulator to the **Move Pivot Tool***.*

- Using the different axes on the manipulator, place the pivot at the desired location.
- Press the **Insert** key again to recover the default manipulator.

  OR

- Select **Modify** → **Center Pivot**.

  Using this command automatically places the pivot at the center of its object.

5   Delete construction history

Construction history is always kept when doing certain operations. This history is sometimes not wanted as it increases file size and loading time. You will now delete the construction history from your scene.

- Select the *door* object.
- To delete the construction history from the selected models, select **Edit** → **Delete by type** → **History**.

  The construction history is now gone from the Inputs section of the Channel Box.

- To delete all the history in the scene, select **Edit** → **Delete All by type** → **History**.

> **Tip:** *Be careful when deleting an entire scene's history since history is sometimes required. For instance, character deformations are done via history. To delete only construction history, use* **Edit → Delete All by type → Non-Deformer History**.

6 Save your scene

- **Save** your scene as *02-addingDetails_02.ma*.

Conclusion

You have begun to develop skills that you will use throughout your work with Maya. Both polygonal and NURBS modeling are entire subjects on their own. You will get to do more in-depth modeling in the next projects, but for now, you will continue experiencing different general Maya topics.

In the next lesson, you will bring colors into your scene by assigning shaders and textures to your objects.

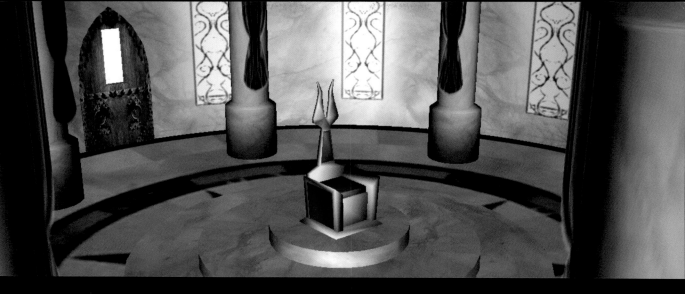

Shaders and Textures

Now that you have created an environment, you are ready to add colors and render your scene. The rendering process involves the preparation of materials and textures for objects.

In this lesson, you will learn the following:

- How to work with a menu-less UI
- How to work with the Hypershade
- How to create shading groups
- About procedural textures
- How to load file textures
- About the alpha channel
- About texture placement
- How to assign shaders to objects and faces
- About hard and soft normals
- How to render a single frame

Hiding the general UI

In the last two lessons, you used menus, numeric input fields, and other UI elements to work with your scene. In this lesson, you will hide most of the user interface and rely more on the hotbox and other hotkeys to access the UI without actually seeing it onscreen.

1 Scene file

- Continue using the file you created from the last lesson or open *02-addingDetails_02.ma* from the *support_files/scenes* directory.

2 Turn off all menus

- If you are in the *four-view* panel layout, position your cursor over the *Perspective* view panel, then tap the **spacebar** quickly to pop up this panel to full screen.

- Press and hold on the **spacebar** to open the hotbox.

> **Tip:** *Tapping the spacebar can be used to toggle between window panes and holding down the spacebar can bring up the hotbox.*

- Click on **Hotbox Controls**.

- From the **marking menu**, go down to **Window Options** and set the following:

  Show Main Menubar to **Off** (Windows only);

  Show Pane Menubars to **Off**.

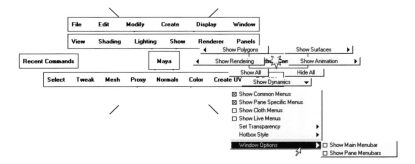

Marking menu

> Now the various menus are hidden and you must rely on the hotbox to access tools.

3 Turn off all the workspace options

- From the **hotbox**, select **Display** → **UI Elements** → **Hide All UI Elements**.

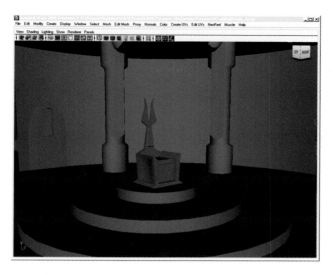

Simplified UI

> You now have a much larger working area that will let you focus more on your work.

> **Tip:** You can also press the **Ctrl+Spacebar** hotkey to toggle between hiding all UI elements and restoring them.

4 Change the panel organization

- Press and hold on the **spacebar** to evoke the hotbox.
- Click in the area above all the menus to apply the north marking menu.
- Select **Hypershade/Render/Persp** from this marking menu.

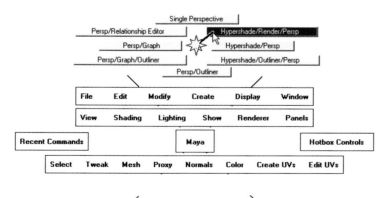

Hypershade/Render/Persp layout

Tip: *Each of the four quadrants surrounding the hotbox and the hotbox's center all contain their own marking menu sets. You can edit the contents of these menus using* **Window → Settings/Preferences → Marking Menu Editor.**

This saved layout puts a Hypershade panel above a Perspective panel and a Render View panel.

The Hypershade is where you will build shading networks, and the Render View is where you will test the results in your scene.

Tip: **Click+drag** *the pane divisions to change the width/height of the different windows in the layout.*

5 **Open the Attribute Editor**

• From the **hotbox**, select **Display → UI Elements → Attribute Editor**.

Now you also have an Attribute Editor panel on the right side of the workspace. This will make it easy to update shading network attributes.

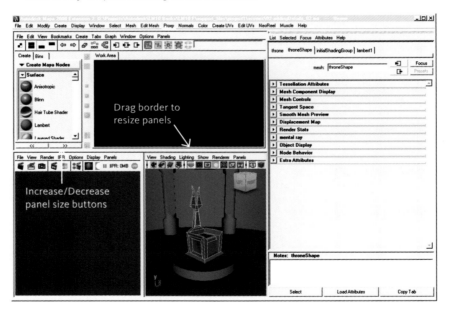

New UI layout

Hotkeys

When working with a minimal UI, you will rely on the hotbox and hotkeys for your work. The following is a list of relevant hotkeys that you may need to use as you work:

spacebar	Hotbox/window popping
Ctrl + a	Show/hide Attribute Editor
f	Frame selected
a	Frame all
q	Pick Tool
w	Move Tool
e	Rotate Tool
r	Scale Tool
t	Show Manipulator Tool
y	Invoke last tool
g	Repeat last command
Alt + v	Start/stop playback
Alt + Shift + v	Go to first frame

> **Note:** *For a complete listing of available hotkeys, go to* **Window → Settings/ Preferences → Hotkey Editor**.

Shading networks

To prepare the environment, room, and objects for rendering, you need to add color and texture. This is accomplished using *shading networks* that bring together material qualities, textures, lights, and geometry to define the desired look.

The Hypershade

The Hypershade panel is made up of three sections—the Create bar, the Hypershade tabs, and the work area. The Create bar allows you to create any rendering nodes required for your scene. The Hypershade tabs list all nodes that make up the current scene, while the work area allows you to look more closely and alter any part of the shading network's graph.

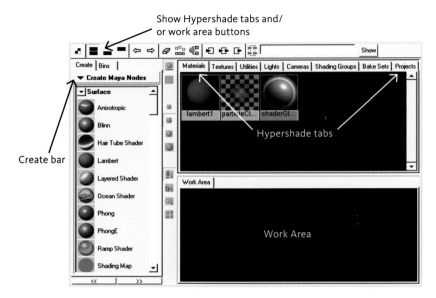

Close-up of Hypershade

Note: *The same mouse and key combinations that you use in the Orthographic viewports can be used for maneuvering in the Hypershade work area.*

Creating shading networks

A shading network consists of a series of nodes that input into a *shading group*. A shading group is a node that defines the various rendering attributes of its related objects, such as surface shading, volumetric shading, displacement shading, etc.

In the following examples, you will create several nodes that define the material qualities of all the different objects, such as the wall, columns, drapes, etc.

1 Sky material

To build a material for the sky, you will use the Hypershade and Attribute Editor.

- Click on the **Show top and bottom tabs** button located at the top left of the Hypershade.

- At the top of the **Create** bar section, click on the tab **Create**.

- Click on the **down arrow** just below the **Create** tab, and make sure **Create Maya Nodes** is selected from the pop-up.

   This offers you a series of icons that represent new Maya nodes, such as surface materials.

- Click on **Lambert**.

   This adds a new Lambert material under the materials' Hypershade tab and in the work area. You will also see the Attribute Editor update to show the new node information.

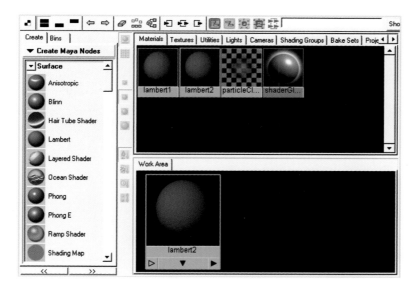

Lambert is a particular type of shader that gives you control over the look of flat materials without shiny highlights.

2 Rename the Material node

- In the **Attribute Editor**, change the name of the **Material** node to *skyM*.

   The M designation is to remind you that this node is a Material node.

Tip:	You can also hold down the **Ctrl** key and double-click on the node in the **Hypershade** to rename it.

3 Edit the material's color

To define how the material will render, you will need to set color attribute.

- In the **Attribute Editor**, click on the color swatch next to the **Color** attribute.

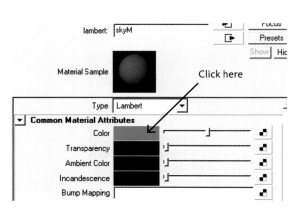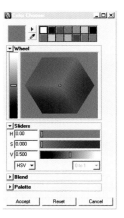

Color swatch in the Attribute Editor   *Color Chooser*

> *This opens the Color Chooser. This window lets you set color by clicking in a color wheel and editing HSV (Hue, Saturation, Value) or RGB (Red, Green, Blue) values.*

- Choose a light blue color and click the **Accept** button.

4 Edit the material's incandescence

Since the sky is irradiating light, it should be self-lit. To further define how the material will render, you can set its incandescence attribute.

- In the **Attribute Editor**, click on the color swatch next to the **Incandescence** attribute.
- Choose a light blue color and click the **Accept** button.

5 Assign the material

- Make sure the sky dome is visible in the viewport.
- With your **MMB**, **click+drag** on the *skyM* node, drag it from the Hypershade panel into the Perspective view and drop it on the *skyDome* object.

  This assigns the material to the object.

Tip: *It is a good idea to be in Hardware Shading mode to ensure that the assignment is correct. The hotkey is **5** on your keyboard.*

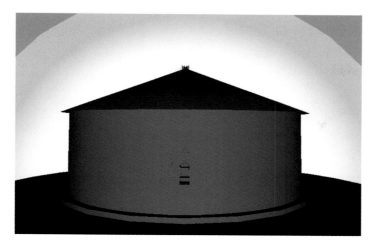

Assigned sky shader

Creating a procedural texture map

To give the ground plane a dirt and grass look, a fractal procedural texture will be added to the *ground's* material color. A procedural texture means the look of the texture is driven by attributes and drawn by mathematical functions. You will also experiment with the drag and drop capabilities of the Hypershade.

1 Ground material

- In the **Hypershade**, clear the work area by holding down the right mouse button and selecting **Graph → Clear Graph** or press the **Clear Graph** button at the top of the Hypershade.

The Clear Graph button

> *This clears the workspace so that you can begin working on a new shading network.*

- From the **Create** bar section, create another *Lambert* material.
- In the **Attribute Editor**, change the name of the *Material* node to *groundM*.

2 Fractal texture

The ground plane looks quite flat in shaded mode, and could use a grainy texture. Adding a fractal procedural texture will greatly help to enhance the look of the ground.

- In the **Create** bar section of the **Hypershade**, scroll down to the **2D Textures** section.

This section allows you to create new textures.

- **MMB+drag** a **Fractal** from the **Create** bar anywhere into the work area.

- In the work area of the **Hypershade**, click with your **MMB** on the **Fractal** icon and drag it onto the *groundM Material* node.

  When you release the mouse button, a pop-up menu appears offering you a number of attributes that can be mapped by the fractal texture.

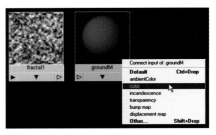

MMB+drag from the fractal onto the material

- Select **color** from the menu to map the *fractal* to the *Material* node's *color* attribute.

- Click on the **Rearrange Graph** button at the top of the *Hypergraph* panel.

The Rearrange Graph button

Tip: *Rearranging the work area will organize the view so connections appear from left to right. This is very useful for following the flow of connections.*

3 Assign the material

- Select the *ground*, then **RMB** on your material *groundM* and select **Assign Material to Selection**.

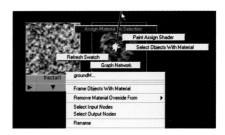

Assign to selection

Tip: *This method of assigning materials works better than the **click+drag** method when you want to assign a material to multiple objects.*

4 View the texture

In order to see the texture in the viewport, you will need to enable hardware texturing.

- Over the Perspective window, click with your **MMB** to make it the active window.

- Open the hotbox and select **Shading → Hardware Texturing**.

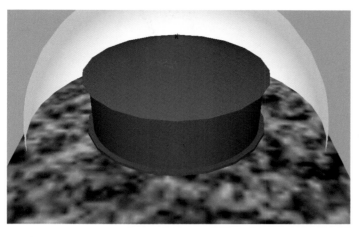

Hardware texturing

> **Tip:** You can also turn on hardware texturing by making the desired panel active and pressing the **6** key.

5 **Edit the fractal attributes**

- In the **Hypershade**, click to select the *Fractal* node.
- In the **Attribute Editor** (**Ctrl+a** to show it if hidden), open the **Color Balance** section.
- Click on the color swatch next to the **Color Gain** attribute.
- Choose any green and click the **Accept** button.
- Click on the color swatch next to the **Color Offset** attribute.
- Choose any brown and click the **Accept** button.
- Under the **Fractal Attributes** section, tweak the attributes to your liking.

  The attributes found in this section control the way the fractal is being evaluated.

- At the top of the **Attribute Editor**, select the *place2dTexture* tab.

  This tab shows different placement options for the fractal texture.

- Change the fractal's placement attributes as shown below:

  Repeat U to **2**;

  Repeat V to **2**.

  The Attribute Editor allows you to easily update the look of a procedural texture to your liking.

Ground texture

 Note: *The viewport texture shading is a representation of what your textures looks like, but it might not reflect perfectly how your scene will render.*

6 Display the whole shading group

- With the *groundM* texture selected in the **Hypershade**, click on **Input and Output Connections**.

Input and Output Connections button

This displays some other nodes that help define this shading group.

- Press the **Alt** key and **click+drag** with your left and middle mouse buttons to zoom out.
- Press the **a** hotkey to frame everything in the view.

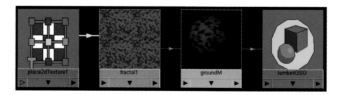

Complete shading network

Texture maps

You will create a material for objects using file textures instead of procedural textures. Many digital artists like to create textures in a 2D paint package. In this example, you will experiment with textures with and without transparency.

Floor texture

1 Create a material for the ground

- From the **Hypershade** panel's work area, **RMB-click** and select **Graph** → **Clear Graph**.
- Scroll to the **Surface** section in the **Create** bar and select **Phong**.

  Phong shaders look like a shiny surface, like plastic or polished marble.

- **Rename** this node *floorM*.

2 Create a File Texture node

To load an external texture, you need to start with a *File Texture* node.

- **Double-click** on the *groundM* material to display its **Attribute Editor** (if hidden).
- In the **Attribute Editor**, click on the **Map** button next to **Color**. The map button is shown with a small checkered icon.

Map button

> *This opens the Create Render Node window.*

- Click on the **Textures** tab.
- In the **2D Textures** section, click on **File**.

  A File node is added to the Lambert material. The appropriate connections have already been made.

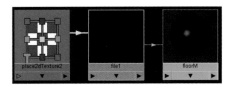

New File Texture node

3   Load the file texture

- In the **Attribute Editor** for the *File* node, click on the **File folder** icon next to **Image name**.
- Select the file named *floor.tif* from your project *sourceimages* directory, then click on the **Open** button.

  The file texture is now loaded into the shading network.

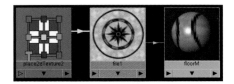

File Texture node

Note: *This file will be available only if you set-up your project correctly from the support_files and if it is set to current.*

Note: *The file texture does not import the image into Maya. Instead, it keeps a path to the specified file and loads it on request from your drive.*

4   Apply the textured material to the ground

- Select the *floor* surface in the *Perspective* view.
- In the **Hypershade**, click on the *floorM* node with your **RMB** and choose **Assign Material to Selection** from the pop-up menu.

  The texture is assigned to the ground surface.

Ground with texture applied

5 Drapes' texture

For the drapes' texture, you will use a texture with an *alpha channel*. This means that the texture contains the regular color channels, plus an alpha channel, which stores the transparency of the texture. This is perfect for the drapes since you will be able to cut out details without having to modify the actual geometry.

Drapes' texture, color, and alpha channel displayed

- **Repeat** the last exercise to create a **Lambert** shader with a mapped **File texture**.
- **Rename** the **Lambert** shader to *drapeM*.
- Open the **Attribute Editor** for the new file texture, and then click on the **Browse** button.
- Select the file named *drapes.tif* from your project *sourceimages* directory, then click on the **Open** button.

  Maya software will automatically detect and connect the alpha channel to the **transparency** *attribute of the Lambert shader.*

- **Assign** the new *drapeM* shader to all the drape objects.

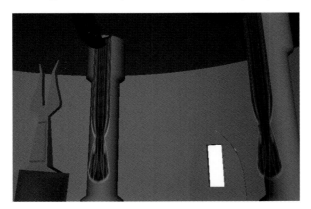

Drapes with transparent texture

6 Texturing polygons

A good thing about polygon geometry is that you can assign different shaders onto different faces of the mesh. In this example, you will texture the throne using two colored shaders.

- Create two **Blinn** shaders in the **Hypergraph**.
- Make one of the new shaders the color **blue** and the other **gold**.
- Select the *throne*, and **assign** the gold **Blinn** to it.
- Press the **F11** hotkey to go into Face Component mode.
- Select the different faces that are to be colored blue using the **Shift** key.
- Press **F8** to go back into Object mode.

7 Soft edges

At this time, the throne looks quite edgy. You can make its appearance smoother and shinier by smoothing the hard edge normals.

- Select the *throne*.
- Press **F3** to select the **Polygon** menu set.
- Select **Normals** → **Soften Edge** from the hotbox.

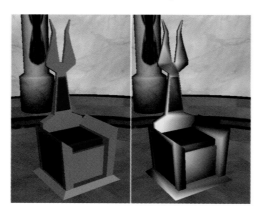

Hard vs. soft edges

8 Texture placement

When loading a texture file, you might want to change the way the texture is placed on the surface. In this example, you will change the repetition of the wall texture so there are several windows all around the room.

- **Create** a new **Blinn** material and map a texture file to its color attribute.
- **Load** the texture file *windows.tif* from the *sourceimages* directory.

  Notice the texture appears stretched and not placed correctly.

- With the new file texture still selected, in the **Attribute Editor**, click on the *place2dTexture* tab near the top of the window.

  This is the node that controls the 2D placement of a texture.

- Set **Repeat UV** to **1.5** and **6.0**.

9 Complete the scene

Before continuing with the next lesson, it is a good idea to assign materials to the remaining objects in your scene. Experiment with 2D procedural Texture nodes such as *Noise, Ramp,* and *Cloth.* You can also map some of the objects with file textures of your own or from those found in the support file directory. The following is an example of the completed room:

The completed scene

> **Note:** *A marble texture and a door texture can be found in the support_files's sourceimages directory.*

Test render

Now that you have materials and textures assigned, it is a good time to do a test render.

1 Display Resolution Gate

Your current view panel may not be displaying the actual proportions that will be rendered. You can display the camera's resolution gate to see how the scene will actually render.

- Make the Perspective view the active panel.

- Use the **hotbox** to select **View → Camera Settings → Resolution Gate**.

  The view is adjusted to show a bounding box that defines how the default render resolution of 640x480 pixels relates to the current view.

- Dolly into the view so that it is well composed within the resolution gate. Try to set-up a view where you see every object.

Keep in mind that only objects within the green surrounding line will be rendered.

The resolution gate displayed

Tip: *Select* **View** → **Camera Settings** → **Resolution Gate** *again to turn off the resolution gate.*

2   Your first render

- In the **Render View** panel, click with your **RMB** and select **Render** → **Render** → **persp** from the pop-up menu.

Render View panel

You can now see a rendered image of your scene. However, because you have not created any lights, the image renders using a default light.

- Try adding lighting to your scene by creating lights from the **Create → Lights** menu.

Note: *Lights are going to be covered later in this book.*

- **Render** your scene again.

3 Zoom into the rendering

You can zoom in and out of the rendered image using the **Alt** key.

- Use the **Alt** key and the **LMB** and **RMB** to zoom in and out of the view.

Now you can evaluate in more detail how your rendering looks at the pixel level.

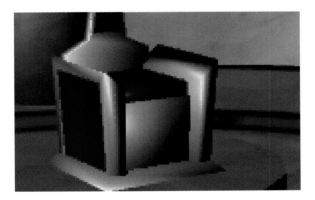

Close-up of rendering

- In the **Render View** panel, click with your **RMB** and choose **View → Real Size**.

4 Save your work

- Through the **hotbox**, select **Save Scene As** from the **File** menu.
- Enter the name *03-textures_01.ma*, then press the **Save** button.

Conclusion

You have now been introduced to some of the basic concepts for texturing and rendering a 3D scene. The Maya shading networks offer a lot of depth for creating the look of your objects. You have learned how to create materials, procedural textures, and file textures, and assign them to objects and faces. Lastly, you rendered a single frame to preview the look of your shaders with default lighting.

In the next lesson, you will learn about animation basics by animating a door that is opening.

Animation Basics

You have built a simple set using various primitive objects and then textured them. You will now learn about the basics of hierarchies and animate the door so that it opens.

In this lesson, you will learn the following:

- How to change and save preferences
- How to group and parent objects
- How to understand parent inheritance
- How to set keyframes
- How to use the Time Slider
- How to use the Graph Editor
- How to select animation curves and keyframes
- How to change keyframe tangents
- How to traverse a hierarchy

Preferences

You can now reset the interface to its default settings. Also, be sure to set your preferences to have an infinite undo queue.

1 Turn on all menus

- From the **hotbox**, click on **Hotbox Controls**.

- From the marking menu, go down to **Window Options** and set the following:

    Show Main Menubar to **On** (Windows only);

    Show Pane Menubars to **On**.

    The menubars are back to normal.

2 Turn on all of the workspace options

- Select **Display → UI Elements → Show All UI Elements**.

    You are now back to the default Maya interface.

 Tip: *You can press the* **Ctrl+spacebar** *hotkey to bring back the interface as it was before you hid everything.*

3 Change the Attribute Editor settings

You might want the Attribute Editor to open in its own window rather than in the Maya interface. The following will show you how to set your preference accordingly.

- Select **Window → Settings/Preferences → Preferences**.

- In the left **Categories** list, make sure **Interface** is highlighted.

- Set **Open Attribute Editor** to **In separate window**.

- You can do the same for **Open tool settings** and the **Open Layer Editor** if wanted.

    The different editors will now open in their own separate windows rather than cluttering the main interface.

4 Infinite undo option

By default, Maya has a limited amount of undo in order to reduce the memory usage of your computer. You will specify here if you want to keep an undo queue larger than the default setting.

- In the **Categories** list, highlight **Undo**.

- Make sure **Undo** is set to **On**.

- Set the **Queue size** to what you think is an appropriate value, such as **50**.

    OR

- Set the **Queue** to **Infinite**.

    The amount of undo is now defined to your liking.

5 Save your preferences
- In order to save these preferences, you must click the **Save** button in the **Preferences** window.

  The next time you open Maya, these settings will be used.

> **Note:** *You can also save your preference by selecting* **File** → **Save Preferences.**

Organize your scene

Before animating objects, you need to make sure that the task will be as simple as possible. You will need to easily find the objects in your scene and animate them as intended. Placing objects logically into hierarchy is going to do just that. To do so, you will learn how to group and parent objects together as well as learn how to use the Outliner.

You can think of scene organization as having groups and sub-groups. For instance, you can have an *environment* group that contains everything in the scene. Then you can have a *room* group, which will contain everything related to the room and in the *room* group, you can have a *columns* group, and so forth.

Thus far you have modeled a bunch of objects, but you haven't looked at how they were organized behind what you saw in the viewports.

1 Hierarchy

It is very important to understand the concept of a hierarchy. A hierarchy consists of the grouping of child nodes under parent nodes. When transforming a parent node, all of its children will inherit its transformation. The following steps explain how to create a hierarchy of objects:

- To better visualize what you are about to do, open the **Outliner** by selecting **Window** → **Outliner**.

  The Outliner lists all the nodes in your scene along with their hierarchies. Currently, in your scene, you can see the default Maya cameras, all of the prior lesson objects, every component of your environment and, at the very bottom, two default sets.

- Scroll in the **Outliner** to see the current organization of the scene.

  The first four nodes in the Outliner are always the default cameras. Following that are your scene contents, and then the different default object sets.

The Outliner

2 Groups

- Hold down the **Shift** key, and **select** all your scene's content from the **Outliner** starting from the *ground* down to *throne*.

  Doing so selects the geometry just like when selecting in a viewport.

- Select **Edit → Group**.

  The selected geometry is now all grouped under a Group node.

- **Double-click** on the newly created group to enable the rename function directly in the **Outliner**.

Expand/collapse button

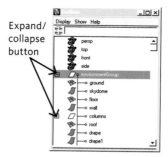

Hierarchy expanded

- Enter the name *environmentGroup*, then hit **Enter** to confirm the name change.

- **Expand** the group to see its content by clicking on the **plus** (+) sign next to *environmentGroup*.

Note: *A new default group has its pivot at the origin and all of its attributes are set to their default values.*

3 Organizing the hierarchy

You will now create a group within the environment group.

- Select all the objects called *drape*.

- Press **Ctrl+g** to group them.

  A new group is created within the environmentGroup, containing only the drape objects.

- **Rename** *group1* to *roomGroup*.

- Select all the remaining house objects that are not already in *roomGroup*.

- Press and hold the **MMB** over the selection and drag them over the *roomGroup*.

  As you can see in the following images, dragging and dropping a node onto another one will set it as the child of the object it was dragged onto.

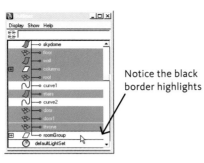 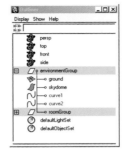

Notice the black
border highlights

Drag

Drop

Note: *Notice the green highlight on the roomGroup, which shows one or more of its*
children is currently selected.

- Select *roomGroup.*
- **MMB+drag** it in the Outliner just under the *environmentGroup* geometry and drop it
  when you see only a single black border highlight.

  Doing so reorders the scene hierarchy.

Tip: *Notice that when dragging objects in the Outliner, one black line shows that it will*
be placed in-between two nodes, while two black lines show that the objects will be
parented.

4 **Parenting**

- Select all the *drape* objects either from the Outliner or from the viewport.
- In the **Outliner**, hold **Ctrl,** then select the *columns group.*

  Make sure the columns group is selected last.

- From the **Edit** menu, select **Parent.**

  OR

- Press **p** on your keyboard.

  Doing so will parent the drape objects to the columns object.

Tip: *Use **Shift+p** to unparent the selected objects.*

5 Completing the hierarchy

- **Delete** the *curves* from the Outliner, since they are no longer required.

- Organize the hierarchy so that it looks like the following:

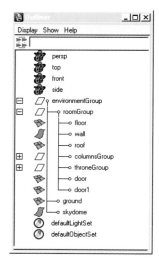

The completed hierarchy

 Tip: To expand a hierarchy along with all the children, hold down the **Shift** key before clicking the **Expand** button in the **Outliner**.

Display layers

In this exercise, you will sort your scene using display layers. A display layer is a grouping of objects which can be hidden, or displayed as reference templates, which makes them unselectable in the viewports.

1 Create a display layer

The first display layer you will create will contain the environment objects, such as the ground and sky dome.

- In the **Layer Editor**, located below the **Channel Box**, select **Layers → Create Empty Layer.**

- **Double-click** on the new layer, and enter *envLayer* as the name.

- Click the **Save** button.

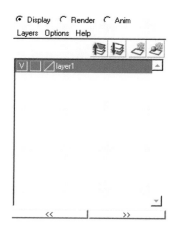

The Layer Editor

2 Add objects to a display layer

- From the **Outliner**, select the *ground* and *skyDome* objects.
- **RMB** on the *envLayer*, and select **Add Selected Objects**.

3 Set the display of the layer

- Toggle the **V** button on the *envLayer* to set the visibility of the objects on that layer.

  Hidden layers are not to be rendered.

- Click in the empty square next to the **V** button to toggle the layer's display between **Normal**, **Template**, and **Reference.**

  When templated, the layer objects are unselectable and displayed as dimmed wireframe. When referenced, the layer objects are unselectable, but displayed normally in the viewport.

- Set the layer to be visible (**V**) and in reference (**R**).

4 Create another layer

In order to simplify any selection process in your scene even more, you will create another layer and add any objects not intended for manipulation.

- **Create** a new layer and rename it to *roomLayer.*
- **Add** the *floor*, *wall*, *roof,* and *columnsGroup* to the *roomLayer.*
- Make the *roomLayer* referenced.

  From now on, when selecting in the viewport, you will be able to select only a reduced amount of objects, which are not on the referenced layers.

Understanding inheritance

Hierarchies are useful to organize your scene, but they also play a role with animation. For instance, if you transform a parent object, all of its children and grandchildren will follow that transformation. Thus, it is essential to freeze transformations of objects to reset their transformation attributes to their default, without moving the object. You must also make sure that all objects' pivots are appropriately placed for your needs.

1 Freezing transformations

At this time, most of your objects have some values in their translate, rotate, and scale attributes. When you animate your objects, those values will come into play and make your task more difficult. To make it easier, you can freeze an object's transformations.

- Select the *environmentGroup.*
- Select **Edit → Select Hierarchy.**
- Select **Modify → Freeze Transformations**.

  Doing so resets all the selected objects' attributes to their default values.

Tip: *If you do not want to freeze all the attributes of an object, you can open the command's option box to specify which attributes need freezing.*

2 Center pivots

Since the groups and objects might not have their pivots at a centered location, it is a good idea to place all the pivots in one easy step.

- Select the *environmentGroup*.
- Select **Edit** → **Select Hierarchy**.
- Select **Modify** → **Center Pivot**.

Every pivot is now located at the best centered location. When an object has children, the command takes into account the entire sub-hierarchy to position the pivot.

3 Child values

When you transform a parent object, none of its children's values change.

- Select the *roomGroup*.
- **Rotate** and **translate** it to modify its positioning.

  Notice that all children are moving along.

- Select any of its children, and notice that all of their values are still zero.
- Select *throneGroup* and **move** it.

  Notice the throne values did not change.

4 Pivot placement

You will now see how the pivot of an object, when well placed, can simplify your task when it comes to moving an object.

- Select the *roomGroup* and set its **scale X, Y,** and **Z** to **1.5**.

  All of the group's children follow the parent scaling, but the floor of the room is going down through the ground.

- **Undo** the previous action.
- Still with the *roomGroup* selected, press the **Insert** key on your keyboard to bring up the **Move Pivot Tool**.
- From the *front* or *side* Orthographic view, place the pivot on the ground plane, near the origin.

Tip: *You can snap it to the grid by holding down the **x** hotkey.*

- Press **Insert** again to exit the tool.

- Set the *roomGroup* **scale X**, **Y,** and **Z** to **0.75**.

  Notice when scaling, you do not have to compensate for the floor moving up or down on the Y-axis.

5 Save your work

- **Save** your scene as *04-animationBasics_01.ma*.

Animating the door

You now have enough knowledge of scene hierarchy and object inheritance to create your first simple animation.

1 Door pivot

Before animating the door, you must consider your needs in animation and make sure that you can achieve such animation with your scene setup. At this time, you need the pivot of that door to be located around the hinge area; otherwise, your door would rotate from its center, which is not ideal for animation.

- With one of the doors selected, press the **Insert** key and move the pivot to where you think the hinges should be.

- Press **Insert** again to exit the **Move Pivot Tool**.

Tip: *You can hold down the **d** hotkey to evoke the **Move Pivot Tool**.*

- **Test** your door by rotating it on its **Y-axis**.

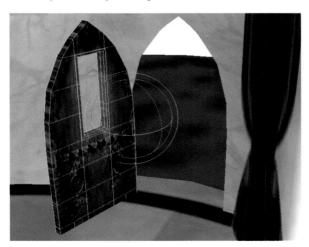

Rotating the door open

- **Undo** the last move to reset the door to its default position.

2 The timeline

The first step with animation is to determine how long you would like your animation to be. By default, Maya software plays animation at a rate of 24 frames per seconds (FPS), which is a standard rate used for film. As such, if you want your animation to last one second, you need to animate 24 frames.

- In the **Time Slider** and **Range Slider** portion of the interface, change **Playback End Time** to **100**.

The frames in the Time Slider now go from 1 to 100. One hundred frames is just above four seconds of animation in 24FPS.

Start time   End time

Playback start time   Playback end time

Time Slider and Range Slider

3 Setting keyframes

Luckily, you do not need to animate every single frame in your animation. When you set keyframes, Maya will interpolate the values between the keyframes, giving you animation.

- Press the **First Frame** button from the playback controls to make the current frame **1**.

First frame   Play   Next key   Next frame

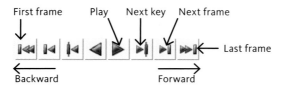

                                Last frame

Backward   Forward

Playback controls

- Select the *door*.
- Make sure all of its rotation and translation values are set to **0**.
- At the top of the interface, change the current menu sets for **Animation**.

 Tip: *The Animation menu set hotkey is* **F2**.

- With the *door* still selected, select **Animate → Set Key**.

 Tip: **Set Key** *can also be executed by pressing the* **s** *hotkey.*

- In the current frame field on the left of the rewind button, type **25** and hit **Enter**.

  Notice the position of the current frame mark in the Time Slider.

Current frame marker   Current frame field

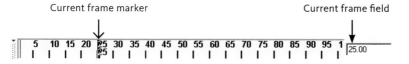

The current frame mark

- Type **-125** in the **Rotate Y** field of the *door* and hit **Enter**.
- Press the **Alt** key while your mouse cursor is over a viewport in order to remove focus from the Y-axis field, then hit the **s** hotkey to **Set Key** at frame **25**.

4 Playback preferences

Before you play your animation, you need to set the Maya playback properly.

- Click the **Animation Preferences** button found at the far right side of the **Range Slider**.

  This opens the preferences window directly on the animation and playback options.

- In the **Time Slider** category, under the **Playback** section, make sure that **Playback Speed** is set to **Real-time (24FPS)**.

  The animation preferences button

- Click the **Save** button.

- Press the **Rewind** button, then press the **Play** button in the playback controls area to see your animation.
- To stop the playback of the animation, press the **Play** button again or hit **Esc**.
- You can also drag the current frame by **click+dragging** in the **Time Slider** area.

Dragging in the Time Slider

Notice the red ticks at frame 1 and frame 25, specifying keyframes on the currently selected objects.

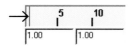

A keyframe tick in the Time Slider

5 Tweak the animation

You now have a partially animated door, but it is still missing refinement. Maybe you think the animation is too slow or too fast. In order to change the timing of the animation, you can drag keyframes directly in the Time Slider.

- With the door still selected, hold down the **Shift** key, then click on frame **25** in the **Time Slider**.

  Doing so highlights frame 25 with a red zone. This zone is actually a manipulator that allows you to translate keyframes in the Time Slider.

- **Click+drag** the red zone to frame **15**.

  The door animation now starts at frame 1 and stops at frame 15.

The keyframe manipulator

- Click anywhere in the **Time Slider** to remove the keyframe selection.

- Go to frame **35**.

- With the *door* still selected, set the **Rotate Y** attribute to **-140**.

- Click on the **Rotate Y** attribute name in the **Channel Box**.

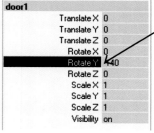

Select only the Rotate Y attribute

Click on the attribute's name

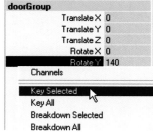

Select Key Selected from the attribute menu

- Click and hold the **RMB** over that same attribute.

  This will pop-up the attribute context menu.

- Select **Key Selected**.

  Doing so will set a keyframe on that attribute for every selected object.

Tip: You can use **Shift+w**, **Shift+e**, and **Shift+r** to keyframe only the translation, rotation, and scale attributes respectively.

- Playback your animation.

  You will notice that the door is opening fast for the first 15 frames and then slows down up to frame 35.

> **Note:** *To delete keyframes in the* **Time Slider,** *simply set the current time marker on a keyframe, then* **RMB** *and select* **Delete.** *To delete multiple keyframes at the same time, select the keyframes using the keyframe manipulator (using the* **Shift** *key), then* **RMB** *and select* **Delete.**

6 Graph Editor

The Graph Editor is the place where you can look at all the keyframes on an object and see their interpolations as curves (function curves or fcurves).

- Select the *door.*

- Select **Window** → **Animation Editors** → **Graph Editor.**

- Select **View** → **Frame All** to frame the entire curve, or press the **a** hotkey.

- Press the **Alt** key and **click+drag** with the **LMB** and **MMB** to dolly in and out of the graph.

- Press the **Shift+Alt** keys and **click+drag** with the **LMB** and **MMB** to constrain the dolly along the dragged axis.

- Press the **Shift+Alt** keys and **click+drag** left and right with the **MMB** to constrain track along the dragged axis.

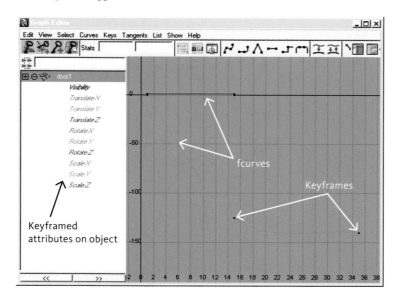

The fcurves on the door

> *The keyframes you have set are represented by black dots. Animation curves of vector attributes are always color coded red, green, and blue for X, Y, and Z axes. The yellow animation curve shows a slope because you have keyframed the rotate Y attribute on the door. All other keyframes were set with their default value of 0.*

7 Selecting keyframes

- Experiment selecting animation curves and keyframes in the Graph Editor.

Note: *You can select an entire animation curve by click+dragging on the curve itself. You can select keyframes by clicking on them. You can also modify the selection using the **Ctrl** and **Shift** hotkeys.*

- With the **Move Tool** selected, **MMB+drag** keys around in the Graph Editor.

Tip: *Use **Shift+MMB-dragging** to constrain the axis of translation of the keyframe.*

8 Modifying keyframes

In order to modify only the Rotate Y keyframes without affecting other animation curves, you can display only the desired curve in the Graph Editor. You will now modify the animation so the door progressively gains speed when it is opening and loses speed once opened.

- In the **Outliner** section located on the left of the **Graph Editor**, highlight the **Rotate Y** attribute.

Only this animation curve is now visible.

- Select the first and last keyframes of the animation curve.

- Select **Tangents → Flat**.

This sets the keyframes to be flat, which causes a gradual acceleration and deceleration of the animation.

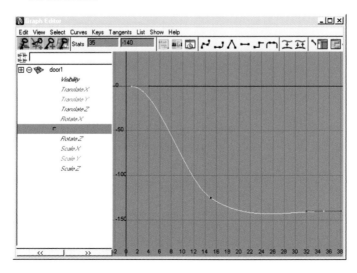

Flat tangents

> **Note:** *Notice how the animation curve goes slightly above 140 around frame 25. This will cause the door to overshoot its animation and rotate a bit further than what was keyed. While this effect is desired in this example, you might want to correct the situation by moving up the keyframe at frame 15, or simply edit its tangent.*

- **Playback** your animation.
- Continue experimenting. Once you like your animation, **close** the **Graph Editor**.

> **Note:** *To delete keyframes, select them in the* **Graph Editor**, *then press the* **Delete** *key.*

9 Traversing a hierarchy

You can traverse hierarchies using the arrows on your keyboard. Traversing a hierarchy is useful for selecting objects without manually picking the object in the viewport or through the Outliner.

- Select the *door.*
- Open the **Outliner** to see the effect of the upcoming steps.
- Press the **Up arrow** to change the selection to the parent of the current selection (*roomGroup*).
- Press the **Up arrow** again to select the *environmentGroup*.

> **Tip:** *You can use the following hotkeys to traverse a hierarchy:*
> **Up arrow**   —*Parent*
> **Down arrow** —*First child*
> **Right arrow** —*Next child*
> **Left arrow**   —*Previous child*
>
>

10 Save your work

- **Save** your scene as *04-animationBasics_02.ma.*

Conclusion

You have now touched upon some of the basic concepts of hierarchies and animation. Maya utilizes more powerful tools than described here to help you bring your scenes to life, but these basic principles represent a great step forward. As well as learning how to group and parent objects together, you also learned about inheritance of transformation and animation and worked with two of the most useful editors—the Outliner and the Graph Editor.

The next lesson is a more in-depth look at most of the tools that you have been using since the beginning of this project. Once you have read this lesson, you will be able to make your own decisions about how to reach the different windows, menu items, and hotkeys.

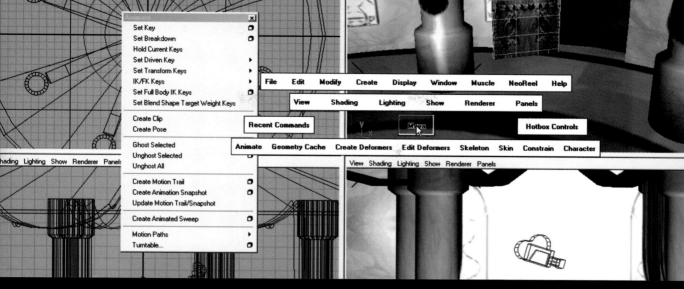

Working with Maya

If you completed the first four lessons, you have worked with Maya software from modeling and animation to shading and rendering. Now is a good time to review some of the UI concepts that you worked with and introduce new concepts in order to provide a more complete overview of how Maya works.

It is recommended that you work through this lesson before proceeding with the subsequent lessons in the book. This lesson explores the basic UI actions that you will use in your day-to-day work.

In this lesson, you will learn the following:

- About the Maya interface
- About the different UI parts
- About the view tools
- About the different hardware displays
- About menus and hotkeys
- About the manipulators and the Channel Box
- About selection and selection masks
- About the difference between tools and actions

The workspace

You have learned how to build and animate scenes using different view panels and UI tools. The panels offer various points of view for evaluating your work—such as Perspective views, Orthographic views, graphs, and Outliners—while the tools offer you different methods for interacting with the objects in your scene. Shown below is the workspace and its key elements:

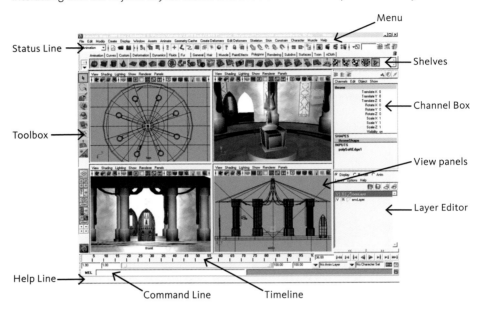

The Maya workspace

Layouts

When Maya is first launched, you are presented with a single Perspective view panel. As you work, you may want to change to other view layouts.

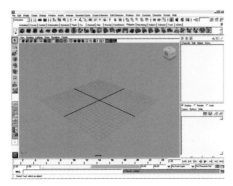

The default layout

1 To change your view layouts

• Go to the view panel's **Panels** menu and select a new layout option from the **Layouts** pop-up menu.

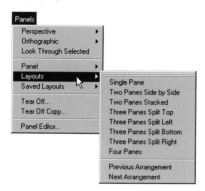

The Layouts pop-up menu

You can set-up various types of layouts ranging from two to four panels.

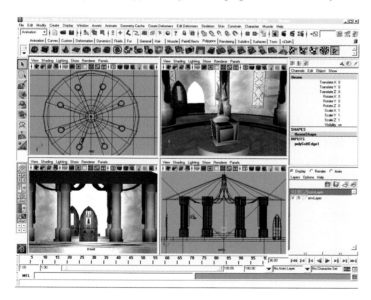

A four-view layout

> **Tip:** *If you are looking at several view panels simultaneously and want to focus on one of them, put your cursor in that view and tap the spacebar. The view will become full-screen. Tap the spacebar again and the panels will return to the previous layout.*

View panels

As you begin to build and animate objects, you will want to view the results from various points of view. It is possible to place either Perspective or Orthographic views in each panel.

1 To change the content of a view panel:

- Go to the view panel's **Panels** menu and select a view type from either the **Perspective** or **Orthographic** pop-ups.

View tools

When you are working with Perspective and Orthographic views, you can change your view-point by using hotkey view tools. The following view tools allow you to quickly work in 3D space using simple hotkeys:

1 To tumble in a Perspective view

- Press the **Alt** key and **click+drag** with the **LMB**.

> **Tip:** The ability to tumble an Orthographic view is locked by default. To unlock this feature, you need to select the desired Orthographic view and under **View**, go to **Camera Tools** and unlock it in the **Tumble Tool** → ❑.

2 To track in any view panel

- Press the **Alt** key and **click+drag** with the **MMB**.

3 To dolly in or out of any view panel

- Press the **Alt** key and **click+drag** with both the **LMB** and **MMB** or only with the **RMB**.

> **Tip:** You can also track and dolly in other view panels, such as the Hypergraph, the Graph Editor, Visor, Hypershade, and even the Render View window. The same view tools work for most panel types.

View Cube

The View Cube appears in the top right corner of any panel view and shows your current camera view.

You can move between views by clicking parts of the View Cube. Clicking any of the cube sections will rotate the current camera view to the selected view. Clicking the home icon will move the camera back to the default Perspective view.

The View Cube

1   **To hide the View Cube in a view**
    - Select **Show → Manipulators**.

2   **To turn the View Cube on and off**
    - Select **Window → Settings/Preferences → Preferences**.
    - In the **Categories** section, select **ViewCube** and choose your favorite settings.

Other panel types

As well, you can change the content of the view panel to display other types of information, such as the Hypershade or Graph Editor.

1   **To change the content of a view panel**
    - Go to the view panel's **Panels** menu and select a panel type from the **Panel** pop-up menu.

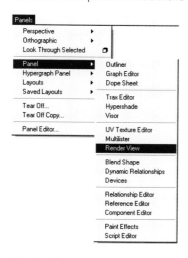

The Panels pop-up menu

In the workspace below, you can see a Hypergraph panel for helping select nodes, a Graph Editor for working with animation curves, and a Perspective view to see the results.

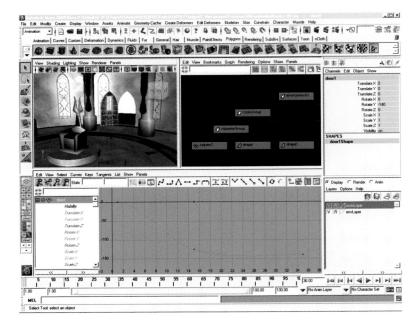

The workspace with various panel types

Saved layouts

As you become more familiar with Maya, you may want to set-up an arrangement of panels to suit a particular workflow. For example, you may want a Dope Sheet, a Perspective view, a top view, and a Hypergraph view all set-up in a certain manner.

1 To add a new layout of your own

- Go to the view panel's **Panels** menu and select **Saved Layouts → Edit Layouts...**

  In the Edit window, you can add a new saved layout and edit the various aspects of the layout.

2 To add a new layout to the list

- Select the **Layouts** tab and click on **New Layout**.

- Select and edit the layout's name.

- Press the **Enter** key.

3 To edit the configuration of a saved layout

- Press the **Edit Layouts** tab.

- Choose a configuration, then **click+drag** on the separator bars to edit the layout's composition.

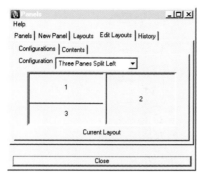

Layout Editor

Layout toolbox

- Press the **Contents** tab.

- Choose a panel type for each of the panels set-up in the configuration section.

> **Tip:** *There is a quicker access to preset layouts, panel types, and layout configuration through the toolbox on the left side of the Maya UI.*

Display options

Using the **Shading** menu on each view panel, you can choose which kind of display you want for your geometry.

1 To change your panel display

- Go to the panel's **Shading** menu and select one of the options.

  OR

- Click the appropriate buttons in the **Panel Toolbar** located under the panel's menu.

  OR

- Click in a panel to set it as the active panel and use one of the following hotkeys to switch display types:

  4 for wireframe;

  5 for smooth shaded.

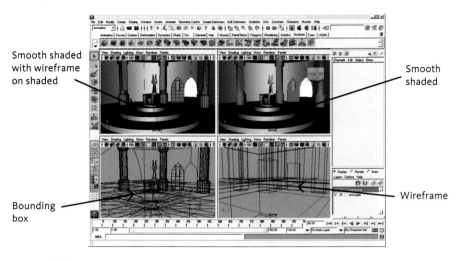

Smooth shaded with wireframe on shaded

Smooth shaded

Bounding box

Wireframe

Various display styles

Texturing and lighting

Another important option found on this menu is hardware texturing. This option allows you to visualize textures and lighting interactively in the view panels.

1   To use hardware texturing

- Build a shader that uses textures.
- Go to the panel's **Shading** menu and select **Hardware Texturing**.

  OR

- Press the **6** hotkey.

2   To display different textures

It is possible to display different texture maps on your surface during hardware texturing. For example, you could display the color map or the bump map if those channels are mapped with a texture.

- Select the material that is assigned to your objects.

- In the Attribute Editor, scroll down to the **Hardware Texturing** section and set the **Textured channel** to the desired channel.

- You can also set the **Texture Resolution** in the **Attribute Editor** for each *Material* node so that you can see the texture more clearly in your viewport.

3   To add hardware lighting to your scene

- Add a light to your scene by going to the panel's **Lighting** menu and select one of the options.

   OR

- Press the **7** hotkey for all lighting.

Hardware lighting and texturing

High quality rendering

When high quality interactive shading is turned on, the scene views are drawn in high quality by the hardware renderer. This lets you see a very good representation of the final render without having to software render the scene.

1   To turn on high quality rendering

- Go to the panel's **Renderer** menu and enable **High Quality Rendering**.

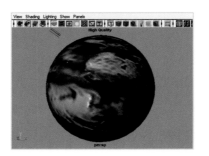

High Quality Rendering

Display smoothness

The viewport display of NURBS and polygonal objects can be changed in the viewport.

1   To change NURBS smoothness

By default, NURBS surfaces are displayed using a fine smoothness setting. If you want to enhance playback and interactivity, you can have the surfaces drawn in a lower quality.

- Go to the **Display** menu and under **NURBS** choose one of the smoothness options.

  OR

- Use one of the following hotkeys to switch display types:

  1 - for rough;

  2 - for medium;

  3 - for fine.

NURBS smoothness

 Tip: To speed up camera movement in a scene with heavy NURBS geometry, go to the **Window → Settings/Preferences → Preferences...** in the **Display** section to enable the **Fast Interaction** option. This option shows the rough NURBS smoothness any time a camera is moving.

2   Smooth Mesh Preview

Use one of the following hotkeys to switch display types of polygonal objects:

  1 - for the polygon display;

  2 - for the polygon cage and smooth preview;

  3 - for the smooth preview only.

Smooth Mesh Preview

 Note: When in smooth display, you can still go into Component mode and tweak the geometry's vertices.

Show menu

The **Show** menu is an important tool found on each view panel's menu. This menu lets you restrict or filter what each panel can show on a panel-by-panel basis.

Restricting what each panel shows lets you display curves in one window and surfaces in another to help edit construction history. Or, you can hide curves when playing back a motion path animation while editing the same curve in another panel.

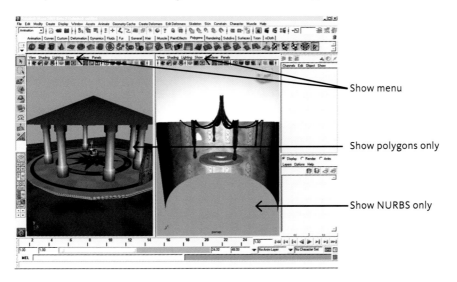

The Show menu

UI preferences

The Maya workspace is made up of various UI elements that assist you in your day-to-day work. The default workspace shows all of them on screen for easy access.

1   To reduce the UI to only view panels and menus

- Go to the **Display** menu and select **UI Elements → Hide All UI Elements**.

  With less UI clutter, you can rely more on hotkeys and other UI methods for accessing tools while conserving screen real estate.

2   To return to a full UI

- Go to the **Display** menu and select **UI Elements → Show All UI Elements**.

Tip: *You can use* **Ctrl+Spacebar** *to toggle between these UI settings.*

Menus

Most of the tools and actions you will use in Maya are found in the main menus. The first six menus are always visible, while the next few menus change depending on which UI mode you are in.

Menus and menu pop-ups that display a double line at the top can be *torn off* for easier access.

1   To tear off a menu

- Open the desired menu, then select the double line at the top of the menu.

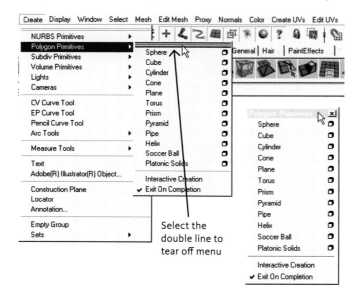

A tear-off menu

Menu sets

There are five menu sets in Maya Complete: *Animation, Polygons, Surfaces, Dynamics,* and *Rendering.* Each menu set allows you to focus on tools appropriate to a particular workflow.

1   To choose a menu set:

- Select the menu set from the pop-up menu found at the left of the **Status Line** bar.

2   To choose a menu set using hotkeys

- While pressing the **h** key, **LMB+drag** over any viewport and choose the desired UI mode from the radial marking menu.

3 To choose a menu set using function keys

- Press **F1** to invoke **Help**
- Press **F2** for **Animation**
- Press **F3** for **Polygons**
- Press **F4** for **Surfaces**
- Press **F5** for **Dynamics**
- Press **F6** for **Rendering**

Shelves

Another way of accessing tools and actions is by using the shelves. You can move items from a menu to a shelf to begin combining tools into groups based on your personal workflow needs.

1 To add a menu item to a shelf

- Press **Ctrl+Shift** and select the menu item. It will appear on the active shelf.

2 To edit the shelf contents and tabs

- Go to the **Window** menu and select **Settings/Preferences** → **Shelf Editor**.

  OR

- Select the **Shelf Editor** from the arrow menu located to the left of the shelves.

3 To remove a menu item from a shelf

- **MMB+drag** the shelf icon to the trash icon located at the far right of the shelves.

Status Line

The Status Line, located just under the Maya main menu, provides feedback on settings that affect the way the tools behave. The display information consists of:

- the current menu set;
- icons that allow you to create a new scene, open a saved one, or save the current one;
- the selection mode and selectable items;
- the snap modes;
- the history of the selected lead object (visible by pressing the input and output buttons);
- the construction history flag;
- the render into a new window and IPR buttons; and
- the Quick Selection field and Numeric Input field.

4 To collapse part of the shelf buttons

- Press the small handle bar next to a button set.

Selection mode

Collapse handle

Select modes before collapsing

Select modes button collapsed

Hotbox

As you learned, tapping the spacebar quickly pops a pane between full screen and its regular size, but if you press and hold the spacebar, you gain access to the hotbox.

The hotbox is a UI tool that gives you access to as much or as little of the Maya UI as you want. It appears where your cursor is located and offers the fastest access to tools and actions.

1 To access the hotbox

- Press and hold the spacebar.

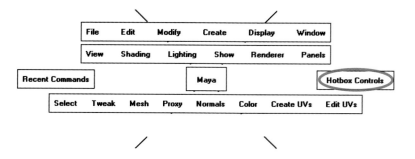

The hotbox with four quadrants marked

The hotbox offers a fully customizable UI element that provides you with access to all of the main menus as well as your own set of marking menus. Use the **Hotbox Controls** to display or show as many or as few menus as you need.

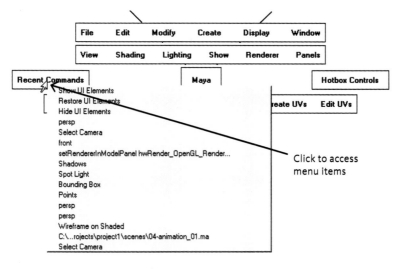

Accessing the recent commands menu

Hotbox marking menus

You can access marking menus in five areas of the hotbox. Since each of these areas can have a marking menu for each mouse button, it is possible to have fifteen menus in total. You can edit the content of the marking menus by going to the **Window** menu and selecting **Settings/Preferences → Marking Menu Editor**.

To access the center marking menu

- Press the **spacebar**.
- **Click+drag** in the center area to access the desired menu.

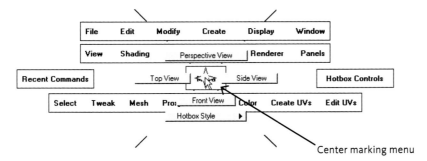

The center marking menu

1. **To access the edge marking menus**
   - Press the **spacebar**.
   - **Click+drag** in either one of the north, south, east, or west quadrants to access the desired marking menu.

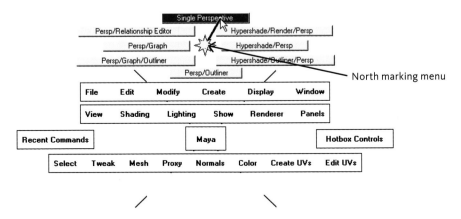

North marking menu

A quadrant-based marking menu

Customizing the hotbox

You can customize the hotbox to make it as simple or complex as you need. You can choose which menus are available and which are not.

If you want, you can reduce the hotbox to its essentials and focus on its marking menu capabilities.

A reduced hotbox layout

Alternatively, you could hide the other UI elements, such as panel menus, and use the hotbox to access everything. You get to choose which method works best for you.

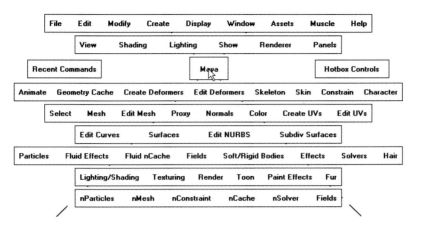

A complete hotbox layout

1   **To customize the hotbox**

- Use the **Hotbox Controls**.

   OR

- Use the center marking menu.

- Choose an option from the **Hotbox Styles** menu.

Tool manipulators

To the left of the workspace you have access to important tools. These include the **Select**, **Move**, **Rotate**, **Scale,** and **Show Manipulator** tools. Each of these is designed to correspond to a related hotkey that can be easily remembered using the QWERTY keys on your keyboard.

These tools will be used for your most common tool-based actions, like selecting and transforming.

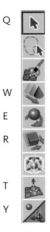

QWERTY tool layout

Note: *The Y key drives the last spot on the QWERTY palette, which is for the last tool used. The advantages of this will be discussed later in this lesson under the heading Tools and Actions.*

Universal Manipulator

The **Universal Manipulator** lets you transform geometry in translation, rotation, or scaling, both manually and numerically. A single click on any of the manipulators will display a numeric field allowing you to type in a specific value.

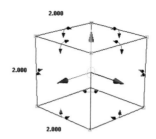

Universal manipulator

Soft Modification Tool

The Soft Modification Tool lets you push and pull geometry as a sculptor would on a sculpture. The amount of deformation is greatest at the center of the push/pull, and gradually falls off further away from the center. The corresponding action is **Deform → Soft Modification**.

Transform manipulators

One of the most basic Maya node types is the *Transform node*. This node contains attributes focused on the position, orientation, and scale of an object. To help you interactively manipulate these nodes, there are three transform manipulators that make it easy to constrain along the main axes.

Each of the manipulators uses a color to indicate their axes. RGB is used to correspond to X, Y, Z. Therefore, red is for X, green for Y, and blue for Z. Selected handles are displayed in yellow.

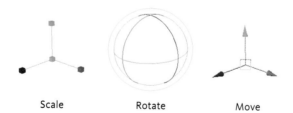

| Scale | Rotate | Move |

To explore some of the options available with manipulators, you will use the transform manipulator.

1 **To use a transform manipulator in view plane**

- **Click+drag** on the center of the manipulator to move freely along all axes.

2   To constrain a manipulator along one axis

- **Click+drag** on one of the manipulator handles.

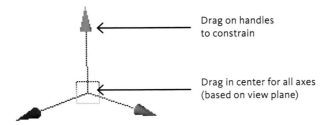

Drag on handles
to constrain

Drag in center for all axes
(based on view plane)

The move manipulator

3   To constrain a manipulator along two axes

- Hold the **Ctrl** key and **click+drag** on the axis that is aligned with the desired plane of motion.

  This now fixes the center on the desired plane, thereby letting you click+drag on the center so that you can move along the two axes. The icon at the center of the manipulator changes to reflect the new state.

4   To go back to the default view plane center

- Press the **Ctrl** key and click on the center of the transform manipulator.

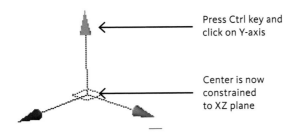

Press Ctrl key and
click on Y-axis

Center is now
constrained
to XZ plane

Working along two axes

> **Note:** *The ability to constrain in two axes at one time is available for the move and scale manipulators.*

Using the mouse buttons

You can interact directly with manipulators by using the left mouse button (LMB) to select objects. The **MMB** is for the active manipulator and lets you **click+drag** without direct manipulation.

1   To select objects

- Set-up selection masks.
- Click with the **LMB**.

2   To select multiple objects

- Use the **LMB** and **click+drag** a bounding box around objects.

3   To add objects to the selection

- Press **Ctrl+Shift** while you select one or multiple objects.

4   To manipulate objects directly

- **Click+drag** on a manipulator handle.

5   To manipulate objects indirectly

- Activate a manipulator handle;
- **Click+drag** with the **MMB**.

Shift gesture

The manipulators allow you to work effectively in a Perspective view panel when transforming objects.

If you want to work more quickly when changing axes for your manipulators, there are several solutions available.

1   To change axis focus using hotkeys

- Press and hold on the transform keys:

    w - for move

    e - for rotate

    r - for scale

- Choose an axis handle for constraining from the marking menu.

2   To change axis focus using the Shift key

- Press the **Shift** key.
- **Click+drag** with the **MMB** in the direction of the desired axis.

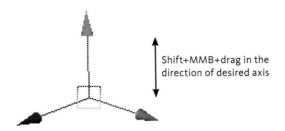

Shift+MMB+drag in the
direction of desired axis

Transform manipulators

Set pivot

The ability to change the pivot location on a Transform node is very important for certain types of animation.

1   To change your pivot point

- Select one of the manipulator tools;
- Press the **Insert** key (**Home** on Macintosh);
- **Click+drag** on the manipulator to move its pivot;
- Press **Insert** to return to the manipulator tool (**Home** on Macintosh).

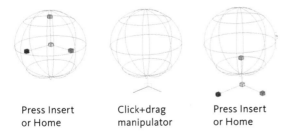

Press Insert   Click+drag   Press Insert
or Home   manipulator   or Home

Setting pivot using Insert / Home key

> **Tip:**   *You can also hold down the **d** hotkey to evoke the **Move Pivot Tool**.*

Channel Box

Another way of entering accurate values is through the Channel Box. This powerful panel gives you access to an object's Transform node and any associated Input nodes.

If you have multiple objects selected, then your changes to a channel will affect every node sharing that attribute.

To put one of the selected objects at the top of the Channel Box so that it is visible, choose the desired node from the Channel Box's **Object** menu.

If you want to work with a particular channel, you can use the **Channels** menu to set keys, add expressions, and complete other useful tasks. You can also change the display of Channel Box names to short MEL-based names.

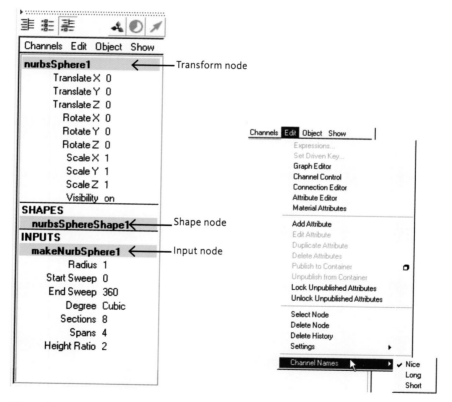

Channel's menu   The Channel Box

Note: *To control what channels are shown in the Channel Box, go to the* **Window** *menu, and choose* **General Editors → Channel Control.**

Channel Box and manipulators

One of the features of the Channel Box is the way in which you can use it to access manipulators at the transform level.

By default, the Channel Box is set to show manipulators every time you tab into a new Channel Box field. You will notice that as you select the channel names such as *Translate Z* or *Rotate X*, the manipulator switches from translate to rotate.

One fast way to edit an attribute is to invoke the virtual slider by selecting the name of the desired channel in the Channel Box, then using the **MMB+drag** in a view panel to change its value.

There are three options for the Channel Box manipulator setting.

Default manipulator setting

This setting lets you activate the appropriate field in the Channel Box, and then modify the values with either the left or middle mouse button.

- Click on the desired channel name or input field, then **click+drag** directly on the active manipulator with the **LMB**.

    OR

- Click on the desired channel name or input field, then **click+drag** in open space with the **MMB**.

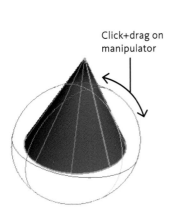
Click+drag on manipulator

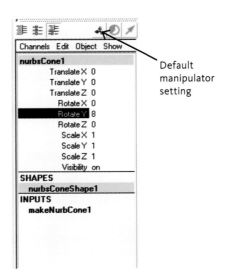
Default manipulator setting

Channel Box default manipulator setting

No-manipulator setting

You can click on the manipulator icon over the Channel Box to turn manipulation off, which leaves the Channel Box focused on coordinate input. With this setting, you cannot use the middle or left mouse buttons for manipulation.

- Click in the channel's entry field and type the exact value.

   OR

- Use one of the normal transform tools such as **Move**, **Rotate,** or **Scale**.

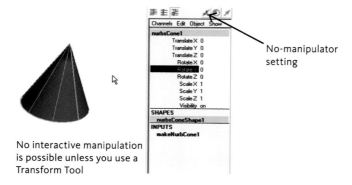

No interactive manipulation is possible unless you use a Transform Tool

Channel Box no-manipulator setting

No-visual manipulator setting

A third option found on this manipulator button returns manipulator capability to the Channel Box—but now you will not see the manipulator on the screen.

- Click on the desired channel name or within the channel's input field.

- **Click+drag** in open space with the **MMB**.

   You can now use the two new buttons that let you edit the speed and drop-off of the manipulations.

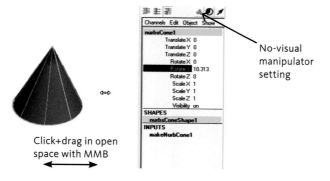

Click+drag in open space with MMB

Channel Box no-visual manipulator setting

The first button that becomes available with the *No-visual* setting is the speed button which lets you **click+drag** with your **MMB** either slow, medium, or fast.

Channel speed controls

Channel drop-off options

The second button is the drop-off button which lets you choose between a linear motion as you **click+drag** with the **MMB**, or a **click+drag** that is slow at first and faster as you drag further.

Attribute Editor

The Channel Box lets you focus on attributes that are keyable using **Set Key**, but the Attribute Editor gives you access to all the other attributes/channels.

The Attribute Editor is used for all nodes in Maya software. This means that shaders, textures, surfaces, lattices, Render Settings, etc., can all be displayed in this one type of window.

1   To open the Attribute Editor window

- Select a node.

- Go to the **Window** menu and select **Attribute Editor**.

2   To open the Attribute Editor panel

- Select a node.

    Go to the **Display** *menu and select* **UI Elements → Attribute Editor**. *The Channel Box is now replaced by an Attribute Editor panel.*

    When you open up the Attribute Editor, you not only get the active node, but also related nodes based on dependency relationships. In the example shown to the right, a sphere's transform, shape, and makeNurbSphere nodes are all present. These are the same Input and Shape nodes shown in the Channel Box.

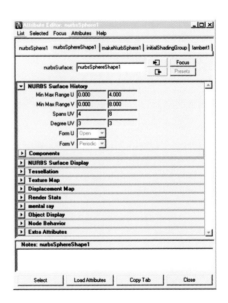

A typical Attribute Editor

Tip: *You can also press the **Ctrl + a** hotkey to open the Attribute Editor. You can set your preference for having the Attribute Editor in a panel or in its own window through **Window → Settings/Preferences → Preferences** and click on the **Interface** section to modify the **Open Attribute Editor** option.*

Numeric input

To add specific values to your transformations, you can use the numeric input boxes. This allows you to apply absolute or relative values to the attributes associated with the current manipulator.

To enter absolute values

- Select the **Absolute Transform** option from the input field menu.

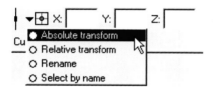

The input field menu

- Enter values and press **Enter** on your keyboard.

   The selected objects will be moved based on the input and the current manipulator.

To enter relative values

- Select the **Relative Transform** option from the input field menu.
- Enter values and press **Enter** on your keyboard.

Note: *You are not required to enter zero values.*

Selecting

One of the most important tasks when using Maya software is your ability to select different types of nodes and their key components.

For instance, you may need to be able to select a sphere and move it, or to select the sphere's control vertices and move them. You may also need to distinguish between different types of objects so that you can select only surfaces or only deformers.

Selection masks

To make selecting work, you have a series of selection masks available to you. This allows you to have one Select Tool that is then *masked* so that it can only select certain kinds of objects and components.

The *selection mask* concept is very powerful because it allows you to create whatever combination of selection types that you desire. Sometimes, you only want to select joints and selection handles, or maybe you want to select anything but joints. With selection masks, you get to set-up and choose the selected options.

The selection UI

The UI for selecting offers several types of access to the selection masks. You can learn all of them now and then choose which best suits your way of working down the line.

Grouping and parenting

When working with Transform nodes, you can create more complex structures by building hierarchies of these node types.

To build these structures, you can choose to *group* the nodes under a new Transform node, or you can *parent* one of the nodes under the other so that the lower node inherits the motion of the top node.

Grouped and parented nodes

Selection modes

At the top of the workspace, you have several selection mask tools available. These are all organized under three main types of select modes. Each type gives you access to either the hierarchy, object type, or components.

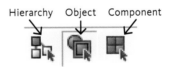

The select modes

Scene hierarchy mode

Hierarchy mode gives you access to different parts of the scene hierarchy structure. In the example shown below, the Leaf node and the Root node are highlighted. This mode lets you access each of these parts of the hierarchy. You can select Root nodes, Leaf nodes, and Template nodes using the selection masks.

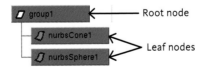

Hierarchy types

Object mode

Object mode lets you perform selections based on the object type. Selection masks are available as icons that encompass related types of objects.

With your **RMB**, you can access more detailed options that are listed under each mask group. If you create a partial list, the mask icon is highlighted in orange.

Object mode with selection masks

> **Tip:** *Once you choose selection masks, Maya software gives priority to different object types. For instance, joints are selected before surfaces. You will need to use the* **Shift** *key to select these two object types together. To reset the priorities, select* **Window → Settings/Preferences → Preferences** *and click on the* **Selection** *section to modify the* **Priority**.

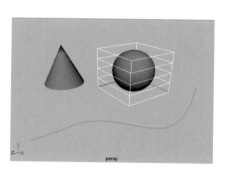

A lattice object and a curve object selected

Selection pop-up menu

Pop-up menu selection

When objects overlap in a view, the pop-up menu selection lets you display a pop-up list of the objects to select. **LMB+click** the overlap area to display the menu. Your selection is highlighted in the scene viewports as you select an item in the list.

- This option is disabled by default. To turn it on, select **Window → Settings/Preferences → Preferences** and click on the **Selection** section to enable **Pick chooser**.

Component mode

The Shape nodes of an object contain various components such as control vertices or isoparms. To access these, you need to be in Component mode.

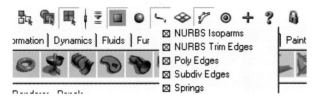

Component selection masks

When you select an object in this mode, it first highlights the object and shows you the chosen component type—you can then select the actual component.

Once you go back to Object mode, the object is selected and you can work with it. Toggling between Object and Component modes allows you to reshape and position objects quickly and easily.

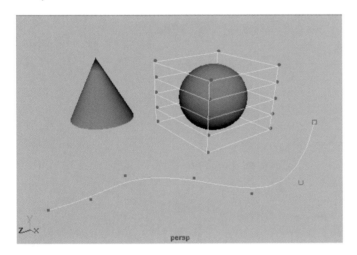

CV components and lattice point components

Tip:	To toggle between Object and Component modes, press the **F8** key.

RMB select

Another way of accessing the components of an object is to select an object, then press the **RMB**. This brings up a marking menu that lets you choose from the various components available for that object.

If you select another object, you return to your previous select mask selection. This is a very fast way of selecting components when in hierarchy mode, or for components that are not in the current selection mask.

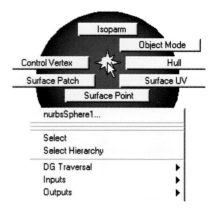

The RMB select menu

Combined select modes

In front of the selection mask mode icons is a pop-up menu that gives you different preset mask options. These presets let you combine different object and component level select options.

An example would be the NURBS option. This allows you to select various NURBS-based mask types such as surfaces, curves, CVs, curve control points, and isoparms.

Note: *In this mode, if you want to select CVs that are not visible by default, you must make them visible by going to the **Display** menu and selecting **NURBS → CVs**.*

When using a combined select mode, objects and components are selected differently. Objects are selected by **click+dragging** a select box around a part of the object, while components can be selected with direct clicking.

Note: *If you have CVs shown on an object and the select box touches any of them, you will select these components instead of the object. To select the object, you must drag the select box over part of the surface where there are no CVs.*

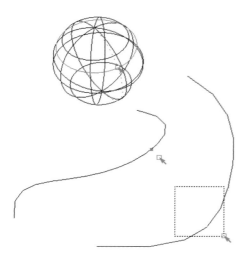

NURBS select options

Tools and actions

In Maya, a large group of menu items can be broken down into two types of commands: *tools* and *actions*, each working in their own particular manner. Almost every function can be set as a tool or action.

Tools

Tools are designed to remain active until you have finished using them. You select a tool, use it to complete a series of steps, then select another tool. In most cases, the Help Line at the bottom of the workspace can be used to prompt your actions when using the tool.

Earlier you were introduced to the **y** key on the QWERTY toolbox. By default, this button is blank because it represents the last tool used. When you pick a tool from the menus, its icon inserts itself into the QWERTY menu.

1   As tool option

- Pick a menu item and select its option box.

- Under the **Edit** menu, select **As Tool**.

    By default you will remain in this tool until you pick another tool. There is also an option that will deselect the tool after completion.

2   To return to the last tool used

- Press the **y** key.

Actions

Actions follow a selection-action paradigm. This means that you first have to pick something and then act on it. This allows you to choose an action, return to editing your work, and refine the results immediately.

Actions require that you have something selected before acting on it. This means that you must first find out what is required to complete the action.

1   To find out selection requirements of an action

- Move your cursor over a menu item.

- Look at the Help Line at the bottom-left of the interface.

  *If you have the Help Line UI element visible, the selection requirements are displayed. For instance, a **Loft** requires curves, isoparms, or curves on surfaces while **Insert Isoparm** requires isoparms to be picked.*

2   To complete the action

- If the tool is not already set as an action, select **Edit → As Action** from the menu item's options.

- Use either the pick mode or the **RMB** pick menu to make the required selections.

- Choose the action using the hotbox, shelf, or menus.

  The action is complete and the focus returns to your last transform tool.

> **Tip:**   *If a menu item contains the word "Tool" such as "Align Curves Tool," it uses tool interaction. If the word "Tool" is not mentioned, the menu item is set as an action. This dynamically updates according to your preferences.*

2D fillet as an action

A good example of a typical action is a 2D fillet. As with all actions, you must start with an understanding of what the tool needs before beginning to execute the action.

1   Draw two curves

- Select **Create → CV Curve Tool**.

- Place several points for one curve.

- Press **Enter** to complete.

- Press the **y** key to refocus on **Curve Tool**.

- Draw the second curve so that it crosses the first.

- Press the **Enter** key to complete.

Two curves for filleting

2 Find out 2D fillet requirements

- In the **Surfaces** menu set, move your cursor over the **Edit Curves** → **Curve Fillet** menu item without executing it.
- Look in the **Help Line** to determine what kind of pick is required.

   The Help Line says: "Select curve parameter points".

3 Pick the first curve point

- Click on the first curve with the **RMB**.
- Pick **Curve Point** from the selection marking menu.
- Click on the curve to place the point on the side you want to keep.

4 Pick the second curve point

- Click on the second curve with the **RMB**.
- Pick **Curve Point** from the selection marking menu.
- Press the **Shift** key and click on the curve to place the point on the side of the curve you want to keep.

   *The **Shift** key lets you add a second point to the selection list without losing the first curve point.*

RMB pick of curve parameter point

> **Note:** *You must first use the marking menu and then the **Shift** key to add a second point to the selection list, otherwise the selection menu will not appear.*

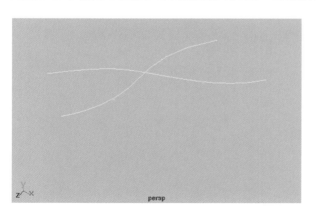

Two curve points in place

5 Fillet the curves

- Select **Edit Curves** → **Curve Fillet** → ❏ to open the tool options.
- Turn the **Trim** option **On**.

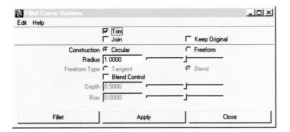

Fillet Tool options window

- Click on the **Fillet** button.

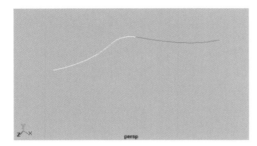

Final filleted curves

2D fillet as a tool

With this example you will use the menu item as a tool rather than an action.

1 Draw two curves

- In a new scene, draw two curves as in the last example.

2 Change curve fillet to tool

- Select **Edit Curves** → **Curve Fillet** → ❏.
- Select **Edit** → **As Tool** from the options window.
- Set **Trim** to **On**.
- Press the **Fillet Tool** button.

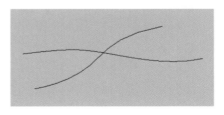

Two curves for filleting

Note: *Notice the menu item now says "Curve Fillet Tool."*

3 Pick the first curve

- Click with the **LMB** on the first curve.

4 Pick the second curve

- Click with the **LMB** on the second curve.

First curve selected

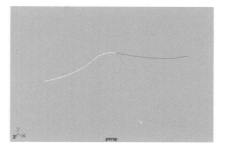

Final filleted curves

Conclusion

You now know how to navigate the Maya UI and how tools and actions work. The skills you learned here will be applied throughout the rest of this book and in your career. You have the knowledge now to determine how you want to use the interface. Experiment with the different techniques taught here as you work through the *Learning Maya* projects.

The instructions for the following projects will not specify whether or not you should use the hotbox or menus to complete an action—the choice will be yours.

In the next lesson, you will explore the Dependency Graph. You will learn about the different nodes and how to build them into hierarchies and procedural animations.

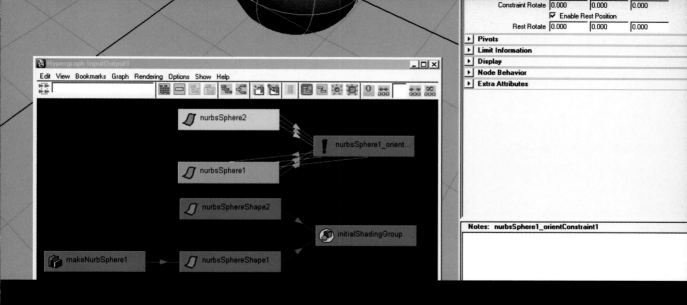

The Dependency Graph

In the first five lessons of this book, you encountered many nodes that helped you animate and render your scene. You were introduced to Input nodes, Hierarchy nodes, shading networks, and Texture nodes. These nodes, among others, represent key elements within Maya software—each node contains important attributes that help you define and animate your scenes.

In this lesson, you are going to explore nodes, attributes, and connections by animating objects at various levels. You will explore how attributes are connected by Maya software and how you can connect them yourself. You will also learn how to distinguish scene hierarchies from object dependencies.

This lesson might seem a bit abstract at first, but in the end you will see how the various nodes contribute to an animated scene that will help you in later lessons.

In this lesson, you will learn the following:

- About hierarchies and dependencies
- About connections
- About construction history

Maya architecture

The Maya architecture is defined by a node-based system, known as the *Dependency Graph*. Each node contains attributes that can be connected to other nodes. If you wanted to reduce Maya software to its bare essentials, you could describe it as *nodes with attributes that are connected*. This node-based approach gives Maya software its open and flexible procedural characteristics.

Hierarchies and dependencies

If you understand the idea of *nodes with attributes that are connected*, you will understand the Dependency Graph. Building a primitive sphere is a simple example involving the Dependency Graph.

1   **Set-up your view panels**

To view nodes and connections in a diagrammatic format, the Hypergraph panel is required along with a Perspective view.

- Select **Panels → Layouts → 2 Panes Side by Side**.
- Set up a Perspective view in the first panel.
- Set up a Hypergraph in the second panel by selecting **Panels → Hypergraph Panel → Hypergraph Hierarchy**.
- Dolly into the Perspective view to get closer to the grid.

2   **Create a primitive sphere**

- Select **Create → NURBS Primitives → Sphere**.
- Press **5** to turn on smooth shading.

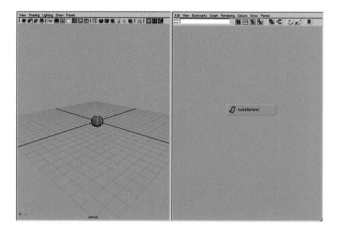

A new sphere

3 View the Shape node

In the Hypergraph panel, you are currently looking at the scene view. The scene view is focused on *Transform nodes*. This type of node lets you set the position and orientation of your objects.

Right now, only a lone *nurbsSphere* node is visible. In fact, there are two nodes in this hierarchy, but the second is hidden by default. This hidden node is a *Shape node* which contains information about the object itself.

- In the **Hypergraph**, select **Options → Display → Shape nodes**.

  You can now see the Transform node, which is the positioning node, and the Shape node, which contains information about the actual surface of the sphere. The Transform node defines the position of the shape below:

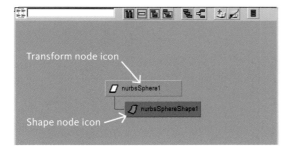

Transform and Shape nodes

- In the **Hypergraph** panel, select **Options → Display → Shape nodes** to turn these **Off**.

  Notice that when these nodes are expanded, the Shape node and the Transform node have different icons.

  When collapsed, the Transform node takes on the Shape node's icon to help you understand what is going on underneath.

Transform node on its own

4 **View the dependencies**

To view the dependencies that exist with a primitive sphere, you need to take a look at the up and downstream connections.

- In the **Hypergraph** panel, click on the **Input and output connections** button.

    The original Transform node is now separated from the Shape node. While the Transform node has a hierarchical relationship to the Shape node, their attributes are not dependent on each other.

    The Input node called makeNurbSphere is a result of the original creation of the sphere. The options set in the sphere's tool option window have been placed into a node that feeds into the Shape node. The Shape node is dependent on the Input node. Changing values for the Input node will affect the shape of the sphere.

    You will also see the initial shading group connected to the sphere. This is the default grey Lambert that is applied to all new objects.

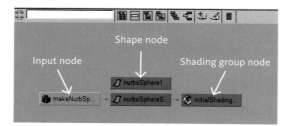

Sphere dependencies

 Tip: *In the previous image, the* **Orientation** *of the graph was changed to* **Horizontal.**

5 **Edit attributes in the Channel Box**

In the Channel Box, you can edit attributes belonging to the various nodes. Every node type can be found in the Channel Box. This lets you affect both hierarchical relationships and dependencies.

If you edit an attribute belonging to the *makeNurbSphere* node, then the shape of the sphere will be affected. If you change an attribute belonging to the *nurbsSphere* Transform node, then the positioning will be altered. Use the Channel Box to help you work with the nodes.

- For the Transform node, change the **Rotate Y** value to **45**.

- For the *makeNurbSphere* Input node, change the **Radius** to **3**.

 Note: *You can set attribute values to affect either the scene hierarchy or the Dependency Graph.*

Shading Group nodes

In earlier lessons, the word *node* was used a great deal when working with shading groups. In fact, Shading Group nodes create dependency networks that work the same way as Shape nodes.

1   Create a shading network

When you create a material, it automatically has a shading group connected to it.

- Select **Window → Rendering Editors → Hypershade.**
- In the **Hypershade** window, select **Create → Materials → Phong**.
- Assign this material to the sphere.
- Select the sphere in the Perspective panel and click on the **Input and output connections** button.

   In the Hypergraph view, you will notice how the Input node is connected to the Shape node, which relates to the Phong shading group.

   A line is now drawn between the sphere's Shape node and Shading Group node. This is because the Shading Group is dependent on the surface in order to render.

   Every time you assign a shading network to an object, you make a Dependency Graph connection.

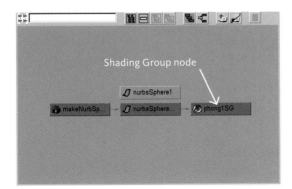

Shading Group dependencies

- Select the *nurbsSphere1* node and the *phong1SG* node in the **Hypergraph**.

- Again, click on the **Input and output connections** button.

  You can now see how the phong Material node and the sphere's Shape node both feed the Shading Group. You can move your cursor over any of the connecting lines to see the attributes that are being connected.

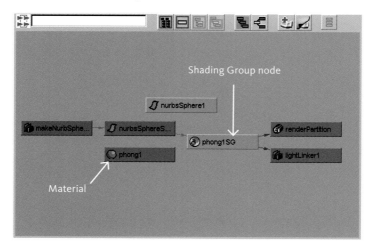

Assigned shading group

2 **Open the Attribute Editor**

You have seen how the nodes in the Hypergraph and Channel Box have been used to view and edit attributes on connected nodes. Now you will see how the Attribute Editor displays nodes, attributes, and connections.

- Click on the **Scene Hierarchy** button in the **Hypergraph** panel to go back to a scene view.

- Select the *sphere*'s Transform node.

- Press **Ctrl+a** to open the **Attribute Editor**.

  In this integral window, you will see several tabs, each containing groups of attributes. Each tab represents a different node. All the tabs displayed represent parts of the selected node's Dependency Graph that are related to the chosen node. By bringing up several connected nodes, you have easier access to particular parts of the graph.

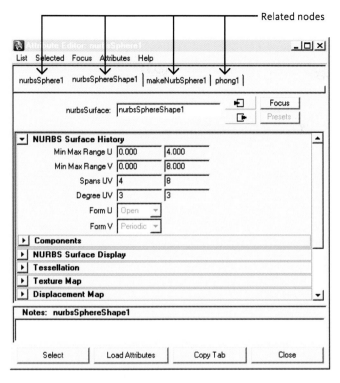

Related nodes

Nodes and attributes in the Attribute Editor

Note: *The Attribute Editor lets you focus on one part of the Dependency Graph at a time.*

Making connections

To help you understand exactly what a Dependency Graph connection is, you are going to make your own connection and see how it affects the graph.

1 **Open the Connection Editor**

- Select the *sphere*.

- Select **Window → General Editors → Connection Editor**.

- Click on the **Reload Left** button.

  The selected Transform node is loaded into the left column. All of the attributes belonging to this node are listed.

Note: *There are more attributes here than you see in the Channel Box. The Channel Box only shows attributes that have been set as keyable. Other attributes can be found in the Attribute Editor.*

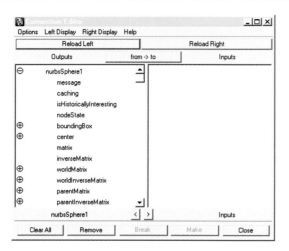

Transform node in the Connection Editor

2 Add phong as the Output node

- In the **Hypergraph**, select **Rendering** → **Show Materials**.

- Select the *phong1* Material node.

- In the **Connection Editor**, click on the **Reload Right** button.

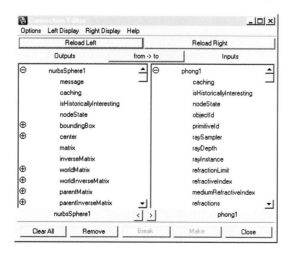

Material node in the Connection Editor

3   Make connections

You will now connect some attributes from the Transform node to the Material node.

- In the left column, scroll down until you find the *Translate* attributes.
- Click on the plus (+) sign to expand this multiple attribute and see the *Translate X, Y,* and *Z* attributes.
- In the right column, scroll down until you find the *Color* attribute.
- Click on the plus (+) sign to expand this multiple attribute and see the *Color R, G,* and *B* attributes.
- Click on the **Translate X** attribute in the left column.
- Click on the **Color R** in the right column.

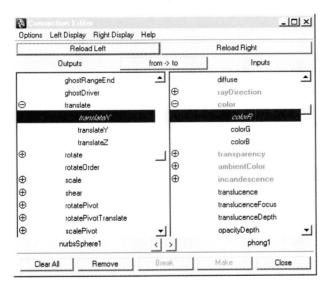

Connected attributes

- Use the same method to connect the following attributes:

    Translate Y to **Color G**;

    Translate Z to **Color B**.

4   View the connections

- In the **Hypergraph** panel, select the *Phong1* node and click on the **Input and output connections** button.
- Move your cursor over the arrow connection between the Transform node and Material node.

The connection arrow is highlighted and the connected attributes are displayed. You now see the diagrammatic results of your action.

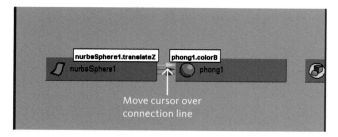

Viewing attribute connections

5   Move the sphere

You should see the effect of your connections when moving the sphere in the Perspective view.

- In the Perspective view, select the *sphere*.
- **Move** the sphere along the **X-axis**.

  The color of the sphere changes to red. By increasing the value of the translation along X, you add red to the color.

- Try moving the sphere along each of the three main axes to see the colors change.

Adding a Texture node

While it is a fun and educational exercise to see the Material node's color dependent on the position of the ball, it may not be very realistic. You will now break the existing connections and map a Texture node in their place.

1   Delete connections

You can delete the connections in the Hypergraph view.

- In the **Hypergraph** view panel, select one of the three connection arrows between the Transform node and the Material node.
- Press the **Backspace** or **Delete** key to delete the connection.
- **Repeat** for the other two connections between these nodes.

Broken connections

2   Add a checkered texture map

You will now use the Attribute Editor to help add a texture to the existing shading group.

- Click on the *phong1* Material node.

- Press **Ctrl+a** to open the **Attribute Editor**.

- Click on the **Map** button next to **Color**.

- Choose a **Checker** texture from the **Create Render Node** window.

- **MMB** in the Perspective view to make it active and press **6**.

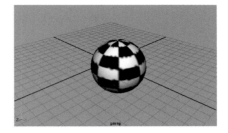

Textured sphere

In the Hypergraph, you can see the dependencies building up for the shading group. The texture is built using two nodes: the Checker node, which contains the procedural texture attributes, and the Placement node, which contains attributes that define the placement of the texture on the assigned surfaces.

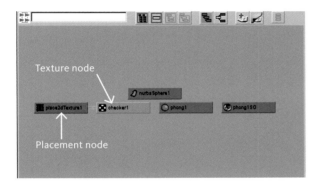

Shading group network

Animating the sphere

When you animate, you are changing the value of an attribute over time. You use keys to set these values at important points in time, then tangent properties to determine how the attribute value changes in-between the keys.

The key and tangent information is placed in a separate Animation Curve node that is then connected to the animated attribute.

1   Select the sphere

- In the **Hypergraph** panel, click on the **Scene Hierarchy** button.

- Select the *nurbsSphere* Transform node.

2   Return the sphere to the origin

Since you moved the sphere along the
three axes earlier, it is a good time to set
it back to the origin.

- Select the sphere's **Translate**
  attributes through the **Channel Box** by
  clicking on the **Translate X** value and
  dragging to the **Translate Z** value.

  *Doing so will highlight all three translate
  values, allowing you to enter a single
  value to change all of them at once.*

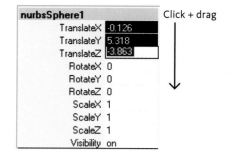

Click + drag

Click+drag on the scale values

- In the **Channel Box**, type **0** and hit **Enter**.

  Make sure all three translation values changed simultaneously.

- Make sure to also set all **Rotate** values to **0** and all **Scale** values to **1**.

3   Animate the sphere's rotation

- In the Time Slider, set the playback range to **120** frames.
- Go to frame **1**.
- Click on the **Rotate Y** attribute name in the **Channel Box**.
- Click with your **RMB** and select **Key Selected** from the pop-up menu.

  This sets a key at the chosen time.

- Go to frame **120**.
- In the **Channel Box**, change the **Rotate Y** attribute to **720**.
- Click with your **RMB** and select **Key Selected** from the pop-up menu.
- **Playback** the results.

  The sphere is now spinning.

4   View the dependencies

- In the **Hypergraph** panel, click on the **Input and output connections** button.

  *You will see that an Animation Curve node has been created and then connected to the
  Transform node. The Transform node is shown as a trapezoid to indicate that it is now
  connected to the Animation Curve node. If you move the mouse cursor over the connection
  arrow, you will see that the connection is to Rotate Y.*

  *If you select the Animation Curve node and open the Attribute Editor, you will see that each
  key has been recorded along with value, time, and tangent information. You can actually
  edit this information here, or use the Graph Editor where you get more visual feedback.*

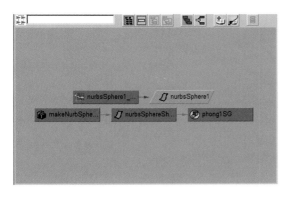

Connected Animation Curve node

Procedural animation

If the Maya procedural nature is defined as *nodes with attributes that are connected*, then a procedural animation would be set-up by animating attributes at various levels of a Dependency Graph network.

You will now build a series of animated events that build on each other to create the final result.

1   Create an edit point curve

- Hide everything in your scene by selecting **Display → Hide → All**.

- Select **Create → EP Curve Tool**.

- Press and hold the **x** hotkey to turn on grid snap.

- Draw a curve as shown below:

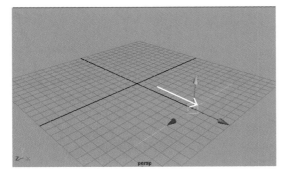

A new curve

- When you are finished, press **Enter** to finalize the curve.
- Select **Modify → Center Pivot**.

 Note: *The pivot of a new curve is centered to the origin by default.*

2 Duplicate the curve
- Select **Edit → Duplicate**.
- **Move** the new curve to the opposite side of the grid.

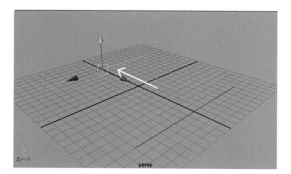

Moved curve

3 Create a lofted surface
A lofted surface can be created using two or more profile curves.

- **Click+drag** a selection box around both of the curves.
- Select **Surfaces → Loft**.

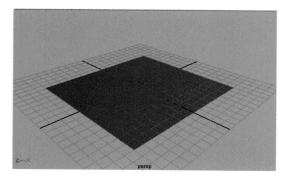

Lofted surface

4 **Change your panel display**

- In the **Hypergraph** panel, select **Panels → Perspective → persp**.

- In the new Perspective panel, select **Show → None and then Show → NURBS Curves**.

  Now you have two Perspective views. One shows the surface in shaded mode and the second shows only the curves. This makes it easier to pick and edit the curves in isolation from the surface itself.

5 **Edit CVs on the original curves**

- Select the first curve.

- Click with your **RMB** to bring up the selection marking menu and select **Control Vertex**.

- **Click+drag** a selection box over one of the CVs and **move** it down.

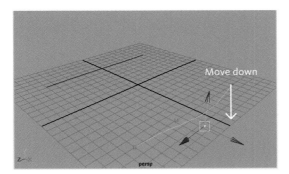

Edited profile curve

In the original Perspective view, you can see the effect on the lofted surface. Since the surface was dependent on the shape of the curve, you again took advantage of the Dependency Graph.

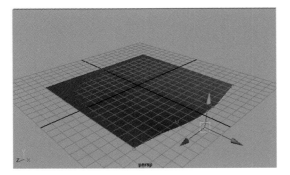

Resulting surface update

Note: *The dependencies associated with models are sometimes referred to as construction history. By updating the input shape, you have updated the history of the lofted surface.*

Curve-on-surface

You will now build a curve directly onto the surface. This curve will become dependent on the shape of the surface for its own shape.

The surface was built as a grid of surface lines called *isoparms*. These lines help define a separate coordinate system specific to each surface. Whereas world space coordinates are defined by X, Y, and Z, surface coordinates are defined by U and V.

1 Make the surface live

So far, you have drawn curves into the world space coordinate system. You can also make any surface into a *live* surface and draw into the UV space of the surface.

- Select the lofted surface.

  The CVs on the curve disappear and you are able to focus on the surface.

- Select **Modify → Make Live**.

  Live surface display changes to a green wireframe.

- Select **Display → Grid** to turn off the ground grid.

2 Draw a curve on the surface

- Select **Create → EP Curve Tool**.

- **Draw** a curve on the live surface.

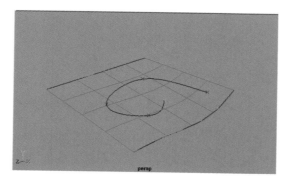

New curve-on-surface

3 Move the curve-on-surface

- Press the **Enter** key to complete the curve.

- Select the **Move Tool**.

  The move manipulator looks a little different this time. Rather than three manipulator handles, there are only two. One is for the U direction of the surface and the other is for the V direction.

- **Click+drag** on the manipulator handles to move the curve around the surface space.

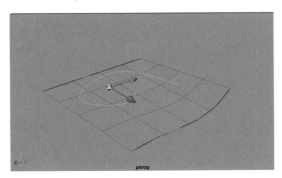

Moving the curve-on-surface

Tip:	*This UV space is the same one used by texture maps when using 2D Placement nodes.*

4 Revert live surface

- Click in empty space to clear the selection.

- Select **Modify → Make Not Live**.

  With nothing selected, any live surfaces are reverted back to normal surfaces.

Tip:	*You can also use the Make Live button on the right of the snap icons in the Status bar.*

Group hierarchy

You are now going to build a hierarchy by grouping two primitives, then animating the group along the curve-on-surface using path animation.

1   **Create a primitive cone**

    • Select **Create → NURBS Primitives → Cone**.

New primitive cone

2   **Create a primitive sphere**

    • Select **Create → NURBS Primitives → Sphere**.

    • **Move** the sphere above the cone.

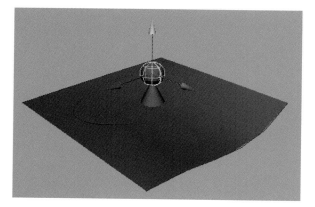

Second primitive object

3   **Group the two objects**

    • Select the cone and the sphere.

    • Select **Edit → Group** or use the **Ctrl+g** hotkey.

- Select **Display** → **Transform Display** → **Selection Handles**.

The selection handle is a special marker that will make it easier to pick the group in Object selection mode.

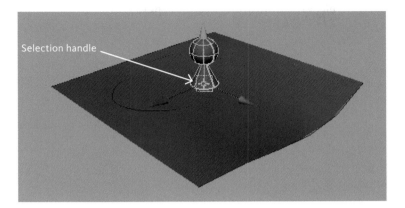

Grouped objects with selection handle

Note: *Selection handles have higher selection priority than curves and surfaces.*

Path animation

To animate the new group, you will attach it to the curve-on-surface. You can use the curve-on-surface to define the group's position over time.

1 Attach to the curve-on-surface

- With the group still selected, press the **Shift** key and select the curve-on-surface.
- Go to the **Animation** menu set.
- Select **Animate** → **Motion Paths** → **Attach to Motion Path** → ❏.
- In the Option window, make sure that the **Follow** option is turned **Off**.
- Click **Attach**.
- **Playback** the results.

As the group moves along the path curve, you will notice that it is always standing straight up.

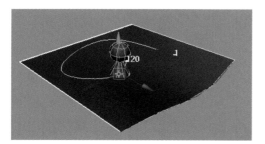

Path animation

2 Constrain to the surface normal

You will now constrain the orientation of the group to the normal direction of the lofted surface. The normal is like the third dimension of the surface's UV space.

- Click on the loft surface to select it on its own.

- Press the **Shift** key and select the grouped primitives using the selection handle.

- Select **Constrain → Normal → ❑**.

- In the **Option** window, set the following:

  Aim Vector to **0, 1, 0**;

  Up Vector to **1, 0, 0**.

- Click **Add** to create the constraint.

- **Playback** the results.

> **Note:** *If your group is upside down, it could be because the surface normals are reversed. To fix this, select your plane and select **Edit NURBS → Reverse Surface Direction**.*

Now the group is orienting itself based on the normal direction of the surface. The group is dependent on the surface in two ways. Firstly, its position is dependent on the path curve, which is dependent on the surface for its shape. Secondly, its orientation is directly dependent on the surface's shape.

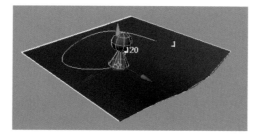

Constrained orientation

Layer the animation

The various parts of the Dependency Graph can all be animated to create exciting results. To see the Dependency Graph in motion, you will animate different nodes within the network to see how the dependencies react.

1 Edit the loft curve shape

Since the shape of the surface is dependent on the original loft curves, you will start by animating the shape of the second curve.

- Select the second loft curve.

> **Tip:** *You may want to use the second Perspective panel, which is only displaying curves.*

- Click with your **RMB** to bring up the selection marking menu and select **Control Vertex**.

  Control vertices define the shape of the curve. By editing these, you are editing the curve's Shape node.

- **Click+drag** a selection box over one of the CVs and move it up to a new position.

  As you move the CV, the surface updates its shape, which in turn redefines the curve-on-surface and the orientation of the group. All the dependencies are being updated.

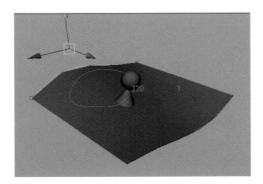

Updating the dependencies

2 Set keys on the CV position

- Go to frame **1**.
- Press **s** to set key.
- Go to frame **120**.
- Press **s** to set key.
- Go to frame **60**.

- **Move** the CV to a new position.
- Press **s** to set key.
- **Playback** the results.

    You can see how the dependency updates are maintained as the CV is animated. You are animating the construction history of the lofted surface and the connected path animation.

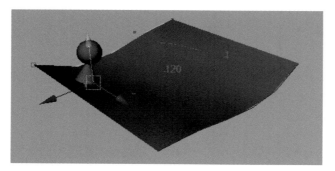

Animated history

3   **Animate the curve-on-surface**

   To add another layer of animation, you will key the position of the curve-on-surface.

- Select the curve-on-surface.
- Go to frame **1**.
- Press **s** to set key.
- Go to frame **120**.
- **Move** the curve-on-surface to another position on the lofted surface.
- Press **s** to set key.

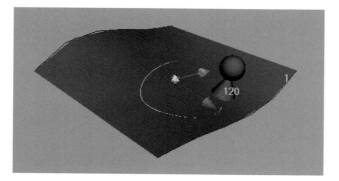

Animated curve on surface

4   **Assign the phong shading group**

To make it easier to see the animating objects, apply the checker shading group created earlier to the primitive group.

- Select the primitive group using its selection handle.
- Go to the **Rendering** menu set.
- Select **Lighting/Shading** → **Assign Existing Material** → **phong1**.
- **Playback** the scene.

5   **View the dependencies**

Of course, you can view the dependency network that results from all these connections in the Hypergraph view, which will probably be a bit more complex than anything you have seen so far.

- Select the primitive group that is attached to the motion path.
- Open the Hypergraph panel and click on the **Input and Output Connections** button.

The resulting network contains the various dependencies that you built during this example.

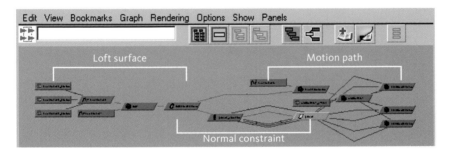

The dependency network

Conclusion

The procedural qualities of Maya software are tied to how the Dependency Graph uses nodes, attributes, and connections. You can see how deep these connections can go and how they are maintained throughout the animation process. Similar techniques can be used on other node types throughout Maya software.

Obviously, you don't have to use the Hypergraph and the Connection Editor to build, animate, and texture map your objects. In most cases, you will be thinking more about the motion of your character's walk or the color of their cheeks. It is still a good idea to know that the Dependency Graph supports everything you do and can always be used to your advantage.

In the next project, you will model, texture, set-up, and animate a scientist character.

Project 02

In this project, you will create a character named Delgo, one of the Lockni from the Fathom Studio movie *Delgo*. You will begin by modeling and texturing his skin using several polygonal tools. Once that is done, you will set-up his skeleton and rig it so that you can fully animate him. You will then test the rig by keyframing a simple walk cycle.

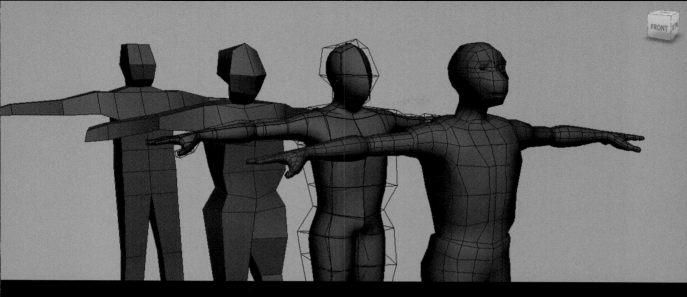

Polygonal Modeling

In this lesson, you will create Delgo, one of the Lockni from the Fathom Studio movie *Delgo*. The character will be created starting from primitives. You will use many polygonal tools and deformers until the desired shape is achieved. As you learned in the first project, it will be possible to edit the construction history of modeling actions to update the model as you go. As well, you can edit the results throughout the lesson until you delete the history.

In this lesson, you will learn the following:

- How to model starting from a cube primitive
- How to model using smooth preview
- How to model with symmetry
- How to work with polygonal components
- How to edit the topology of a polygonal model
- How to work with procedural modeling attributes
- How to change edge normals
- How to use a lattice deformer

Set-up your project

Since this is a new project, you must set a new directory as your current project directory. This will let you separate the files generated in this project from other projects. If you want to look at the final scene for this lesson, refer to the scene *07-delgo_06.ma*.

1 Set the project

As you have already learned, it is easier to manage your files if you set a project directory that contains sub-directories for different types of files that relate to your project.

- If you copied the support files onto your drive, go to the **File** menu and select **Project → Set...**

  A window opens, pointing you to the projects directory.

- Click on the folder named *project2* to select it.

- Click on the **OK** button.

  This sets the project2 directory as your current project.

  OR

- If you did not copy the support files on your drive, create a new project called *project2* with all the default directories.

2 Make a new scene

- Select **File → New Scene**.

Starting the character

You will build the character starting from a polygonal cube primitive. Facets will be extruded to create the more complex biped shape required and will then be refined to create the character shape.

It is important to understand what you will be doing throughout this lesson, so you must plan ahead and breakdown the task into simple stages. The following explains how you will approach the character modeling.

Torso

The cube primitive will be the pelvis area of the character. You will then extrude faces up to create the torso, neck, and head.

Legs

Starting from the pelvis geometry, you will extrude the polygon faces to create the legs.

Arms

Starting from the torso geometry, you will extrude polygon faces to create and refine the arms and hands.

Later in the lesson, you will ensure that your model is symmetrical by mirroring it.

> **Tip:** *It is a good idea to look at reference images from this project and from the gallery in this book to give you an idea of the finished product.*

1 Primitive cube

- Select **Create → Polygon Primitives → Cube**.

- Press **5** to **Smooth Shade All**.

- **Rename** the cube to *body*.

- From the **Inputs** section of the **Channel Box**, set the **Subdivisions Width** of the *polyCube1* node to **2**.

  Doing so will define polygonal edges going down the central line of the character.

> **Tip:** *As a general convention, you should always model your characters facing the scene's positive **Z-axis**.*

- Move the cube up by about **10 units** and **scale** it to roughly match the following, which represents the waist of the character:

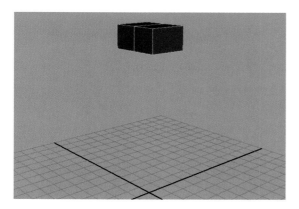

Start primitive cube

> **Tip:** *When modeling, don't be afraid to model big. You do not want to be stuck working on a tiny model. Use the grid as a reference to represent the floor. You can always edit the proportions of your character later on.*

2 Extrude faces

Before extruding the faces, you need to make sure that the **Keep Faces Together** option is enabled. When this option is **On**, it extrudes chunks of facets instead of each facet individually. The following is an example of **Keep Faces Together** both **On** and **Off**:

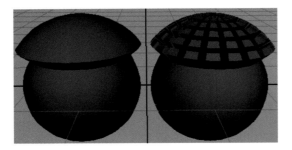

The Keep Faces Together effect

Note: *During the process of modeling the character, make sure that you do not accidentally select, deselect, or modify facets that are on the opposite side of the object. If you do, use Ctrl to deselect unwanted components.*

- Select the **Polygons** menu set by pressing **F3**.
- Make sure the option **Edit Mesh → Keep Faces Together** is set to **On**.
- Go into **Component** mode with faces displayed by pressing **F11,** or by setting the selection mask in the **Status Bar** as follows:

Component mode with faces enabled

Tip: *You can turn On or Off the preselection highlight in the preferences, under the Selection category.*

- Select the two top faces on the cube, then select **Edit Mesh → Extrude**.
- **Move** the faces up in the **Y-axis**.
- **Scale** them down uniformly a little bit.

- **Repeat** the last three steps to get geometry similar to the following:

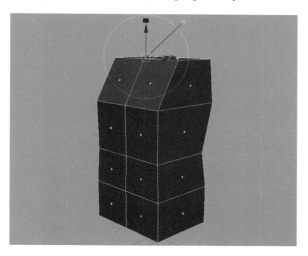

Waist and torso of the character

- **Extrude** four more times to make the neck, the chin, the middle of the head, and the top of the head of the character.

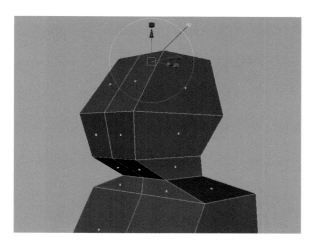

Neck and head of the character

Note: *You can preview smooth geometry by pressing the 1, 2, or 3 hotkeys with polygonal geometry selected.*

3   Smooth Mesh Preview

So far, you need a bit of imagination in order to see the character's shape. Smooth Mesh Preview is a simple tool that allows you to see a smoothed version of your model while still modeling on the cube from the previous steps.

- Go into Object mode.
- With the *body* selected, press the **2** hotkey.

Doing so displays the original geometry, known as the cage, in wireframe and displays the smoothed resulting geometry within it. Whenever you update the cage geometry, the smoothed version will automatically update. Once you have refined the cage to your needs, you can either go back to the unsmoothed version, or convert the geometry to the smooth version using **Modify → Convert → Smooth Mesh Preview to Polygons***.*

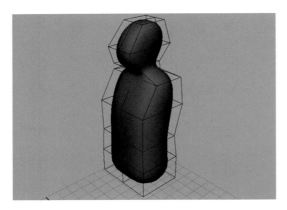

The cage and smoothed preview geometry

Tip: *You can tweak the smoothed version directly by pressing the* **3** *hotkey.*

4   Extruding the legs

Now that you can see the rough shape of the character's body, you need to extrude the legs. Here, you will extrude both legs at the same time.

- Select the cage geometry and display its faces.
- Select the two faces from underneath the pelvis to start extruding the legs.
- Turn **Off** the **Edit Mesh → Keep Faces Together**.

You will now be able to extrude both faces at the same time, still creating independent legs.

- Select **Edit Mesh → Extrude**.
- **Move** and scale the extruded faces down to the character's knees.

- **Extrude** again to create the bottom of the pants near the ankles.
- **Rotate** the faces from the last extrusion by about **45 degrees** in order to flow the next extrusion into the feet.
- **Extrude** and **move** the faces down to create the heels.
- **Extrude** to create the base of the toes.

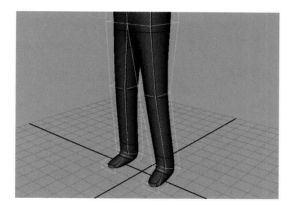

Leg extrusions

5 **Extruding the arms**

Since you should be concentrating only on the basic shape of the character, you will stop refining the legs here and go into extruding the arms.

- Select the faces on either side of the top torso.

- **Extrude** once and **scale** the faces down so the arms start with small shoulders.
- **Extrude** the arms up to the elbows.

- **Extrude** again up to the wrists.
- **Extrude** one last time to create the palm of the hand.

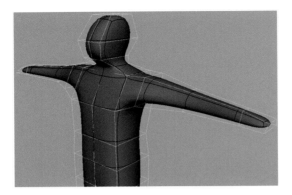

The extruded arms

6 Save your work

- **Save** your scene as *07-delgo_01.ma*.

Shaping the character

Now that the basic shape of the character is established, you can concentrate on moving polygonal vertices around to refine the general silhouette of the character.

Tip: *For a quick look at the silhouette of the character, you can press 7 on your keyboard. Without lights in your scene, this makes an instant black silhouette, allowing you to concentrate on contours.*

1 Tweak the proxy

In order to define the shape of the character a little better, you do not need to add geometry yet. Instead, you can edit the proxy geometry's vertices.

- Select the *body* geometry.
- Go into **Component** mode with **vertices** displayed.

Component mode with vertices enabled

- **Double-click** on the **Move Tool** in the toolbox to bring up its options.

- In the **Move Tool** options, set the following:

    Reflection to **On**;

    Reflection space to **World**;

    Reflection axis to **X**;

    Tolerance to **0.1**.

- Click on the **Close** button.

- Select a vertex on the proxy geometry and **move** its position.

    Because of the reflection option in the Move Tool, the corresponding symmetrical vertex is also moved.

Tip: *You should try to do symmetrical edits for this section of the lesson. It is not critical to always do them, but it will help you experience different tools and workflows. If you don't do symmetrical edits, try to always modify the same side of the model.*

- **Tweak** the global shape of the character using the cage geometry, until you cannot improve it anymore unless adding vertices.

Tip: *It is important to tweak the cage geometry so the smoothed geometry looks good and not the reverse.*

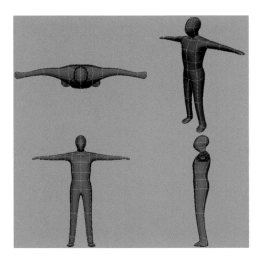

The refined shape

Tip: *The wireframe lines on the smoothed mesh are excellent guidelines to place articulations.*

2   Modeling tips

- With vertices selected, you can press the arrows on your keyboard to traverse the geometry components.

- Make sure to always look through different views when modeling. You can stay in the Perspective view, but be sure to use the **View Cube** located in the upper right corner.

The View Cube

- You can turn on the wireframe on shaded option by selecting **Shading → Wireframe on Shaded**. This will allow you to see the underlying geometry on the smoothed geometry.

- Try to not move the central line of vertices on their X-axis. This will make your work easier when you mirror the geometry.

Refine the character

You should now need more geometry to play with in order to get the character to the next level. Here, you will add to the existing geometry in order to better define key areas such as the arms, legs, feet, and hands. Here, you will only refine one half of the model; you will then mirror the geometry to make both sides identical.

1   Shape the bicep

The arm is very simplistic and the first step is to add more geometry to play with. You will add several edge loops to define the muscles.

Note: *An edge loop is defined by a continuous line of connected edges. The edges perpendicular to an edge loop are called edge rings.*

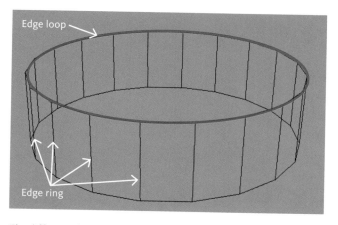

The difference between an edge loop and an edge ring

- With the *body* geometry selected, select **Edit Mesh → Insert Edge Loop Tool**.
- **Click+drag** on any horizontal edge in the upper arm bicep area.

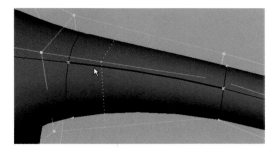

Insert an edge loop

- **Release** the mouse button to execute the tool.
- **Repeat** the last step to insert another edge loop next to the one you just inserted.

> **Tip:** *You can offset the edge loop by changing the* **Weight** *attribute for the polySplitRing node in the* **Channel Box**.

- **Tweak** the new vertices to shape the bicep.

2 Shape the forearm

- Insert a new edge loop in the middle of the forearm.
- Select **Edit Mesh → Offset Edge Loop Tool**.

  This tool allows you to simply add two edge loops on either side of an existing edge loop.

- **Click+drag** on any edge from the edge loop you just inserted.

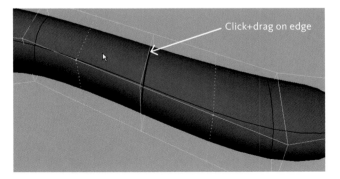

Click+drag on edge

Offset edge loop

- **Release** the mouse button to execute the tool.

3 Delete edges

By inserting two new edge loops, you can now delete the edge loop in the middle of the forearm, which is no longer required.

If you need to delete edges, it is possible to simply select them and press the delete key on your keyboard. However, working this way leaves vertices on the perpendicular edges that are not wanted. In order to compensate for this, there is a specialized command that can be used to correctly delete edges and vertices.

- Press **F10** to go into **Component** mode with the edge mask.
- **Double-click** on any of the vertical edge loops in the middle of the forearm.

  Doing so automatically selects the associated edge loop.

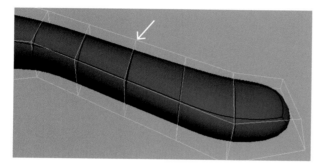

The edge loop to delete

- Select **Edit Mesh → Delete Edge/Vertex**.

  The entire edge loop is properly deleted.

- **Tweak** the new vertices to shape the forearm.

4 Sliding edges

At some point, you might want to offset edges or edge loops. The following shows a tool meant to do just that.

- **RMB** on the geometry and select **Edge**.
- **Double-click** on the edge loop that you want to slide.
- Select **Edit Mesh → Slide Edge Tool**.
- With the edge loop still selected, **MMB+drag** in the viewport to slide the edges.

 Tip: *Hold down the **Shift** key to slide the edges along their normals.*

5 Shape the leg

Using what you have just learned, shape the leg so it has more muscle mass.

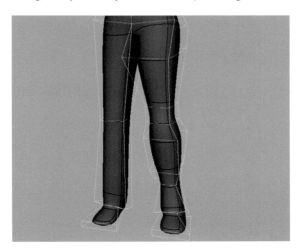

The shaped leg

> **Note:** *Don't forget to tweak only the leg on the same side as you just refined the arm.*

6 Flatten the feet

As you can see, the smoothed character model does not have flat feet. This can be fixed by extruding an additional face underneath the foot.

- Select the face under the foot.

- Select **Edit Mesh → Extrude**.

  Doing so forces the smoothed version of the geometry to be flatter in that area.

- Using the extrude manipulator, scale the face so it is a little smaller.

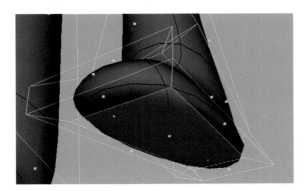

The flat foot sole

7 Splitting polygons

The Delgo character has two toes. In order to extract the toes, you will need to split polygonal faces at the front of the foot in order to create faces at specific locations to use for extrusions.

- Select **Edit Mesh → Split Polygon Tool**.
- **Click** on the edge on the inner side of the foot and then drag up so the new edge starts at an already existing vertex.
- **Click+drag** on the edge at the front of the foot to define a new vertex.
- **Click+drag** on the edge at the bottom of the foot to define a new vertex.
- **Click+drag** on the edge underneath the foot so the last edge ends at an already existing vertex.

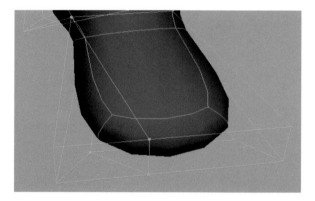

The toe split

- Hit **Enter** to complete the action.

  Doing so inserts a new set of edges that will split in two the face at the front of the foot so you can extrude the toes.

8 Toes

You will now extrude the toes.

- Select the two faces on the front of the foot where the toes should be extruded.
- **Extrude** twice to create the toes.
- **Tweak** the resulting vertices to your liking.

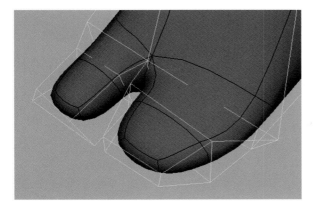

The extruded toes

9 Shape the hand

You can now take some time to extrude Delgo's five fingers out of his palm. His fingers are similar to human hands, so make sure to create three segments for each finger and two for the thumb.

- **Split** the palm **three** times as follows:

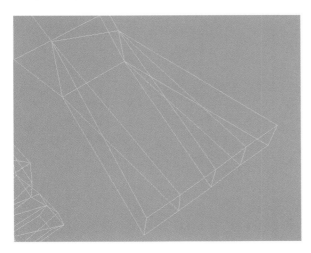

The finger splits

- **Extrude** the fingers **three** times.
- **Extrude** the thumb **three** times out of the face on the side of the palm.
- **Tweak** the resulting geometry to your liking.

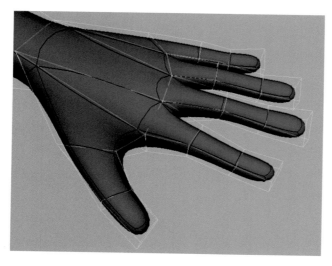

The refined hand

- **Split** across the inside of the palm, starting from the thumb and going to the pinky.
- **Tweak** the resulting geometry to your liking.

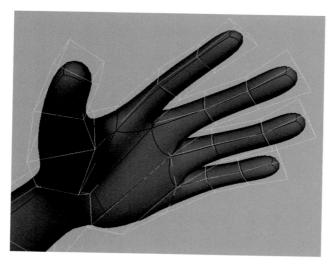

The refined palm

10 Save your work

- **Save** your scene as *07-delgo_02.ma.*

Mirror geometry

Mirroring geometry is a very important step when modeling since it saves you a lot of time when creating a symmetrical model.

The last few steps were not reflected on the other half of the character, so rather than redoing all the work for the other side, it is simpler to create a mirrored version of your geometry. This will also simplify your work once you begin modeling the character's face.

1 Delete one half

You will now delete one half of the model and duplicate the remaining half using instance geometry.

- Display the original *body* geometry by pressing the **1** hotkey.
- From the *front* view, press **4** to display the model in wireframe.
- Select all the faces on the left side of the character as in the following image:

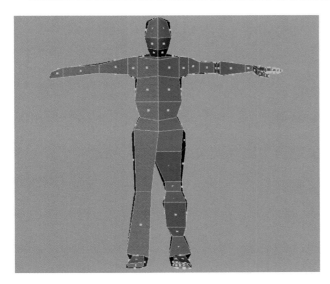

All the left faces selected

> **Tip:**   *Be careful to select faces that might be part of the right side.*

- Hit the **Delete** key on your keyboard.

2 Duplicate instance

- Go back into **Object** mode and select the *body* geometry.
- Select **Edit → Duplicate Special → ❏**.

- In the duplicate options, select **Edit → Reset Settings**, and then set the following:

    Geometry Type to **Instance**;

    Scale X to **-1**.

- Click the **Duplicate Special** button.

    The model is duplicated as a mirrored instance. An instanced object uses the same geometry as the original object, except that it can have a different position, rotation, and scaling in space. Any adjustments done on one side will simultaneously be done on the other side.

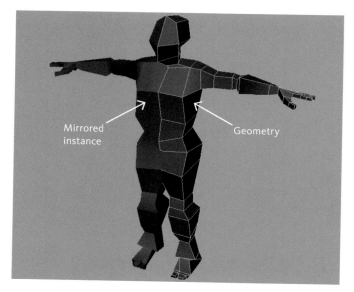

The model and its instance

3 Delete the history

At this point, your model might start to be heavy because of all the construction history involved with your model. The construction history list for the model in the Channel Box is starting to look impressive, but it is useless. Now is a good time to delete the history on your model and from the entire scene in order to speed up your work.

- Select **Edit → Delete All by Type → History**.

4 Save your work

- **Save** your scene as *07-delgo_03.ma*.

Refine the head

Perhaps the most important part of the character is the face. This exercise will go through some steps in order to refine the head, but most of the work will have to be done by yourself, since this is an artistic task which cannot easily be explained step–by-step.

Several new tools will be explained here with some key examples that will require experimentation. If you would like to use the final scene of this exercise as a reference, look for the scene *07-delgo_04.ma* from the support files.

1   Split an edge ring

There are several ways to access the different modeling commands other than with the menus. If you like working with the menus, keep doing so, but the following is an alternative that involves a hotkey and a marking menu.

- Deselect any edges from the *body* geometry.
- **Pick** one of the horizontal edges on the side of the head.
- Hold down the **Ctrl** key and then **RMB** on the geometry.

  This brings up a polygonal modeling marking menu.

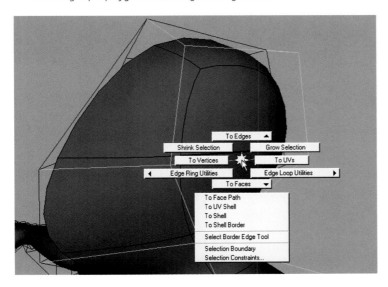

The modeling marking menu

- From the marking menu, select **Edge Ring Utilities**.

  Doing so automatically pops up a second marking menu related to edge rings.

- Select **To Edge Ring and Split**.

  The command automatically selects the related edge ring around the chosen edge, and then does a split on those edges.

  Notice that when inserting and splitting edge loops or rings, the tool keeps splitting across polygonal faces with four sides. If it encounters polygonal faces with more than or fewer than four sides, the tool stops splitting more edges. This can be very useful, but it can also go through your entire character before it stops splitting edges. In this example, notice how the edges split the middle finger and the toes, thus adding unwanted extra geometry.

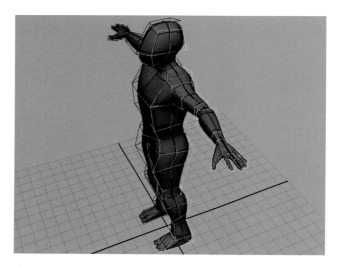

The edge ring split goes across the entire model

2 Control splitting polygons

In order for you to control how many edges are split as well as the path the tool is taking, there is an option that allows you to pick the edge to split. The following is an example of such an application.

- **Undo** the last command.
- Select **Edit Mesh → Insert Edge Loop Tool → ❏**.
- In the **shown** window, turn **Off** the **Auto Complete** option.
- Click the **Close** button.
- **Pick** the central horizontal edge on the top of the head.

  The tool now requires you to pick subsequent edges in order to define an edge loop.

- **Pick** an edge on the wrist of the model.

  The tool displays the solved edge loop.

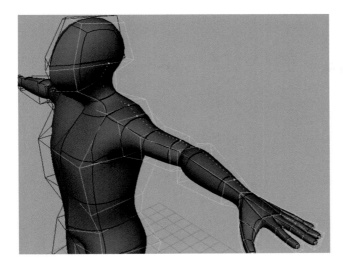

The solved edge loop

> **Note:** *You can keep selecting other edges to define a longer edge loop. The edges do not need to be part of the same edge ring.*

- **Pick** an edge on the top of the head of the model.
- Press the **Enter** key when you are ready to insert the proposed edge loop.
- Select **Edit Mesh → Split Polygon Tool**.
- Split from the new vertex at the wrist to the vertex between the middle fingers.
- **Delete** the edge beside it to make a quad instead of two triangles.

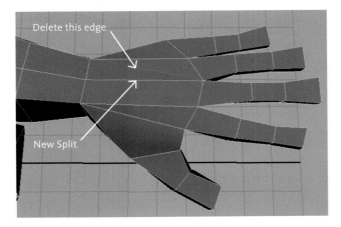

The new split and edge to delete

Tip: *When modeling, it is preferable to try building quad polygons rather than triangles.*

3 Splitting the lower body

You will now propagate a new edge loop split from the palm, along the side of the body, to the foot, and in-between the legs.

- Select **Edit Mesh → Insert Edge Loop Tool**.
- **Pick** the central edge at the base of the palm.
- **Pick** the edge on the side of the ankle.
- Instead of going into the toes like the automated results, **split** straight down into the foot sole edge.
- Continue splitting across the foot sole and up into the crotch.

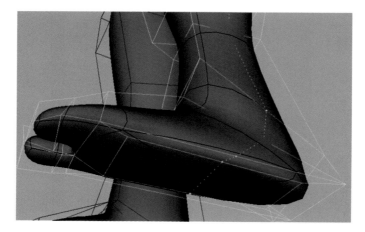

The specific path to split the foot

- Hit the **Enter** key when you are ready to insert the proposed edge loop.
- Split from the new vertex in the palm to the vertex between the middle fingers.
- **Delete** the edge beside it to make a quad instead of two triangles.

4 Tweak the inserted vertices

There is now much more geometry to refine all over the character. The further you will get into the modeling, more and more artistic work comes into play. You must use your own judgment to define the geometry to your liking.

5 Save your work

- **Save** your scene as *07-delgo_04.ma*.

Keep on modeling

You now have a good understanding of polygonal modeling basics. By continuing to refine the character, you will see that the time spent experimenting will provide invaluable experience. Throughout the modeling process, you can explore trial and error processes that will eventually achieve great solutions. At some point, you will be able to visualize the different steps to take without ever touching the model.

The following are some general directions to finish modeling the character. To see the final scene of this exercise, look for the scene *07-delgo_05.ma* from the support files.

1   Snap the central axis of the body

The following will ensure that all the vertices on the central axis of the body are correctly aligned on the X-axis.

- Select the mirrored instance and then hit the **Delete** key.
- With the *body* selected, select **Display → Polygons → Border Edges**.

  Doing so shows any edges that are located on borders in the geometry with thicker lines.

- From the *front* view, select all the vertices that are on a border.

> **Tip:** *Confirm in the Perspective view that you have selected all the required vertices.*

- **Double-click** on the **Move Tool** to bring up its options.
- In the **option** window, scroll down and turn **Off** the **Retain component spacing** option.

  Doing so will allow you to snap the vertices to the X-axis all at once.

- Hold down the **x** hotkey to snap to grid, then **click+drag** on the X-axis of the move manipulator to snap all the selected vertices to the central **X-axis**.
- Make sure that no vertex crosses the central X-axis. If so, translate them back on the left side of the body.

2   Mirror the geometry

You can now make the entire body a single polygonal mesh.

- While in **Object mode** with the *body* selected, select **Mesh → Mirror Cut.**

  A plane will be added to your scene, which is used as a mirror to make your model symmetrical.

- With the *mirrorCutPlane* selected, set its **Translate X** attribute to **0.0.**

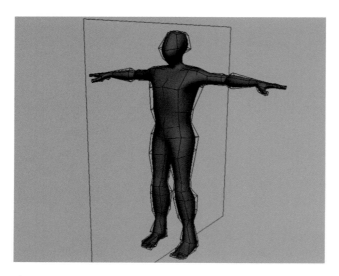

The mirrored geometry

- Select **Edit → Delete All by Type → History**.

  Doing so will allow you to finalize the geometry and delete the mirror plane.

- **Delete** the *mirrorCutPlane*.

3 Smooth the geometry

The Smooth Mesh Preview is a great way to create a general shape for your character, but at some point, you will need to tweak the smoothed geometry rather than continuing to work on the low resolution cage.

In the following, you will smooth the geometry to get a higher resolution and start refining the higher resolution model.

- Select the *body* geometry and press the **3** hotkey.

- Select **Modify → Convert → Smooth Mesh Preview to Polygons**.

  You now have a higher resolution model to work with, but the default smoothing value is higher than you require.

- Highlight the *polySmoothFace1* node in the **Channel Box**, and set **Divisions** to **1**.

  The geometry is now less dense, but perfect for your needs.

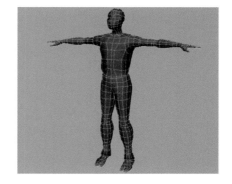

The high resolution model   High resolution refinements

4   Tweak the vertices

Now that you have more vertices defining your character, you can play with the shape of the character.

- Make sure the **Reflection** option for the **Move Tool** is turned **On** so that any modifications are made on both sides of the model.

Tip: *Don't be afraid of moving vertices one by one. You will most likely end up moving each vertex by hand for the entire model anyway.*

While you are tweaking the vertices around the eyes, try to define the different facial areas with edges. Doing so will help you see the different parts of the face, and it will also make it easier to split polygons to get even more resolution.

5   Removing definition

When working with a model that was automatically smoothed, you might end up with edge loops that are absolutely necessary to better define the model. For instance, the toes might have too much resolution for your needs. Here you will learn a quick way to delete edge loops.

- Identify an edge loop to be deleted.

- While in **Component mode** with the edge mask enabled, select a single edge of the edge loop to be deleted.

- Hold down the **Ctrl** key and click your **RMB** to select **Edge Loop Utilities → To Edge Loop and Delete**.

  The edge loop is automatically deleted.

- Experiment with other edge loop and edge ring utilities.

6 Add divisions

You must now concentrate on splitting and refining only one half of the model.

- **Delete** half the model and create a mirrored **instance** as previously shown.
- Use the **Split Polygon Tool** to insert new edges where required in order to better define certain areas.
- Use the **Delete Edge/Vertex** to remove unwanted edges where you will split new faces.

Tip: As a rule, try to always create four-sided polygons when splitting geometry. Doing so will spare you problems later on.

- **Extrude** the eye socket faces and **scale** them slightly toward the inside to add circular edges in the eye area.

Edges inserted

- **Split** the mouth area to refine the lips.

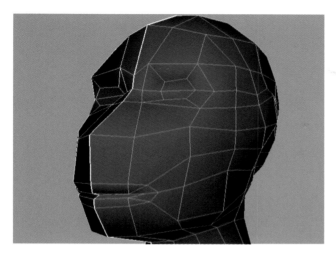

The final head

7 **Soft normals**

The extrusion and polygon splits create hard edges by default. The following shows how to soften the edges of the entire model at once.

- With the *body* geometry selected, select **Normals → Soften Edge**.

8 **Merging the model**

At this point, you can continue refining the model, or call it final and go on with the rest of the project.

- **Delete** the instanced geometry.
- Select the *body* geometry.
- Select **Mesh → Mirror Geometry → ❏**.
- In the options, specify the **Mirror Direction** to be **–X**.
- Click the **Mirror button**.

    The geometry is mirrored and then merged together to create a full body.

9 Merging edges

It is possible that, through the process of modeling, you moved central vertices off the mirror plane, causing the geometry to have open edges along the central axis. The following shows how to merge those edges.

- Select the *body* geometry.
- Select **Display → Polygons → Border Edges**.

  Doing so causes border edges to be displayed with a thicker wireframe line.

- Press **4** to see your model in wireframe.

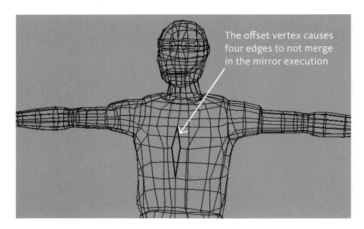

The offset vertex causes four edges to not merge in the mirror execution

An open edge

- Select **Edit Mesh → Merge Edge Tool**.

  This tool allows you to pick two edges and force them to merge together.

- **Pick** any of the opened thicker edges.

  Possible edges to be merged are highlighted in pink.

- **Pick** the pink edge located on the other half of the model.
- Hit **Enter** to merge the edges.

  The edges should now be closed.

- **Repeat** the previous steps for any other open edges.

10 Final steps

- With the *body* geometry selected, select **Normals → Soften Edge**.
- Select **Edit → Delete All by Type → History**.

11 Save your work

- **Save** your scene as *07-delgo_05.ma*.

Proportions

Sometimes when modeling, you sit back and look at your work thinking you could improve the proportions of the model. An easy way to change a model's proportions is to create and modify a lattice deformer. A lattice surrounds a deformable object with a structure of points that can be manipulated to change the object's shape. Once you are happy with the new proportions, you can simply delete the history, thus freezing the deformations on the model.

1 Create a lattice deformer

- Select the *body* geometry.

- From the **Animation** menu set, select **Create Deformers → Lattice**.

  A large lattice box is created around your model.

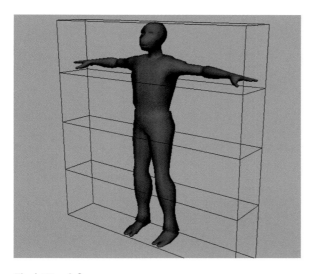

The lattice deformer

- In the **Channel Box** with the lattice selected, set the *ffd1LatticeShape* node as follows:

  S Divisions to **9**;

  T Divisions to **9**;

  U Divisions to **3**.

  Doing so will change the amount of subdivisions in the lattice deformer, which in turn adds more lattice points to deform the surface with. This will allow more control over the deformations.

> **Tip:** *You may adjust these settings to better fit your geometry and divide the model into body part sections, but only do so before you start tweaking the lattice box.*

2 Deform the lattice box

- **RMB** on the lattice object in the viewport to bring up the lattice context menu, and select **Lattice Point**.

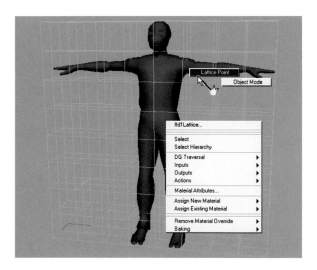

The lattice context menu

- **Transform** the lattice points just as you would do with vertices.

  Notice how the lattice points deform the geometry.

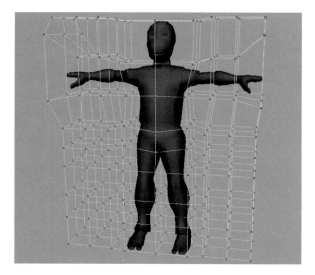

Delgo proportions

- Find the best proportions possible.

3 Delete the deformer

If you simply deleted the lattice deformer, the geometry would snap right back to its original shape. In order to keep the deformation and freeze the geometry with that shape, you need to delete its history, which will automatically delete the deformer.

- Select the *body* geometry.
- Select **Edit → Delete by Type → History**.

Final touches

The body of the character looks great, but Delgo is still missing key components, such as eyes. The eyes will be created in a simplistic manner, starting from NURBS primitives.

Just like the rest of this lesson, you will model only half the geometry and then mirror it over to the other side.

1 Eyeball

- Select **Create → NURBS Primitives → Sphere**.
- **Rename** the sphere to *eyeball*.
- **Rotate** the *eyeball* by **90** degrees on its **X-axis**.
- **Translate** and **scale** the *eyeball* to the proper eye location.

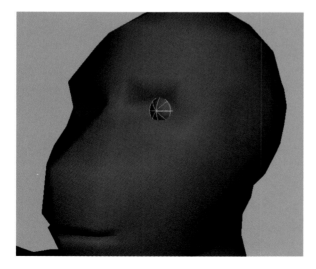

The eyeball in place

2 **Eyelid**

- With the *eyeball* selected, select **Edit → Duplicate Special → ❑**.

- In the shown window, select **Edit → Reset Settings**, then turn **On** the **Duplicate input graph** option.

    This option duplicates the geometry along with all its inputs, such as construction history, which will be used here.

- Click the **Duplicate Special** button.

- **Rename** the duplicate to *eyelid*.

- From the **Channel Box**, **rotate** the eyelid by **-90** degrees on its **Y-axis**.

- **Scale** the *eyelid* so that it is a little bigger than the *eyeball*.

- In the **Channel Box**, highlight the *makeNurbsSphere2* Input node.

- Set the **Start Sweep** to **20** and the **End Sweep** to **340**.

    The eyelid will use its construction history in order to simplify the eye blinks.

The eyelid

Note: *Advanced modelers should be creating realistic looking eyes by modeling the eyelids starting from the original polygonal geometry. This will not be covered in this book.*

3 **Mirror the eyeball**

- Select the *eyeball* and *eyelid*.

- Press **Ctrl+g** to **group** them all together.

- With the new group selected, select **Edit → Duplicate Special**.

  Doing so will duplicate the required construction history on the eyelid, which will be needed later for eye blinking.

- In the **Channel Box** with the duplicated group still selected, set **Scale X** to **-1**.

  You now have eyes for both sides of the character.

> **Note:** *From now on, do not delete the construction history for the entire scene since the eyelids require it for blinking. If you want to delete the history, do it only for the selected models.*

4 Save your work

- **Save** your scene as *07-delgo_06.ma*.

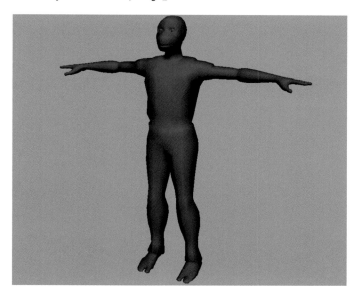

The final model

Conclusion

In this lesson, you learned how to model a complete character out of basic polygonal primitives. In the process, you used several polygonal modeling tools to create the shape and details. As you noticed, each tool created an Input node for which you were able to modify the construction history. You also used the lattice deformer, which is a great tool to know about.

In the next lesson, you will texture the character. This will allow you to experiment with polygonal texture tools and techniques.

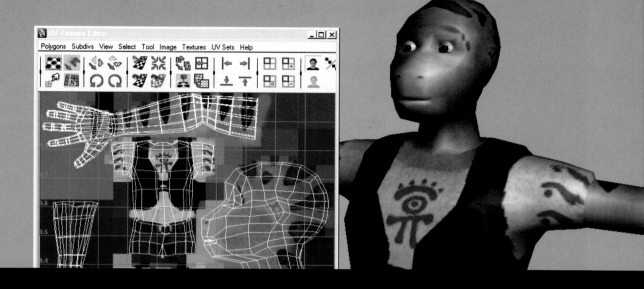

Polygonal Texturing

You now have a polygonal mesh that requires texturing. Even though polygons have a default setting for UV parameters onto which textures can be applied, in this lesson you will adjust these to get the best possible result. You can use special polygon tools to assign and modify these kinds of values on the model.

You will first apply texture projections in order to create UV coordinates on the mesh. Then, you will texture the character using the 3D Paint Tool to paint directly on the model.

In this lesson, you will learn the following:

- How to use the UV Texture Editor
- How to project UVs on polygons
- How to manipulate projections
- How to grow and reduce the current selection
- How to assign and paint textures using the 3D Paint Tool
- How to remove unused shading groups

Texturing polygonal surfaces

The character will be textured using multiple shading groups and texture maps. You will start by positioning a texture on the main body geometry, which will be accomplished using constructive polygon texturing tools. Once that is done, you will texture the eyes of the character. Feel free to continue using your own file, or start with *07-delgo_06.ma* from the last lesson.

1 UV Texture Editor

The UV Texture Editor is where you can see the UVs of your model. UVs are similar to vertices except that they live in a flat 2D space. The UVs determine the coordinates of a point on a texture map. In order to properly assign a texture to a polygonal model, the UVs need to be unfolded somewhat like a tablecloth.

- Select the *body* geometry.
- Select **Window → UV Texture Editor**.

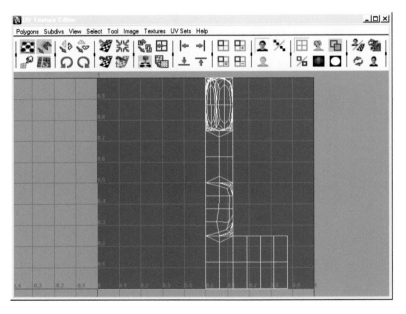

The UV Texture Editor

Displayed in the UV Texture Editor are the UVs for the selected geometry. Those UVs are now irregular and will result in a very poor texture mapping.

2   **Create and assign a body shader**

   • **Open** the **Hypershade** window.

   • **Create** a *blinn* Material node.

   Blinn is the simplest material that once properly set-up can look like skin.

   • **Rename** the Material node to *bodyM*.

   • **Assign** the *bodyM* material to the *body* geometry.

   • To view the upcoming steps, press **6** on your keyboard to turn **On** the **Hardware Texturing** in the Perspective view.

3   **Map a checker to the color**

   • Open the **Attribute Editor** for the *bodyM* material.

   • **Map** the **Color** attribute with a **Checker** Texture node.

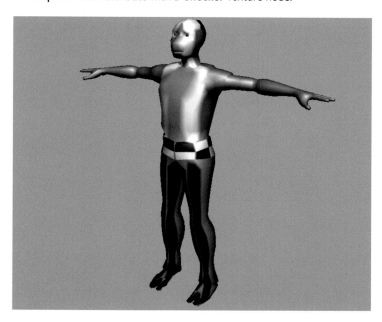

Irregular texture placement due to poor UVs

> **Note:** *The checker texture is just a temporary texture in order to better see the UV placement on the model.*

4 Planar mapping

In order to start correcting the texture mapping of the character, you will use a planar projection.

- With the *body* geometry selected, select **Create UVs** → **Planar Mapping** → ❑ from the **Polygons** menu set.
- In the option window, select **Project** from **Z-axis**.
- Click the **Project** button.

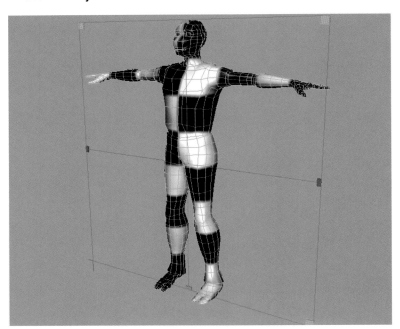

Planar projection

> *A large projection plane icon surrounds the object, which projects the texture map along the Z-axis. You can see the texture mapped onto the surface with hardware texturing.*

5 Projection manipulators

The projection manipulator allows you to transform the projection to better suit your geometry.

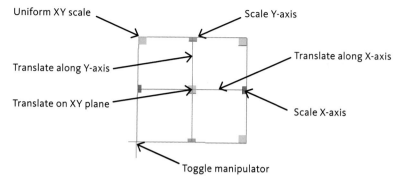

Planar projection manipulator

You can toggle the manipulator type for a conventional all-in-one manipulator by clicking on the *red T*.

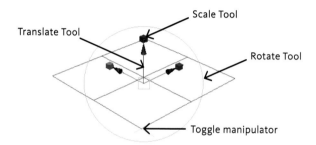

Other planar projection manipulator

> **Note:** *If the projection manipulator disappears, reselect the geometry, click on the polyPlanProj Input node in the Channel Box, and select the Show Manipulator Tool, or press the **t** hotkey.*

6 **UV Texture Editor**

If you change the positioning of the manipulator from the previous step, you will see that the UVs of the model in the UV Texture Editor have been updated to be projected according to the manipulator in the viewport.

- In the UV Texture Editor menubar, select **Image → Display Image** to toggle the display of the checker texture to **Off**.

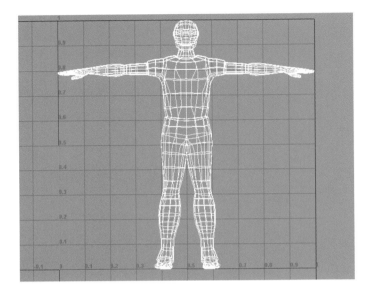

The projected UVs

Modifying UVs

It is important to prevent overlapping of the UVs where it is not wanted. For instance, if you make a planar projection from the front of the model, the UVs would overlap on the front and back of the model. If you make the chest of the character another color, the back would also change.

1   **Projection for the head**
  - **RMB** on the *body* geometry and select **Face**.
  - Select the faces of the head and neck.
  - Select **Create UVs** → **Planar Mapping** → ❑.
  - In the option window, select **Project** from **X-axis**.
  - Click the **Project** button.

    Doing so will make the head symmetrical across the X-axis.

2   Moving the UVs

- In the UV Texture Editor with the character's head faces still selected, **RMB** and select **UV** from the context menu.

  Doing so sets the current selection mask to UVs only.

- **Click+drag** a selection rectangle over the entire head.

  The UVs of the head are now selected.

- **Scale** and **move** the UV shell under the arm of the character.

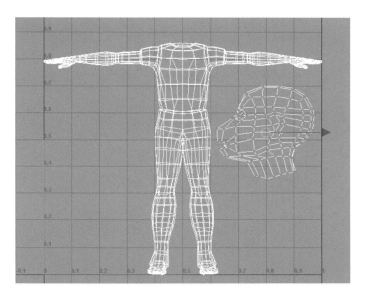

Tweaked UV shell

Note: *Individual* **UV** *groups are called* **UV shells**.

3   Projection for the arms

- Select the faces of the hands of the character in the Perspective view.

- From the main Maya interface, select **Select → Grow Selection Region**.

  The neighbor UVs on the model are selected, which increases the current selection.

Tip: *You can press* **Shift+>** *to increase the selection and* **Shift+<** *to shrink the current selection.*

- Select **Select** → **Grow Selection Region,** or press **Shift+>** a few more times until you have the arm selected up to the sleeves.
- Select **Create UVs** → **Planar Mapping** → ❏.
- In the option window, select **Project** from **Y-axis**.
- Click the **Project** button.

  Doing so will make the head symmetrical across the Y-axis.
- Select **Select** → **Convert Selection** → **To UVs**.
- Place the UV shells in the **UV Texture Editor** like the following:

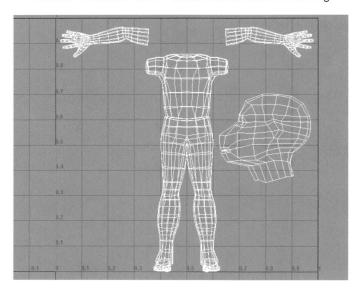

All of the arm UVs selected

4 Projection for the legs

- **Repeat** the previous step to create a projection across the **X-axis** for the legs**.**

5 Layout UVs

At this time, the UVs of the character are good enough to start texturing except for one thing. The front and back of the torso are overlapping, which would cause undesirable effects when texturing. The following shows a simple solution to solve this.

- In the **UV Texture Editor**, select a few UVs of the torso UV shell.
- Still in the **UV Texture Editor**, choose **Select** → **Select Shell**.

  Doing so selects all the UVs that are part of the same continuous group of UVs.
- Select **Polygons** → **Layout** → ❏.

- In the option window, set the following:

  Layout objects to **Per object (overlapping)**.

  Separate shell to **Folds**.

- Click the **Layout UVs** button.

  Doing so separates the overlapping UVs into two distinct UV shells.

- Manually layout the UV shells to look like the following:

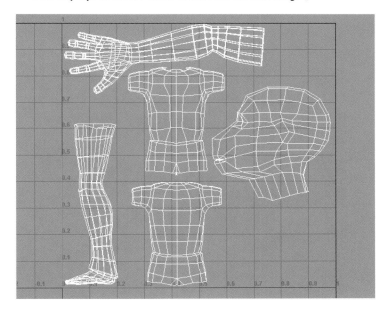

Unfolding and scaling the UVs

> **Note:** *The arms were moved on top of each other so you only have to texture one of them in the next exercise.*

- Close the UV Texture Editor.

6 Save your work

- **Save** your scene as *08-delgoTxt_01.ma*.

3D Paint Tool

A great way to create custom texture is to paint a texture directly on a model in the viewport. The 3D Paint Tool allows you to paint using default paintbrushes or Paint Effects' brushes. You can use the tool to outline details to be painted in separate software, or to create a final texture directly in the Maya software.

Tip: *As you are working with the 3D Paint Tool, you might want to change the way the UVs are laid out to minimize texture stretching and overlapping.*

1 **Open the 3D Paint Tool**
   - Select the *body* geometry.
   - Select the **Rendering** menu set by pressing **F6**.
   - Select **Texturing** → **3D Paint Tool** → ❏.

     This will open the tool's option window.
   - Scroll down to the **File Textures** section.
   - Make sure **Attribute to Paint** is set to **Color**.
   - Click the **Assign/Edit Textures** button.

     This will open the new texture creation options.
   - Set **Image Format** to **Tiff (tif)**.
   - Set both the **Size X** and **Size Y** to **512**.

Tip: *For more definition in your textures (if your computer can handle it), you might want to boost up the texture resolution to 1024x1024 or even 2048x2048.*

   - Click the **Assign/Edit Textures** button.

     Doing so will duplicate the currently assigned texture and save it in your project in the 3dpainttextures folder. As you paint on the geometry, only this new texture will be automatically updated.

2 **Set the initial color**
   You will now paint a color over the old checkered pattern.
   - In the **3D Paint Tool settings**, change the **Color** attribute in the **Flood** section to be **green**.
   - Click on the **Flood Paint** button.

     The character is now totally green.

3 Set erase image

To make sure that you can erase your drawing and come back to the original texture, you need to set the erase image as the current texture.

- Scroll to the **Paint Operations** section and click on the **Set Erase Image** button.

4 Paint on geometry

- Under the **File Textures** section, turn **On** the **Extend Seam Color** option.

  This option will make sure that there are no visible seams when painting.

- Scroll at the top of the **3D Paint Tool** and make sure the second **Artisan** brush is enabled in the **Brush** section.

- When you put your mouse cursor over the geometry in the viewport, if the brush size is too big or too small for painting, set its **Radius (U)** in the option window, or hold the **b** hotkey and **drag** the radius of the brush in the **viewport**.

- Change the **Color** attribute from the **Color** section to **orange**.

- **Paint** directly on the geometry to define the character's shirt.

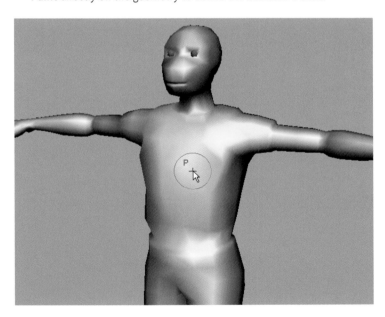

The painted shirt

Tip: *Undoes are supported when painting strokes, or you can erase them by setting the Paint Operation to Erase. When erasing, you are reverting to the texture saved when you clicked the* **Set Erase Image** *button in the previous step.*

5 Reflection

Since the shirt is to be symmetrical, it is a good idea to turn on the reflection capability of the 3D Paint Tool.

- Under the **Stroke** section, turn **On** the **Reflection** option, and make sure the **Reflection axis** is set to **X**.

- Paint the character's vest **black**.

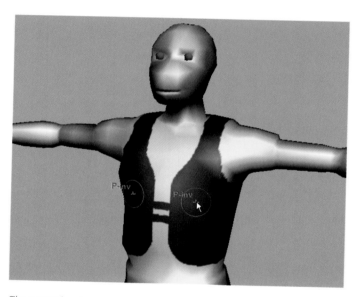

The painted vest

6 Paint options

Under the **Paint Operations** section, you can set various paint operations like Paint, Erase, Clone, Smear, and Blur. You can also set the Blend Mode, which affects the way new strokes are painted on your texture. Those options can be very useful for tweaking your texture.

- Continue painting the character with different colors on the different parts of his body such as the head, eyebrows, ears, arms, feet, pants, and belt.

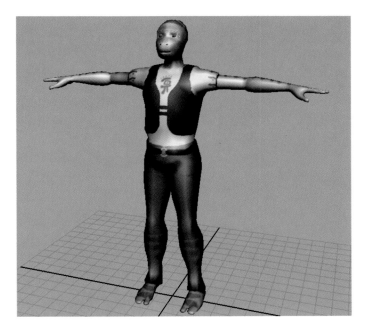

Fully painted character

> **Note:** *Sometimes, painting directly on the geometry creates artifacts due to things such as seams, color, texture resolution, UV placement, UV overlapping, etc. One way of correcting this is by editing the texture later in a paint program.*

7 Paint Effects

- Scroll to the **Brush** section of the tool and enable the first **Paint Effects** brush.
- To choose a template brush, click on the **Get Brush** button to pull up the **Visor**.

Get Brush button

- In the **Visor**, scroll to the *Watercolor* directory and choose the brush called *spatterMed.mel*.
- Experiment by painting on Delgo's skin to give it some definition.

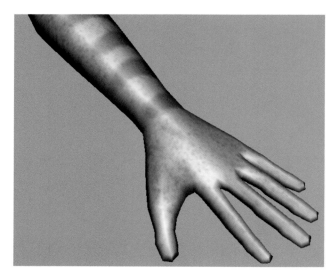

Paint Effects' strokes

8 Screen projection

When painting with a Paint Effects brush, you will notice that the brush icon in the viewport looks stretched. This is because the brush bases itself on the object's UVs, which are stretched. To correct the problem, you need to enable the screen projection option.

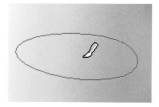

Stretched brush

- Expand the **Stroke** section in the **3D Paint Tool** window.
- Turn **On** the **Screen Projection** attribute.
- **Paint** on geometry.

> **Note:** *When painting with Screen Projection, you are painting using the current camera view. This can be very useful in some cases, but can also create stretched textures when painting on geometry parallel to the view.*

9 Reference strokes

You might find it easier to draw only reference strokes in the Maya software and then use a paint program to refine the look of the texture. To do so, you will draw where you want to add texture details on the object, and then open the texture in a paint program. Once you are finished with the texture, you can reload it in the Maya software.

10 Save textures

You have not yet saved to disk the texture just drawn, making it inaccessible to another program.

- To save the texture manually, click the **Save Textures** button in the **File Textures** section.

  OR

- To save the texture automatically on each stroke, turn **On** the **Save Texture on Stroke** checkbox in the **File Textures** section.

11 Edit the texture

You can now edit your texture from the *3dpainttextures* directory in a paint program. When you have finished modifying the texture, save the new image.

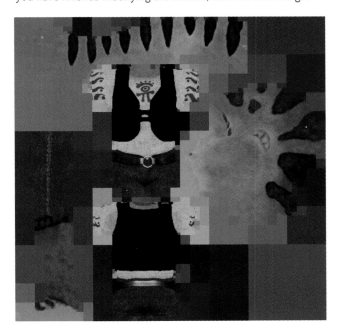

The final texture

- Back in Maya, in the texture's **Attribute Editor**, click the **Reload File Textures** button to update the skin texture for the new version.

The final texture on the model

Tip: *If you saved the file under a different name or in a different location, browse to get the modified texture.*

Final touches

In order to finish texturing the character, you must texture the eyeballs and eyelids. Note that the eyes were made out of NURBS surfaces, so they will not require extra UV steps. The texturing of NURBS surfaces will be shown in more detail in the third project.

1   **Create and assign an eye shader**
   - **Open** the Hypershade window.
   - **Create** a *phong* Material node.

     Phong is the material that suits the shiny eyes best.
   - **Rename** the Material node to *eyeM*.
   - **Assign** the *eyeM* material to both *eyeballs*.

2   **Map a ramp to the color**
   - Open the **Attribute Editor** for the *eyeM* material.
   - **Map** the **Color** attribute with a **Ramp** Texture node.

- **Rename** the Ramp node to *eyeColor*.

3 Tweak the ramp

- In the **Attribute Editor** for the *eyeColor*, set **Type** to **U Ramp**.
- **Tweak** the ramp's colors as in the following image:

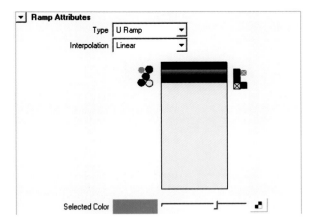

4 Create and assign an eyelid shader

- **Create** a *Blinn* material and **rename** it to *eyelidM*.
- Set the **Color** of the material to be a color similar to the surrounding eye color of the character.

- **Assign** the *eyelidM* to the *eyelid* objects.

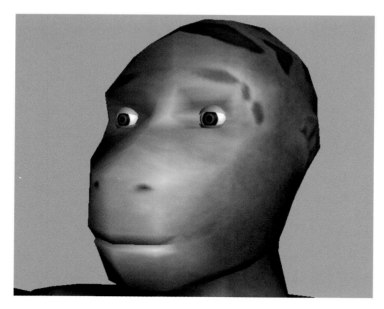

The textured eyes

Optimizing the scene

To maintain a good workflow, you should clean up your scene once texturing is complete. For instance, you might want to delete all unused shading networks in the scene.

5 Delete unused nodes

- From the **Hypershade** window, select **Edit → Delete Unused Nodes**.

  Maya will go through the list of Render nodes and delete anything that is not assigned to a piece of geometry in the scene.

6 Optimize scene size

- Select **File → Optimize Scene Size**.

  Maya software will go through the entire scene and remove any unused nodes.

7 Delete the history

- Select all the objects except the *eyelids*.

- Select **Edit → Delete by Type → History**.

8 Save your work

- The final scene, *08-delgoTxt_02.ma*, can be found in the support files. Delgo's texture is called *body.tif* and is located in the *3dpainttextures* directory.

Conclusion

You now have a good understanding of texturing polygons. You have experimented with a projection and some polygonal tools and actions. There is much more to learn concerning polygonal texturing, so feel free to experiment on your own.

In the next lesson, you will learn about creating joint chains, which is the first step for animating a character.

Lesson 09

Skeleton

In this lesson, you will create the skeleton hierarchy to be used to bind the geometry and to animate Delgo. In order to create a skeleton, you need to draw joints to match the shape of your character. The geometry is then bound to the skeleton and deformations are applied.

In this lesson, you will learn the following:

- How to create skeleton joints
- How to navigate around a joint hierarchy
- How to edit joint pivots
- How to mirror joints
- How to reorient joints
- How to edit the joint rotation axis

Drawing a skeleton chain

In this exercise, you will draw skeleton chains. Even if this operation appears to be simple, there are several things to be aware of as you create a joint chain.

1 **Joint Tool**

   - **Open** a new scene and change the view to the *side Orthographic view.*
   - From the **Animation** menu set, select **Skeleton → Joint Tool → ❑**.

     The tool's option window is displayed.
   - Change the **Orientation** attribute to **None**.

Note: *This attribute will be explained later in this exercise.*

   - Click the **Close** button to close the tool window.
   - In the side *view,* **LMB+click** two times to create a joint chain.
   - Press **Enter** to exit the tool.

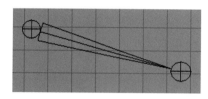

A simple joint chain

Joint hierarchy

2 **Joint Hierarchy**

   - Open the **Hypergraph**.

     Notice the joint hierarchy, which is composed of two nodes.

3 **Adding joints**

   - Click on the **Joint Tool** icon in the toolbox or press the **y** hotkey to access the last tool used.
   - **LMB** on the end joint of your previous chain.

     The tool will highlight the end joint.
   - **LMB+click** two times to create a Z-like joint chain.

     The new joints are children of the joint selected in the previous step.
   - You can **MMB+drag** to change the last joint placement.
   - Press **Enter** to exit the tool.

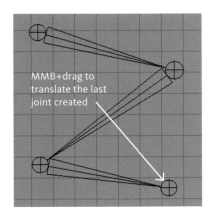

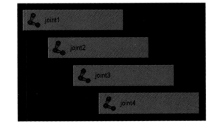

New joint chain   *Joint hierarchy*

4 Automatic joint orientation

When using the automatic orientation, all three joint axes are aligned according to the right-hand rule. For example, if you select an orientation of XYZ, the positive X-axis points into the joint's bone and toward the joint's first child joint, the Y-axis points at right angles to the X-axis and Z-axis, and the Z-axis points sideways from the joint and its bone.

> **Note:** *If you look closely at the joints in the Perspective view, you can see these axes and where they are pointing.*

- **Double-click** on the **Joint Tool** icon in the toolbox.

  The tool's option window is displayed.

- Change the **Orientation** attribute to **XYZ**.

- **Close** the tool window.

- Create a second joint chain similar to the first one.

  Notice that as you draw the joints, they are automatically oriented toward their child.

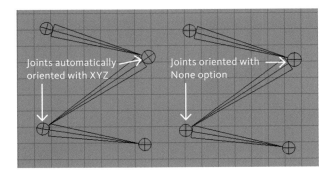

Joint orientation

5 Joint rotation axis

To better understand the effect of the joint orientation, you need to rotate in local mode and compare the two chains you have created.

- **Double-click** on the **Rotate Tool** icon in the toolbox.

  The tool's option window is displayed.

- Select **Local** as the **Rotation Mode**.

  This specifies that you want to rotate nodes based on their local orientation rather than using the global world axis.

- **Close** the tool window.

- Select the second joint of both chains and see the difference between their rotation axes as you rotate them.

  Notice that when the joint is properly oriented, it moves in a more natural way.

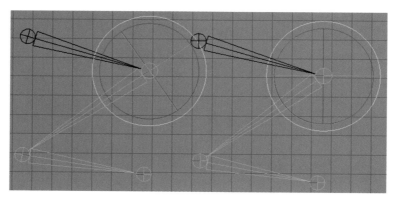

Joint rotation axis

Complex joint chain

When you create a complex joint chain, you can use some features intended to simplify your work. For instance, you can navigate in a hierarchy of joints as you create them. You can also use a command to reorient all the joints automatically.

1 Navigate in joint hierarchy

- **Delete** all the joint chains in your scene.

- Make the *top view* active.

- Press the **y** hotkey to access the **Joint Tool**.

 Note: *Make sure the tool* **Orientation** *is set to* **XYZ**.

- **Draw** three joints as follows:

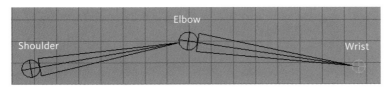

Arm chain

- **Draw** a thumb made of two joints.

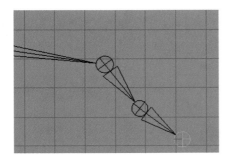

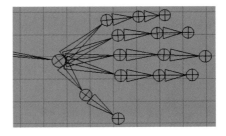

Thumb joints

Completed hand

- Press the **up arrow** twice on your keyboard to put the selection on the wrist joint.

  The arrows let you navigate in the hierarchy without exiting the Joint Tool.

- **Draw** the index joints and press the **up arrow** again.

- **Draw** the remaining fingers as above.

2 **Snap to grid**

- Press the **up arrow** until the selection is on the shoulder joint.

- Hold down the **x** hotkey to snap to grid and add a spine bone.

- Press **Enter** to exit the Joint Tool.

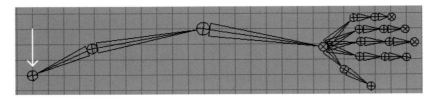

Spine bone

3 Reroot a skeleton

In the last step, you created a spine bone that is the child of the shoulder bone. This is not a proper hierarchy since the spine should be the parent of the shoulder. There is a command that allows you to quickly reroot a joint chain.

- Select the *spine* bone, which was the last joint created.
- Select **Skeleton** → **Reroot Skeleton**.

The spine is now the root of the hierarchy.

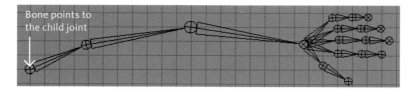

Spine joint as root

4 Mirror joints

Another very useful feature is the ability to mirror a joint chain automatically.

- Select the *shoulder* bone.
- Select **Skeleton** → **Mirror Joint** → ❑.
- In the option window, specify **Mirror Across** the **YZ** plane.
- Click the **Mirror** button.

Both arms

Skeleton

You are now ready to create a skeleton for the character from the last lesson. To do so, you need to determine the proper placement of each joint. Once that is done, you will need to set a proper joint orientation so that when you rotate a joint, it rotates in an intuitive manner. If you do not take great care for placement and orientation, you will have difficulty animating the character later.

1 Open scene

- **Open** the file *08-delgoTxt_02.ma*.

- While in **Hardware Texturing** mode, select **Shading** → **X-Ray Joints** from the panel menu.

  This shading mode shows the joints on top of the geometry, helping you place the joints accurately.

2   Character spine

In this step, you need to determine a good placement for the pelvis bone, which will be the root of the hierarchy. Once that is done, it will be easy to create the rest of the spine bones.

- Select **Skeleton** → **Joint Tool**.
- Make the *side view* active.
- **LMB** to create the *pelvis* joint.

  It is recommended that the pelvis joint be aligned with the hips.

- **LMB** to draw **three** equally spaced joints, which will represent the *spine*, *spine1*, and *neck* joints.
- **LMB** to draw **two** equally spaced joints, which will represent the *neck1* and *head* joints.
- Lastly, **LMB** to draw the *nose* joint.
- Hit **Enter** to complete the joint chain.

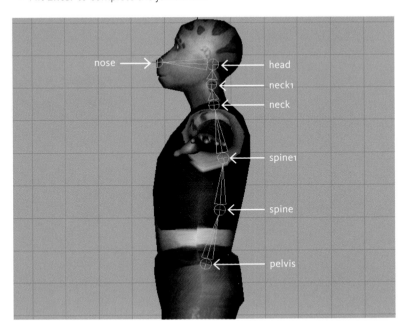

Pelvis, spine, and head joints

Tip: *If you find the displayed joints to be too big or too small, this is a visual representation that can be changed by setting* **Display → Animation → Joint Size** *to your liking.*

- **Rename** each joint properly.

Note: *A spine could be made of more bones, but this is not required in this example. The nose joint would normally be used only to get a visual representation of the head when the geometry is hidden, but you might as well use it to deform the nose to create a cartoon-y animation.*

3 Create a leg

You now need to create the legs of the character. The new joint chain will be in a separate hierarchy, but you will connect it to the pelvis later on.

- Select **Skeleton → Joint Tool**.
- **Click+drag** the *hip* joint to its proper location.

  The hip joint should be centered on the hip geometry, very close to the pelvis joint.

- **Draw** the remaining *knee, ankle,* and *toe* joints, and create an extra joint on the tip of the foot, which should be called *toesEnd*.

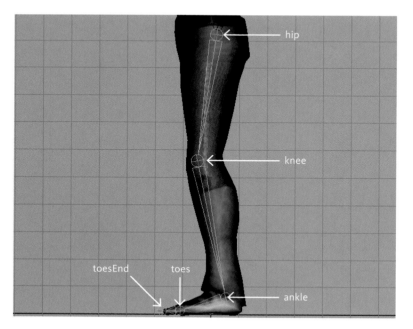

Leg joints

- Press **Enter** to exit the tool.
- Change to the *front view*.

  Notice that all the bones you created were drawn centered on the X-axis. That was correct for the spine, but not for the leg.

- On the *hip* joint, **Translate** on the X-axis and **rotate** on the Y-axis to fit the geometry as follows:

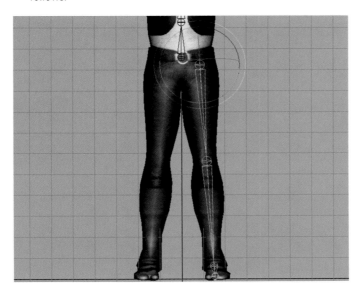

Front view

4 Connect and mirror the leg

- Select the *hip* joint, then **Shift-select** the *pelvis* joint.
- Select **Skeleton → Connect Joint → ❑**.
- Change the **Mode** option to **Parent Joint**.
- Hit the **Connect** button.

  The leg is now parented to the pelvis.

> **Note:** *You could also parent using the* **p** *hotkey.*

- Select the *hip* joint.
- Select **Skeleton → Mirror Joint → ❑**.

- Set the following:

    Mirror across to **YZ**;

    Mirror function to **Behavior**.

    This option will cause the legs to have the same behavior.

- Click on the **Mirror** button.

    If your character was modeled symmetrically, it should now have two legs properly placed.

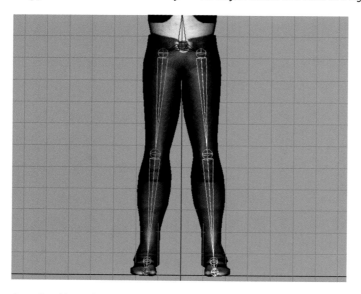

Completed lower body

- **Rename** all the joints appropriately.

Tip: *Make sure to prefix the joints on the left side with **l**, and the ones on the right side with **r**. For example, if you name the ankle, you may want to call it lAnkle.*

5 Arm and hand joints

- Select **Display → Animation → Joint Size...**

- Set the **Joint Size** to **0.25**.

    Doing so will reduce the display size of the joints in the viewport, making it easier to place joints close together, such as the finger joints.

- From the *front view*, draw a joint to represent the *clavicle* between the *spine1* and *neck* joints, then draw the *shoulder* joint.

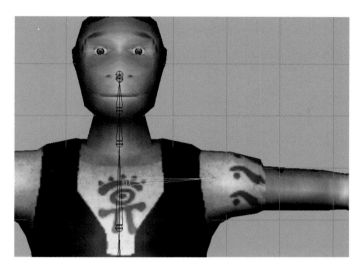

The clavicle and shoulder joints

- Change to the *top view*.
- **Move** the *clavicle* on the **Z-axis** to better fit the geometry.
- **Draw** the character's *elbow* and *wrist* joints.

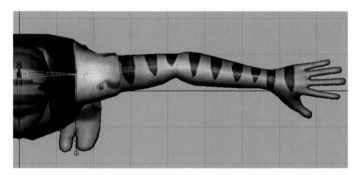

The arm and hand joints

- Change to the *front view*.
- **Rotate** down the joints on the **Z-axis** to better fit the geometry.

Tip: *It is a better workflow for joint placement to rotate the joints rather than translating them.*

- From the *top view*, draw the finger and thumb joints.
- Make sure the joints are properly positioned in the *Perspective view*.

- **Rename** all the joints correctly.

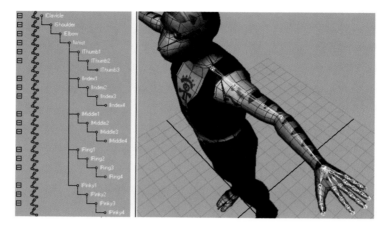

Joints correctly placed and named

> **Tip:** *It might be easier to set the display in the viewport as* **X-Ray Joints** *with* **Wireframe on Shaded**.

6 Joint pivot

In some cases, you might want to adjust the position of a joint without moving all of its children. You can use the **Insert** key (**Home** key on Macintosh) to move a joint on its own, or hold down the **d** hotkey.

For instance, if the angle defined by the shoulder, elbow, and wrist joints is not appropriate, you can correct the problem by moving a joint on its own.

- Select the *elbow* joint.
- Select the **Move Tool**.
- Press the **Insert** key (**Home** on Macintosh).
- **Move** the pivot of the *elbow* joint.
- Press the key again and exit the Move Pivot manipulator.

7 Connect and mirror the arm

- Select the *clavicle* joint, then **Shift-select** the *spine1* joint.
- Press **p** to parent the joints.

  The arm is now parented to the spine1 joint.

- Select the *clavicle* joint.
- Select **Skeleton → Mirror Joint → ❏**.

- In the option window, make sure to set **Mirror** function to **Behavior**.

  This option will cause the arms to have mirrored behavior.

- Click on the **Mirror** button.

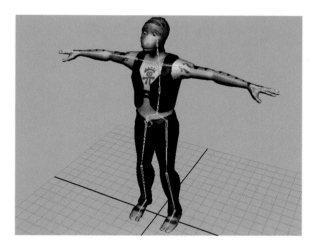

Proper arms

8 **Details**

- Select the **Joint Tool**.

- From the *side view*, click on the *head* joint to highlight it.

  Doing so tells the tool that you want to start drawing joints from the head joint.

- **Draw** one joint for the *eye* and two for the *jaw* as follows:

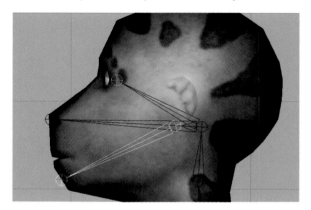

The new head joints

- **Rename, translate,** and **mirror** the new joints when needed.

Tip: *When mirroring the eye joint, make sure to set the **Mirror** function to **Orientation** so the eyes move together and are not mirrored.*

9 Save your work

- **Save** your scene as *09-delgoSkeleton_01.ma*.

Joint orientation

Now that the character has a skeleton, you need to double-check all the joint orientations using the Rotate Tool. In this case, most of the joint orientations will be correct by default, but there will be times when you will need to change some orientations to perfect your skeleton.

1 Hide the geometry

- From the *Perspective view*, select **Show** → **Polygons** and **Show** → **NURBS Surfaces** to hide them.

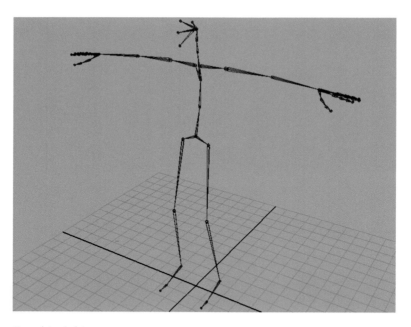

Complete skeleton

2   Default rotation values

It is recommended that all rotations of a joint hierarchy be zeroed out. This means that when the skeleton is in the current default position, all the joint rotations are zero.

- Select the *pelvis* joint.

- Select **Modify → Freeze Transformations**.

  If you rotated bones in previous steps, their rotations are now zeroed out.

Note: *Unlike geometry, joint translations cannot be zeroed or else they would all be at the origin.*

3   Reorient all joints

You can reorient all the joints in a hierarchy automatically to your preferred orientation, such as XYZ.

- Select the *pelvis* joint.

- Select **Skeleton → Orient Joint → ❏**.

- Make sure the **Orientation** is set to **XYZ**, then click the **Orient** button.

  All the joints are now reoriented to have their X-axis pointing toward their first children.

Note: *When reorienting joints, you might lose inserted mirrored behavior when mirroring the joints. A good workflow is to mirror the joints only after making sure half the skeleton was perfectly created with proper local rotation axes.*

4   Local rotation axes

The automatic orientation of the joints is not always perfect. Depending on how your skeleton was built, it can flip certain local rotation axes and you need to manually fix those pivots.

- Select the *pelvis* joint.

- Press **F8** to go into **Component mode** and enable the **?** mask button.

Local rotation axes mask

  All the local rotation axes are displayed in the viewport for the selected hierarchy.

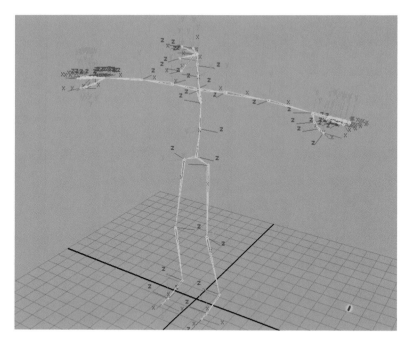

Local rotation axes in the viewport

5 Manually set the local rotation axes

It might seem confusing at the moment, but changing the local rotation axes is quite easy. There is one axis per joint, and if you dolly closer to a joint, you will see that the axis respects the left-hand rule, where the X-axis points toward the first child joint.

In certain cases, you will not want the automatic orientation setting. Problems usually arise when you select multiple bones and rotate them at the same time. For instance, if you selected all of the spine and neck joints, you would notice an odd rotation shaped like an accordion, since their Z rotation axes point in different directions.

The left-hand rule

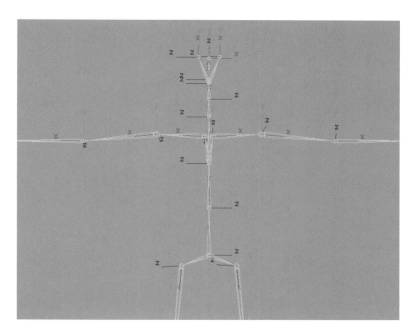

Bad rotation axes

To fix the problem, manually select an incorrect local rotation axis and rotate it into a good position.

- Still in Component mode with the local rotation axis displayed, select the *pelvis, spine,* and *neck1* local rotation axes (in this case), by clicking on them and holding down the **Shift** key.

- **Double-click** the **Rotate Tool**.

- In the tool's options, set **Snap rotate** to **On** and **Step size** to **90**.

- **Rotate** on the **X-axis** by **180 degrees**.

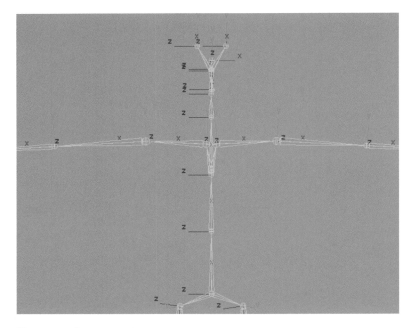

The corrected rotation axis

- In the **Rotate Tool's** options, set **Snap rotate** to **Off**.
- Go back into **Object mode** and try rotating the hips, spine, neck, and head together.

  The problem seen earlier is now solved.

Note: *It is normal that mirrored joints have an inverted local rotation axis. This is a welcome behavior set in the Mirror Joint command, which allows animation to be mirrored from one limb to another.*

6 **Test the skeleton**

You should now test your skeleton to see if everything is rotating as expected. If you notice incorrect local rotation axes, attempt to correct them manually by following the steps outlined above. Typical problematic areas are the knees and ankles, since the joint chains are made in a Z shape.

Note: *The end joint's local rotation axis usually is not important since it might not be intended for animation.*

7 **Save your work**

- Save your work as *09-delgoSkeleton_02.ma*.

Conclusion

You now have greater experience creating skeleton chains and navigating skeleton hierarchies. You have learned how to move and rotate joints, and how to use joint commands such as reroot, connect, mirror, and orient. Finally, you have manually changed local rotation axes, which is the key to creating a good skeleton for animation.

In the next lesson, you will bind the character geometry to the skeleton and explore different techniques and tools used for character rigging.

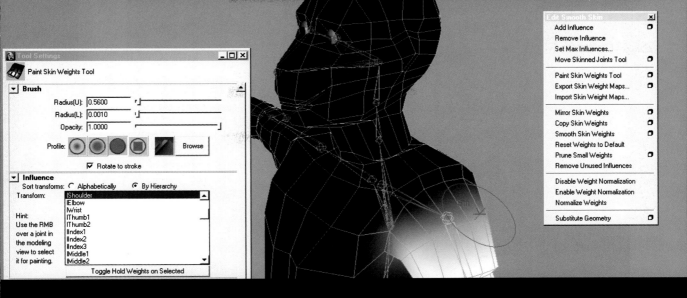

Skinning

To get your character's geometry to deform as you move joints, you must bind it to the skeleton. There are many skinning techniques to bind a surface. In this lesson, you will first experiment with basic examples, which will help you to understand the various types of skinning. You will then use this understanding to bind the Delgo character.

In this lesson, you will learn the following:

- How to bind using parenting

- How to use rigid binding

- How to use the Edit Membership Tool

- How to edit rigid bind membership

- How to use flexors

- How to use lattice binding

- How to use smooth binding

- How to access skin influences

- How to set and assume a preferred angle

- How to set joint degrees of freedom and limits

Parent binding

Perhaps the simplest type of binding is to parent geometry to joints. This type of binding is very fast and needs no tweaking, but requires the pieces of a model to be separate. For instance, an arm would need to be split into two parts: an upper arm and a lower arm. There are other scenarios where parenting is appropriate, for example, a ring on a finger, or the eyes of a character.

1 Create a simple scene

- Open a new scene and change the view to the *top* Orthographic view.
- **Draw** three joints defining an arm.
- Change the view to the *Perspective* view.
- Create two polygonal cylinders and place them over the bones, as follows:

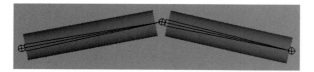

Basic parenting setup

2 Parent the geometry

- Select the *left cylinder*, then **Shift-select** the *left bone*.
- Press the **p** hotkey to **parent** the cylinder to the bone.
- Repeat the last two steps to **parent** the *right cylinder* to the *right bone*.

 Note: *Notice that the geometry is now a child of the joints in the Outliner.*

3 Test joint rotations

- Select the bones and rotate them to see the result of the parenting.

Joints' rotation

Note: *Notice that when selecting, bones have a higher selection priority than geometry. To select a bone, simply make a bounding box selection over the bone and geometry.*

Rigid binding

Rigid binding works like the parenting method, except that it affects the geometry's components. By rigid binding geometry on bones, the vertices closer to a certain bone will be instructed to follow that bone. This type of binding usually looks good on low resolution polygonal geometry or NURBS surfaces, but can cause cracking on dense geometry. The following are two examples using rigid binding:

1 Create a simple scene

- Open a new scene and change the view to the *top* Orthographic view.
- Draw **three** joints to define an arm.
- Select the **first** joint and press **Ctrl+d** to duplicate the joint chain.
- **Move** the joint chains side-by-side.
- From the *Perspective* view, create a *polygonal cylinder* and a *NURBS cylinder*.
- Place each cylinder so it entirely covers a joint chain.
- Set the polygonal cylinder's **Subdivisions Height** to **10**.
- Set the NURBS cylinder's **Spans** to **10**.

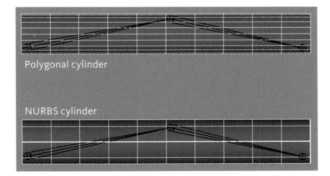

Example scene setup

2 Rigid bind

- Select the *first joint chain*, then **Shift-select** the *polygonal cylinder*.
- Select **Skin → Bind Skin → Rigid Bind**.
- Select the *second joint chain*, then **Shift-select** the *NURBS cylinder*.
- Select **Skin → Bind Skin → Rigid Bind**.

3 Test joint rotations

- Select the bones and rotate them to see the result of the rigid binding on both geometry types.

The polygonal object appears to fold in on itself, since a vertex can only be assigned to one bone. The NURBS object seems much smoother because the curves of the surface are defined by the CVs, which are bound to the bones just like the polygonal object.

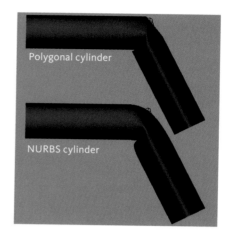

Rigid binding

Note: *Notice in the Outliner that the geometry is not parented. The binding connects the geometry's vertices to the joints.*

4 Edit Membership Tool

When using rigid bind, you might want to change the default binding so that certain points follow a different bone. The Edit Membership Tool allows you to specify the cluster of points affected by a certain bone.

- Select **Edit Deformers → Edit Membership Tool**.

- Click on the *middle bone* of the first joint chain.

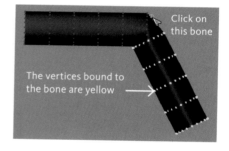

The Edit Membership Tool

You should see all the vertices affected by that joint highlighted in yellow. Vertices affected by other bones are highlighted using different colors to distinguish them.

- Using the same hotkeys as when you select objects, toggle points from the cluster using **Shift**, remove points from the cluster using **Ctrl** and add points to the cluster using **Shift+Ctrl**.

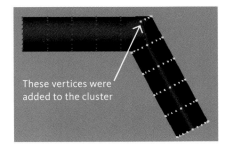

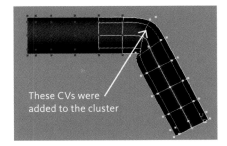

Added polygon vertices   *Added NURBS vertices*

- **Repeat** the same steps for the NURBS geometry to achieve a better deformation.

Flexors

Flexors are a type of deformer designed to be used with rigid bound surfaces. By creating a flexor for a joint, you can smooth out the binding region between two bones, thus preventing geometry from cracking. Flexor points can also be driven by Set Driven Keys to modify their positions as the bone rotates. For instance, you can refine an elbow shape when the elbow is folded.

1   Creating flexors

- From the previous scene, reset the rotations of the bones to their default positions.
- Select the *middle joint* for the first joint chain.
- Select **Skin → Edit Rigid Skin → Create Flexor...**

  An option window is displayed.
- Make sure the **Flexor Type** is set to **Lattice**.
- Turn **On** the **Position the Flexor** checkbox.
- Click the **Create** button.

  A flexor is created at the joint's position and is selected so that you can position it correctly.

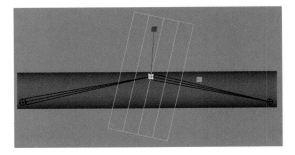

The flexor deformer

- **Translate** and **scale** the flexor to cover the bending region.

2 Test joint rotations

- Select the *middle bone* and rotate it to see the result of the flexor on the geometry.

  Notice that the bending area of the polygonal geometry is now much smoother.

 Tip: *If necessary, hide the flexor object by toggling* **Show → Deformers** *so you can see the deformations more clearly.*

3 Set Driven Keys

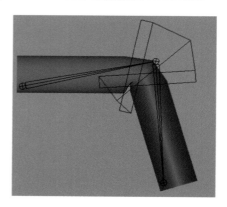

- **Zero** the rotation of the bones.

- Select **Animate → Set Driven Key → Set...**

- In the **Driver** section, load the *middle joint* and select the **Rotate Y** attribute.

- Select the *flexor* and press **F8** to display its points.

- Select all the flexor's lattice points and click the **Load Driven** button in the **Set Driven Key** window.

- Highlight all the driven objects in the **Driven** section and highlight the **XYZ values** on the right side.

The bent geometry using a flexor

- Click the **Key** button to set the normal position.

- Go back into **Object mode** and **rotate** the *middle joint* on the **Y-axis** by about **80 degrees**.

- Select the *flexor* and press **F8** to display its points.

- **Move** the flexor points to confer a nice elbow shape on the cylinder.

- Click the **Key** button to set the bent position.

 Note: *The points on the flexor might not move exactly as expected since they are using the local space of the middle bone.*

4 **Test joint rotations**

- Select the *middle bone* and rotate it to see the result of the driven flexor on the geometry.

  Notice that you can achieve a much better crease by using a driven flexor.

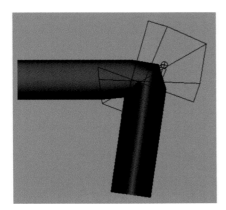

Driven flexor

Lattice binding

Another way to achieve nice skinning using rigid bind is to create a lattice deformer on the geometry and rigid binding the lattice to the bones. This technique can achieve a very smooth binding, using the simplicity of the rigid binding to your advantage.

1 **Detach a skin**

- Select the *polygonal cylinder* from the previous exercise.
- Select **Skin → Detach Skin**.

  The geometry returns to the original shape and position it was in before being bound.

- Select the *middle joint* and **zero** its rotation.
- Select the *flexor* and press **Delete** on your keyboard, as it is no longer required.

2 **Create a lattice**

- Select the *polygonal cylinder*, then select **Deform → Create Lattice**.

  A lattice is created and fits the geometry perfectly.

- Increase the number of lattice subdivisions by going to the **Shapes** section in the **Channel Box** and setting its **T Divisions** attribute to **9**.

3 Rigid bind the lattice

- With the lattice still selected, **Shift-select** the *first bone* of the joint chain.

- Select **Skin** → **Bind Skin** → **Rigid Bind**.

4 Test joint rotations

- Select the *middle bone* and rotate it to see the result of the lattice on the geometry.

  At this time, the binding is not much different than a normal rigid binding.

5 Adjust the lattice

- Select the *lattice* object.

- In the **Outputs** section of the **Channel Box**, highlight the *ffd1* node.

- Set the following:

    Local Influence S to **4**;

    Local Influence T to **4**;

    Local Influence U to **4**.

  The deformation of the geometry is now much smoother.

6 Edit membership

It is now much easier to edit the membership of the lattice points rather than the dense geometry vertices.

7 Driven lattice

If the Edit Membership Tool does not provide enough control over the deformation of the geometry, you can use driven keys to achieve a much better deformation for the elbow and the elbow crease, just like in the previous flexor exercise. You can also use driven keys to bulge the bicep.

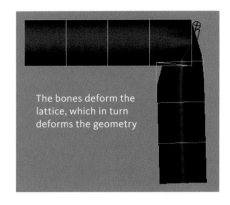

The bones deform the lattice, which in turn deforms the geometry

The bound lattice

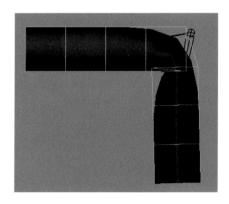

The smoothed influences of the lattice

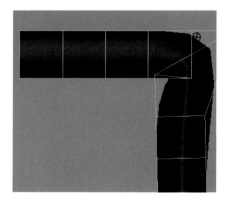

The edited rigid bind membership

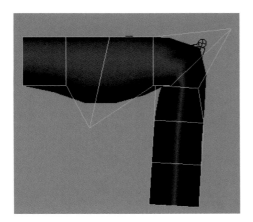

Driven lattice

Smooth binding

The most advanced type of skinning is called smooth binding. Smooth binding allows an object vertex or CV to be influenced by multiple bones, according to a certain percentage. For instance, a vertex's influence can follow a particular bone at 100%, or that influence can be spread across multiple bones in varying percentages, such as 50%-50% or 25%-75%. Doing so will move the vertex accordingly between all the influence bones.

1   Set-up the scene

- Using the scene from the previous exercise, set the *middle joint* rotation to **zero**.

- Select **Edit → Delete All by Type → History** to remove the lattice object.

2   Smooth bind

- Select the *first joint*, then **Shift-select** the *polygonal cylinder*.

- Select **Skin → Bind Skin → Smooth Bind**.

3   Test joint rotations

- Select the *middle bone* and rotate it to see the result of the smooth binding on the geometry.

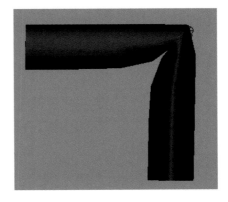

Default smooth binding

4   Edit smooth bind influence

Modifying the influences of each bone on each vertex can be a tedious task, but you can use the *Paint Skin Weights Tool* to paint the weights of the vertices directly on the geometry in the viewport. The *Paint Skin Weights Tool* will display an influence of 100% as white, an influence of 0% as black, and anything in-between as grayscale. This makes it easier to visually edit the influence of bones on the geometry.

- Select *polyCylinder* and go to **Shading → Smooth Shade All**.

- Select **Skin → Edit Smooth Skin → Paint Skin Weights Tool → ❏**.

  The painting option window opens and the geometry gets displayed in grayscale.

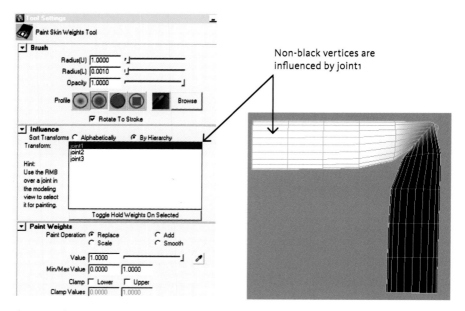

The Paint Skin Weights Tool and the weights on the geometry

Painting skin weights requires a solid understanding of bone influences. Since the tool is based on the Artisan Tool, you can edit the skin weighting on your own. Smooth binding, along with its various related tools, will be covered in greater detail in the intermediate *Learning Maya 2009 | The Modeling & Animation Handbook.*

Binding the character

Since the character is mostly composed of deformable skin objects, you will bind its geometry using smooth binding. You will also use binding for the eyes and claws. You could parent those objects directly to the skeleton, but it is an easier workflow to keep geometry in one hierarchy and the character skeleton in another.

1 Open the scene from the last lesson

- **Open** the file *09-delgoSkeleton_01.ma*.

2 Set Preferred Angle

When binding geometry on a skeleton, you need to test the binding by rotating the bones. By doing so, you should be able to return the skeleton to its default position quickly. Maya software has two easily accessible commands called *Set Preferred Angle* and *Assume Preferred Angle*. These commands allow you to first define the default skeleton pose, then return to that pose whenever you want.

Note: *The preferred angle also defines the bending angle for IK handles.*

- Select the *pelvis* joint.
- In the viewport, **RMB** over the *pelvis* joint to pop-up the contextual marking menu.
- Select **Set Preferred Angle**.

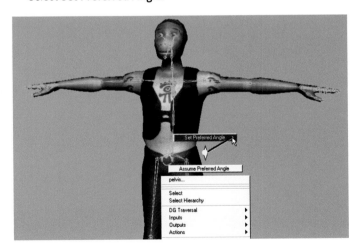

Joint marking menu

Note: *These commands are also available in the **Skeleton** menu.*

3 Assume Preferred Angle

- **Rotate** several joints to achieve a pose.
- Select the *pelvis* joint.
- In the viewport, **RMB** over the *pelvis* joint and select **Assume Preferred Angle**.

  The skeleton should return to its preferred angle (set in the previous step).

4 Bind the body

- Select **Skin → Bind Skin → Smooth Bind → ❑**.
- In the smooth bind options, change **Bind To** to **Selected Joints**.

 Tip: *It is recommended that you select the joints to which you want to bind the geometry, in order to avoid having unwanted influence from other bones.*

- Select the following joints, which should play an important role in the binding of the character:

	lClavicle	lHip
pelvis	lShoulder	lKnee
spine	lElbow	lAnkle
spine1	lWrist	lToes
neck		
neck1	rClavicle	rHip
head	rShoulder	rKnee
jaw	rElbow	rAnkle
	rWrist	rToes

- Also select all the finger and thumb joints, except the ending ones, which will not be used.
- **Shift-select** the *body* geometry.
- Click the **Bind Skin** button in the **Smooth Bind** option window.

  You will notice that the wireframe of the bound geometry is now purple, which is a visual cue to show the connection to the selected joint.

- **Rotate** the *pelvis* joint to see if the geometry follows correctly.

5 Smooth bind the eyeballs

- Select the *lEyeball* geometry, then **Shift-select** the *lEye* joint.
- Select **Skin → Bind Skin → Smooth Bind**.
- **Repeat** to bind the right eyeball.
- **Rotate** the *eye* joints to see if the geometry follows correctly.

6 Rigid bind the eyelids

- Select the *lEyelid* and *rEyelid* geometry, then **Shift-select** the *head* joint.
- Select **Skin → Bind Skin → Rigid Bind → ❑**.
- In the **Rigid Bind** options, change **Bind To** to **Selected Joints**.
- Click the **Bind Skin** button.
- **Rotate** the *head* joints to see if the geometry follows correctly.

7 Ensure everything is bound

- To ensure all the geometry is bound, select the *pelvis* joint and **translate** it.

  You will easily notice if a piece is left behind.

- Pose the character to see the effect of the binding and note problematic areas.

> **Note:** *Do not translate any bones except the root joint (pelvis). The preferred angle command only keeps rotation values.*

8 Reset the skeleton position

- **Undo** the last movement to bring the skeleton back to its original position.

  OR

- Select the *pelvis* joint, then select **Skeleton → Assume Preferred Angle**.

  Doing so will ensure all the skeleton rotations are set to their preferred values.

9 Save your work

- **Save** your scene as *10-delgoSkinning_01.ma*.

The entirely bound character

10 Paint Skin Weights Tool

Once the geometry is bound to the skeleton, you must refine the weighting so that every joint bends the geometry as expected. Perhaps the easiest way to edit a smooth skin is to use the Paint Skin Weights Tool. As mentioned earlier, this tool works just like the 3D Paint Tool, except that you paint bone influences in grayscale instead of colors, where white is fully influenced by a joint and black is not influenced at all by a joint.

Since painting skin weights is considered an advanced topic, this lesson will not cover the painting weights workflow. Consider experimenting on your own with this tool.

- To see the final skinned character scene file, open the scene *10-delgoSkinning_02.ma*.

Joint degrees of freedom and limits

A character is usually unable to achieve every possible pose. In this case, the character's articulation works in a similar way to the human body. Some joints cannot be rotated a certain way or exceed a certain rotation limit. Bending joints too much or in the wrong way might cause the geometry to interpenetrate or appear broken. Joints have many options to let you control how they are bent by the animator.

1   Degrees of freedom

By default, all three rotation axes on a joint are free to rotate. If you need to, you can limit the degrees of freedom on a joint. In the case of the character, the elbows and knees cannot bend in all three directions due to the nature of a biped skeleton. Therefore, you need to limit these joint rotations to a single axis.

- Select the *lElbow* joint.

- Notice on which axis the joint should be allowed to bend.

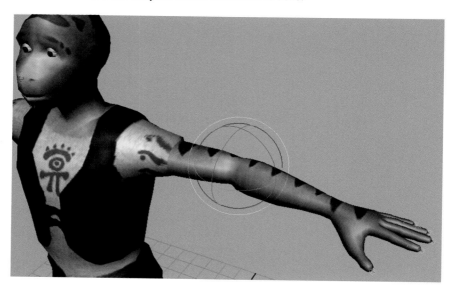

The elbow rotation axes

 Tip: *The* **Rotate Tool** *must be in* **Local** *mode.*

- Open the **Attribute Editor** and scroll to the **Joint** section.

- Turn **Off** the **X** and **Z** checkboxes for the **Degrees of Freedom** attribute.

Notice that the **Rotate X** *and* **Rotate Z** *attributes in the* **Channel Box** *are now locked.*

2 **Joint limits**

A joint limit allows you to specify the minimum and maximum values allowed for a joint to rotate. In this case, the elbow joint needs to stop rotating when it gets fully bent or fully extended.

- Select the *lElbow* joint.

- **Rotate** the joint to bend it on the **Y-axis** and stop just before it interpenetrates with the upper arm.

- In the **Attribute Editor**, open the **Limit Information** section.

- In the **Rotate** section, turn **On** the **Rot Limit Y Min** attribute.

- Click on the **<** button to put the **Current** value in the **Min** field.

- **Rotate** the *lElbow* joint on the **Y-axis** the other way, and stop when the arm is perfectly straight.

- Back in the **Attribute Editor**, turn **On** the **Rot Limit Y Max** attribute.

- Click on the **>** button to put the **Current** value in the **Max** field.

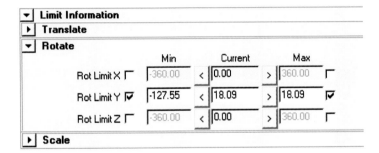

The lElbow rotation limits

3 **Remainder of skeleton limits**

You can now set the freedom and limitations on the character skeleton as you would like them to be.

4 **Save your work**

The completed version of the bound character can be found in the support files as *10-delgoSkinning_03.ma*.

Conclusion

You have now explored the various skinning types required to bind a character to its skeleton. You have also learned how to change a joint's degrees of freedom and set limit information.

In the next lesson, you will learn about the Blend Shape deformer, which will be used for facial animation.

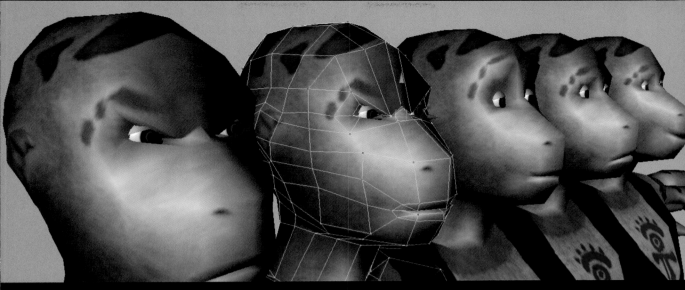

Blend Shapes

In this lesson, you will create a blend shape deformer, which is a type of deformer that blends between different geometry shapes. This will allow you to model facial expressions for the character to be used for animation.

In this lesson, you will learn the following:

- How to sculpt surfaces by painting with Artisan
- How to use different brush operations
- How to create Blend Shapes
- How to mix Blend Shapes

Sculpting a surface

You will now test the Artisan Sculpt Tool. You will use the tool on a sphere to get a feel for it. Once you are more familiar with the tool, you will apply brush strokes to the character geometry.

1   Make a test sphere

- **Create** a polygonal primitive sphere.

- Set its construction history for both **Subdivisions Axis** and **Subdivisions Height** to **60**.

- To better see the effect of your painting in the viewport, assign a new *phong* material to the sphere by selecting **Lighting/Shading → Assign New Material → Phong** from the **Rendering** menu set.

- Press the **5** key to turn on **Smooth Shade All**.

2   Open the Sculpt Geometry Tool

- With the *pSphere* selected, select **Mesh → Sculpt Geometry Tool → ❑** from the **Polygons** menu set.

    This opens the **Tool Settings** *window, which includes every Artisan sculpting option.*

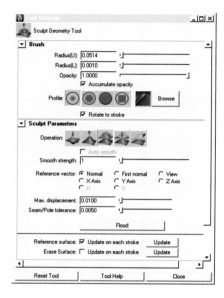

Tool Settings window

- Click on the **Reset Tool** button to make sure that you are starting with Artisan's default settings.

- Set the following attributes:

    Under **Brush***:*

    Radius (U) to **0.2**.

    Under **Sculpt Parameters***:*

    Max Displacement to **0.1**.

- Place the **Tool Settings** window to the right of the *sphere* and keep it open.

3 Paint on the surface

- Move your cursor over the *pSphere* geometry.

  The cursor icon changes to show an arrow surrounded by a red circular outline. The arrow indicates how much the surface will be pushed or pulled, while the outline indicates the brush radius. Artisan's brush icon is context sensitive. It changes as you choose different tool settings.

- **Click+drag** on the *sphere*.

  You are now painting on the surface, pushing it toward the inside.

Tip: *Artisan works more intuitively with a tablet and stylus, since the input device mimics the use of an actual paintbrush.*

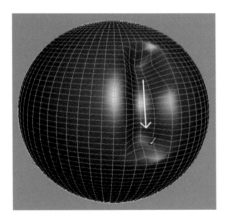

First brush stroke

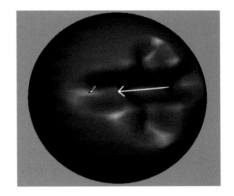

Second brush stroke

4 Change the Artisan display

- Open the **Display** section in the **Tool Settings** window.
- Click on **Show Wireframe** to turn this option **Off**.

  Now you can focus on the surface without displaying the wireframe lines.

5 Paint another stroke

- Paint a second stroke across the mask surface.

  Now it is easier to see the results of your sculpting.

The sculpting tools

You will now explore some of the Artisan sculpting operations to see how they work. So far, you have been pushing on the surface. Now you will learn how to pull, smooth, and erase.

1 Pull on the surface

- In the Tool Settings window, scroll to the **Sculpt Parameters** section.

- Under **Operation**, click on **Pull**.

- **Tumble** around to the other side of the sphere.

- **Paint** on the surface to create a few strokes that pull out.

2 Smooth out the results

- Under **Operation**, click on **Smooth**.

- Under **Brush**, change the **Radius (U)** to **0.6**.

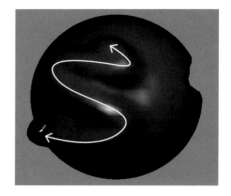

Pulling the surface with several brush strokes

This increases the size of your brush. You can see that the red outline has increased in size. This is the brush feedback icon.

 Tip: *You can hold the **b** hotkey and **click+drag** in the viewport to interactively change the brush size.*

- **Paint** all of the strokes to smooth the details.

If you stroke over an area more than once, the smoothing becomes more evident.

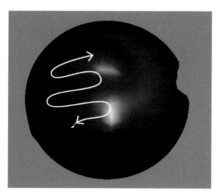

Smoothing the brush strokes

Erasing the brush strokes

3   Erase some of the brush strokes

- Under **Operation**, click on the **Erase** option.
- Paint along the surface to begin erasing the last sculpt edits.

4   Flood

- Under **Operation**, click on the **Pull** option.

- In the **Sculpt Parameters** section, click on the **Flood** button.

  This uses the current operation and applies it to the entire surface using the current opacity setting.

- Under **Operation**, click on the **Erase** option.

- In the **Sculpt Parameters** section, click on the **Flood** button.

  The sphere comes back to its orginal shape.

Fully erased surface

Updating the reference surface

When you paint in Artisan, you paint in relation to a *reference surface*. By default, the reference surface updates after every stroke so that you can build your strokes on top of one another. You can also keep the reference surface untouched until you decide to update it manually.

1   Change the brush attributes

- Under **Operation**, click on **Pull**.
- Set the following attributes:

  Under **Brush***:*

    Radius (U) to **0.2**.

  Under **Sculpt Parameters:**

    Max Displacement to **0.2**.

2   Pull the surface with two strokes

- Paint on the surface to create **two** crossing strokes that pull out.

  The second stroke is built on top of the first stroke. Therefore, the height of the pull is higher where the two strokes intersect.

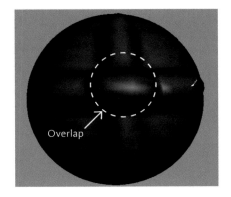

Painting with reference update

3 **Change the reference update**

- In the **Tool Settings** window, scroll down in the **Sculpt Parameters** section and turn **Off** the **Reference Surface: Update On Each Stroke**.

4 **Paint more overlapping strokes**

- Paint on the surface to create a few strokes that pull out.

  This time, the strokes do not overlap. The reference surface does not update, therefore, the strokes can only displace to the **Maximum Displacement** *value. You cannot displace beyond that value until you update the reference surface.*

5 **Update the reference layer**

- Still in the **Sculpt Parameters** section, click on the **Update** button next to **Reference Surface**.

6 **Paint on the surface**

- **Paint** another stroke over the last set of strokes.

  The overlapping strokes are again building on top of each other.

7 **Flood erase the surface**

- Under **Operation**, click on the **Erase** option.
- Click on the **Flood** button.

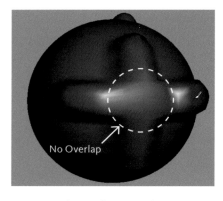

Painting with no reference update

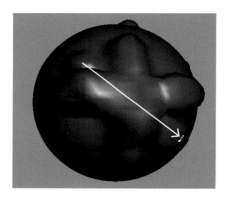

Painting on updated reference layer

Sculpting the character

You will now use the Artisan Sculpt Tool to create a few facial shapes for the Delgo character. You will first duplicate the body of the character in order to have multiple copies to use for the blend shape deformer.

1   **Scene file**

• Continue with your own scene file from the previous lesson.

   OR

• Continue with *10-delgoSkinning_03.ma*.

2   **Skin envelope**

Before you start making blend shapes, you must ensure that the geometry is in its original position. One way to get the skin back to its exact original position is to turn off the skin's influence.

• Select the character's *body*.

• In the Channel Box, highlight the *skinCluster1*node.

• Set **Envelope** to **0**.

   Doing so temporarily turns off the skinCluster, thus removing any influence of the skeleton and placing the geometry back to its exact original position.

3   **Duplicate the character**

The blend shape deformer requires that the original untouched character and character duplicates be deformed.

• **Hide** the joints in the viewport.

• Select all of the character's geometry.

• Press **Ctrl+d** to **Duplicate** it all.

• Highlight every locked attribute in the Channel Box, then **RMB** and select **Unlock Selected**.

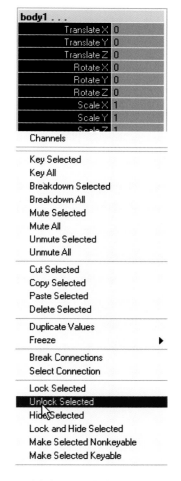

Highlight and unlock the attributes

- Press **Ctrl+g** to **group** all the geometry together.
- **Move** the new group next to the original character.
- **Rename** the new *body* geometry to *smile*.
- **Duplicate** the group you have just created and **rename** the *body* geometry for the following:

    sad;
    browUp;
    browDown.

The duplicates

Tip: *It is good to duplicate the other objects like the eyes, since you will be able to use them as a reference for when you model the Blend Shapes. Never modify an object other than the one intended for deformation.*

- Select the character's original *body*.
- In the **Channel Box**, highlight the *skinCluster* node.
- Set **Envelope** to **1**.

4 Sculpt the smile shape

You will use Artisan to paint and deform the smile geometry.

- With the *smile* geometry selected, select **Mesh → Sculpt Geometry Tool → ❑** from the **Polygons** menu set.
- Click on the **Reset Tool** button to make sure that you are starting with Artisan's default settings.

- Set the following attributes:

Under **Brush**:

> **Radius (U)** to **0.2**.

Under **Sculpt Parameters:**

> **Operation** to **Pull**;

> **Reference Vector** to **Y-axis**;

> **Max Displacement** to **0.1**.

Under **Stroke:**

> **Reflection** to **On**.

This option allows you to sculpt only one side of the geometry to create the complete shape.

Under **Display:**

> **Show Wireframe** to **Off**.

This last option will turn off the wireframe display on the geometry. It is up to you whether to turn this on or off.

Note: *In the previous test sphere example, you were painting using the normals of the surface as the direction to be pushed and pulled. In this case, you will pull along the Y-axis, which will move the vertices up.*

- **Paint** directly on the model to get a shape similar to the following:

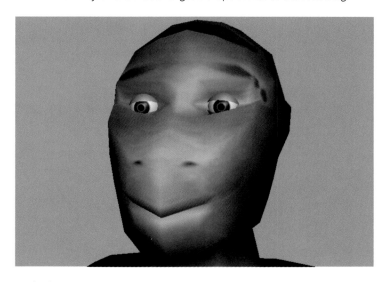

Smile shape

5 Sculpt the other shapes

- **Repeat** the previous steps to sculpt the three other shapes and any other shape you would want.

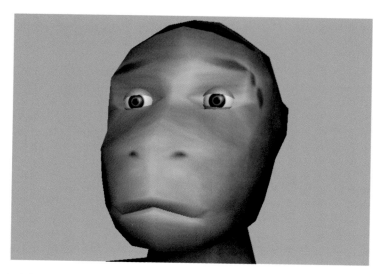

Sad shape

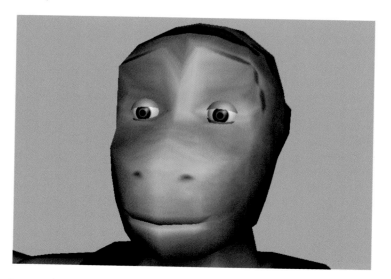

Brow up shape

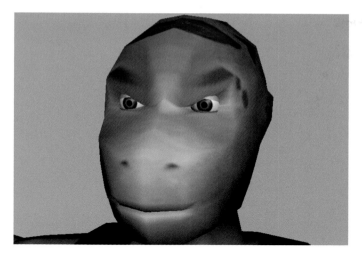

Brow down shape

Blend Shape deformer

In order to make character animation more realistic, you will need facial animation. This will be done using a deformer that will blend between the original character geometry and the geometry displaying emotion that you just created. That kind of deformer is called a *Blend Shape deformer*. Blend Shapes are very useful in 3D, especially to animate facial expressions on characters, but they can also be used for plenty of other things.

1   Creating the deformer

- Select, in order, the *smile*, *sad*, *browUp*, and *browDown* shapes, and then **Shift-select** the original *body* shape.

Note: *It is important to select the original object last.*

- From the **Animation** menu set, select **Create Deformers → Blend Shape → ❑**.
- In the Blend Shape option window, make sure to set **Origin** to **Local**.
- Select the **Advance** tab and make sure **Deformation Order** is set to **Front of chain**.

  The Front of chain option tells Maya that you need the Blend Shape deformer to be inserted before any other deformers, such as the skinCluster.

- Click the **Create** button.

2 Testing the deformer

- Select the original *body* geometry.

  In the Channel Box, you should see a blendShape1 node and its construction history.

- Highlight the *blendShape1* node.

  Notice that the attributes have the same names as the geometry you duplicated earlier. These attributes control the blending between the original shape and the sculpted ones.

- Highlight the *smile* attribute's name.

- **MMB+drag** from left to right to access the virtual slider and see the effect of the deformer on the geometry.

- Experiment blending more than one shape at a time to see its effect.

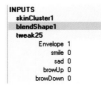

The Blend Shape node

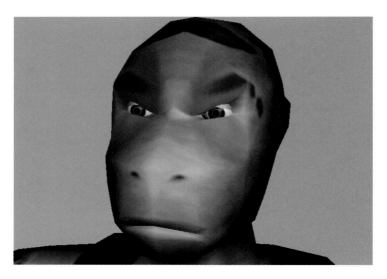

Sad and browDown shapes mixed together

3 Tweaking the Blend Shape

Since construction history still links the Blend Shape with the deformed surface, you can still tweak the sculpted geometry as needed.

- Make modifications on any of the sculpted geometry with the Artisan Sculpting Tool.

 Tip: *Your changes must be made on the sculpted blend shape geometry and not on the original geometry.*

4 Delete targets

- Select all the duplicated groups used to create the Blend Shapes.

- Press **Backspace** or **Delete** to dispose of them.

> **Note:** *When you delete Blend Shape targets, Maya keeps the blend values in the Blend Shape node instead of using the geometry in the scene. Because of this, it is important to not delete the history on the model unless you want to get rid of the Blend Shapes.*

5 Save your work

- **Save** your scene as *11-delgoBlendshapes_01.ma*.

Conclusion

You are now more familiar with the very useful Blend Shape deformer, as well as the Artisan Sculpting Tool. You now have the skills to create extremely powerful deforming animations, such as lip-synching, facial expressions, and reactive animations.

In the next lesson, you will refine your character setup by using IK handles, constraints, and custom attributes. You will also create a reverse foot setup that will help maintain the character's feet on the ground.

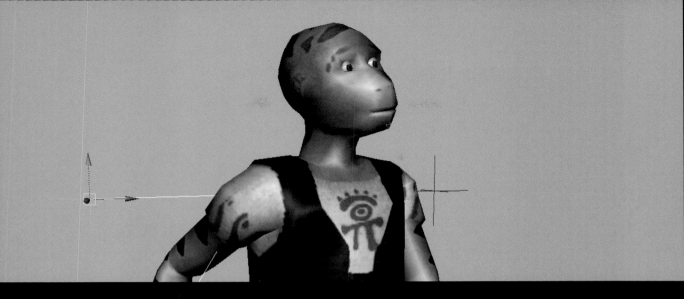

Inverse Kinematics

In this lesson, you will add IK (inverse kinematics) handles and constraints to the existing character skeleton in order to make the character easier to animate. You will also create a reverse foot setup, which simplifies floor contact when animating, and hand manipulators, which will help lock hands upon contact with the environment. Lastly, you will learn about pole vector constraints.

In this lesson, you will learn the following:

- How to add single chain IK handles
- How to add rotate plane IK handles
- How to create a reverse foot setup
- How to use point, orient, and parent constraints
- How to use pole vector constraints

IK handles

There are several types of IK handles and you will experiment with two types in this lesson: the *single chain IK* and the *rotate plane IK*. The difference between these two is that the single chain IK handle's end effector tries to reach the position and orientation of its IK handle, whereas the rotate plane IK handle's end effector only tries to reach the position of its IK handle.

Single Chain IK

A single chain IK handle uses the single chain solver to calculate the rotations of all joints in the IK chain. Also, the overall orientation of the joint chain is calculated directly by the single chain solver.

1 **Open the last character scene**

- **Open** the file *11-delgoBlendshapes_01.ma*.

2 **Joint rotation limits**

For better results using IKs, it is not recommended to have rotation limits on joints that are part of an IK handle. Limiting joint rotations will prevent the IK solver from finding good joint rotations and may cause it to behave unexpectedly.

- **Remove** rotation limits and enable all degrees of freedom for the arm and leg joints, if any.

> **Note:** *Rotation limits and degrees of freedom are especially useful on joints intended to be animated manually.*

3 **Single Chain IK**

- Select **Skeleton → IK Handle Tool → ❑**.

  The tool's option window will be displayed.

- Change the **Current Solver** to **ikSCsolver**.

- Click on the **Close** button.

- In the viewport, click on the *lShoulder* bone.

  The joint will be highlighted. This is the start joint.

- Click on the *lWrist* bone.

  The IK handle is created, starting at the shoulder and going down to the wrist of the character.

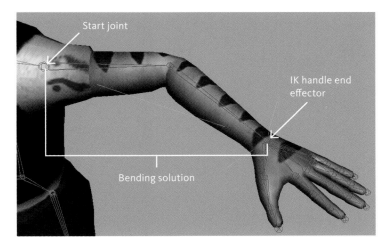

Single chain IK

In the Hypergraph, you can see the end effector connected to the hierarchy and the IK handle to the side. The end effector and the IK handle are connected, along with the appropriate joints at the dependency node level. When you control the handle, you control the whole IK chain.

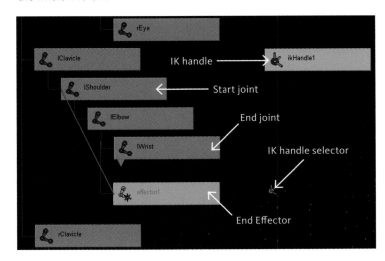

IK chain and nodes in Hypergraph

4 **Experiment with the IK handle**

• Press **w** to enter the **Translate Tool**.

• **Translate** the IK handle and notice the resulting bending of the arm.

Tip: *If the IK handle does not bend the arm or if it bends it the wrong way, it is because the angle in the arm joint chain was not appropriate. To remedy the situation, delete the IK handle, bend the arm appropriately, and then recreate the IK.*

- Press **e** to enter the **Rotate Tool**.
- **Rotate** the IK handle and notice the resulting bending of the arm.

  Rotating the IK handle will change the bending solution, but will not affect the wrist's rotation. You will create a hand setup in a later exercise.

- **Rename** the IK handle *lArmIk*.

5 Preferred angle

- With the IK selected, **RMB** in the viewport and select **Assume Preferred Angle**.

  The arm joints and the IK handle will move back to the preferred angle set in the previous lesson.

6 Right arm IK

- **Create** another single chain IK for the right arm and rename it *rArmIk*.

Tip: *IK handles have a higher selection priority than joints and geometry. To pick an IK handle, simply make a selection bounding box over it.*

Rotate Plane IK

A rotate plane IK handle uses the rotate plane solver to calculate the rotations of all joints in its IK chain, but not the joint chain's overall orientation. Instead, the IK rotate plane handle gives you direct control over the joint chain's orientation via the pole vector and twist disk, rather than having the orientation calculated by the IK solver.

Note: *The twist disk is a visual representation showing the vector defining the chain's overall orientation. You will experiment with the twist disk in the following steps.*

1 Rotate Plane IK

- Select **Skeleton → IK Handle Tool → ❑**.
- Change the **Current Solver** for **ikRPsolver**.
- Turn **On** the **Sticky** option.

  This option snaps the IK to its effector at all times.

- Click on the **Close** button.
- In the **viewport**, click on the *lHip* bone.

- Click on the *lAnkle* bone.

  The IK handle gets created, starting at the hip and going down to the ankle of the character.

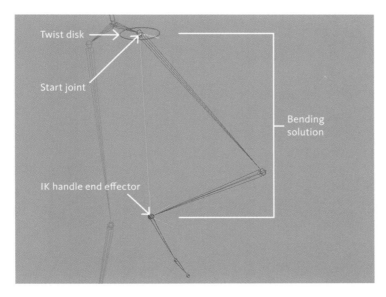

Rotate plane IK

2 Experiment with the IK handle

One differentiating feature of this type of IK handle is the ability to control the twist of the solution using the *twist* and *pole vector* attributes.

- **Move** the IK handle up.
- Press **t** to show the IK handle manipulators.
- **Move** the pole vector manipulator located next to the twist disk.

  This manipulator affects the pointing direction of the IK chain.

- Highlight the **Twist** attribute in the Channel Box and **MMB+drag** in the viewport.

  This attribute also affects the pointing direction of the IK chain, but overrides the pole vector attributes.

- **Rename** the IK handle *lLegIk*.

3 Reset the IK handle's position

- With the IK selected, **RMB** in the viewport and select **Assume Preferred Angle**.

4   **Right leg IK**

- **Create** another rotate plane IK for the right leg.

- **Rename** the IK handle *rLegIk*.

5   **Save your work**

- **Save** the file as *12-delgoIK_01.ma*.

Reverse foot

When you animate a walking character, you need one of the character's feet to plant itself while the other foot is lifted into position. In the time it is planted, the foot needs to roll from heel to toe. A reverse foot skeleton is the ideal technique for creating these conditions.

1   **Draw the reverse foot skeleton**

- Change the viewport to a *four-view* layout.

- Dolly on the feet of the character in all views.

- Select **Skeleton → Joint Tool**.

  *The **Orientation** of the tool should be set to* **XYZ***.*

- In the *side* view, create the first joint on the heel of the character's foot geometry.

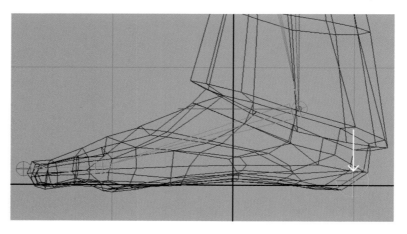

The heel joint

- In the *front* view, **MMB+drag** the new joint to align it with the rest of the foot joints.

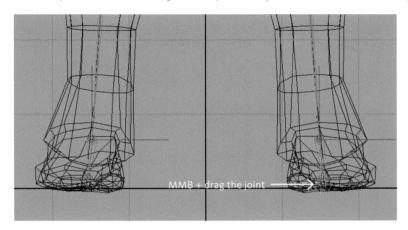

Move the heel joint

- In the *Perspective* view, turn **Off** the geometry display by selecting **Show** → **Polygons**.
- Hold down the **v** hotkey to enable **Snap to Point**.
- **Draw** three other bones, snapping them to the *toesEnd*, *toe* and *ankle* joints respectively.

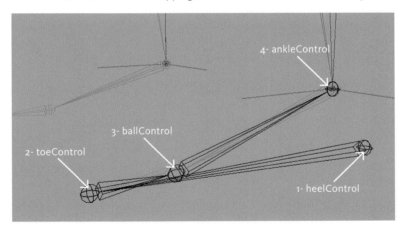

The complete reverse foot

- Press **Enter** to exit the tool.
- **Rename** the joints as shown in the previous image.

Set-up the reverse foot

To control the foot and have a proper heel-to-toe rotation, you will now constrain the IK handle, ankle, and toe joints to the reverse foot chain. This will allow you to use the reverse foot chain to control the foot and leg.

1 Point constrain the IK handle

- Select the *ankleControl* joint on the reverse foot chain.

- **Shift-select** the IK handle.

> **Tip:** *You may want to use the Hypergraph panel to help you select the joint.*

- Select **Constrain → Point**.

  The point constraint forces an object to follow the position of a source object. The IK handle is now positioned over the reverse foot's ankleControl joint.

2 Test the reverse foot chain

- Select the *heelControl* joint.

- **Move** the joint to test the foot setup so far.

  The ankle moves with the reverse foot chain, but the joints do not stay properly aligned.

- **Undo** your moves.

3 Orient constrain the toes

To align the rest of the foot, you will orient constrain the *toes'* joint to the reverse foot.

- Select the *toeControl* joint on the reverse foot chain.

- **Shift-select** the *toes'* joint from the leg chain.

- Select **Constrain → Orient → ❑**.

- In the **orient constraint** options, turn **On** the **Maintain Offset** option.

- Click the **Add** button.

  The orient constraint forces an object to follow the rotation of a source object. The Maintain Offset option forces the constrained object to keep its position.

- **Rotate** the *heelControl* joint to test the foot setup so far.

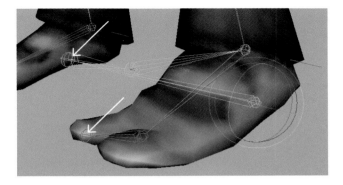

Orient constrained toes' joint

- **Undo** your moves.

4 **Orient Constrain the ankle joint**

You will now repeat these last few steps for the *ankle* joint.

- Select the *ballControl* joint on the reverse foot chain.

- **Shift-select** the *ankle* joint from the leg chain.

- Select **Constrain → Orient**.

Now the foot joints and reverse foot joints are aligned.

5 **Test the movement of the reverse foot**

- **Rotate** the different joints of the foot setup to test them.

Notice how you can easily achieve the motion of peeling the foot off the floor. You can also easily roll the toes or the heel on the floor, which would otherwise be very difficult to achieve.

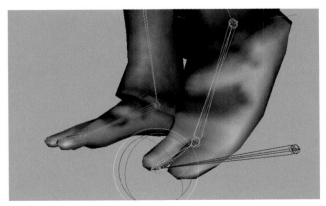

Orient constrained foot setup

- **Undo** your moves to bring the foot setup back to its original position.

Creating the heel-to-toe motion

You can now control the rotation of the foot by rotating the various control joints on the reverse foot. Instead of requiring the rotation of several joints to achieve a heel-to-toe motion, you will use Set Driven Key to control the roll using a single attribute on the *heelControl* joint.

1   Add a Roll attribute

- Select the *heelControl* joint.

- Select **Modify → Add Attribute...**

- Set the following values in the Add Attribute window:

    Long Name to **roll**;

    Data Type to **Float**;

    Minimum to **-5**;

    Maximum to **10**;

    Default to **0**.

- Click **OK** to add the attribute.

    You can now see this attribute in the Channel Box. The minimum and maximum values give reasonable boundary values for the roll.

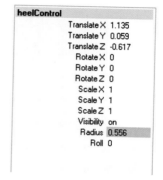

The roll attribute in the Channel Box

2   Prepare the Set Driven Key window

- Select **Animate → Set Driven Key → Set...**

- Select the *heelControl* joint and click **Load Driver**.

- In the **Driver** section, highlight the **roll** attribute.

- Select the *heelControl*, *ballControl*, and *toeControl* joints and click **Load Driven**.

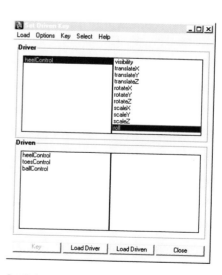

Set Driven Key window

3 Key the heel rotation

- In the **Driven** section, highlight **heelControl** and the **rotate Z** attribute.
- Click on the **Key** button to set the starting rotation.
- In the Channel Box, set the **roll** value to **-5**.
- Set the **Rotate Z** to **20**.

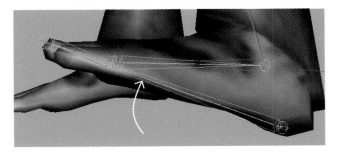

Foot rotated back on heel

- Again, click on the **Key** button.
- You can now test the **roll** attribute by clicking on its name in the **Channel Box** and **MMB+dragging** in the viewport. You can see that the foot rolls from the heel to a flat position.
- Set the **Roll** attribute to **0**.

4 Key the ball rotation

- In the **Driven** section, click on **ballControl** and then on **rotate Z**.
- Click on the **Key** button to set the starting rotation.
- Click on **heelControl** in the **Driver** section and set the **roll** value to **10**.
- Click on **ballControl** and set the **Rotate Z** to **30**.

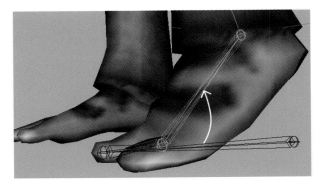

Foot rotated forward on ball

- Again, click on the **Key** button in the **Set Driven Key** window.
- Click on **heelControl** and set the **Roll** value back to **0**.

Tip: When working with Set Driven Key, always set the value of the driver before setting the driven. If you set the driver second, it will reset your driven value because of earlier keys.

5 Key the toe rotation

- In the **Driven** section, click on **toeControl** and then on **rotate Z**.
- Click on the **Key** button to set the starting rotation.
- Click on **heelControl** and set the **roll** value to **10**.
- Click on **toeControl** and set the **Rotate Z** to **30**.

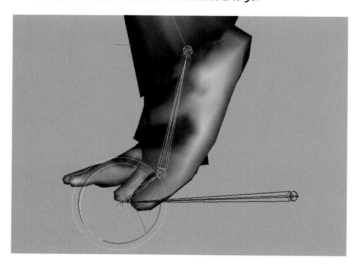

Foot rotated forward on toe

- Again, click on the **Key** button.

6 Test the foot roll

- Select the *heelControl* joint.
- Click on the **roll** attribute name in the **Channel Box** and **MMB+drag** in the viewport to test the roll.
- Set the **roll** back to **0**.
- Click the **Close** button in the **Set Driven Key** window.

7 Right foot setup

Create another reverse foot setup for the right leg.

- Select the *heelControl* joint.
- Select **Edit** → **Duplicate Special** → ❏.
- In the options, turn **On** the **Duplicate input graph** option.
- Click the **Duplicate Special** button.

  By duplicating the input graph, you will keep the driven keys you have just made.

- In the **Channel Box**, change the value of the **TranslateX** attribute to be the same value, but **negative**.
- Snap the reverse foot joints to their respective joint.
- **Recreate** the different constraints for the right foot.
- **Rename** all the joints appropriately with their left and right prefixes.

8 Test the setup

- Select the *pelvis* joint.
- **Move** and **rotate** the *pelvis* to see the effect of the constrained IK handles.

Moving the pelvis joint

- **Undo** the last step to bring the pelvis back to its original position.

9 Save your work

- **Save** the scene as *12-delgoIK_02.ma*.

Hand setup

It is good to be able to plant the feet of your character, but it would also be good to control the hand rotations. In this exercise, you will create a basic hand setup that will allow you to control the hand rotations.

1   Change the arm IK type

Single plane IKs are best used when you don't need to bother with the hands' rotation or with the bending solution. This means that they are not ideal for the type of control you are looking for in this case. You will need to delete the ones you have on the arms and create new rotate plane IKs.

- Select the two arm IK handles.
- Press **Delete** on your keyboard.
- Select **Skeleton → IK Handle Tool**.

  The IK type should already be set to ikRPsolver.

- **Create** IK handles for both arms.
- **Rename** the IK handles properly.

2   Create a hand manipulator

- Make sure **Show → NURBS Curves** is turned on in the viewport.
- Select **Create → NURBS Primitives → Circle**.
- **Rename** the circle *lHandManip*.
- Press **w** to access the **Translate Tool**.
- Hold down the **v** hotkey and snap the *circle* to the *lWrist* of the skeleton.
- **Rotate** and **scale** the circle to fit the wrist.

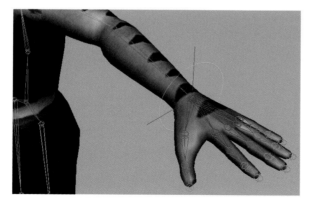

The hand manipulator

- Select **Modify → Freeze Transformations**.

3 Constrain the IK handle

- With the *circle* still selected, **Shift-select** the *lArmIk* handle.

- Select **Constrain → Parent**.

  The parent constraint forces the constrained object to follow a source object, just as if it were parented to it.

4 Constrain the wrist

- Select the *circle*, then **Shift-select** the *lWrist* joint.

- Select **Constrain → Orient**.

5 Test the wrist manipulator

- **Move** and **rotate** the *lHandManip* to see how it affects the arm and hand.

- **Move** and **rotate** the *pelvis* joint to see how it affects the arm and hand.

  Notice how the hand stays planted wherever it is. This is exactly the behavior you are looking for.

- **Undo** the last steps to return the *pelvis* and *lHandManip* to their original locations.

6 Create a pole vector constraint

- Select **Create → Locator**.

- Hold down **v** to enable **Snap to Point**, then snap the locator on the *lElbow* joint.

- **Move** the *locator* back on the **Z-axis** by about **5 units**.

- Select **Modify → Freeze Transformations**.

- With the *locator* selected, **Shift-select** the *lArmIk* handle.

- Select **Constrain → Pole Vector**.

  *The pole vector constraint will connect the locator's position to the IK handle's **Pole Vector** attribute. By doing this, you can now control the rotation of the arm using a visual indicator.*

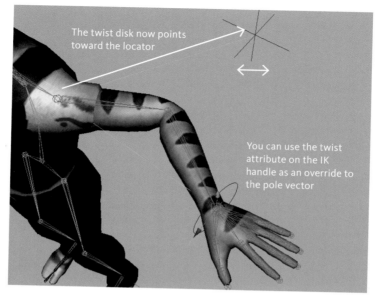

The twist disk now points toward the locator

You can use the twist attribute on the IK handle as an override to the pole vector

A pole vector locator

- **Rename** the locator to *lArmPv*.

7 **Right hand manipulator**

- **Create** the same type of manipulator on the right hand.

The completed IK setup

8 Save your work

- **Save** the scene as *12-delgoIK_03.ma*.

Conclusion

In this lesson, you learned the basics of how to use IK handles in a custom setup. You experimented with some of the most popular tricks, such as the reverse foot setup and manipulators. You also used the twist attribute and pole vector constraints, which are required for any good IK handle animation.

In the next lesson, you will refine the current character setup even more. Steps will include creating an eye setup, locking and hiding non-required attributes, adding and connecting custom attributes, and creating a character set. Doing so will make your character rig easier to use, limiting manipulation errors that could potentially break it. You will also generate a higher resolution version of the geometry.

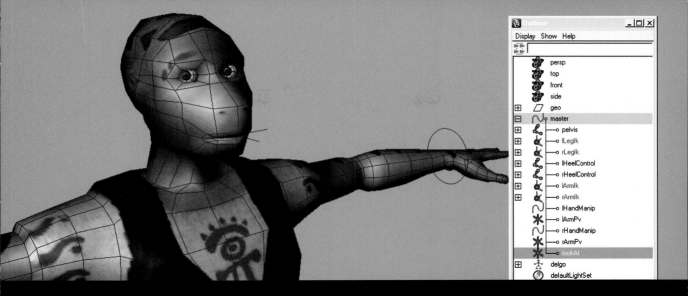

Rigging

Character rigging requires a thorough knowledge of Autodesk® Maya® objects and lots of experimentation. The more you experiment with creating and animating character rigs, the better you will become at producing first-rate setups.

In this lesson, you will finalize the character rig by making it animator friendly. This means that you will make the various useful setups and attributes easy to find, as well as hiding unnecessary ones. You will also create a high resolution polygonal version of the character, in order to get better visualization once you are finished animating.

In this lesson, you will learn the following:

- How to organize the rig's hierarchy
- How to create selection sets
- How to create visibility layers
- How to strategically place attributes
- How to use aim constraints
- How to use the jiggle deformer
- How to lock and hide nodes and attributes
- How to create a Smooth node and hook it to the rig
- How to create a character set for keyframing

Rig hierarchy

When you look in the Outliner, your character's hierarchy should be clean, well-named, and simple to understand. For instance, all the Setup nodes should be parented together under a Master node. You can then use that Master node for the global placement of the character in a scene.

1   Open the last scene

• **Open** the file *12-delgoIK_03.ma*.

2   Geometry group

• Select all the bound geometry in your scene.

 Tip: *It might be simpler to select the geometry and geometry groups from the* **Outliner***.*

• Press **Ctrl+g** to group it all together.

• **Rename** the group *geo*.

3   Create a Master node

• Change the current view to the *top* view.

• Select **Create → EP Curve → ❑**.

• Change the **Curve Degree** for **1 Linear**.

• Click the **Close** button.

• Hold down **x** and draw a four-arrows shape as indicated:

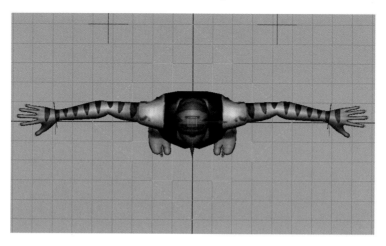

The Master node curve

- Hit **Enter** to complete the curve.
- **Rename** the curve *master*.

4 Hierarchy

- Select **Panels → Saved Layouts → Persp/Outliner**.
- In the Outliner, select all character Setup nodes and **Parent** them to the *master* node.

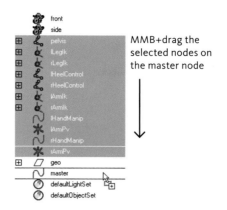

MMB+drag the selected nodes on the master node

Parent setup nodes to master

Note: *Do not parent bound geometry or the geometry group to the master node.*

There should now be only two main groups in the Outliner, which are geo and master.

5 Node names

- Make sure all nodes are named correctly.

Note: *It is recommended to have unique names for all your objects.*

6 Visibility layers

- In the Layer Editor, click on the **Create a new layer** button.
- **Rename** the new layer *setupLayer*.
- Select the *master* node in the *Perspective* view, then **RMB** on the *setupLayer* and select **Add Selected Objects**.

  All the character rig nodes can now be hidden by hiding the setupLayer.

- Click the **Create a new layer** button and **rename** the new layer to *geoLayer*.
- Select the *geo* node in the *Perspective* view, then **RMB** on the *geoLayer* and select **Add Selected Objects**.

Selection sets

Selection sets are meant to simplify the selection process of multiple objects. In the character setup, it would be nice to select all the spine and neck joints at once in order to be able to bend the character's back easily.

1 Select the spine and neck

- Select the *spine, spine1, neck, neck1,* and *head* joints.

2 Create a set

- Select **Create → Sets → Quick Select Set**...

- In the **Create Quick Select Set** window, enter the name *spineSet*.

- Click the **OK** button.

    If you scroll down in the Outliner, there will be a set called spineSet.

The new set

3 Use the selection set

- Select *spineSet* in the **Outliner**.

- **RMB** to pop-up a contextual menu and choose **Select Set Members**.

    All the objects in the set are selected.

- Press **e** to access the **Rotate Tool**.

- **Rotate** all the joints simultaneously.

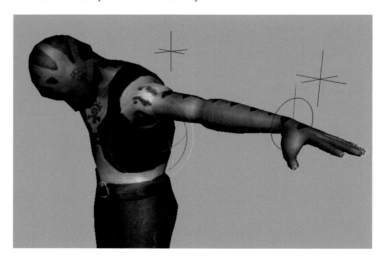

Rotate all joints simultaneously

4   **Edit a selection set**

It would probably be best if the head was not selected at the same time as the other joints when you need to rotate the character's back. The following will remove the head from the selection set.

- **Undo** the last rotation.

- Select **Window** → **Relationship Editors** → **Sets**.

- On the left side of the **Relationship Editor**, click on the **+** sign next to the *spineSet* to expand it.

  All the objects in that set are displayed.

- Still in the left side of the **Relationship Editor**, highlight the *head* joint from the set *spineSet*.

- Select **Edit** → **Remove Highlighted from Set**.

Note: *When you highlight a set in the Relationship Editor, its members are highlighted on the right side of the panel. Toggle objects on the right side to add them to or remove them from the current set.*

- **Close** the Relationship Editor.

5   **Save your work**
- **Save** your scene as *13-delgoRig_01.ma*.

Custom attributes

As you will notice by working in the current rig, some attributes are not easy to access. You should place useful attributes on strategic nodes for easy access.

Since you control the arm and leg IK handles using custom setups, it is a good idea to place useful IK attributes on the hand manipulator and the reverse foot bones.

1   **Add new attributes**
- Select the *lHandManip*, the *rHandManip*, the *lHeelControl*, and the *rHeelControl*.

- Select **Modify** → **Add Attribute...**

- Set the following:

  Long Name to **twist**;

  Data Type to **Float**;

  Default to **o**.

- Click the **Add** button.

  This will add the Twist attribute to all selected nodes. The Add Attribute window will remain open for further attribute additions.

- Set the following:

  > **Attribute Name** to **ikBlend**;
  >
  > **Data Type** to **Integer**;
  >
  > **Minimum** to **0**;
  >
  > **Maximum** to **1**;
  >
  > **Default** to **1**.

- Click the **OK** button.

2   Connect the new attributes

- Select **Window → General Editors → Connection Editor**.
- Select the *lHandManip*.
- In the **Connection Editor**, click on the **Reload Left** button.
- Scroll down and highlight the **Twist** attribute.
- Select the *lArmIk*.
- In the **Connection Editor**, click on the **Reload Right** button.
- Scroll down and highlight the **Twist** attribute.

  You have just connected the Twist attribute of the hand manipulator to the left arm IK handle Twist attribute.

- Highlight the **ikBlend** attribute on the left side of the editor.
- Highlight the **ikBlend** attribute on the right side of the editor.

  The ikBlend attribute of the hand manipulator is now connected to the left arm IK handle ikBlend attribute.

3   Repeat

- **Repeat** the previous steps in order to connect the remaining *rHandManip*, *lHeelControl*, and *rHeelControl* attributes to their respective IK handles.
- Click the **Close** button to close the Connection Editor.

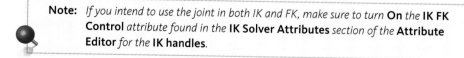

Note: *If you intend to use the joint in both IK and FK, make sure to turn **On** the **IK FK Control** attribute found in the **IK Solver Attributes** section of the **Attribute Editor** for the **IK handles**.*

4 Hide the IK handles

Since you have connected the *Twist* and *IK Blend* attributes of the IK handles to their manipulators, the IK handles can now be hidden since they are no longer required to be visible or selected.

- Select the *lArmIk*, the *rArmIk*, the *lLegIk,* and the *rLegIk*.
- Set the **Visibility** attribute in the Channel Box to **Off** by typing in **o** in the **Channel Box**.

  All the IK handles are now hidden.
- Highlight the **Visibility** attribute's name.
- **RMB** in the **Channel Box** and select **Lock Selected**.

  Doing so will prevent the IK handles from being displayed, even when using the **Display** → **Show** → **All** *command.*

Selection handles

There are several nodes that you will need to select when animating the character. Unfortunately, these nodes can be hidden under geometry or difficult to pick in the viewport. This is where a selection handle becomes helpful.

1 Show selection handles

- Select the *lHeelControl*, the *rHeelControl*, and the *pelvis* joints.
- Select **Display** → **Transform Display** → **Selection Handles**.
- Clear the current selection.
- **Click+drag** a selection box over the entire character in the viewport.

  Since selection handles have a very high selection priority, only the three selection handles get selected.

2 Move selection handles

- Go into **Component** mode.
- Make sure only the selection handle mask is enabled.

The selection handle mask

- Choose the selection handles for the *lHeelControl*, the *rHeelControl,* and the *pelvis* joints.
- Press **w** to enable the **Translate Tool**.

- **Translate** the selection handles toward the back of the **Z-axis** until they are outside the geometry.

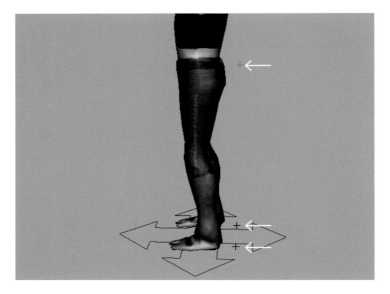

The selection handle outside the geometry

- Go back into **Object** mode.

3 **Save your work**
   - **Save** your scene as *13-delgoRig_02.ma*.

Eye setup

The eyes of the character need to be able to look around freely. To do so, you will create an aim constraint, which forces an object to aim at another object. You will also need to define a new attribute for blinking.

1 **LookAt locator**

   A locator will be used to specify a point in space where the eyes will be looking.

   - Select **Create** → **Locator** and **rename** it *lookAt*.
   - **Snap** the locator to the *head* joint.
   - **Move** the locator in front of the character about **10 units** on the **Z-axis**.

The lookAt locator

- **Parent** the *lookAt* locator to the *master* node.

2 **Freeze transformations**

In order to be able to easily place the *lookAt* locator at its default position, you should freeze its transformations.

- Select the *lookAt* locator.
- Select **Modify → Freeze Transformations**.

3 **Aim constraint**

- Select *lookAt,* then from the **Outliner**, **Ctrl-select** the *lEye* joint.

Note: *You might have to expand the hierarchy in the Outliner using the **+** sign to reach the desired node.*

- Select **Constrain → Aim → ❑**.
- Turn **On** the **Maintain Offset** checkbox, then click the **Add** button.
- **Repeat** for the *rEye* joint.

4 **Experiment with lookAt**

- Select the *lookAt* locator and **move** it around to see how the *eyeball* reacts.

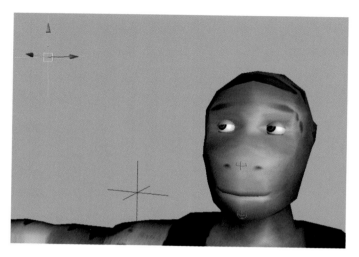

The eyes looking at the locator

5 Eye blink attribute

It would be good to have a *blink* attribute on the locator, to make it easy to blink the character's eyes.

- Select the *lookAt* locator and select **Modify → Add Attribute...**
- Set the following in the new attribute window:

    Long Name to *blink*;

    Data Type to **Float**;

    Minimum to **0**;

    Maximum to **2**;

    Default to **1**.

- Click the **OK** button to add the new attribute.

6 Eye blink driven keys

- Select the **Animate → Set Driven Key → Set...**
- Load the *lookAt* node and the *blink* attribute as the driver.
- Select both *eyelid* geometries, then highlight the *makeNurbsSphere* in the **Channel Box**.

> **Note:** *If the makeNurbsSphere node is not listed in the Channel Box, it means that you have deleted the history on the eyelid. To remedy the situation, rebuild the eyelid starting from a new primitive sphere.*

- Click on the **Load Driven** button.
- Highlight the two *makeNurbsSphere* nodes and highlight their *startSweep* and *endSweep*.
- Click the **Key** button.
- Set the **blink** attribute to **0**, then set the **sweep** attributes to set the eye closed.
- Click the **Key** button.
- Set the **blink** attribute to **2**, then set the **sweep** attributes to set the eye wide open.
- Click the **Key** button.

7 Test the eye blink
- Test the **Blink** attribute using the virtual slider.

Jiggle deformer

The Jiggle deformer will make vertices jiggle as the geometry is moving. You will use a jiggle deformer on the sleeves of the character so that it wobbles as he is walking.

1 Paint Selection Tool
- Select the *body* geometry.
- In the toolbox, **double-click** on the **Paint Selection Tool**.
- **Paint** on the *body* geometry to easily select the belly vertices.

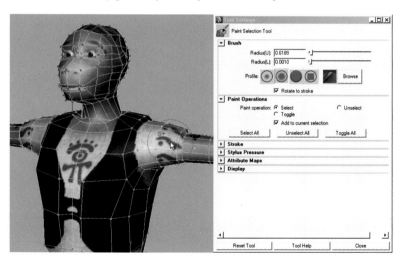

The vertices to be used with the jiggle deformer

Tip: *Use the* **Unselect** *paint operation to select unwanted vertices.*

2 **Create a jiggle deformer**

- With the wanted vertices still selected, select **Create Deformers** → **Jiggle Deformer** → ❑.
- In the option window, set the following:

    Stiffness to **0.2**;

    Damping to **0.2**;

    Ignore Transform to **On**.

- Click the **Create** button.

    The jiggle1 deformer will be added to the character's input history in the Channel Box.

3 **Smooth the jiggle influence**

With the default value, all the vertices selected are fully affected by the jiggle deformer. It is better to create a nice gradient effect by smoothing the jiggle's weight.

- Go into **Object mode** and select the *body* geometry.
- Select **Edit Deformers** → **Paint Jiggle Weights Tool** → ❑.
- Change the **Paint Operation** to **Smooth**.
- Paint on the geometry to smooth out the jiggle weight to get the following:

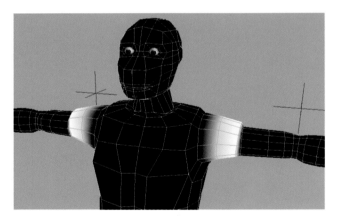

The jiggle influence

- **Close** the tool window.

4 **Test the jiggle deformer**

In order to test the jiggle deformer, take some time to keyframe a very simple animation and then playback the scene. The attributes of the jiggle deformer to tweak can be found in the Channel Box, when the *body* geometry is selected.

Once testing is over, remove the animation and make sure all the joints are at their preferred angle.

> **Tip:** *Make sure to always set your **Playback Speed** to **Play Every Frame** and **Max Playback Speed** to **Real-time** when playing a scene with dynamics. Doing so will ensure an accurate representation of the final effect.*

5 Save your work

- **Save** your scene as *13-delgoRig_03.ma*.

Lock and hide nodes and attributes

Many nodes and attributes in the character rig are not supposed to be animated or changed. It is recommended that you double-check each node and attribute to see if the animator requires them. If they are not required, you can lock and hide them.

The Channel Control window allows you to quickly set which attributes are displayed in the Channel Box and which ones are locked.

1 Lock geometry groups

Since all the geometry is bound to the skeleton, it must not be moved. All the geometry attributes should, therefore, be locked.

- Select **Window → Hypergraph: Hierarchy**.
- Make sure all nodes are visible in the **Hypergraph** by enabling **Options → Display → Hidden Nodes** to **On**.
- Select the *geo* group.
- Select **Edit → Select Hierarchy** from the main menu.
- In the **Channel Box**, highlight the **Translate**, **Rotate,** and **Scale** attribute names.
- **RMB** in the **Channel Box** and select **Lock and Hide Selected**.

Doing so will leave only the visibility attribute in the Channel Box for the Geometry nodes.

2 Channel Control Editor

- Select **Window → General Editors → Channel Control**.

*Under the **Keyable** tab, all the keyable attributes shown in the Channel Box are displayed. If you highlight attributes and then click on the **Move >>** button, the selected attributes will be moved in the **Nonkeyable Hidden** column. Notice that only the **Visibility** attribute is still visible in the Channel Box.*

*In the same manner, under the **Locked** tab, you can move the wanted attributes from the **Locked** column to the **Non-Locked** column and vice versa.*

![The Channel Control Editor window showing Keyable, Nonkeyable Hidden, and Nonkeyable Displayed columns]

The Channel Control Editor

3 Hide end joints

End joints are usually not animated.

- Select all the end joints on your skeleton, except the eye joints.

- Set their **Visibility** attributes to **Off**.

- **Lock and hide** all the end joints on your skeleton.

  An end joint is the last joint in a joint chain. They are usually created only for visual reference and often never used.

Tip: *Try using* **Edit → Select All by Type → Joints,** *then press the* **down arrow** *repeatedly until all the end joints are selected.*

4 Lock joints

Joints can usually rotate, but should not be translated or scaled. There are exceptions, such as *joint* roots, that usually need to be able to translate.

- **Lock and hide** the **Translate, Scale,** and **Visibility** attributes for all the joints in the scene, except for *pelvis, lHeelControl,* and *rHeelControl,* which require translation.

Tip: *Try using* **Edit → Select All by Type → Joints.**

- **Lock and hide** the **Scale** and **Visibility** attributes for the *pelvis, lHeelControl,* and *rHeelControl.*

5 Rest of setup

You should spend some time checking each node in your character rig hierarchy to lock and hide unwanted attributes or nodes. When you don't know what an attribute does, you should at least set it to non-keyable, so that it doesn't appear in the Channel Box. This will prevent it from being keyframed accidentally.

6 Master scale

You should make sure to set the *master*'s scaling attributes to non-keyable, but you should not lock these attributes. By doing so, you can be sure no keyframes will be made on the global scaling of the character, but you will still be able to change the character's scaling to fit its environment.

7 Save your work

- **Save** your scene as *13-delgoRig_04.ma*.

High resolution model

When animating a character, it is good to have the choice of displaying either the high resolution or low resolution model. In this case, the character geometry is already quite low resolution and it would be good to have a high resolution version of the model to visualize the final result of your animation.

Here you will use a polygonal Smooth node and connect it to a new attribute on the character's master. Once that is done, you will be able to crank up the character's resolution easily.

1 Smooth polygons

- Select the *body* geometry.

- Select **Mesh → Smooth**.

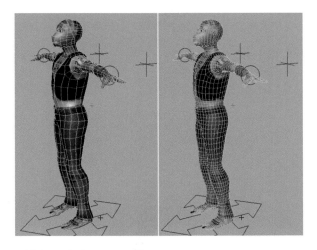

High resolution geometry

2 Smooth attribute

- Select the *master* node.

- Select **Modify → Add Attribute...**

- Set the following in the new attribute window:

  Long Name to *smooth*;

  Data Type to **Integer**;

  Minimum to **0**;

  Maximum to **2**;

  Default to **0**.

- Click the **OK** button to add the new attribute.

- Using the **Connection Editor**, connect the new **Smooth** attribute to the *polySmoothFace1*'s **Divisions** attribute.

- **Test** the new attribute.

  You can now easily increase or decrease the resolution of the model.

Creating character sets

In the next lesson, you will use keyframing techniques to make the character walk. To organize all animation channels needed for keyframing, you can create character sets. These sets let you collect attributes into a single node that can then be efficiently keyed and edited as a group.

1 Create a main character node

- Select the *master* node.

- Select **Character → Create Character Set → ❑** from the **Animation** menu set.

- Set the following:

  Name to *delgo*;

  Hierarchy below selected node to **On**;

  All keyable to **On**.

- Click **Create Character Set**.

  This character is now active and visible next to the Range Slider. It was created with all the keyframable attributes for the entire master hierarchy.

Character menu

2 Remove unnecessary attributes from the character set

- Select the *character* set from the **Outliner**.

The character node

> All the character's attributes are listed in the Channel Box.
>
> If you scroll in the Channel Box, you will notice that some attributes are already connected (colored). They are being driven by constraints, therefore, they are not needed in the character.

- Use the **Ctrl** key (**Apple** key on Macintosh) to highlight all of the colored attributes in the Channel Box for the *character* set.

- Select **Character → Remove from Character Set**.

  Those attributes are now removed from the character set.

- Also remove the master's **Smooth** attribute from the character set since it is not intended for animation.

3 Save your work

- **Save** your scene as *13-delgoRig_05.ma*.

Conclusion

You now have a biped character all hooked up and ready for a stroll. You made your character rig simpler for an animator to use and virtually unbreakable. You also created an attribute to set the resolution of the model, which will be very useful for visualizing animation.

In the next lesson, you will animate Delgo using the character rig and character set. It will put both your rigging and animation skills to the test.

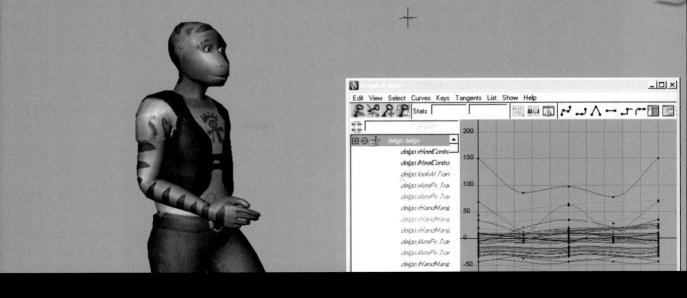

Animation

The character you built is now ready to be animated. To create a walk cycle, you will build up the motion one part at a time. Starting with sliding the feet, you will then lift the feet, use the roll attribute and set the twist of the pelvis. When that is done, you will animate the upper body accordingly.

In this lesson, you will learn the following:

- How to reference a scene
- How to use a character set
- How to animate the character's legs and arms
- How to animate the twist of the pelvis, shoulders, and head
- How to create a cycle using the Graph Editor
- How to bake animation channels
- How to create a Trax clip
- 'How to export a Trax clip

Reference

Instead of working directly with the file from the last lesson, you will reference Delgo. A reference refers to another scene file that is set to read-only and loaded into the current scene. It allows you to animate the character, leaving the rig file untouched. That way, if you update the rig file the file referencing will also get updated.

1   Create a reference

- Select **File → New Scene**.

- Select **File → Create Reference → ❑**.

  Doing so will open the Create Reference options.

- Under **Name Clash Options**, set **Resolve all nodes with this string:** *delgo.*

  This will prefix all the Reference nodes with the string delgo.

> **Note:**   *For simplicity, the Delgo prefix will not be cited.*

- Click on the **Reference** button.

- In the browse dialog that appears, select the file *13-delgoRig_05.ma*, then click **Reference**.

  The file will load into the current one.

  Notice the small diamond icon in the Outliner and the red names in the Hypergraph. This means that Delgo nodes are loaded from a reference file as read-only.

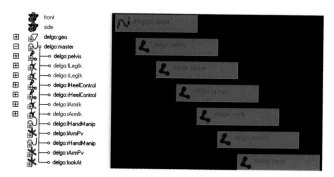

Referenced nodes in the Outliner and Hypergraph

> **Note:**   *If you need to bring changes to the character setup from the last lesson, you will need to open the rig file, make your changes, then save the file. Once that is done, you will need to open the animation file again so the new referenced rig gets reloaded. Be careful—if you remove nodes or attributes in the rig file that are animated in the animation file, their animation will be lost.*

2 Layers

- Turn the visibility **On** for the *geoLayer* and the *setupLayer*.
- Make sure the **smooth** attribute on the *master* node is set to **0**.

  You should now see only the low resolution model along with its rig.

3 Change the view panels

- Select **Panels → Layouts → Two Panes Stacked**.
- Change the top panel to a *side* view and the bottom panel to a *Perspective* view.
- For the *side* view, select **View → Predefined Bookmarks → Left Side**.

Tip: *You can also use the view cube to interactivly choose the proper camera view.*

- In the *side* view, turn **Off** both **Show → NURBS Surfaces** and **Show → Polygons**.

  This panel will be used to watch the movements of the rig.

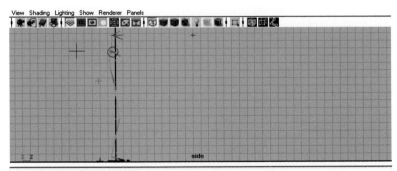

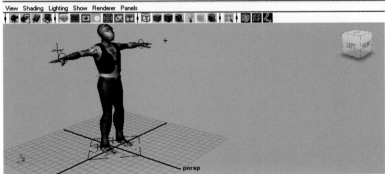

View panel layout

Animating a walk cycle

To create a walk, you will start with a single cycle. To create a cycle, you will need the start position and end position to be the same. There are several controls that need to be keyed, including the position of the feet, the roll of the feet, and the rotation of the pelvis.

Animate the feet sliding

You will now key the horizontal positions of the feet to establish their forward movement. This will result in a sliding motion of the feet.

> **Note:** *The animation values specified here depend on the scale of your character. To follow this lesson properly, either open the required support file or adjust the values to compensate.*

1 **Set your time range**

- Set the **Start Time** and **Playback Start Time** to **o**.
- Set the **End Time** and **Playback End Time** to **20**.

  This will give you a smaller time range to work with as you build the cycle. The cycle will be a full stride, using two steps of 10 frames each.

2 **Active character**

- In the **Current Character** menu next to the Range Slider, select *delgo*.

  Now any keys you set will be set on all the attributes of this Character node.

Active Character menu

3 **Position and key the lower body start pose**

You will key the starting position of the character in the position of a full stride.

- Go to frame **o**.
- Select the *lHeelControl* selection handle and set the following:

  Translate Z to **9** units;

  Roll to **-5**.

- Select the *rHeelControl selection handle* and set the following:

    Translate Z to **0** units;

    Roll to **10**.

Tip: *Make sure the Translate Tool is set to be in World coordinates.*

- Set the *pelvis* **translate Z** to **6** units.
- **Move** the *pelvis* down until the knees bend.

Note: *Leave the arms behind for now. Later, you will add secondary animation.*

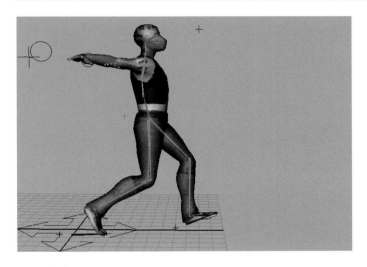

Lower body position

- Press **s** to set a key on all the channels of the *Delgo* character.

    The entire character gets keyframed since the Delgo character is selected in the Current Character menu at the bottom right of the interface.

4   **Position and key the right foot**

- Go to frame **10**.
- Set the *rHeelControl* **translate Z** to **18** units and **roll** to **-5**.

    This translation value is exactly double the value of the initial left foot key. This is important to ensure that the two feet cycle together later.

- Set the *lHeelControl* **roll** to **10**.
- Set the *pelvis* **translate Z** to **15** units.

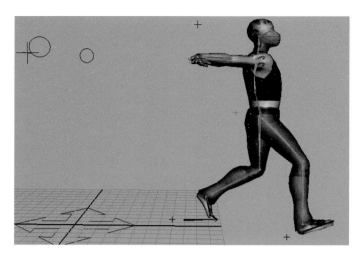

Right leg position

- Press **s** to set a key on all the channels of the *Delgo* character.

5 **Position and key the left foot**

You will move the left foot into a position that is similar to the starting position.

- Go to frame **20**.
- Set the *lHeelControl* **translate Z** to **27** units and **roll** to **-5**.

  Again, the value is set using units of 9. This will ensure a connection between cycles later.

- Set the *rHeelControl* **roll** to **10**.
- Set the *pelvis* **translate Z** to **24** units.

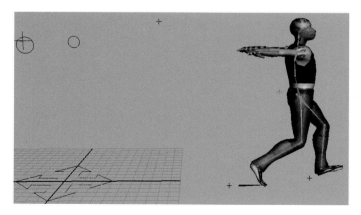

Left leg position

- Press **s** to set a key on all the channels of the *Delgo* character.

Edit the animation curves

To refine the in-between motion of the feet, you can use the animation curves to view and change the tangent options for the feet.

1   View the curves in the Graph Editor

You will edit the animation curves produced by the keys in the Graph Editor.

- Clear the selection.

- Select **Window** → **Animation Editors** → **Graph Editor**.

- Press the **Ctrl** key (**Apple** key on Macintosh) to select *lHeelControl.TranslateZ* and *rHeelControl.TranslateZ* in the Outliner section of this window.

- Select **View** → **Frame Selection**.

The pattern of the animation curves you have created should look as follows:

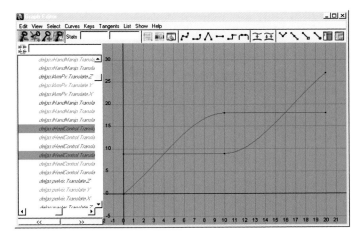

Animation curves in Graph Editor

- **Playback** the animation to see the motion.

> **Note:**   *If you open the Graph Editor when the feet are selected, you will see an animation channel with keys set in the negative direction. This is the animation curve connecting the Rotate Z of the foot to the Roll attribute.*

2   Edit the curve tangents on the feet

The curve tangent type should be changed so that the steps cycle smoothly. The default tangent type is *Clamped*.

- Select the two animation curves for *lHeelControl.TranslateZ* and *rHeelControl.TranslateZ*.

- Select **Tangents → Flat**.

  The visual difference between clamped and flat tangents in the Graph Editor is subtle. Look at the start and end keyframes on the curves. The flat tangents will create a smooth hook-up for the cycle between the start frame and end frame.

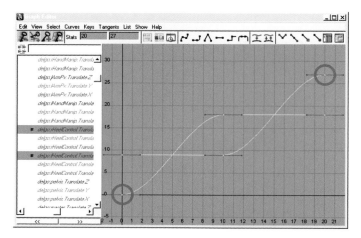

Flat tangents

Animate the feet up and down

You will now key the vertical raising and lowering of the feet to establish the stepping action.

1 Turn on Auto Key

You will now use **Auto Key** to help with the raising of the feet. The Auto Key feature will automatically keyframe any attributes on the selected nodes that already have at least one keyframe, and for which the value is changing.

- Click on the **Auto Keyframe** button in the right side of the **Time Slider** to turn it **On**.

- Open the **Animation Preferences** window, using the button just to the right of the **Auto Keyframe** button.

- In the **Timeline** category, make sure the **Playback speed** is set to **Play every frame** and that **Max Playback Speed** is set to **Real-time**.

- Click on the **Animation** category under the **Settings** category and set the following under the **Tangents** section:

    Default in tangent to **Flat**;

    Default out tangent to **Flat**.

  This will set all future tangents to flat.

- Click on the **Save** button.

2   Raise the right foot at mid-step

Key the high point of the raised foot in the middle of a step.

- Go to frame **5**.
- Select the *rHeelControl*.
- **Translate** the foot about **1** unit up along the **Y-axis**.

  This sets a new key for the Y-axis channel of the foot using Auto Key.

3   Raise the left foot at mid-step

- Go to frame **15**.
- Select the *lHeelControl*.
- **Move** the foot about **1** unit up along the **Y-axis**.

  Again, a key is automatically set.

- **Playback** the results.

4   Save your work

- **Save** your scene as *14-delgoWalk_01.ma*.

Animate the pelvic rotations

To create a more realistic action, the pelvis' position and rotation will be set to work with each step. You will again set keys for the translation and rotation of the pelvis using Auto Key.

1   Set the pelvis Y rotation

You will now animate the pelvis rotation to give the walk a little more motion.

- Go to frame **0**.
- Select the *pelvis* node using its selection handle.
- In the *top* view, **rotate** the *pelvis* using the outer rotation handle in a clockwise direction by about **-10 degrees**.

  This points the left hip towards the left foot and the right hip towards the right foot.

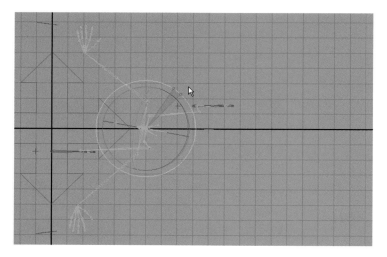

Rotate pelvis toward left foot

2 **Rotate in the opposite direction**

- Go to frame **10**.

- **Rotate** the pelvis in the opposite direction by about **10 degrees**.

3 **Copy the first Y rotation**

- Go to frame **0**.

- In the Time Slider, **MMB+drag** the current time to frame **20**.

  The display has not changed, but the time has changed.

- With the *pelvis* still selected, highlight the **Rotate** attribute in the **Channel Box**, then **RMB** and select **Key Selected**.

  *By doing so, you have manually set a keyframe on the rotation value of the pelvis from frame **0** to frame **20**.*

- **Refresh** the Time Slider by dragging anywhere in the time indicator.

  *Notice that the pelvis' **Rotate** attributes have the exact same value at frame **20** that they do at frame **0**.*

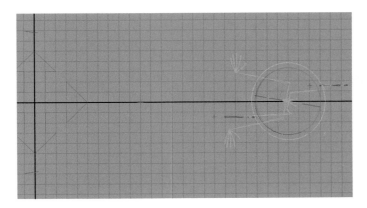

Copied rotation value at frame 20

4 Pelvis in front view

- Go to frame **5**.
- In the *front* view, **Rotate** the *pelvis* on its **Y-axis** by about **-3 degrees** so that the right hip is rising with the right leg.
- **Translate** the *pelvis* on the **X-axis** by about **0.5** units so that the weight of Delgo is on the left leg.

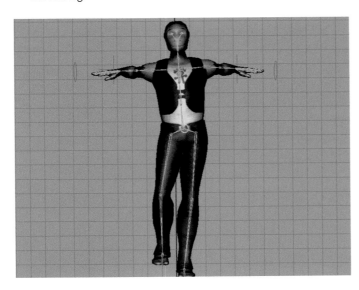

Offset pelvis with right foot raised

- Go to frame **15**.
- **Rotate** the *pelvis* on the **Y-axis** in the opposite direction as the left foot raises.

· **Translate** the *pelvis* on the **X-axis** so that the weight of Delgo is on the right leg.

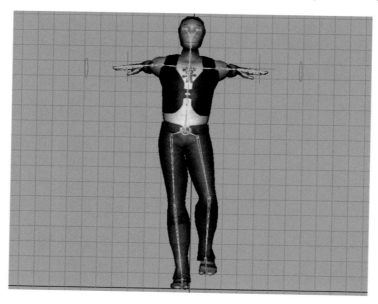

Offset pelvis with left foot raised

5 Edit the keys

To prepare the file for creating cycles later, you will need to ensure that the rotations match at the start and end of the cycle.

· Make sure the *pelvis* is selected.

· In the **Graph Editor**, press the **Ctrl** key and highlight the **Translate X**, **Rotate X,** and **Rotate Y** attributes.

· Select **View → Frame All**.

Since you copied frame 0 of the pelvis' X rotation onto frame 20 in Step 3, the start and end values of the animation curve are a perfect match. If they were different, you could have fixed the curve in the Graph Editor so that the cycled motion is smooth.

- Change the tangents so the curves look like the following:

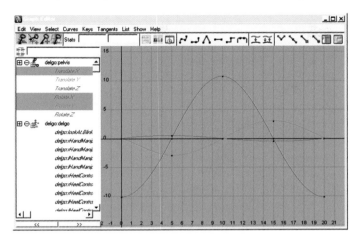

Pelvis curves

Add a bounce to the walk

To create a bouncing motion for the walk, you will add keyframes to the Y translation of the *pelvis* node.

1 Edit the pelvis height

- In the **Graph Editor**, highlight the *pelvis.TranslateY* channel.

2 Insert keys

- Select the **Insert Keys Tool** found in the **Graph Editor**.

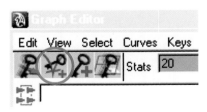

The Insert Key Tool

- Select the **translateY** curve, then with your **MMB** insert a key at frame **5** and frame **15**.

3   **Edit the Y translation value of the keys**

- Press **w** to select the **Move Key Tool**.

- Select the new keys at frame **5** and frame **15** by holding down **Shift,** and select the two keyframes.

- **Click+drag** with the **MMB** to move these keys to a value of about **10.4** to add some bounce to the walk.

Tip: *If the current time in the Time Slider is either on frame 5 or 15, you will see the effect of the change directly on the character. Make sure the value you are using doesn't hyperextend the legs.*

- Press **a** to frame the curve.

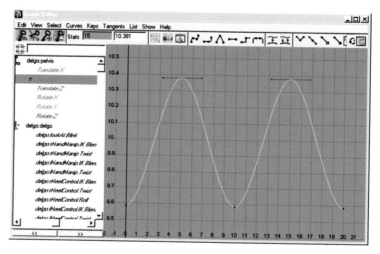

Pelvis Y Translate channel

Refine the feet rotation

When you created the reverse foot setup, you spent a great deal of time preparing the foot for the *heel-to-toe* motion that occurs when walking. So far, you have only rolled the feet so the legs would not snap. You are now going to refine the animation of the foot rotations.

1   **Set a key on the left foot's roll**

As you playback, you will notice that the feet don't pound on the ground after the heel contact.

- Select the *lHeelControl* using its selection handle.

- Go to frame **2**.
- Set the *lHeelControl*'s **Roll** attribute to **0**.
- Go to frame **5**.
- Set the *lHeelControl*'s **Roll** attribute to **0**.

2   Set a key on the right foot's roll
- Select the *rHeelControl* using its selection handle.
- Go to frame **12**.
- Set the *rHeelControl*'s **Roll** attribute to **0**.
- Go to frame **15**.
- Set the *rHeelControl*'s **Roll** attribute to **0**.

3   Walking on a line

Take some time to animate the feet on their X-axes so Delgo appears to be walking in a straight line.

- Set the *lHeelControl* **Translate X** to be **0.5** at frame **0**, **5**, **10**, and **20** and **1.0** at frame **15**.
- Set the *rHeelControl* **Translate X** to be **-0.5** at frame **0**, **10**, **15,** and **20** and **-1.0** at frame **5**.
- Set the **Twist** attribute on the *lHeelControl* to be **-10** for the whole animation.
- Set the **Twist** attribute on the *rHeelControl* to be **10** for the whole animation.

4   Playback the results

You have now covered most of the leg animation. Playback the results and try to fix the lower body animation so it appears like a natural walk.

Do not try to add more keyframes at this time. Instead, try to tweak the existing animation until you have no choice but to add more keyframes.

> **Tip:**   *You should always try to keep the required amount of keyframes to a minimum and group them on the same frame if possible. Later in the animation process, the animation curves can become quite complex and having fewer keyframes makes them easier to modify.*

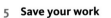

5   Save your work
- **Save** your scene as *14-delgoWalk_02.ma*.

Animate the arm swing

The character needs some motion in his arms. To do this, you will animate the translation of the arm manipulators to create an animation that can be cycled.

To add some secondary motion, you will also set keyframes on the rotation of the head.

1 Set keys for the start position

- Go to frame **0**.
- **Rotate** the clavicles down on their **Z-axes** by about **-10 degrees**.
- **Move** and **rotate** the *lHandManip* behind the body and low down.

Tip: *Make sure to not keyframe the arms while they are hyperextended. They should always be sligthly bent.*

- **Move** the *lArmPv* to bend the elbow to a good angle pointing slightly out.
- **Move** and **rotate** the *rHandManip* in front of the body and up.
- **Move** the *rArmPv* to bend the elbow to a good angle.

  Now the arms are opposite to how the feet are set-up. This makes the swinging motion work with the feet.

- **Rotate** the fingers to get a natural, relaxed hand pose.

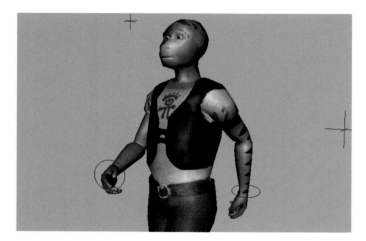

Arm positions

- Select the *head* joint and **rotate** it around the **Y-axis** by about **10-degrees**.

  This has the head and hips moving in opposite directions, where the head always aims straight forward.

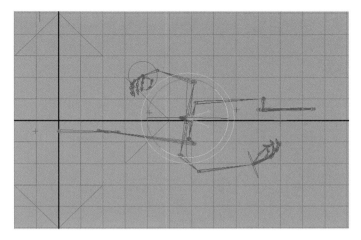

Top view of head rotation looking straight forward

2 Copy keys for the end position

In order to create a smooth transition for the arm cycle, you must have matching values at the start and end of the cycle.

- Select the *lClavicle, lArmPv, lHandManip, rClavicle, rArmPv,* and *rHandManip.*
- In the timeline, **MMB+drag** the **Time Slider** from frame **0** to frame **20**.

*The character will not move when you scrub along the timeline when the **MMB** is pressed.*

- Highlight the **translation** and **rotation** attributes in the **Channel Box**.
- **RMB** and select **Key Selected** from the pop-up menu.

This sets keyframes only on the attributes you have selected in the Channel Box.

Note: *Because you have multiple nodes selected, you can see three dots after the node's name in the Channel Box. This indicates that other nodes are active, and that they will also receive the keyframes.*

- **Refresh** the **Time Slider** at frame **20**.

You will see that you have set keyframes at the current position on the manipulators, but they are not following Delgo.

Note: *You can also use the Dope Sheet to copy and paste selected keyframes, or you can cut and paste keyframe values from the Graph Editor.*

3 **Add to attributes**

You must now set the right offset to the values already in the Translate Z attributes of the arm manipulators and pole vectors. The Channel Box can allow you to enter a simple mathematical expression in the attribute value field.

- Go to frame **20**.

- With the *lArmPv, rArmPv, lHandManip,* and *rHandManip* nodes selected, type **+=18** in the **Translate Z** attribute in the **Channel Box**, then hit **Enter**.

  Doing so adds 18 units to whatever value is in the attribute for each node.

4 **Set keys for the head**

Use the method outlined in **Step 2** to set the last keyframe for the head rotation.

- Select the *head* joint.

- **MMB+drag** the **Time Slider** from frame **0** to frame **20**.

- **LMB** over the *head* **Rotate Y** attribute in the **Channel Box** to highlight it.

- **RMB** and select **Key Selected** from the pop-up menu.

5 **Set keys for the middle position**

- Go to frame **10**.

- **Move** the arm manipulators opposite to the *legs*.

- **Rotate** the *head* joint opposite to the *hips*.

6 **Fix the fingers**

- Select the *lWrist* and *rWrist* joints.

- Select **Edit → Select Hierarchy**.

  Doing so selects all the fingers for which you need to tweak the animation.

- **Open** the **Graph Editor** and select all the keyframes at frame **0**.

- In the **Graph Editor**, select **Edit → Copy**.

- Go to frame **10**.

- In the **Graph Editor**, select **Edit → Paste → ❏**.

- In the option window, set the **Paste** method to **Merge**.

- Click the **Paste Keys** button.

- Go to frame **20**.

- In the **Graph Editor**, select **Edit → Paste**.

  The fingers should now have a proper position throughout the animation.

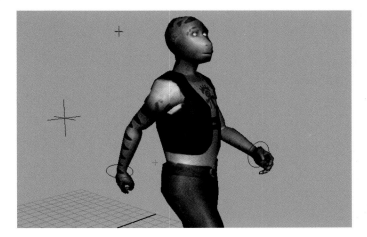

Arm positions at frame 10

7   Keyframe the in-between

- Make sure to set a good position for the arms at frames **5** and **15**.

8   Fix the arm manipulator curves

- In the **Graph Editor**, select the arm manipulator's **Translate** and **Rotate** attributes.
- Select all keyframes between frames **5** and **15**.
- Select **Tangents → Spline**.

9   The lookAt manipulator

- Go to frame **0**.
- Set the *lookAt* **Translate Z** attribute to **5**.
- Go to frame **10**.
- Set the *lookAt* **Translate Z** attribute to **14**.
- Go to frame **20**.
- Set the *lookAt* **Translate Z** attribute to **23**.

10 Refine the animation

Take some time to refine the actual animation without adding any keyframes. Look at the character's walk and try to figure out what could be improved. For instance, Delgo's chest should counter-animate the pelvis Y rotation, so his back stays straight and facing right in front of the character.

When viewed from the front, a human skeleton will compensate the hips' animation with the shoulders while the head tries to stay straight, as in the following image:

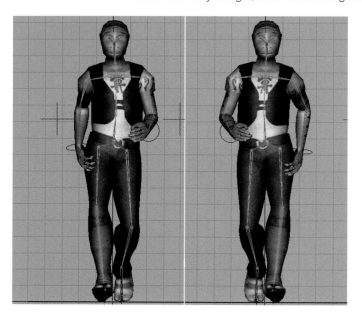

The hips and shoulders relation

 Tip: *For a more cartoon-y look, exaggerate the hips and shoulder compensation. For a more feminine look, reduce the shoulder animation, but exaggerate the hips' motion.*

11 **Make sure the animation cycles**

A quick trick to see if an animation cycles is to look at your character from the front view and toggle between frame 0 and 20. If nothing appears to be moving, your animation is probably a perfect cycle; if, however, the character is slightly changing position, then you need to copy the keyframes from frame 0 to frame 20 or vice versa.

12 **Delete the static channels**

If a curve is flat its whole length, the value of the attribute it represents does not change. This attribute is a static channel. Static channels slow Maya processing, so it is beneficial to remove them.

• Select **Edit → Delete All By Type → Static Channels**.

13 Turn off Auto Key

14 Save your work

- **Save** your scene as *14-delgoWalk_03.ma*.

Cycle the animation

So far, you have animated one full step for the walk cycle. Next, you will use the Graph Editor to complete the cycle.

1 Set your time range

- Set the **Start Time** and **Playback Start Time** to **0**.
- Set the **End Time** and **Playback End Time** to **300**.

2 View all curves in the Graph Editor

- Select **Window → Animation Editors → Graph Editor**.
- Select *delgo* from the **Outliner** portion of the window, then press the **a** hotkey to see all the animation curves for the character.

3 View the cycle

In order to check if the cycle works smoothly, you can display the curves' infinity and set it to cycle.

- In the **Graph Editor**, select **View → Infinity** and zoom out to see the dotted infinity curves.
- Select all the animation curves.
- Select **Curves → Pre Infinity → Cycle with Offset**.
- Select **Curves → Post Infinity → Cycle with Offset**.

  Cycle with Offset appends the value of the last key in the cycled curve to the value of the first key's original curve. You can now see what the curves are like when cycled.

- **Play** the animation for the entire **300** frames.

4 Adjust the curves

As the animation plays, make sure nothing moves increasingly away from the character. If an object gets out of control, you need to tweak the original animation between frame **0** and **20**.

- Zoom on the curves and adjust the tangency of the keyframes on frames **0** and **20** so that the connection between the curves and cycle is smooth.
- If needed, adjust the in-between keyframe tangencies.

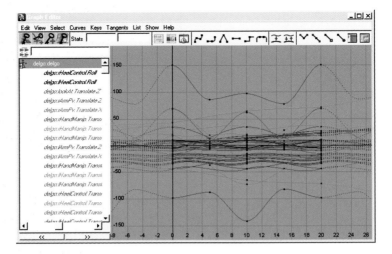

Animation cycle

- **Go to frame 300**.

  At this frame, you should clearly see if there are any problems with the offset of your cycle where an object keeps moving farther and farther away.

- Fix any problems in your cycle by changing either frame **0** or **20**.

Tip: *You should not set a keyframe outside the cycle's boundary, otherwise, you will break up the cycle.*

Bake the keyframes

Ultimately, you will use this animation inside the Trax Editor, so you will bake the keyframes of the post infinity onto the curves. The Trax Editor cannot use post infinity curves from the Graph Editor, so you will generate the actual keyframes by baking them.

1   **Select the character**
   - In the Graph Editor, select *delgo*.

2 **Bake the keyframes**

    • In the Graph Editor, select **Curves → Bake Channel → ❏**.

    • Set the following options:

        Time Range to **Start/End**;

        Start Time to **0**;

        End Time to **120**;

        Sample by **5**;

        Keep Unbaked Keys to **On**;

        Sparse Curve Bake to **On**.

    • Click the **Bake** button.

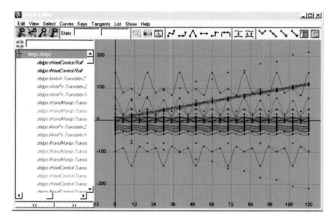

Baked curves

3 **Save your work**

    • **Save** your scene as *14-delgoWalk_04.ma*.

Create a Trax clip file

The animation is finished, but since you will be working with the Trax Editor later in this book, you will now create a Trax clip file and export it for later use.

1 **Open the Trax Editor window**

    • Select **Window → Animation Editors → Trax Editor**.

    • Make sure the *delgo* character is set as current.

    • In the **Trax Editor**, enable **List → Auto Load Selected Characters**.

    You should not see anything in the Trax Editor at this time.

2   **Create a clip**

- From the **Trax Editor**, select **Create** → **Animation Clip** → ❏.

- Set the following options:

  Name to *walk;*

  Leave Keys in Timeline to **Off**;

  Clip to **Put Clip in Trax Editor and Visor**;

  Time Range to **Animation Curve**;

  Include Subcharacters in Clip to **Off**;

  Create Time Warp Curve to **Off**;

  Include Hierarchy to **On**.

- Click the **Create Clip** button.

- Press **a** in the **Trax Editor** to frame all.

  A clip is created and placed in the Trax timeline. A corresponding clip source file called walkSource is also placed in the Visor.

  Until you export the clip, it can only be accessed through this scene file.

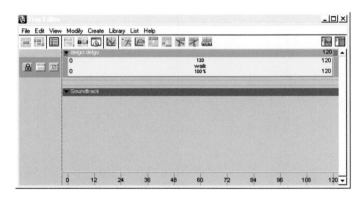

Walk clip in the Trax Editor

3   **Export the clip**

- Select **File** → **Visor...**

- Select the **Character Clips** tab to see the clip source.

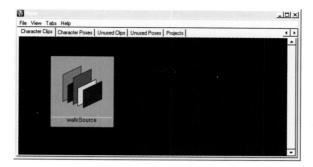

Walk source clip in Visor

- Select the *walkSource* clip.
- **RMB** on the clip and select **Export**.

  A pop-up menu will browse to the clips directory of your current project.

- **Export** the clip as *delgoWalkExport*.

  Now you can import this clip into another scene. You will do so later in this book.

- **Close** the Visor**.**

4 Save your work

- **Save** your scene as *14-delgoWalk_05.ma*.

Conclusion

Congratulations, you have completed a walk cycle! You learned how to reference a file, and then you animated Delgo using a character set. You produced a perfect cycle and exported a Trax clip.

In the next project you will build a catapult from NURBS, texture it, and rig it up so that Delgo can interact with it.

Project 03

In this project, you will model a catapult, which Delgo will interact with. You will begin by modeling, texturing, and rigging the NURBS catapult. Once that is done, you will test various deformers and use Paint Effects to add vegetation to the set built in the first project. Finally, you will add lights to your scene and experiment with the different renderers available in Autodesk™ Maya® software.

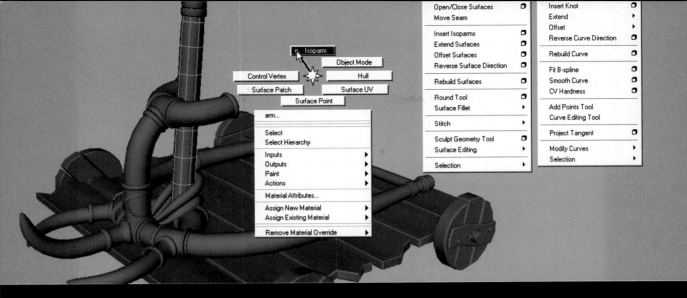

NURBS Modeling

This lesson will introduce you to modeling with NURBS (non-uniform rational b-spline) surfaces. You will create curves and build surfaces to construct a catapult as see in the movie *Delgo*.

In this lesson, you will learn the following:

- How to attach curves
- How to extrude a surface at path
- How to move the seam of a surface
- How to detach and attach surfaces
- How to duplicate curves from a surface
- How to use loft surface tools

Lesson 15

Set-up your project

Since this is a new project, it is recommended to set a new current project directory.

1 Set the project

- If you copied the support files onto your drive, go to the **File** menu and select **Project → Set...**

  A window opens, pointing you to the Maya projects directory.

- Click on the folder named *project3* to select it.

- Click on the **OK** button.

  This sets the project3 directory as your current project.

  OR

- If you did not copy the support files on your drive, create a new project called *project3* with all the default directories.

2 Make a new scene

- Select **File → New Scene**.

Base armature

The first step for modeling the catapult is to create the base frame. This will be a simple exercise that will introduce several useful NURBS tools.

1 Base curve

You will now create the catapult's base curve.

- Select **Create → EP Curve Tool → ❏**.

- In the option window, make sure **Curve degree** is set to **3 Cubic**.

- Close the tool option window.

- From the *top* view, draw half a horseshoe-like curve, making sure to snap to the **X-axis** the first curve point.

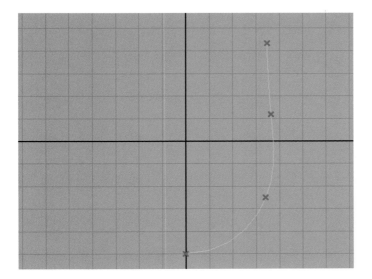

The base curve

2   Duplicate and attach curves

In order to ensure that the base curve is symmetrical, you will now duplicate the existing curve and attach the two curves together.

- With the curve selected, press **Ctrl+d** to duplicate it.
- Set the new duplicate's **Scale X** to **-1**.
- Select both curves.
- From the **Surfaces** menu set, select **Edit Curves → Attach Curves → ❏**.
- In the option window, set the following:

    Attach method to **Connect**;

    Multiple knots to **Remove**;

    Keep originals to **Off**.

- Click the **Attach** button to execute the tool.

    You should now have a single curve, perfectly symmetrical, in the shape of a horseshoe.

Tip: *If for some reason the curves do not attach correctly, highlight the attachCurve node in the Channel Box and toggle the Reverse1 or Reverse2 attribute.*

- **Delete** the **history** for the curve.

3   Profile curve

You will use a circle to be extruded along the base curve to create the base's geometry.

- Select **Create** → **NURBS Primitives** → **Circle**.
- With the *circle* selected, hold down the **c** hotkey to snap to curve.
- Using the center of the **Move Tool**, **click+drag** the circle on top of the base curve.
- Still holding down the **c** hotkey, **click+drag** again in the middle of the **Move Tool manipulator**.

  If done correctly, the Move Tool manipulator should snap to the base curve.

- **Click+drag** the *circle* to one end of the base curve.
- **Rotate** the *circle* by **90 degrees** on its **X-axis**.
- **Scale** the *circle* on all axes to about **0.5**.

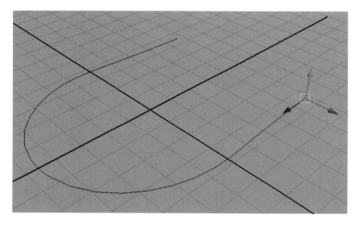

The profile curve in place

4   Extrude at path

You will now extrude the profile curve along the base curve.

- Select the *circle*, then **Shift-select** the *base* curve.
- Select **Surfaces** → **Extrude** → ❏.
- In the option window, set the following:

  Style to **Tube**;

  Result position to **At path**;

  Pivot to **Closest end point**;

  Orientation to **Profile normal**.

- Click the **Extrude** button.

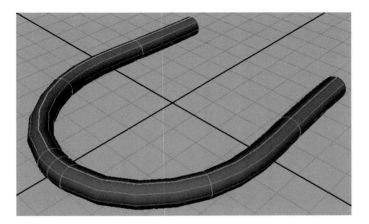

The base surface

- **Rename** the new surface to *base*.

5   Moving the seam

Notice the NURBS seam on the base surface. The seam is shown as a thicker line on the wireframe while in shaded mode.

When modeling with NURBS, it is important to carefully place the seam for two reasons. First, when attaching and detaching surfaces, it is better to have seams aligned on every surface. Second, when texturing, it is better to hide the seams as much as possible since this is where the opposite texture edges meet. For this piece of geometry, the seam will be placed underneath it so that it is never visible.

- In the *Perspective* view, look under the *base* surface.

- **RMB** on the *base* and select **Isoparm**.

  Isoparms are similar to edge loops on polygonal geometry. They define continuous lines going across the entire NURBS surface.

> **Note:** *When you click directly on an isoparm to select it, the isoparm gets highlighted with a continuous yellow line. If you **click+drag** on an isoparm, a dotted yellow line shows you the isoparm at the cursor's position.*

- **Click** to highlight in yellow the isoparm located at the bottom of the *base* surface.

- Select **Edit NURBS → Move Seam**.

  The seam should now be located under the base surface.

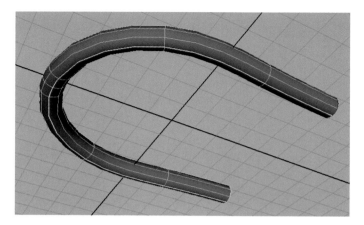

The moved seam

6 Shape the base

- **Double-click** on the **Move Tool** and enable its **Reflection** option.
- **Tweak** the shape of the base surface to your liking.
- When you are done, **delete** the **history** for the *base* surface.
- **Delete** the *base* and *profile* curves.

7 Create a cap

You will now use a profile curve to revolve a cap to cover the extremity of the base surface.

- From the *top* view, **draw** a curve as follows:

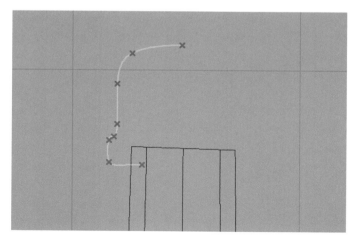

The cap profile curve

- Select **Modify → Center Pivot.**
- Press the **Insert** key to enter the **Move Pivot Tool**.
- **Holding** down the **c** hotkey to snap to curve, **click+drag** the pivot to the top end of the cap curve.

  Doing so will define the proper location to revolve the cap.
- Press **Insert** again to exit the **Move Pivot Tool**.
- Select **Surface → Revolve → ❑**.
- In the option window, set the **Axis preset** to be **Z**.
- Click the **Revolve** button.

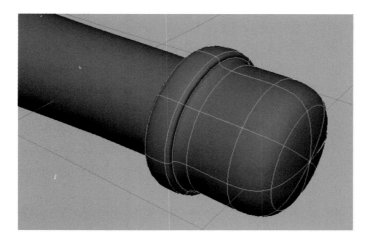

The revolved cap surface

- **Rename** the new surface to *cap*.
- **Duplicate** the *cap*, and set its **Scale X** to **-1**.

Note: *New curves and surfaces always have their pivots at the origin.*

8 Clean up

- Select the *base* and *cap* surfaces, then select **Modify → Freeze Transformations**.
- Select **Modify → Center Pivot**.
- **Delete** all the construction curves.
- **Delete** all the construction history in the scene.

9 Save your work

- **Save** your scene as *15-catapult_01.ma*.

Catapult basket

Next, you will model the catapult's arm and basket. These will be first modeled in two separate pieces, but then joined together.

1 **Create the arm**

- Select **Create → NURBS Primitives → Cylinder**.

- In the **Inputs** section of the **Channel Box**, set the following for the *makeNurbCylinder* node:

    Radius to **0.4**;

    Sections to **8**;

    Spans to **8**;

    Height Ratio to **18**.

    The arm needs more spans because it will later be deformed as it bends backwards, ready to fire.

- **Translate** the *cylinder* up by about **3.5** units.

- **Rotate** the *cylinder* by **90 degrees** on its **Y-axis**.

    Doing so will place the seam in the back of the arm.

2 **Create the basket**

- Select **Create → NURBS Primitives → Sphere**.

> **Note:** *Note that both the arm and basket have eight isoparms. Making sure the two surfaces have the same amount of isoparms will allow you to attach them together without problems.*

- **Translate** the *sphere* up by about **9** units.

- **Rotate** the *sphere* by **90 degrees** on its **Y-axis**.

    Doing so will place the seam in the back of the basket.

- **RMB** on the *sphere* and select **Control Vertex**.

- From the *side* view, select the following CVs:

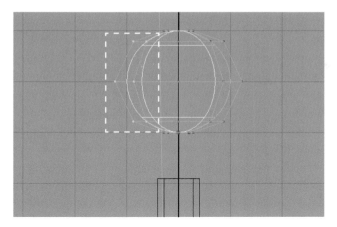

The CVs to select

- **Scale** and **move** the selected CVs towards the inside of the *sphere* to create a basket.
- **Tweak** the shape of the basket to your liking.

3 **Connect the arm and basket**

You will now cut the bottom pole of the basket and connect it to the arm surface.

- **RMB** on the *sphere* and select **Isoparm**.
- **Click+drag** on the horizontal isoparm to define a new isoparm near the bottom pole.

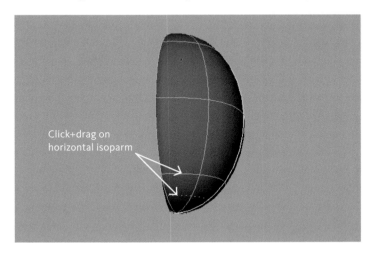

Click+drag on
horizontal isoparm

The defined isoparm

- Select **Edit NURBS → Detach Surfaces.**
- **Delete** the separated surface located at the bottom pole.

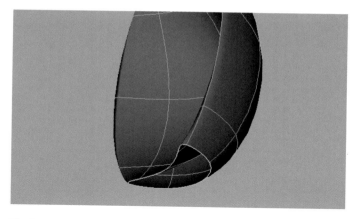

The bottom opening

4 **Duplicate surface curve**

At this point, you have two piece of geometry with eight spans each, which will allow you to connect them. Since there is quite a lot of distance between the two pieces, you will now duplicate the isoparm from the basket opening.

- **RMB** on the *sphere* and select **Isoparm**.
- Click on the isoparm at the opening to select it.
- Select **Edit Curves → Duplicate Surface Curves**.

   A curve is created, representing exactly the surface isoparm. Doing so will spare you the trouble of using a NURBS circle to create the in-between profile.

- Select **Modify → Center Pivot**.
- **Translate** the curve down between the two surfaces.

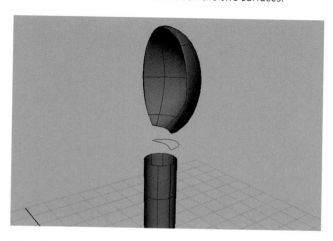

The middle curve

5 Loft

The Loft Tool creates a surface by linking several profile curves. This is the perfect tool to generate the linking surface.

- **RMB** on the *sphere* and select **Isoparm**.
- Click on the isoparm at the bottom opening to select it.
- **Shift-select** the middle curve.
- **RMB** on the *cylinder* and select **Isoparm**.
- **Shift-select** the isoparm at the top opening to select it.

> **Note:** *You must select the curves or isoparms in appropriate order so that the loft is created correctly.*

- Select **Surfaces → Loft**.

  The new surface is created by linking the selected curves.

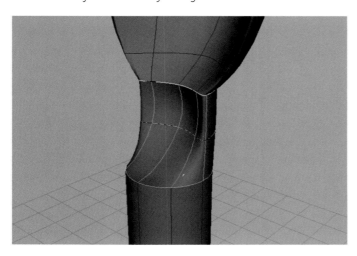

The connecting loft

- **Tweak** the shape of the in-between profile curve to refine the loft shape.

  Because of construction history, you can still manipulate the curve, arm, or basket surfaces, and the lofted surface will update properly.

6 Attach surfaces

You will now attach the three surfaces together so the entire arm is a single piece of geometry.

- Select the *cylinder* and the *lofted* surfaces.

- Select **Edit NURBS → Attach Surfaces → ❑**.
- In the option window, set the following:

    Attach method to **Blend**;

    Blend bias to **0.5**;

    Keep originals to **Off**.
- Click the **Attach** button.

    The two pieces should now have become a single surface.
- Select the *arm* and the *sphere* surfaces.
- Select **Edit NURBS → Attach Surfaces**.

    The entire arm is now a single surface.

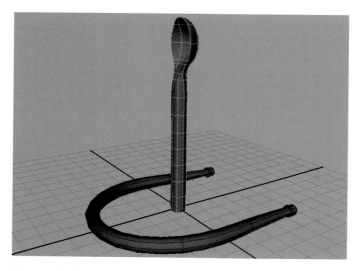

The completed arm surface

- **Rename** the surface to *arm*.
- **Tweak** the *arm* shape to your liking.

7 Clean up

- With the *body* selected, select **Modify → Freeze Transformations**.
- Select **Edit → Delete All by Type → History**.
- **Delete** any obsolete nodes from the **Outliner**.

8 Save your work

- **Save** the scene as *15-catapult_02.ma*.

Finish the catapult frame

The remaining steps to create the catapult frame should be pretty straightforward. The following steps overview the rest of the frame creation.

1 Build the arm stopper

- From a cylinder and half a torus, create the arm stopper.

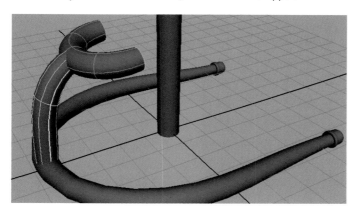

The arm stopper

2 Connect the arm to the base

- Using NURBS cylinders, create the connection between the arm and the base and also the two elastics that will power up the catapult.

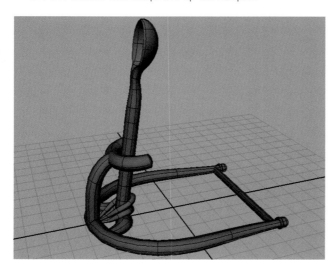

The arm connection

Tip: *You can model only half the surfaces, and then mirror them and attach them. Doing so will ensure that you model symmetrically.*

3 Decorative horns

- Using a NURBS cone, create a decorative horn coming out in front of the catapult.

- **Revolve** a profile curve to create the socket in which the horn is inserted.

- **Duplicate** and **modify** the first horn to make two smaller ones on either side of the catapult.

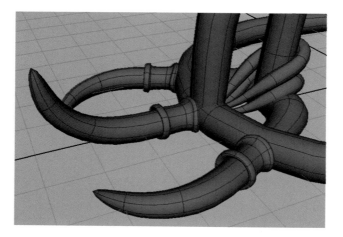

The decorative horns

Tip: *Always make sure to move the seam of any NURBS surfaces to where it is the least likely to be seen.*

4 Decorations

- Take the catapult model as far as you would like by adding decorative ropes, sockets, and caps.

- **Project** curves on the different surfaces and then **extrude** a profile curve to create ropes forming X patterns.

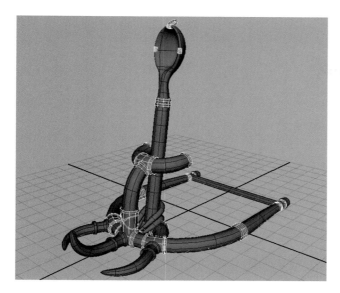

The catapult with decorations

5 Hook

The catapult is missing one last object to make it functional; it is the hook used to attach the arm when the arm is bent backwards. This piece of geometry is somewhat more complex than what has been created so far, so you should build it with polygons rather than NURBS.

• Starting from a primitive polygonal cube, extrude faces to create a hook.

• Finalize the hook by applying a **Mesh** → **Smooth** on it.

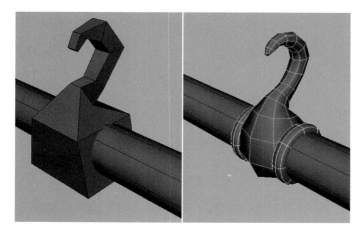

The hook geometry

6 **Clean up**
  - **Rename** each node correctly.
  - Use **Modify → Freeze Transformations** on all nodes.
  - Select **Edit → Delete All by Type → History**.

    Since you don't require any construction history, it is good to frequently clean up your scene.

  - **Delete** any obsolete nodes from the **Outliner**.

7 **Save your work**
  - **Save** the scene as *15-catapult_03.ma*.

Wagon

You will now model a wagon on which the catapult will be placed. This will allow you to easily move it on the ground.

Since the wagon will have a mechanical look, it will be built from polygons.

1 **Planks**
  - **Create** a polygonal cube.
  - Change the *polyCube* Input node to have **3** in **Subdivisions Width** and **4** in **Subdivisions Depth**.
  - **Rename** the cube to *plank*.
  - **Scale** and **tweak** the *plank* as follows:

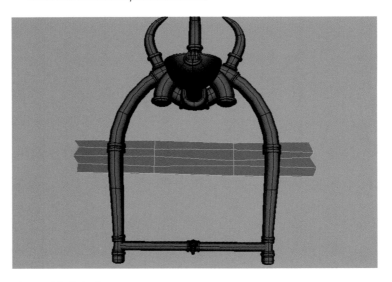

The modified plank

- **Duplicate** and **move** the *planks* to cover the size of the catapult base.
- **Tweak** the *planks* to randomize their look.

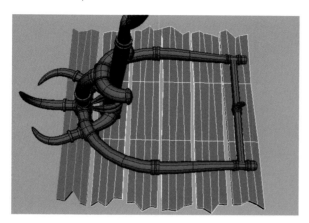

The complete wagon surface

2 **Bevel**

You will now bevel the edges of the planks to give them a better look.

- Select all the *planks*, and then go into **Component** mode with the **Edge** mask enabled.
- From the **Polygons** menu set, select **Select → Select Using Constraints...**
- Set **Constrain** to **Next Selection** and **Smoothing** to **Hard**.
- **Click+drag** around all the *planks* to select all the hard edges.
- Click the **Close and Reset** button.
- Select **Edit Mesh → Bevel**.

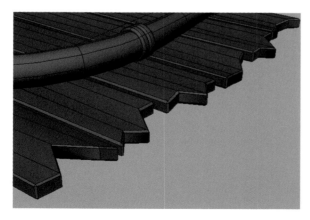

The beveled planks

3   Wheels

The wagon wheels will also be created from polygons using the same technique as in the previous step.

- Using three polygonal cubes, build the following:

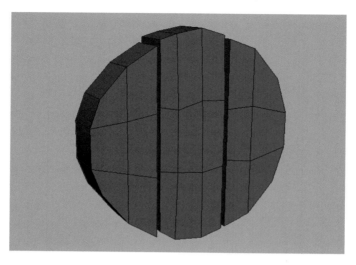

The wheel

- Finish the wheel as you would like it.
- **Bevel** the hard edges.

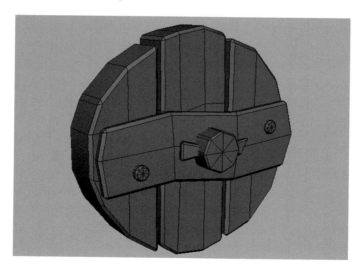

The finished wheel

- **Combine** all the wheel pieces together and **rename** it to *wheel*.
- Make sure the wheel's pivot is centered on its axel.
- **Duplicate** and place the wheels to finish the wagon.

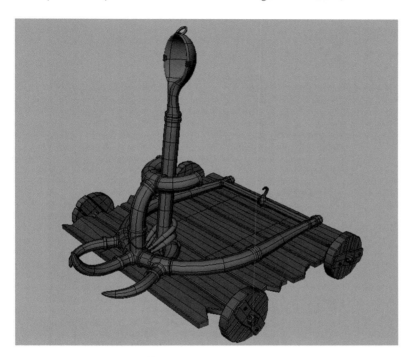

The final catapult

4 **Create a projectile**

You will now model a rock to use as a projectile with the catapult.

- Select **Create → Polygon Primitives → Platonic Solids**.
- In the **Channel Box**, highlight the *polyPlatonicSolid* node and make sure **Solid Type** is set to **Dodecahedron**.
- **Rename** the solid to *rock*.
- **Move** the *rock* beside the catapult.
- **RMB** on the *rock* and select **Vertex**.
- Randomly tweak the vertices so the model looks like a rock.
- Go back into **Object mode** and select **Normals → Harden Edge**.

- **RMB** on the *rock* and select **Face**.
- Select all the faces and **Extrude** them with the **Keep Faces Together** turned **Off**.
- **Scale** them down by half their size and **move** them in slightly.
- Using the selection constraints, select all the hard edges.
- Deselect any unwanted edges, and then select **Edit Mesh → Bevel**.
- **Select the** *rock* and select **Normals → Soften Edge**.

The rock with Smooth Preview enabled

- Place the *rock* on the *wagon*.

5 Finalize the model

Tip: *To speed up the display in the viewport, you can select NURBS surfaces and press 1 to set the NURBS display to coarse.*

6 Clean up the scene

7 Save your work

- **Save** the scene as *15-catapult_04.ma*.

Conclusion

In this lesson, you experimented with several NURBS curves and surface tools. NURBS modeling for simple objects can be straightforward, but modeling organic and complex shapes requires much more experience and planning.

In the next lesson, you will assign materials and textures to the catapult.

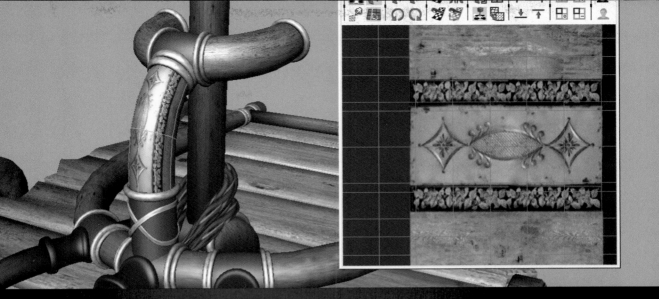

NURBS Texturing

In this lesson, you will learn about NURBS texturing and other generic workflows. NURBS surfaces use a different UV system than polygons because they are always square and can automatically compute square UV mapping.

In this lesson, you will learn the following:

- About NURBS surface UVs
- How to texture using procedural textures
- How to break connections in the Attribute Editor
- How to save color presets
- How to place a texture using the Interactive Placement Tool
- How to convert a shading network to a file texture
- About texture reference objects
- How to export and import a shading network

Texturing NURBS

Unlike polygonal geometry, UV mapping is not required on NURBS geometry since texture coordinates are determined by the U and V directions of the NURBS surface itself.

1   Scene file

- **Open** the scene from the last lesson.

2   Checker texture

In order to view the default UV maps, you will create both a Lambert and checker texture, and then assign them to the catapult geometry.

- In the **Hypershade**, create a **Lambert** material.
- **Map** the **Color** of the new material with a **Checker** texture.

 Tip: *Make sure the create option at the top of the Create Render Node window is set to* **Normal***.*

- Press **6** on your keyboard to enable the **Hardware Texturing**.
- **Assign** the new material to the entire *catapult*.
- See how the texture is mapped on every object.

On equally proportionate surfaces (as close to square as possible), the checker texture will not appear to be too stretched, but on long and thin surfaces, such as the ropes, the texture will look stretched. Also, where a NURBS surface has a pole, the texture will look pinched.

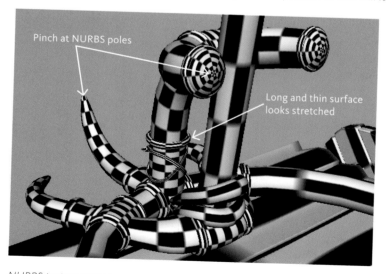

NURBS texture mapping

3 Assign a file texture

- Open the Attribute Editor for the Lambert material created in the last step.
- At the top of the attribute list, set **Type** to **Blinn**.

  Doing so changes the type of the material without creating a new shader.

- Still in the Attribute Editor, **RMB** on the **Color** attribute's name and select **Break Connection**.

  This breaks the link between the shader and the checker.

- **Map** the **Color** of the material with a **File** texture.
- **Browse** to the *sourceimages* directory of the current project and choose *woodPlank.tif* for the file texture.

The assigned wood texture

  Notice how the texture is automatically mapped on the NURBS surfaces.

- **Rename** the material *woodM*.
- **Tweak** the *woodM*'s **Specular Shading** to your liking.

4 Arm ramp

The catapult looks quite plain at this time, so you will improve the texturing of various pieces. You will be able to texture the catapult's arm quite well using procedural textures.

- In the **Hypershade**, select the *woodM* shader, and select **Edit** → **Duplicate** → **Shading Network**.
- Select **Graph** → **Rearrange Graph**.
- In the **Attribute Editor** for the *woodM1* shader, break the connection for the **Color** attribute.
- **Map** the **Color** attribute with a **Ramp** texture.
- **Assign** the new shade to the *arm* surface.
- Set the *ramp* **Type** to **U Ramp**.

The assigned ramp texture

 Note: *In this example, the red color is at the top of the surface, but at the bottom of the ramp texture. It is possible that on your surface, the automatic UV mappings differ.*

- Select the color marker at the top of the ramp widget.
- Click in the color swatch of the **Selected Color** attribute.
- Set a **dark brown** color.
- Before accepting the color, click the **arrow** button at the top of the Color Chooser window.

  Doing so will save the color in one of the color presets for future usage.

- Select the color marker at the bottom of the ramp widget.
- Map this marker with a **Fractal** texture.
- Under the **Color Balance** section, click to choose the **Color Gain**.
- Click the color preset you have just saved.

  You are now certain that the top and bottom of the ramp have the exact same color.

- Click the **Accept** button.
- Highlight the color marker in the middle of the ramp widget.
- With the Attribute Editor and the Hypergraph side-by-side, **MMB+drag** the *file2* wood texture onto the **Selected Color** attribute of the *ramp*.

  Doing so will map the wood texture in the ramp texture, allowing you to do gradients between the different ramp markers.

- **Tweak** the color markers for the ramp so the gradient between the wood texture and fractal texture is made under the decorative rope in the middle of the arm.

The modified ramp texture

5 Horn color

Another technique for using a ramp texture to change the color of a texture is to map the texture in the Color Gain attribute rather than directly in the ramp's color markers.

- **Create** a new **Phong** material.
- **Rename** the shader to *hornM*.
- **Map** the **Color** attribute with another **Ramp** texture.
- In the Attribute Editor for the ramp texture, scroll down to the **Color Balance** section.

- **Map** the **Color Gain** attribute with a **Noise** texture.

  Notice how the entire ramp texture is now affected by the noise texture. The colors mapped into the Color Gain of a texture act as multipliers to the existing colors.

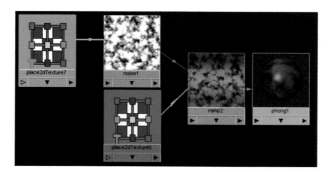

Noise texture assigned to the color gain

- **Assign** the *hornM* shader to the *horn* surfaces.
- Set the ramp texture's **Type** to **U Ramp**.
- **Tweak** the *ramp* texture so it looks as follows:

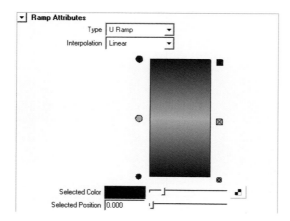

The new ramp colors

- **Tweak** the *noise* texture to your liking.

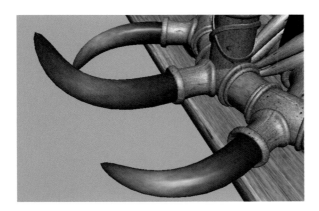

The horn color

6 **Elastic material**

- **Create** a **Lambert** material.

- **Assign** the new shader to both *elastics*.

- **Map** the **Color** attribute with a **Cloth** texture, and set the following:

  U **Color** to **Beige**;

  V **Color** to **Brown**;

  U **Width** to **0.3**;

  V **Width** to **1.0**;

  U **Wave** to **0.2**;

  V **Wave** to **0.3**;

  Bright Spread to **0.3**.

The elastic texture

7 **Save your work**

- **Save** your file as *16-catapultTxt_01.ma*.

Interactive Placement Tool

The Interactive Placement Tool is designed to ease the placement of textures onto NURBS surfaces. This tool allows you to interactively set the different placement values of a 2D texture using an all-in-one manipulator.

1   Arm base material

- Select a NURBS surface for which you want to change the texture. In this case, the *armBase* surface texture is to be changed.

- In the **Hypershade**, select **Graph → Graph Materials on Selected Objects**.

- **Select** the shader and select **Edit → Duplicate → Shading Network**.

- **Assign** the new shader to the *armBase*.

  You are duplicating the shading network on the surface because other surfaces with the same shader will also be affected by the upcoming steps.

2   Interactive Placement Tool

- Select the *place2dTexture* node of the wood file texture used by the *armBase* surface.

- In the Attribute Editor, with the file texture's *place2dTexture* tab selected, click on the **Interactive Placement** button.

  *Doing so will access the **NURBS Texture Placement Tool**. This tool displays a red manipulator on the NURBS geometry, which allows you to interactively place the texture in the viewport.*

Note: *You can also access the **NURBS Texture Placement Tool** via the **Texturing** menu when a NURBS surface is selected.*

- **MMB+drag** on the manipulator's red dots to change the placement of the texture.

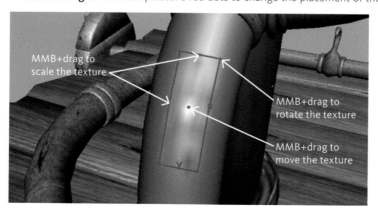

The interactive placement manipulator

> **Note:** *Notice the value of the place2dTexture node updates as you drag the manipulator. You can also set the place2dTexture values manually.*

> **Tip:** *This technique is perfect for placing a logo or image at a specific location on a NURBS surface.*

3 Tweak the texture

- To better see the texture in the viewport, select the shader, and set **Texture resolution** to **Highest** under the **Hardware Texturing** section.

- To change the default gray color of the region outside the texture, select the texture, and set or map the **Default Color** under the **Color Balance** section.

Ramp texture mapped in the default color

Convert to texture

If you would like to paint details on a procedural texture, you will have to convert the shading network to a file texture. The following shows the basic workflow to do so.

1 Convert to shading network

Autodesk® Maya® software can convert a complex shading network into a single texture file.

- Select the shader from the previous exercise and **Shift-select** its corresponding surface.

- From the **Hypershade**, select **Edit → Convert to File Texture (Maya Software) → ❏**.
- In the option window, set the following:

    UV Range to **Entire Range**;

    X Resolution to **512**;

    Y Resolution to **512**;

    Image Format to **Tiff (tif)**.

- Click the **Convert and Close** button.

    Maya will convert the network to a texture and will create and assign a new network using only a single texture. The new texture is automatically saved in the current project's sourceimages folder.

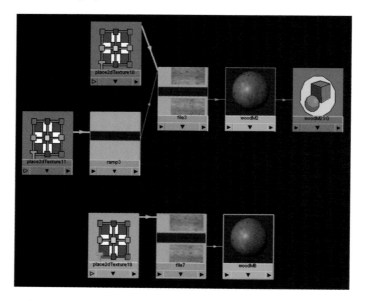

Before and after the conversion

> **Tip:** *When converting textures assigned to polygonal objects, you must make sure that the UVs of the surface can accommodate a single texture to cover all of its geometry. If some UVs overlap, the texture might not reflect exactly what you were expecting.*

2 Delete unused Render nodes

Since the original shading network for the surface is no longer used, you can automatically delete unused Rendering nodes.

- In the **Hypershade**, select **Edit → Delete Unused Nodes**.

3 **Edit the converted texture**

If required, you can edit the converted texture found in the *sourceimages* folder of the current project to fix any problems with the projections and then reload your file texture to see your changes.

Texture reference objects

If while texturing you used projected textures or 3D textures, the results might be good on static geometry, but there can be unintended results when the surface is moving or deforming. This is because the object is moving without the 3D Placement node, which causes a texture sliding problem. To correct this, you can set-up a non-deformed reference object to lock the texture on the geometry.

1 **Rock texture**

- **Create** a *Blinn* material and **assign** it to the *rock*.

- **Map** the **Color** attribute with a **Brownian** from the **3D Textures** section.

- **Tweak** the 3D texture to your liking so it looks like granite.

- With the *rock* selected, select **Create UVs → Automatic Mapping**.

  Doing so will simplify the UV layout of the polygonal rock to minimize texture stretching and overlapping.

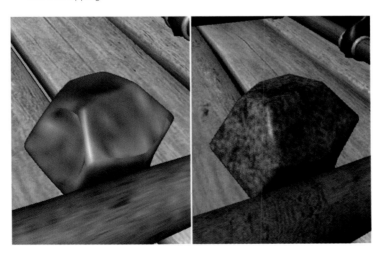

Viewport vs. rendered procedural texture

Note: *You will need to render the scene in order to see the exact effect of procedural textures on the surfaces. Displayed in the viewport is only an approximation of the actual rendered effect.*

2 Texture reference object

Using texture reference objects is best when an object is deforming. Otherwise, it is easier to simply parent the Projection node to the model itself, or convert the 3D texture to a file texture.

- Select the *rock*, which has projected texture assigned to it.

- Under the **Rendering** menu set, select **Texturing → Create Texture Reference Object**.

  An unselectable and unrenderable object duplicate will appear as wireframe in the viewport. This object is only selectable through the Outliner or the Hypergraph.

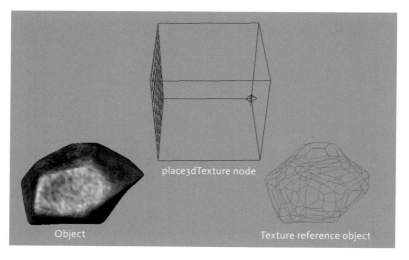

place3dTexture node

Object

Texture reference object

The object, its texture reference object, and place3dTexture

- **Group** the *place3dTexture* and *rock_reference* objects from the **Outliner**.

- **Rename** the group to *txtRefGrp* and **hide** it.

Note: *By converting a shading network to a texture, you do not require a texture reference object.*

Finish texturing the catapult

You can now spend some time shading and creating textures for the remaining pieces of the catapult's geometry. Once you are satisfied with the results, you will make sure your scene is cleared of obsolete Shading nodes.

1   Texture the rest of the catapult

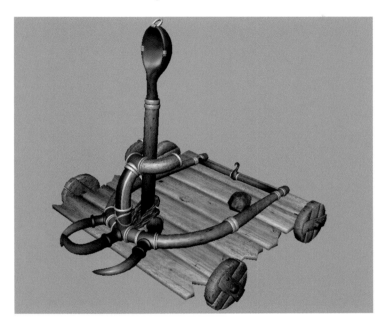

The final catapult

Import export of a shading network

When you need to texture lots of objects, it might be a good idea to build a library of shaders for generic materials such as metals, woods, rocks, etc. The following shows you how to export a material and import it when required without needing to recreate it from scratch.

1   Exporting shading networks

If you want to export one or more of your shading networks, do the following:

• Open the **Hypershade** and select the shader of your shading network. If you select more than one shader, they will all get exported at the same time in the same file.

• Still in the Hypershade, select **File → Export Selected Network**.

- Choose a file name that reflects the selected shaders and click the **Export** button.

The shaders are exported by themselves in a Maya file located in the renderData/shaders of the current project.

2 Import shading networks

If you want to import a shader, do the following:

- From the **Hypershade**, select **File → Import...**
- In the browse window, select the file named *golden.ma* from the folder *renderData\ shaders* from the current project's *support_files*.
- Click the **Import** button.

The shaders from this scene file are now in your scene.

3 Assign the shaders

- Under the **Materials** tab in the Hypershade, **MMB+drag** the *goldenM* shader onto a surface in your scene.

Doing so assigns the shader to the object.

The imported shader

4 Optimize scene size

- **Delete** all the **history** in the scene.
- Select **File → Optimize Scene Size**.

Doing so will remove any unused nodes in your scene.

5 Save your work

- **Save** your file as *16-catapultTxt_02.ma*.

Conclusion

You now have experience texturing NURBS surfaces and have learned how to use procedural textures. You should now be comfortable creating textures from scratch using Maya nodes and converting networks to file textures.

In the next lesson, you will set-up the catapult for animation.

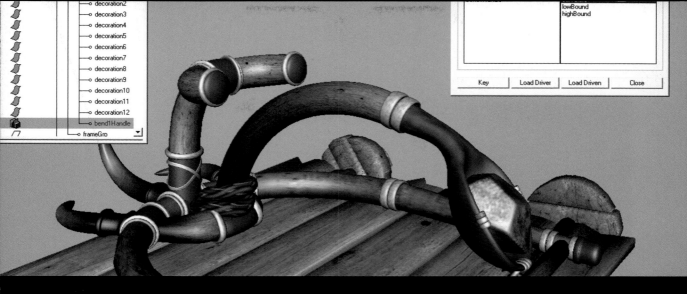

Rigging

In this lesson, you will rig the catapult for animation. This rig will be slightly different from the Delgo character since the geometry is mechanical and, hence, you can have some automation built into it. You will first organize the catapult's hierarchy. Once that is done, you will set-up driven keys that will automate some movements, such as the wheels turning automatically when moving the wagon.

In this lesson, you will learn the following:

- How to rename multiple objects all at once
- How to add animation overrides in hierarchies
- How to set-up reactive driven keys
- How to use the Distance Tool
- How to add non-linear deformers
- How to disable inherited transformations

Hierarchy

The first thing to do before rigging a model is to make sure that all of its nodes are in a good hierarchy where everything is easy to find and well named.

1 Scene file

- **Open** your scene from the last lesson.

  OR

- **Open** the scene file named *16-catapultTxt_02.ma* from the support files.

2 Rename multiple objects

When you create content, you should be renaming nodes fairly frequently. Since you usually need to rename all the nodes one-by-one, you will learn a way to rename several nodes simultaneously.

- Select all the objects that should have similar names, such as the planks.

- In the top right corner of the interface, set the **Rename** option in the input field as shown to the right:

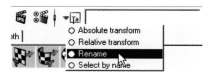

Rename option

- Enter *plank* in the input field and press **Enter**.

  Each and every selected object will be assigned a unique name starting with the defined string, followed by a unique number.

 Note: *The order of selection defines the order of the numbers appended to each name.*

- Take some time to appropriately **rename** every node in the scene.

3 Hierarchy

- **Group** basic, related objects together, such as *wagonGrp*, *catapultGrp*, *armGrp*, and *frameGrp*, leaving the *rock* on its own.

  The idea is to define a hierarchy in which you could animate each group of objects individually, without modifying the hierarchy.

- **Group** everything together into a new group called *geo* as shown to the right:

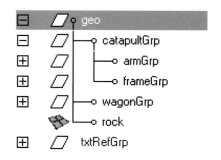

The grouped hierarchy

Tip: *Leave the txtRefGrp on its own since it is not intended to be part of the animation rig.*

4 Pivots

- Make sure every group's pivot is properly placed.

  To do this, make sure you look at every group and determine how it could be moving when animated. Once you know where a group should be moving from, place its pivot to that location. Doing so will allow you to animate any part of the catapult easily.

Note: *Unlike skinned characters, mechanical geometry and groups can be directly animated without a skeleton structure controlling them.*

5 Overrides

When animating any object as a whole, such as the wagon, it is important to have animation overrides on the top group. These overrides can then be used individually to isolate certain animation. For instance, the top Group node will later be animated from path animation. Since this node will be controlled by its connection, you can then use lower overrides to add some custom animation such as rotations or translations.

- Select the *geo* group.

- Press **Ctrl+g** to group the hierarchy **three times**.

- **Rename** the top group to *master*.

- **Rename** the group below it to *transOverride*.

- **Rename** the group below *transOverride* to *rotOverride*.

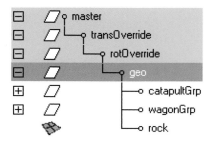

The overrides

6 Save your work

- **Save** your scene as *17-catapultRig_01.ma*.

Automation

Sometimes, when creating rigs, you need to add some automation to ease the work of the animator. In this exercise, you will automate the wheel rotations using Set Driven Keys.

Automation is usually considered a good thing from the point of view of the set-up artist, but can also introduce limitations for the animator. For instance, if a wheel movement is automated, the animator doesn't have the ability to spin the wheel or break it manually. Adding animation overrides, however, will allow the animator to gain control over the automation.

Note: *For simplicity reasons, this setup will only work when the wagon is rotated between 0 and 90 degrees on its Y-axis and translated forward. Having the wheels work in all possible directions would require a more complex exercise.*

1   Wheel overrides

- Select one of the *wheels*.
- Select **Edit → Group → ❏**.
- In the options, set **Group** pivot to **Center**.
- Press the **Group** button.

   The wheel is now grouped and the new group's pivot is centered with the wheel geometry.

- Make sure the group's pivot is centered on the wheel axel.
- **Rename** the new group appropriately with the *auto* prefix to clearly identify this group as being an automated node.
- **Repeat** for the other wheels.

Tip: *Using animation overrides, such as groups, is an inexpensive way to give more control to the artist. Consider adding animation overrides even where it is not required; you will succeed in giving even more control over the rig.*

2   Set Driven Keys

You will now animate the wheels to rotate when the catapult moves forward.

- Select **Animate → Set Driven Key → Set...**
- Select the *master* node, and then click on the **Load Driver** button.
- Highlight the **master** node and its **translateZ** attribute.
- Select all four wheel *auto* groups, and then click on the **Load Driven** button.
- Highlight all four wheel nodes and their **rotateX** attributes.

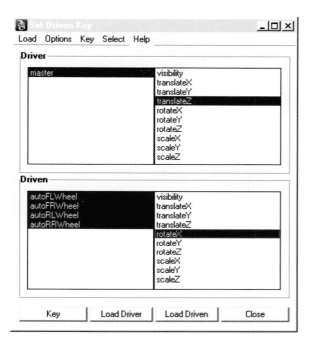

The correct attributes highlighted

- Click on the **Key** button in the Set Driven Key window.

  This sets the initial keyframe in the default position.

3 Mathematics

Trial and error is helpful for determining the proper rotation on the wheels, but you can also use a simple formula to get the proper values.

Following is the formula for finding the distance when rotating a wheel by 360 degrees:

```
pi * diameter = distance
```

You will now use the Distance Tool to get the diameter of a wheel.

- Select **Create → Measure Tools → Distance Tool**.

  The Distance Tool shows in the viewport the distance between two points. Those two points are defined by locators.

- From the *side* view, click at the center of a wheel and then click on its perimeter to create the Distance nodes.

  You now have the radius of the wheel. You need to double that value to get the diameter of the wheel.

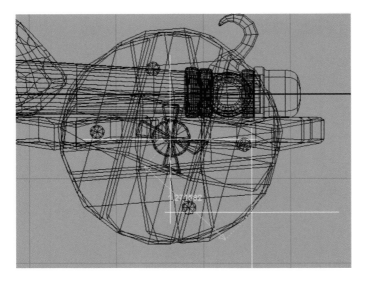

The Distance Tool

- If you solve the above formula with the returned value, you get:

```
3.14 * (1.27 * 2) = 7.98
```

- **Note** down this value.
- **Delete** the Distance node along with its two locators from the **Outliner**.

4 **Set keys**

- Select the *master* node by clicking on it in the **Set Driven Key** window.
- **Move** the *master* on its **Z-axis** by **7.98** units.
- Select all four wheel groups.
- **Rotate** them on their **X-axes** by **360 degrees**.
- Click the **Key** button.

5 **Animation tangent**

Since you have set the default tangent type to be flat in the animation preferences, the animation curves need to be changed.

- Select all four wheel groups.
- Open the **Graph Editor**.
- Select all the animation curves that are visible.
- Select **Tangents → Spline**.
- **Translate** the *master* on its **Z-axis** to test the setup.

    The wheel should rotate correctly within the translation keys set above.

6 Infinity

The current driven animation curves are finite, and that is why when you translate the catapult, at some point the wheels stop turning. To correct this, you need to change the infinity of the animation curve.

- Select all four wheel groups.
- Select all the animation curves that are visible in the **Graph Editor**.
- Select **Curves** → **Pre Infinity** → **Linear**.
- Select **Curves** → **Post Infinity** → **Linear**.
- To make sure the curves are set correctly, select **View** → **Infinity**.
- **Translate** the *master* on its **Z-axis** to test the setup.

  The wheels should no longer stop when you move the master.

7 More driven keys

The wheels are now rotating correctly when you move the master on its Z-axis, but odds are that the catapult will not only move in a straight line. For instance, if you rotate the master on its Y-axis and translate it, the wheels will now slide or not rotate at all. The following will correct this behavior.

- Make sure to place the *master* back at the origin.
- Set its **rotateY** to **90 degrees**.

  *Now if you translate the catapult forward, the wheels will not turn at all. As a result, you need to set new driven keys for the **translateX** attribute.*

- Still in the Set Driven Key window, highlight **translateX** as the driving attribute.
- Click the **Key** button to set the initial keyframe.
- **Move** the *master* on its **X-axis** by **7.98** units.
- Select all four wheel groups.
- **Rotate** them on their **X-axes** by **360 degrees**.
- Click the **Key** button.
- Set the tangents of the new animation curves to **Spline**.
- Set the **infinity** of the new animation curves to **linear**.
- Close the Set Driven Key window.

8 Test the driven keys

The automation you have done so far now allows you to translate the catapult forward in any direction with its wheels moving correctly.

- **Double-click** on the **Move Tool** in the toolbox.
- Set **Move** to **Object**.

- **Rotate** the catapult *master* and test the wheels by **translating** the catapult on the manipulator **Z-axis**.
- Place the *master* back at the origin.

9 Save your work

- **Save** your work as *17-catapultRig_02.ma*.

Non-linear deformers

The arm of the catapult will require some deformation when the catapult will be in loaded position. This is a perfect opportunity to use a non-linear deformer. Non-linear deformers will deform objects according to a mathematical formula such as bend, sine, wave, squash, etc.

In this exercise, you will use a bend deformer.

1 Assign a bend deformer

- Select the *armGrp*.
- Select **Create Deformers** → **Nonlinear** → **Bend**.

  The bend deformer is created and displayed as a single straight line.
- In the **Channel Box**, highlight the *bend1* node.
- To make the tweaking of the deformer easier, set **Curvature** to **1**.

  The deformer doesn't deform as intended just yet.

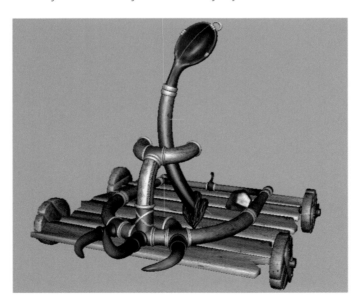

The effect of the bend deformer

2   **Tweak the deformer**

- **Rotate** the bend deformer handle by **90 degrees** on its **Y-axis**.

- Set **Low Bound** in the **Channel Box** for the *bend1* to **0**.

- **Translate** the bend deformer handle down to match the anchor of the arm.

- **Increase** the **High Bound** attribute so that it is longer than the arm geometry.

- **Rotate** the bend deformer handle on its **Z-axis** so the tip of the deformer passes in the middle of the basket.

- Test the **Curvature** attribute to see if it bends the arm correctly.

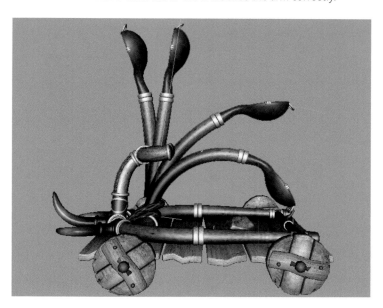

The final bending effect

3   **Custom attribute**

When an attribute is hard to find, it is a good idea to make sure it is easily accessible.

- Select the *catapultGrp*.

- Select **Modify → Add Attribute...** and set the following:

    Attribute name to *load*;

    Data Type to **Float**;

    Default to **0**.

- Click on the **OK** button.
- **RMB** on the new **Load** attribute in the **Channel Box** and select **Editors** → **Connection Editor**.

  This is another way of opening the Connection Editor.
- Click **Reload Left** with the *catapultGrp* selected.
- Click **Reload Right** with the *bend1* node highlighted in the **Channel Box**.
- Highlight the **load** attribute in the left column, then highlight the **curvature** attribute in the right column.

  Doing so connects the load *attribute to the* curvature *attribute.*
- **Close** the Connection Editor.

4 Parent the deformer

In order for the bend deformer to act as intended, its handle needs to be parented into the catapult hierarchy.

- Select the bend deformer handle, then **Ctrl-select** the *armGrp* from the **Outliner**.
- Press **p** to **parent** the handle to the *armGrp*.
- **Hide** the bend deformer by pressing **Ctrl+h**.

 Tip: *Deleting the history on the armGrp or its pieces would delete the bend deformer effect. Make sure to keep the history on the affected surfaces.*

5 Lock and hide attributes

- Make sure to **lock and hide** attributes that are not required to be changed by the animator.

6 Visibility layer

- **Create** a **new layer** and **rename** it to *setupLayer*.
- Select the *master* node and add it to the *setupLayer*.

7 Character set

- Select the *master* node and select **Character** → **Create Character Set** → ❑.
- Select the **Name** to *catapult*.
- Click the **Create Character Set** button.

8 Save your work

- **Save** your scene as *17-catapultRig_03.ma*.

Conclusion

The catapult is now ready to be animated. You have created some automation, but you also made sure that the animator could override that animation by placing the automation on groups. As well, you used a non-linear deformer, which in this case was much easier to use than any other setup.

In the next lesson, you will learn how to fill your environment with one of the most powerful Maya software tools—Paint Effects.

Paint Effects

For this next stage, you will generate lots of content for Delgo's environment. The Paint Effects Tool gives you access to preset brushes ranging from grasses to trees and buildings to lightning bolts, which can be customized for your own scenarios.

In this lesson, you will use several Paint Effects brushes and test render your scene.

In this lesson, you will learn the following:

- How to paint on canvas
- How to paint on geometry
- How to optimize the way Paint Effects are displayed in the viewport
- How to share, blend, and customize brushes
- How to save brush presets
- How to auto-paint a surface

Paint on canvas

In order to experiment with various Paint Effects brushes, you will create a nature scene with trees, flowers, and grass. First, you will test the tool on a canvas.

1 Open a new scene

2 Paint in the Paint Effects window

- Press **8** on your keyboard to display the Maya Paint Effects Canvas window.
- Select **Paint → Paint Canvas**.

  This will set the canvas to a 2D paint mode.

- In the **Paint Effects** window, select **Brush → Get Brush...**

  The Visor will open, letting you browse through the various template Paint Effects brushes.

- Open any brush folder, select a brush and paint on the canvas.

  You can now experiment with different brushes.

- Select **Canvas → Clear**.

3 Change the background color

- Select **Canvas → Clear → ❏**.
- Set the **Clear Color** to **light blue**, then press the **Clear** button.

 Note: *You can also import an image as a starting point by selecting* **Canvas →** **Open Image**.

4 Paint your image

- In the Visor window, open the *clouds* folder.

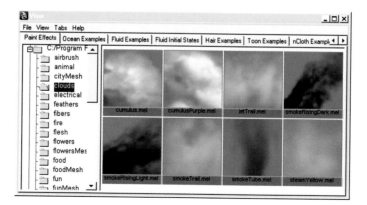

The Visor

- Select the *jetTrail.mel* brush and paint some clouds onto your image.

- Continue painting elements onto your image using the different preset brushes.
- If you make a mistake, you can **undo** the last brush stroke by selecting **Canvas** → **Canvas Undo**.

Test image

5 **Save the image**

- When you are finished with your image, you can save it by selecting **Canvas** → **Save As** → ❏.
- In the **Option** window, you can decide whether or not you want to use the **Save Alpha** option.
- Click on **Save Image** and name your image.

If you want, you can then use this image as an image plane or as a texture.

- Return to a single Perspective layout by clicking its icon in the toolbox.

Paint Effects strokes

You will now learn how to paint strokes on geometry and how strokes can share the same brush. As well, you will learn how to scale Paint Effects.

The following scenery will take place outside the throne room built in the first project.

1 Scene file

- **Open** the scene *04-animationBasics_02.ma* from the first project's *scenes* directory.

2 Delete the animation

- Go to frame **1**, then select **Edit → Delete All by Type → Channels.**

  Doing so will delete the animation in the entire scene.

3 Prepare the set

- Select the *wall* surface and open its Attribute Editor.

- Under the **Render Stats** section, turn **On** the **Double Sided** attribute.

- Select the *environmentGroup* and **scale** it to **5** on all axes.

 Tip: *Make sure the pivot is located at the origin before scaling the group.*

- Select the *roomGroup*, **scale** it to **0.3** on all axes, and **move** it by **-20** units on its **Z-axis**.

  Doing so will give you room to eventually bring in the catapult.

- **RMB** on the *ground* plane and select **Vertex**.

- **Tweak** the surface to create a hill as follows, on which the catapult will eventually be placed.

A hill next to the throne room

> **Tip:** *Keep the ground next to the throne room perfectly flat since this is where the character will be walking.*

4 Paint trees

- Press **F6** to select the **Rendering** menu set.
- With the *ground* selected, select **Paint Effects → Make Paintable**.

  Doing so will allow you to paint directly on the surface.

- Select **Paint Effects → Get Brush...**
- In the Visor, select the *funMesh* directory, then click on the *gloppy.mel* brush preset.

  Clicking on a brush preset in the Visor automatically accesses the Paint Effects Tool.

- Hold down **b** and **click+drag** to resize the brush.
- **Paint** a single stroke on the *ground* to create a weird looking tree.

A Paint Effects gloppy tree

5 Optimized display

When working with Paint Effects, you can clutter your scene and computer with a lot of objects in no time. The following will change the display of a stroke in the viewport.

- Select the gloppy stroke.
- In the **Shapes** section of the **Channel Box**, set **Draw As Mesh** to **Off**.

  Rather than displaying meshes when painting the Paint Effects, only reference lines will be used. This drastically reduces the display refresh of the viewport, but does not affect the scene rendering.

- Select **Paint Effects → Paint Effects Tool → ❏**.
- In the option window, turn **Off** the **Draw as Mesh** option.
- **Paint** some more gloppy trees around the room.

More trees

Tip: *To reduce the viewport refresh rate even more, you can also set the stroke's Display Percent to a lower value. This attribute specifies how many of the Paint Effects you want to see interactively in the viewport.*

6 Share one brush

At the moment, every stroke that you have drawn uses a different brush, letting you customize each one individually. To modify the trees simultaneously, you can set-up the strokes so they share the same brush.

- Open the **Outliner**.

  You should see all the different strokes you have drawn on the ground.

- Select all the *strokeGloppy* strokes.

- Select **Paint Effects → Share One Brush**.

  Now all the strokes use the same brush. Modifying this brush will change all the trees at the same time.

7 Scale the trees

- Press **Ctrl+a** to open the **Attribute Editor** for any of the selected strokes.

- Select the *gloppy* tab.

  This is the brush shared among all the strokes.

- Set the **Global Scale** attribute to your liking.

8 Offset the trees

- Select all the *strokeGloppy* strokes.

- In the **Channel Box**, under the **Shapes** section, set **Surface Offset** to **-2**.

  Doing so will have the trunk of the gloppy tree inside the ground.

9 Test render the scene

- Select **Render → Render Current Frame**.

The rendered Paint Effects

10 Save your work

- **Save** your scene as *18-paintEffects_01.ma*.

Customize brushes

In this exercise, you will blend brushes together and customize your own brushes. You will also save your custom brush presets on your shelf for later use.

1 Blending brushes

- Select **Paint Effects → Get Brush...**
- In the **Visor**, select the *grasses* directory, then click on the *astroturf.mel* brush preset.
- Still in the Visor, **RMB** on the *grassBermuda.mel* brush preset.

  This will display a menu letting you blend the current brush with the new one.

- Select **Blend Brush 50%**.

  This will blend the second brush with the first brush, giving the stroke a little bit of profile from both brushes.

- **RMB** again on the *grassBermuda.mel* brush preset and select **Blend Shading 5%**.

  This will blend the shading of the two brushes together.

2 Paint the new brush

- **Paint** one stroke of the new brush on the ground on either side of the room.
- In the **Channel Box**, set the **Display Percent** attribute of the Paint Effects stroke to **50**.
- Set the **Global Scale** of the Paint Effects brush as desired.

The painted grass

- Select all the *strokeGrassBermuda* strokes.
- Select **Paint Effects** → **Share One Brush**.

3 Customizing brushes

- In the **Attribute Editor**, select the *grassBermuda* tab.

  Doing so will display all the Paint Effects attributes for the current brush and the current stroke.

- Try changing some of the values to see their affect on the current stroke. The following are some examples:

      Tubes → **Creation** → **Tubes Per Step**;

      Tubes → **Creation** → **Length Min**;

      Tubes → **Creation** → **Length Max**;

      Tubes → **Creation** → **Tubes Width1**;

      Tubes → **Creation** → **Tubes Width2**;

      Tubes → **Creation** → **Width Rand**;

      Tubes → **Creation** → **Width Bias**;

      Behavior → **Forces** → **Gravity**.

Tip: *You may have to render the stroke in order to see changes.*

- **Reduce** the quality of the brush to speed up rendering time:

    Brush Profile → **Brush Width** to **3**;

    Brush Profile → **Flatness1** to **1**;

    Brush Profile → **Flatness2** to **1**;

    Tubes → **Creation** → **Tubes per Step** to **25**;

    Tubes → **Creation** → **Segments** to **1**;

    Tubes → **Growth** to **Branches only**.

4 Get brush settings from stroke

In order to draw more customized grass, you need to update the current template brush with the settings of the stroke you just modified.

- With the stroke selected, select **Paint Effects** → **Get Settings from Selected Stroke**.

    This will set the customized grass brush as the current template brush.

5 Save custom brushes

You can save the current template brush for later use. The brush can be saved either to your shelf or the Visor.

- Select **Paint Effects** → **Save Brush Preset...**
- Set the following in the **Save Brush Preset** window to save to current shelf:

    Label to **Custom Grass**;

    Overlay Label to **grass**;

    Save Preset to **To Shelf**.

Note: *The preset will be saved to the currently selected shelf, so make sure you select the appropriate shelf before executing these steps.*

OR

- Set the following in the **Save Brush Preset** window to save to a *Visor* directory:

    Label to **Custom Grass**;

    Overlay Label to **grass**;

    Save Preset to **To Visor**;

    Visor Directory to *brushes* from your *prefs* directory.

- Click the **Save Brush Preset** button.

Note: *You can obtain an image for your new brush only through the Paint Effects Canvas panel.*

6 **Automatically paint a surface**

If you do not need to paint strokes by hand, you can use the **Paint Effects → Auto Paint** command. This will automatically paint onto a surface according to the options set. For instance, you could cover a rock with lichen or flowers in a single click.

7 **Paint some more plants**

Add to your scene some weird looking vegetation achieved by blending brush presets.

An example render

Note: *Several Paint Effects brushes are pre-animated so when you play your scene, some Paint Effect strokes might be animated.*

8 **Scene set-up**

- Open the **Outliner**.
- **Group** the strokes together and **rename** the group to *pfxGroup*.
- **Parent** the *pfxGroup* to the *environmentGroup*.

  Since the Paint Effect strokes rely on the position of the ground plane, do not move the environmentGroup since it would cause the strokes to double transform and offset themselves from the ground plane.

- **Create** a new layer called *pfxLayer* and add *pfxGroup* to it.

> **Tip:** *To speed up the rest of the project, you can hide the pfxLayer.*

9 Save your work

- **Save** your scene as *18-paintEffects_02.ma*.

Conclusion

You have now experienced one of Maya software's greatest tools, but you have only scratched the surface of the power available in Paint Effects. Learning how to use the Paint Effects Canvas, how to paint on objects, and how to customize your brushes will serve you well as you become more and more familiar with the tool. There are so many ways to use Paint Effects to generate scene content that there should be no reason for your future scenes to look dull and empty.

In the next lesson, you will learn how to convert Paint Effects and how to use deformers.

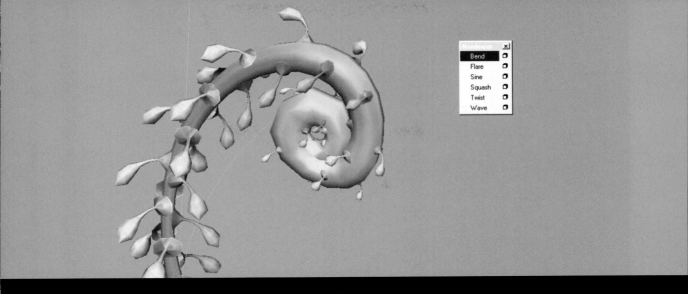

Deformers

Deformers can be used for numerous reasons: for character set-up and animation, for facial expressions, for modeling, and for creating dynamic surfaces. In this lesson, you will be introduced to various deformers to experiment with using a Paint Effects tree converted to polygons. These deformers will change the tree's shape while still keeping an organic feel to the geometry.

In this lesson, you will learn the following:

- How to convert Paint Effects to polygons
- How to use wire deformers
- How to use point on curve deformers
- How to use clusters
- How to use the Soft Modification Tool
- How to use non-linear deformers
- How to change the deformation order

Convert Paint Effects

To begin, you will need geometry to deform. In this lesson, you will be using a polygonal tree originally from Paint Effects. Most Paint Effects' strokes can be converted to geometry and even animated dynamically.

For the sake of this lesson, you will only be using the output geometry of the conversion as a surface to deform.

1 Open a new scene

2 Paint a tree

- From the **Rendering** menu set, select **Paint Effects → Get Brush**.
- Under the *FunMesh* directory, click on the *gloppy.mel* brush preset.
- **Paint** a single gloppy tree at the origin.

3 Convert to polygons

- With the stroke selected, select **Modify → Convert → Paint Effects to Polygons → ❑**.

- In the options, turn **On** the **Quad output** option.

- Click on the **Convert** button.

4 Combine the model

If your model is composed of multiple meshes, for instance, the leaves, branches, and trunk, it will be simpler to combine them all together.

- Select all the meshes.

- Select **Mesh → Combine**.

Paint Effects gloppy

5 Delete history

Some Paint Effects' brushes are animated by default, and when you convert the Paint Effects to polygons, the construction history keeps the ability to animate the mesh automatically. In this lesson, you will not require construction history.

Note: *Try to play your scene to see the Paint Effects' animation. If the playback is too slow, try to display the stroke as wireframe or playblast the scene.*

- Select **Edit → Delete All by Type → History**.

The mesh has now lost its connection to the Paint Effects' stroke and is now a static model.

- **Delete** the stroke and curve from the **Outliner**.

6   Center the tree

- Select the mesh and move it so it grows straight up from the origin.
- **Freeze** its transformations.
- **Rename** it to *tree*.

7   Save your work

- **Save** the scene as *19-deformers_01.ma*.

Wire deformer

You will now modify the tree using a wire deformer. A wire deformer is used to deform a surface based on a NURBS curve. You will use that type of deformer on the tree trunk.

1   Draw a curve

- Select **Create → EP Curve Tool**.
- From a *side* view, **draw** a curve along the trunk, then press **Enter**.
- **Tweak** the curve to follow the trunk in other views.

2   Create the wire deformer

- From the Animation menu set, select **Create Deformers → Wire Tool**.

  The Wire Tool requires two steps. First, you must select the deformable surfaces, then you must select the NURBS curve to be the deformer.

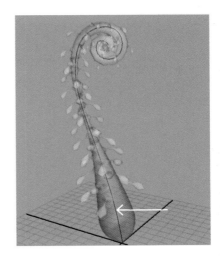

The curve to be used as a deformer

> **Note:**   *You can read the tool's directives in the Help Line at the bottom of the main interface. The tool automatically sets the proper picking masks so you don't actually pick unwanted object types.*

- Select the *tree* geometry and press **Enter**.
- Select the NURBS curve and press **Enter**.

  The wire deformer is created.

3   Edit the shape of the curve

- With the *curve* selected, press **F8** to go into **Component mode**.
- Select some CVs and **move** them to see their effect on the geometry.

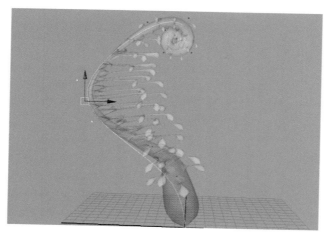

The default wire deformer effect

4 Edit the deformer attribute

As with any other deformers, the attributes of the wire deformer can be changed through the **Channel Box**.

- In the **Channel Box**, select the *wire1* history node.
- Highlight the **Dropoff Distance** attribute in the **Channel Box**.
- Hold down **Ctrl**, then **MMB+drag** in the viewport to see its effect.

  The effect of the wire deformer changes across the geometry.

Note: *Holding down the **Ctrl** key makes the virtual slider change with smaller increments.*

5 Edit the deformer membership

The **dropoff** has a nice effect, but the deformer might be affecting some undesired components. You can correct that by defining the membership of the geometry to the deformer.

- Select **Edit Deformers → Edit Membership Tool**.
- Select the *curve* to highlight the vertices affected by it.

  All the vertices of the tree geometry will be highlighted yellow.

- Hold the **Ctrl** key and **deselect** the branch vertices.

  Vertices that are no longer deformed will move back to their original positions.

The deformer's membership

> **Tip:** *You can also use* **Edit Deformers** → **Paint Set Membership Tool** *to easily define the membership of the vertices.*

6 Experiment

Now that the deformer no longer affects the branches, you can set its **dropoff** to a higher value.

- Go back to **Object mode**.
- Press **q** to exit the **Edit Membership Tool** and enable the **Pick Tool**.
- Select the *curve* and try to change other deformer attributes from the **Channel Box**.
- Experiment with moving the *curve*'s CVs to see the effect of the deformer.

Point on curve and cluster deformer

The wire deformer is working well to deform the tree, but it is not practical to deform the curve for animation. Several other types of deformers can be used to deform the curve itself. Here you will experiment with the *point on curve* deformer and the *cluster* deformer.

1 Point on curve deformer

The point on curve deformer will create a locator linked to a curve edit point.

- **RMB** on the *NURBS curve* and select **Edit Point**.

  Unlike CVs, edit points are located directly on the curve.

- Select the edit point located at the base of the trunk.

- Select **Create Deformers** → **Point on Curve**.

  A locator is created at the edit point's position.

- Select **Modify** → **Center Pivot** to center the pivot of the *locator*.

- **Move** the locator to see its effect on the curve.

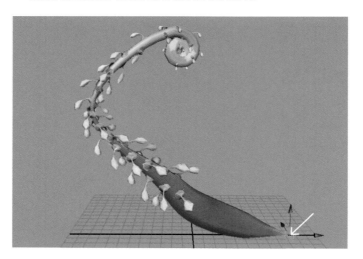

The point on curve deformer

 Note: *Rotating a point on curve deformer has no effect on the curve.*

2 Cluster deformer

The point on curve works well, but has its limitations. For instance, it can only control one edit point at a time, and it cannot be used for rotation. The cluster deformer will create a handle that controls one or more vertices. When a cluster has multiple vertices in it, it can also be rotated.

- **RMB** on the *NURBS curve* and select **Control Vertex**.

- Select the two CVs in the middle of the trunk.

 Tip: *It might be easier to locate the CVs by also displaying hulls. If you select only one CV, rotating the CV would have no effect.*

- Select **Create Deformers** → **Cluster**.

  *A cluster handle is displayed with a **C** in the viewport.*

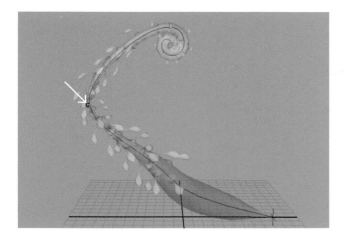

The cluster handle

- **Move** and **rotate** the *cluster handle* to see its effect on the curve and the tree.

> **Note:** *Both the point on curve locator and cluster handle can be animated like any other node.*

Soft Modification Tool

The *Soft Modification Tool* lets you push and pull geometry as a sculptor would push and pull a piece of clay. By default, the amount of deformation is greatest at the center of the deformer, and gradually falls off moving outward. However, you can control the fall-off of the deformation to create various types of effects.

1 Scene file

- **Open** the scene *19-deformers_01.ma* without saving your previous changes.

2 Create the deformer

- **RMB** on the *tree* surface and select **Vertex**.

- Select the tree's lower half vertices.

- Click on the **Soft Modification Tool** in the toolbox, or select **Create Deformers → Soft Modification**.

  An **S** *handle similar to the cluster handle will be created. The tool's manipulator will also be displayed, and the influence of the deformer is shown. Yellow indicates areas that are fully deformed, while black areas are not deformed at all.*

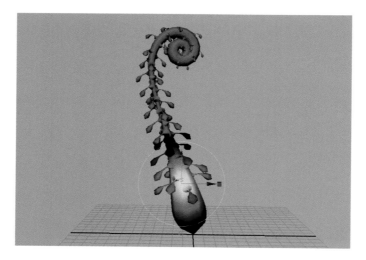

The influence of the deformer

3 **Edit the deformer**

- **Move**, **rotate,** and **scale** the deformer to see its effect on the geometry.

- Press **Ctrl+a** to open the **Attribute Editor** for the deformer.

  The various deformer options can be edited here.

- Set the **Falloff Radius** to **2.0**.

- Click on the button next to the **Falloff Curve** graph.

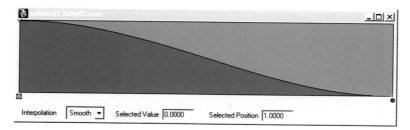

Falloff curve

- See the effect of the deformer on the geometry.

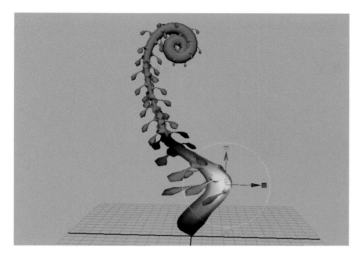

The modified influence

> **Note:** *The Soft Modification effect works best on high resolution models.*

4 Modeling with Soft Modification Tool

When modeling a high resolution model, such as a character's face, you can create multiple Soft Modification deformers to achieve a final shape. The deformers can even overlap.

5 Delete Soft Modification deformers

If you want to delete the deformer, simply select its **S** handle and **delete** it. If you want to keep the shape of the geometry but remove the deformers, you must delete the model's history.

Non-linear deformers

Maya software has several *non-linear deformers*. Non-linear deformers can affect one surface, multiple surfaces, or parts of a surface, and are very simple to use. In this exercise, you will experiment with all the non-linear deformers.

1 Scene file

- **Open** the scene *19-deformers_01.ma* without saving your previous changes.

2 Bend deformer

- Select the *tree* geometry, then select **Create Deformers → Nonlinear → Bend**.

  The Bend handle is created and selected.

- In the **Attribute Editor**, highlight the *bend₁* input.

  All the attributes for this deformer type are listed.

- Experiment and combine the different attributes to see their effect on the geometry.

> **Tip:** Most of the attributes have visual feedback on the deformer's handle in the viewport. You can also use the **Show Manipulator Tool** to interact with the deformer in the viewport.

- **Moving**, **rotating,** and **scaling** the handle will also affect the location of the deformation.

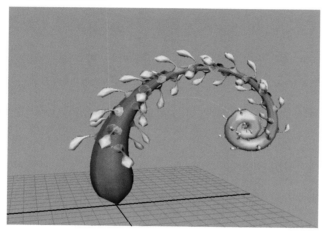

Bend deformer

> This deformer can have several uses, including simplifying modeling tasks, which would be otherwise difficult to achieve. In this case, it could be used to simulate wind animation.

- When you finish experimenting, select the deformer and **delete** it.

3 Flare deformer

- Select the *tree* geometry, then select **Create Deformers → Nonlinear → Flare**.

  The Flare handle is created and selected.

- In the **Attribute Editor**, highlight the *flare₁* input.

- Experiment by moving, rotating, scaling, and combining the different attributes to see their effect on the geometry.

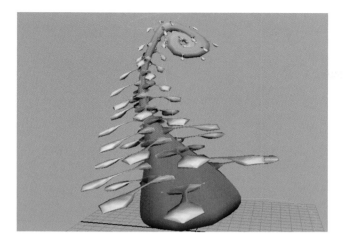

Flare deformer

> *This deformer is also versatile and can be used to simplify modeling tasks.*

- When you finish experimenting, select the deformer and **delete** it.

4 Sine deformer

- Select the *tree* geometry, then select **Create Deformers → Nonlinear → Sine**.

  The Sine handle is created and selected.

- In the **Attribute Editor**, highlight the *sine1* input.

- Experiment by moving, rotating, scaling, and combining the different attributes to see their effect on the geometry.

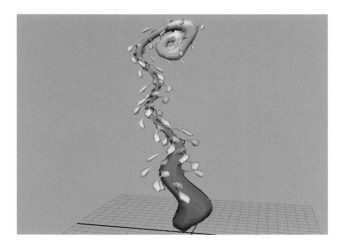

Sine deformer

Tip: *The **Offset** attribute is great for animating a waving effect.*

This deformer can help achieve refined randomization and could be used to simulate a flag animation or waves on a shore.

- When you finish experimenting, select the deformer and **delete** it.

5 Squash deformer

- Select the *tree* geometry, then select **Create Deformers** → **Nonlinear** → **Squash**.

The Squash handle is created and selected.

- In the **Attribute Editor**, highlight the *squash1* input.
- Experiment by moving, rotating, scaling, and combining the different attributes to see their effect on the geometry.

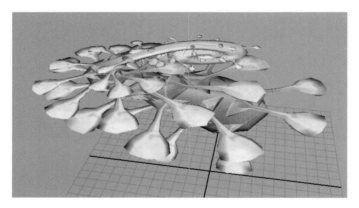

Squash deformer

This deformer is useful for adding stretch and squash to an animated object.

- When you finish experimenting, select the deformer and **delete** it.

6 Twist deformer

- Select the *tree* geometry, then select **Create Deformers** → **Nonlinear** → **Twist**.

The Twist handle is created and selected.

- In the **Attribute Editor**, highlight the *twist1* input.
- Experiment by moving, rotating, scaling, and combining the different attributes to see their effect on the geometry.

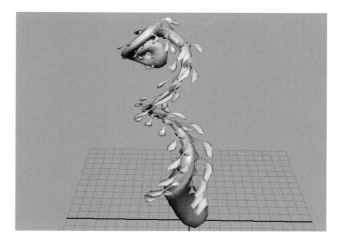

Twist deformer

> This deformer can add twisting animation to an object, among other uses.

- When you finish experimenting, select the deformer and **delete** it.

7   **Wave deformer**

- Select the *tree* geometry, then select **Create Deformers → Nonlinear → Wave**.

   The Wave handle is created and selected.

- In the **Attribute Editor**, highlight the *wave1* input.

- Experiment by moving, rotating, scaling, and combining the different attributes to see their effect on the geometry.

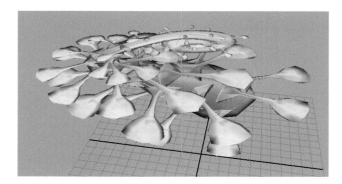

Wave deformer

> As you can see, this deformer can have several uses, such as creating a rippling effect for water.

- When you finish experimenting, select the deformer and **delete** it.

8   Experiment

Spend some time deforming the tree as you wish. Keep in mind that you can add multiple deformers to the same object.

If you want to animate the tree later, consider keeping the deformers in the scene and making an animation setup.

Deformation order

The deformation order of a surface is very important to take into consideration. For instance, if you apply a *sine* deformer and then a *bend* deformer, the results are very different than if you apply a *bend* deformer and then a *sine* deformer.

The deformation order does not only apply to non-linear deformers. For instance, a rigid binding and a polygonal smooth will have a very different effect than a polygonal smooth and a rigid bind.

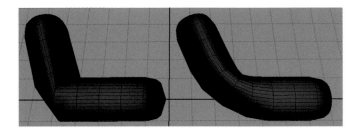

Smooth/Rigid bind vs. Rigid bind/Smooth

Note: *In the previous statement, a rigid bind followed by a smooth would evaluate much faster and give better results than a smooth followed by a rigid bind, since the rigid binding would have to skin a higher resolution model.*

1   New Scene

- Select **File → New**.

2   Create a cylinder

- Select **Create → Polygon Primitives → Cylinder**.

- Edit the *cylinder* as follows:

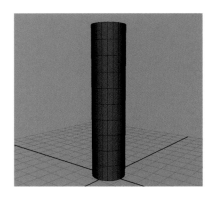

Example cylinder

3   **Apply deformers**

  - Select the *cylinder*, then select **Create Deformers** → **Nonlinear** → **Bend**.
  - Select the *cylinder*, then select **Create Deformers** → **Nonlinear** → **Sine**.

4   **Edit the bend deformer**

  - Select the *cylinder*.
  - In the **Channel Box**, highlight the *bend1* deformer.
  - Set the **Curvature** attribute to **2**.

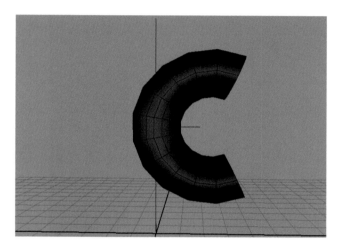

Bend deformer effect

5   **Edit the sine deformer**

  - Select the *cylinder*.
  - In the **Channel Box**, highlight the *sine1* deformer.
  - Set the **Amplitude** attribute to **0.1**.
  - Set the **Wavelength** attribute to **0.35**.

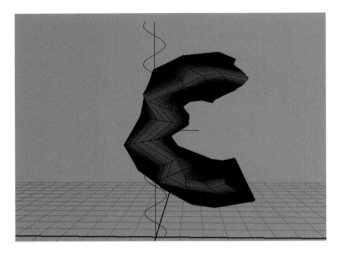

Sine and bend deformer effect

6 List input for the cylinder

- **RMB** on the *cylinder*.

- Select **Inputs → All Inputs**...

    Doing so will display a window with all the History nodes affecting the cylinder.

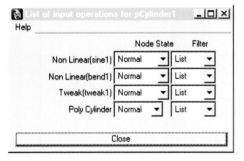

List of input for cylinder

7 Change the order of deformation

- In the **Input** window, **MMB+drag** the *Non Linear(sine1)* item over the *Non Linear(bend1)* item to change their order.

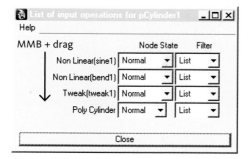

List of input for cylinder

8 Result of the new order of deformation

New deformation order effect

Conclusion

You should now be comfortable using basic deformers. Being aware of the results created by the deformation order will allow you to reorder them if needed.

In the next lesson, you will learn about lighting and effects, which can greatly improve the quality of your rendered scene.

Lights and Effects

In the real world, it is light that allows us to see the surfaces and objects around us. In computer graphics, digital lights play the same role. They help define the space within a scene and, in many cases, help to set the mood or atmosphere. As well, several other effects besides lighting can be added to the final image in order to have it look more realistic. This lesson explores and explains some of the basic Maya effects.

In this lesson, you will learn the following:

- How to add lighting to your scene
- How to enable shadows
- How to add light fog and lens flare
- How to set-up motion blur
- How to batch render an animation
- How to use fcheck

References

When you first animated Delgo, you saw how to create a reference. You will now open that same animation file, but this time you will also reference the environment.

1   Scene file

- **Open** the scene file *14-delgoWalk_05.ma* from the second project's *scenes* directory.

2   Create references

- Select **File** → **Reference Editor** from the main interface menu.
- Select **File** → **Create Reference** → ❑ from the main interface menu or from the **Reference Editor**.
- Set **Resolve all nodes with this string:** *set*.

  This will prefix all the Reference nodes with the string set.

- Click on the **Apply** button.
- In the browse window, select the file *18-paintEffects_02.ma*, and then click **Reference**.

  The file will load into the current one.

- Set **Resolve all nodes with this string:** *catapult*.
- Click on the **Reference** button.
- In the browse dialog that appears, select the file *17-catapultRig_03.ma*, and then click **Reference**.

> **Note:** *You may have to re-link textures that are not automatically found. To do so, simply open the **Hypershade**, select the **Texture** tab, and change the path of the texture through the **Attribute Editor**.*

3   Scaling

Looking at the three elements in your scene, you can clearly see that there is a scaling issue between the files.

- Select the *environmentGroup*.

> **Tip:**   *Make sure the group's pivot is located at the origin before scaling.*

- Set its **scale X**, **Y**, and **Z-axes** to **4.0**, or any other appropriate value.
- Select the Delgo *master*.
- Set its **scale X**, **Y**, and **Z-axes** to **0.5**, or any other appropriate value.

Note: *You are not scaling the catapult since it would break the wheel automation you created earlier that was based on the wheel diameter.*

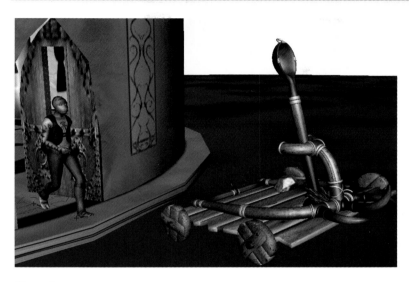

The entire scene

Note: *If the top node's scale attributes are non-keyable and unlocked, they will not show in the Channel Box, but the Scale Tool will still work. Alternatively, you can access the scale attributes in the Attribute Editor. If the scale attributes of the node are locked, you need to unlock them in the referenced file and re-open this file again.*

4 **Placing the characters**

- **Move** the Delgo *master* in the doorway and set a **keyframe** in **Translation**.

  Since the character is controlled by a Trax clip, setting a keyframe will prevent it from snapping back at the origin.

- **Move** the catapult *master* next to the door.

5 **Save your work**

- **Save** this scene to *20-lightsEffects_01.ma*.

Placing a point light

To create the primary light source in the scene, such as the sun, you will use a point light. This light type works exactly like a lightbulb, with attributes such as color and intensity.

1 Create a point light

- Select **Create** → **Lights** → **Point Light**.

  This places a point light at the origin.

- With the light still selected, **translate** the point light high up in the sky, in front of the room.

The light placement

 Tip: *Make sure that you don't place the light outside the sky dome.*

2 Turn on hardware lighting (if possible)

One step beyond hardware texturing is *hardware lighting*. This lets you see how the light is affecting the surface that it is shining on.

- Press the **6** hotkey to display textures in the viewport.
- Select **Lighting** → **Use All Lights** or press the **7** hotkey.

  You will see the scene being lit by the point light.

The hardware lighting enabled

3 Test render the scene

- From the **Rendering** menu set, select **Render → Render Current Frame**.

  Notice the rendered image is dark without much contrast.

The rendered scene

Placing a directional light

So far, you used a point light to create a sun, but this kind of light is not adequate for sunlight and shadows because in reality, the sun is so far away that the rays coming from it are parallel to each other.

As a second light source in the scene, you will use a directional light. This light type mimics a light source so far away that rays are parallel, which is exactly what you need.

1   Create a directional light

- Select **Create** → **Lights** → **Directional Light**.

This places a directional light at the origin.

2   Edit the directional light's position

The Show Manipulator Tool provides a manipulator for the light's *look at point* and *eye point*. You can edit these using the same method as you would with a typical transform manipulator.

- Press the **t** key to access the **Show Manipulator Tool**.

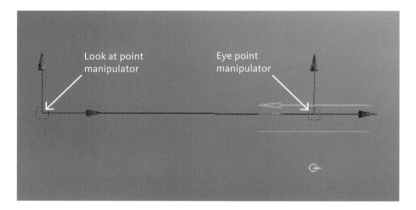

Show Manipulator Tool

- **Click+drag** on the manipulator handles to reposition the light in the direction in which the sunlight should hit the set.

New light position

3 **Shadows**

- In the **Attribute Editor**, expand the **Shadows** section for the directional light.
- **Enable** shadow casting by checking the **Use Depth Map Shadows** attribute.
- **Render** the scene.

  Notice that you don't see the effect of the directional light anymore. This is because the directional light is from an infinite distance, so the sky dome places the entire set in shadow. To correct this, you can disable shadow casting on the sky dome surface.

- Select the *skydome* surface and open its **Attribute Editor**.
- Under the **Render Stats** section, set the following:

  Casts Shadows to **Off**;

  Receive Shadows to **Off**.

- **Render** the scene again.

  You should now see shadows.

Shadows in the rendered image

4 **Refine the shadows**

Right now, the shadow resolution is coarse. The following shows how to increase the depth map shadow resolution:

- Open the **Attribute Editor** for the *directionalLight1*.

- In the **Depth Map Shadow Attributes** section, set the following:

    Resolution to **1024** or even **2048,** rather than **512;**

    Filter Size to **2.**

    Doing so will first increase the resolution of the shadow maps, and will then apply a blur filter to smooth out the shadow even more.

- **Render** the scene again to see how this makes the shadow smoother.

5 **Adding ambient lighting**

In the real world, light rays bounce off surfaces, particles, and atmosphere, making the global lighting level of a set brighter. In order to mimic this, you could add several directional lights pointing from the back and from below, but instead you will use an ambient light, which can accomplish this effect.

- Select **Create → Lights → Ambient Light**.

- In the **Channel Box**, set the **Intensity** attribute to **0.5**.

- **Place** the light at the opposite side of the scene.

- **Render** the scene.

    Notice how the geometry that previously had a side in complete shadow is now much more visible. Also notice how the global light level raised to what you would think of as daylight.

The ambient light effect

Light effects

The point light used for the sun doesn't help much at this time. When the rendered camera is looking directly at bright light, a light glow and lens flare would add realism to your renders. You will now add light effects to your point light.

1 Light FX

- Open the **Attribute Editor** for the *pointLightShape1*.
- Scroll down to the **Light Effects** section.
- Click on the **map** button next to the **Light Glow** attribute.

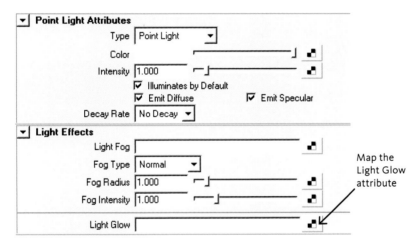

Light Glow attribute

> *Maya software will automatically create, select, and display an opticalFX node in the Attribute Editor.*

- Set the *opticalFX1* attributes as follows:

      Lens flare to **Enabled**;

      Glow Type to **Linear**;

      Halo Type to **Lens Flare**.

      Under **Lens Flare Attributes,** set **Flare Intensity** to **2**.

- **Place** the camera to look directly at the sun from inside the room.
- **Unhide** the *pfxLayer* if it is not visible already.
- **Render** your scene to see the lens flare.

Never look directly at the sun!

2 Save your work

- **Save** your scene as *20-lightsEffects_02.ma*.

Rendering animation

Now that you have defined the lighting in your scene and you are happy with your test rendering, it is time to render an animation. This is accomplished using the Maya *batch renderer*. In preparation, you will add motion blur to your scene, in order to simulate the blur generated in live action film and video work.

1 Render Settings

Render Settings are a group of attributes that you can set to define how your scene will render. To define the quality of the rendering, you need to set the Render Settings.

- In the **Render View** window, click with your **RMB** and choose **Options** → **Render Settings...**

  OR

- Click the **Render Settings** button located at the top right of the main interface.
- Select the **Maya Software** tab.
- Open the **Anti-aliasing Quality** section if it is not already opened.

- Set the **Quality** preset to **Intermediate quality**.

Anti-aliasing is a visual smoothing of edge lines in the final rendered image. Because bitmaps are made up of square pixels, a diagonal line would appear jagged unless it was anti-aliased.

2   Set the image output

To render an animation, you must set-up the scene's file extensions to indicate a rendered sequence. You must also set-up the start and end frames.

- Select the **Common** tab in the **Render Settings** window.

- From the **File Output** section, set the following:

> **File name prefix** to *scenery*.
>
> *This sets the name of the animated sequence.*
>
> **Frame/Animation ext** *to:*
>
> **name.#.ext**.
>
> *This sets up Maya to render a numbered sequence of images.*
>
> **Start frame** to **1**;
>
> **End frame** to **50**;
>
> **By frame** to **1**.
>
> *This tells Maya to render every frame from 1 to 50.*

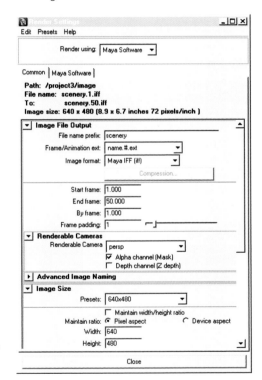

3   Turn on motion blur

- Select the **Maya Software** tab.

- Under the **Motion Blur** section, click on the **Motion blur** button to turn it **On**.

- Set the **Motion blur type** to be **2D**.

  This type of motion blur renders the fastest.

Render Settings

Motion blur on Delgo

Tip: *If you want to see more or less motion blur in your renders, you can set the* **Blur** *length in the* **Motion Blur** *section of the* **Render Settings.**

4 Place your camera

- In the Perspective view panel, select **View → Camera Settings → Resolution Gate**.
- **Place** the camera so you can see your animation from frames **1** to **50**.

5 Save your work

- **Save** your scene as *20-lightsEffects_03.ma*.

6 Batch render the scene

- Press **F6** to change to the **Rendering** menu set.
- Select **Render → Batch Render**.
- If for any reason you want to cancel the current batch render, select **Render → Cancel Batch Render**.

7 Watch the render progress

- The sequence will be rendered as a series of frames. You can look in the Command Feedback line or through the **Window → General Editor → Script Editor** to see the status of the current rendering process.

Tip: *Once a batch render is launched, you can safely close Maya without interrupting the batch render.*

8 View the resulting animation

After the rendering is complete, you can preview the results using the *fcheck* utility.

- To open the *fcheck* utility, go into your programs, and then go to **Autodesk → Autodesk Maya 2009 → FCheck.**
- In **FCheck**, select **File → Open Sequence**.
- Navigate to the *project3\images* folder.
- Select the file *scenery.1.iff* and click **Open**.

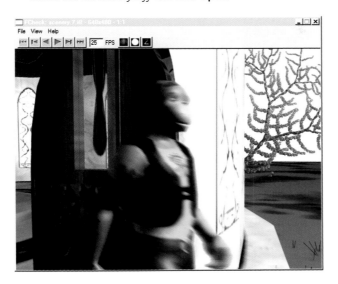

Animation previewed with fcheck utility

The animation will load one frame at a time, and once in memory, it will play it back in real time.

> **Tip:** To learn more about the capabilities of fcheck for previewing your animations, enter the `fcheck -h` in a command shell or select the Help menu.

Conclusion

You are now familiar with the basic concepts of lighting and rendering a scene. You began by enabling various light options such as shadows, light glow, and lens flare. Then, you added 2D motion blur just before launching your first animation batch render. Once your render was complete, you viewed it in the fcheck utility.

In the next lesson, you will learn about rendering tasks and experiment with different renderers.

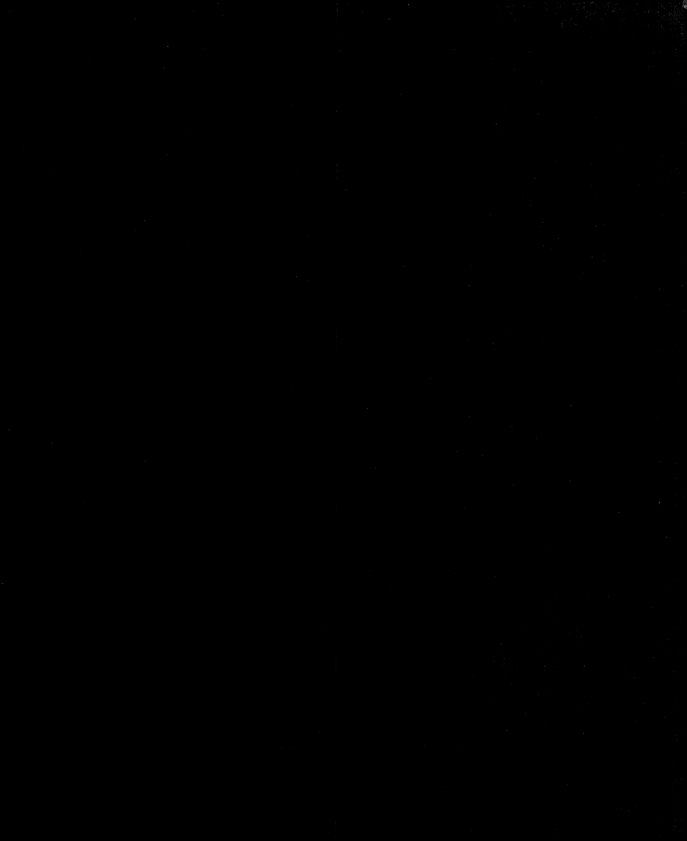

Rendering

This lesson will make extensive use of the Maya Interactive Photorealistic Renderer (IPR). This tool allows you to create a rendering of the scene that can then be used to interactively update changes to the scene's lighting and texturing. You will see how fast and intuitive it is to texture your scene with the IPR.

So far, you have been using only the Maya software renderer to render your scenes. In this lesson, you will also learn about three additional rendering types: Maya Hardware, Maya Vector, and mental ray® for Maya. Each has its own strengths and you should determine which rendering engine to use on a per project basis, depending on the final application.

In this lesson, you will learn the following:

- How to render a region and display snapshots
- How to open and save images
- How to display an image's alpha channel
- How to start the IPR
- How to make connections in the Hypershade
- How to enable high quality rendering in a viewport
- How to render with mental ray
- How to render with Maya Vector
- How to render with Maya Hardware

Rendering features

You are now ready to refine the rendering of your scene. In this section, you will experiment with the Render view features, such as snapshots, image storage, and region rendering.

1 Scene file

- Continue with the scene file you were using in the last lesson.

  OR

- **Open** the scene *20-lightsEffects_03.ma*.

2 Render set-up

- In the *Perspective* view, select **Panels → Saved Layouts → Hypershade/Render/Persp**.
- Frame Delgo's *eyes* in the *Perspective* view.
- **Hide** the *pfxLayer* to speed up the rendering process.
- Turn **Off** the **Motion blur** in the render settings.
- **RMB** click in the *Render* view and select **Render → Render → Persp**.

Note: *You can change the size of the panels by* **click+dragging** *on their separators.*

3 Keep and remove image

When test rendering a scene, it is good to be able to keep previously rendered images for comparison with the changes you implement.

- To keep the current render for reference, select **File → Keep Image in Render View** or click the **Keep Image** button.

  Notice a slider bar appears at the bottom of the Render view.

- In the *Perspective* view, select the eyeball geometry.
- In the **Hypershade**, click on the **Graph material on selected objects** button.

Note: *You will be modifying the eyeball textures when the character is referenced. This way, your changes will only be in that scene file and not in the original scene file.*

- In the **Create Maya Node** section, scroll down to the **2D Textures** section and click on the **File** node.
- **Double-click** on the *file1* node to open the **Attribute Editor**.
- Click the **Browse** button and select the *eyeball.tif* texture from the *sourceimage* folder.
- In the **Hypershade** work area, **MMB+drag** the *file1* node onto the *eyeM* material.

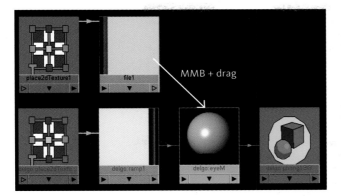

Dragging to create a connection

- Choose **Color** from the context menu to map the file in the color of the material.
- Make sure the *place2dTexture* node places the iris correctly on the eyeball.
- In the *Render* view, **render** the model again.
- Click the **Keep Image** button.
- Open the Attribute Editor for the *file1* node.
- Under the **Color Balance** section, change the **Color Offset** to change the eye color.
- **Render** the model again.
- Once the rendering is done, scroll the image bar at the bottom of the *Render* view to compare the previous render results.
- Scroll the image bar to the right (the older image), and select **File → Remove Image from Render View** or click the **Remove Image** button.

  This will remove the currently displayed image stored earlier.

The eye render

> **Note:** You can keep as many images as you want in the Render view. The images will be kept even if you close and reopen the Render view window.

4 Region rendering

You might think it is a waste of time to render the entire image again just for the small portion of the image that changed. With the Render view, you can render only a region of the current image.

- Select a region of the current image by **click+dragging** a square directly on the previously rendered image.

Select a region of the rendered image

- Click on the **Render Region** button to render the selected region.
- To automatically render a selected region, **RMB** and enable the **Options → Auto Render Region**.

With this option, every time you select a region on the rendered image, it will automatically be rendered.

 Note: *You can still keep an image that has a region render in it.*

5 Snapshots

If your scene is long, you might not want to wait for a complete render before selecting a region to render. The Render view allows you to take a wireframe snapshot of the image to render so that you can easily select the region you want.

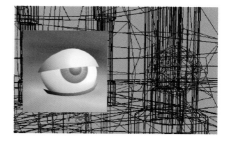

- **RMB** in the *Render* view and select **Render → Snapshot → Persp**.

  A wireframe image is placed in the Render view for reference.

A snapshot in the Render view

- Select the region you would like to render.

6 Open and save images

You can open renders or reference images directly in the Render view.

- To open a reference image, select **File → Open Image**.

- **Browse** to the reference image *eyeReference.tif* located in the *images* folder of the current project.

The eye reference

Tip: *Keep reference images in the Render view to easily compare them with the render.*

You can also save your renders to disk from the Render view.

- To save your current Render view image, select **File → Save Image**.

7 Display the alpha channel

When rendering, you often want to display the image's alpha channel to see if it will composite well onto another image.

- Select the Delgo geometry group.

- Select **Display → Hide → Hide Unselected Objects**.

- Select **Display → Show → Lights**.

- Frame the character and render your scene.

- Once the render is finished, click on the **Display Alpha Channel** button located at the top of the Render view.

The character's alpha channel

Note: *In an alpha channel, black is totally transparent, white is completely opaque, and grey tones are semi-transparent. The above image is slightly blurred because of motion blur.*

- To go back to the colored images, click on the **Display RGB channels** in the Render view.

IPR

To give you access to interactive updating capabilities, you will set-up an IPR rendering. An IPR rendering creates a special image file that stores not only the pixel information about an image, but also data about the surface normals, materials, and objects associated with each of these pixels. This information is then updated as you make changes to your scene's shading.

1   IPR set-up

- From the *Render* view panel, click on the **Render Settings** button.
- Click on the **Maya Software** tab.
- From the **Anti-aliasing Quality** section, set **Quality** to **Production quality**.

  For IPR, you can use the best settings if desired. Your initial IPR rendering will be slower, but the interactive updates will still be fast.

- Close the **Render Settings** window.

2   IPR render

- From your *Render* view panel, select **IPR** → **IPR Render** → **persp**.

  Now what seems to be a regular rendering of the scene appears. Notice the message at the bottom of the Render view saying: Select a region to begin tuning.

- **Click+drag** to select an area of the IPR rendering that will cover the entire character.

  This is the area that will be updated as you make changes.

Initial IPR rendering

Note: *You can still change the region by* **click+dragging** *again in the Render view.*

3 Tweak your materials

- In the rendered IPR image, **click** directly on the character's *body*.

  Doing so will automatically select the body shading group.

- In the **Hypershade**, click the **Input and output connections** button to graph the shading network.

- **Drag** the *delgo file1* onto the *bodyM* material and **drop** it in the **specularColor** attribute.

  Notice how the IPR updates every time you bring a change to the shading network.

- **Drag** the *delgo file1* onto the *bodyM* material and **drop** it in the **bump map** attribute.

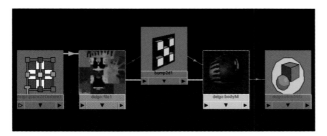

The updated shading network

- Select the *bump2D* node and change the **Bump Depth** to **-0.3**.

IPR update

4 **Stop the IPR**

- **Stop** the IPR by clicking on the button located at the top right of the Render view.

5 **Drag and drop feature**

- Select the *eyeball* geometry and **graph** its shading network.

- In the **Hypershade**, select the *eyeM* material.

- Select **Edit → Duplicate → Shading Network** in the **Hypershade**.

IPR functions

Doing so duplicates the entire selected shading network(s).

- Click the **Rearrange graph** button to order the work area.

- Frame the eyes in the *Perspective* view and **launch** another IPR.

- Select the render region surrounding the eyes.

- **MMB+drag** the duplicated *eyeM* and drop it on one of the *eyeballs* in the Render view.

Each eye now has a separate material assigned.

Note: *Dropping a material directly in the IPR has the same effect as dropping it on a model in a viewport.*

6 **IPR and the Attribute Editor**

- Open the **Attribute Editor**.

- Single click on any object in the IPR image and see the Attribute Editor update to show the related material node.

The IPR updates the Attribute Editor

7 Refresh the IPR image

When you have models outside the IPR region, you can refresh the entire image without losing your selected region.

- To refresh the entire image, click on the **Refresh the IPR Image** button.

The entire image gets redrawn and your original region is maintained.

8 IPR lighting

You can also use the IPR window to explore different lighting scenarios. Changing the light direction or properties will cause the IPR to redraw accordingly.

> **Note:** *When you don't have any lights in your scene, the IPR creates a directional light for you by default. The defaultLight node gets deleted when you stop an IPR rendering.*

- Select any light from the **Outliner**.
- Change the light intensity or color to see the IPR update with the new lighting.

New light color and intensity in IPR

9 IPR shadows

The IPR might not update certain shadow tweaks. To correct this, do the following:

- Select **IPR → Update Shadow Maps**.

The IPR updates and the shadows are re-rendered.

- **Stop** the IPR.

High quality rendering

When high quality rendering is turned on, the scene views are drawn in high quality by the hardware renderer. This lets you see a very good representation of the final render's look without having to software render the scene.

1   **Enabling high quality rendering**

- In the Perspective view, press **5, 6,** or **7**.

Note: *High quality rendering is not available while in wireframe, and not compatible with all graphic cards.*

- Enable **Renderer → High Quality Rendering**.
- Enable **Lighting → Shadows**.

High quality rendering

Tip: *If you require faster playback or camera tumbling while using high quality rendering, turn on* **Shading → Interactive Shading**.

Note: *If the surfaces appear black even when you have lights in your scene, you might need to reverse the surface so the normals point outwards.*

mental ray

Perhaps the most complex and powerful rendering type available in Maya software is mental ray. It offers many solutions for the creation of photorealistic renders, such as Global Illumination, caustic reflections and refractions, support for High Dynamic Range Imaging (HDRI), custom shaders, and motion blurred reflections and shadows.

In this exercise, you will open an existing scene that includes the Delgo with animation, reflection, and lighting. Using mental ray, the shadows will have motion blur, and the motion blur on Delgo will be reflected in a mirror.

1   Scene file

- Select **File → Open** and choose *21-rendering_01.ma* without saving changes to the previous scene.

2   Set-up the depth map shadows

- Select *pointLight1* and open the Attribute Editor.
- Under the *spotLightShape1* tab, expand the **Shadows** section.
- Set **Use Depth Map Shadows** to **On**.
- Change the **Shadow Color** to a **dark grey**.

3   Open the Render Settings

- Select **Window → Rendering Editors → Render Settings**...
- In the **Render Settings** window, select **Render Using → mental ray**.

  Doing so changes the renderer to mental ray instead of Maya software.

> **Tip:**   *If mental ray is not available, you must load the Mayatomr.mll plug-in in the* **Window → Settings/Preferences → Plug-ins Manager**.

4   Set the rendering options

To render the animation, you must set-up the scene's file extensions to indicate a rendered sequence. You must also set-up the start and end frames.

- Click on the **Common** tab.

- From the **Image File Output** section, set the following:

  File Name Prefix to *mentalRay*

  This sets the name of the animated sequence.

  Frame/Animation Ext *to:*

  name.#.ext

  This sets up mental ray to render a numbered sequence of images.

  Start Frame to **1**;

  End Frame to **10**;

  By Frame to **1**.

5 **Set-up the mental ray Render Settings for motion blur**

- Under the **mental ray** tab, select **Quality Presets** → **Production: Motion Blur**.

  This image quality preset automatically turns on high quality motion blur. It also sets up raytracing, as well as high quality anti-alias and texture sampling values for mental ray.

6 **Perform a test render**

- Go to frame **5**.
- Make the *Perspective* view active.
- Select **Render** → **Render Current Frame...**

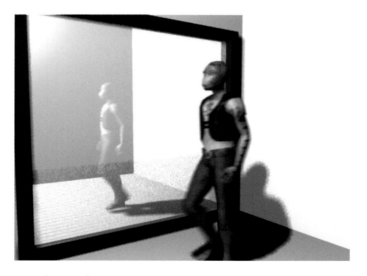

mental ray rendering

Note: *Notice that the reflection and shadows in the scene have a motion blur.*

7 Batch render

• Select **Render** → **Batch Render**.

Tip: *If you have a computer with multiple processors, it is recommended that you set* **Use all Available Processors** *to* **On** *in the batch render options, since the render can be time-consuming.*

• When the render is complete, select **Render** → **Show Batch Render...** This will activate the fcheck utility to playback the animated sequence.

OR

• From the browser, select one of the frames of the animation, then click **Open**.

Maya Vector

The Maya Vector renderer can output files in 2D vector format. It can also be used to create stylized flat renderings seen in illustrations and 2D animation.

Using the previous scene, you will set-up a Maya Vector render.

1 Open the Maya Vector Render Settings

• Select **Window** → **Rendering Editors** → **Render Settings...**

• In the **Render Settings** window, select **Render Using** → **Maya Vector**.

2 Set-up the Maya Vector options

• Select the **Maya Vector** tab.

• In the **Fill Options** section, set the following:

> **Fill objects** to **On**;
>
> **Fill style** to **Single color**;
>
> **Show back faces** to **On**;
>
> **Shadows** to **On**;
>
> **Highlights** to **On**;
>
> **Reflections** to **On**.

• In the **Edge Options** section, select the following:

> **Include edges** to **On**;
>
> **Edge weight preset** to **3.0 pt**;
>
> **Edge style** to **Outlines**.

3 Perform a test render

- Make the Perspective view active.
- Select **Render → Render Current Frame...**

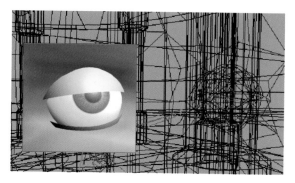

Maya Vector rendering

4 Batch render

- **Repeat** step **7** from the previous exercise to render the sequence.

 Note: *You might experience compatibility issues with the Maya Vector renderer on Intel-based Macs.*

Maya Hardware

Not to be confused with the Hardware Render Buffer, which will be introduced in the next project, the Maya hardware renderer allows you to create broadcast resolution images faster than with the software renderer.

In many cases, the quality of the output will be high enough to go directly to broadcast, but some advanced shadows, reflections, and post-process effects cannot be produced with the hardware renderer. The final image quality of the Maya hardware renderer is significantly higher than that of the viewport and Hardware Render Buffer.

1 Set-up the depth map shadows

- Make sure the **Use Depth Map Shadows** attribute for the *pointLight1* is still **On** from the previous exercise.

2 Open the Maya Hardware Render Settings

- Select **Window → Rendering Editors → Render Settings...**
- In the **Render Settings** window, select **Render Using → Maya Hardware**.
- Select the **Maya Hardware** tab.

- Under the **Quality** section, set **Presets** to **Production Quality.**
- Under the **Render Options** section, set **Motion Blur** to **On.**

3 **Perform a test render**

- Make the *Perspective* view active.
- Select **Render → Render Current Frame...**

  You cannot see a reflection in the mirror since the raytracing feature is unavailable with the hardware renderer. However, the renderer is otherwise capable of fast, high quality rendering, including texture mapped reflections, depth map shadows, and motion blur.

Maya hardware render

Note: *You might need to reverse some surfaces in order to render them correctly.*

4 **Batch render**

- **Repeat** step **7** from the mental ray exercise to render the sequence.

Conclusion

You have now completed this short introduction to the rendering engines available in the Maya software. The Maya IPR helps speed up the creative process and allows you to explore fast shading, lighting, and texturing possibilities. For more mental ray, Maya Vector, Maya hardware, and Maya software rendering tutorials, see the Maya online documentation.

In the next project, you will experiment with more animation techniques, rigid bodies, and particles.

Project 04

In this project, you will try more animation techniques using animation layers, Trax, motion paths, particles, and dynamics. You will also learn about MEL scripting, so you can automate some tasks and simplify your everyday work.

More Animation

Since you have created the catapult model, you can now practice animation skills from a more artistic point of view. In this lesson, you will animate Delgo picking up a rock and placing it in the catapult. This time, rather than approaching animation from a mathematical standpoint, you will have to establish key poses based on artistic knowledge to generate the animation.

In this lesson, you will learn the following:

- How to update a reference
- How to establish key poses
- How to refine in-betweens
- How to playblast an animation
- How to fix the timing of your animation

Set-up your project

Since this is a new project, it is recommended to set a new current project directory.

1 Set the project

- If you copied the support files onto your drive, go to the **File** menu and select **Project → Set...**

  A window opens, pointing you to the Maya projects directory.

- Click on the folder named *project4* to select it.

- Click on the **OK** button.

  This sets the project4 directory as your current project.

  OR

- If you did not copy the support files on your drive, create a new project called *project4* with all the default directories.

2 Scene file

- **Open** the scene file *20-lightsEffects_03.ma* from the last project's *scenes* directory.

> **Note:** *You may have to relink textures that are not automatically found. To do so, simply open the* **Hypershade**, *select the* **Texture** *tab, and change the path of the texture through the* **Attribute Editor**.

Picking the rock up

Now that your scene is properly set-up, you will animate Delgo picking up a rock. Once this is done, the new sequence will be saved as a Trax clip.

1 Active character

- In the **Active Character** menu next to the **Range Slider**, select the *delgo* character set.

2 Set the time range

- Set the **Start Time** and **Playback Start Time** to **1**.

- Set the **End Time** and **Playback End Time** to **70**.

3 Current time

- Move the current time indicator to frame **1**.

4 Clear the Trax Editor

As you may notice, Delgo is already animated in this scene. This is because the Trax Editor still contains the Trax walk cycle clip you create earlier. You will now clear the Trax Editor and start a new animation.

- Open the **Trax Editor** by selecting **Window** → **Animation Editors** → **Trax Editor**.
- If the walk clip is not visible, make sure to turn on the **List** → **Auto Load Selected Characters** options.
- Press **a** to frame all in the **Trax Editor**.
- Click on the *walk* clip to highlight it.
- Press **Delete** to remove it.

  The animation has now been removed, but the character has kept its initial step position, which will be used as the starting pose of the new animation.

- Close the Trax Editor.

5 Start pose

- Press the **s** hotkey to keyframe the entire *character*.
- Enable the **Auto Key** button.
- **Translate** and **rotate** the character *master* so Delgo is next to the catapult.
- Set the **Load** attribute on the *catapultGrp* to about **1.5** so it is in loaded position.

The start pose

Tip: *Change display layers to be **Reference** layers to avoid accidentally picking unwanted objects.*

6 Bending forward pose

- Go to frame **10**.
- Hold down the **w** hotkey, click in the view, and choose **Object** from the marking menu.

  This changes the Move Tool's option to be oriented with the object rather than with the world.

- Bring the *rHeelControl* up on the catapult, as Delgo is anticipating the weight of the rock.
- Place the character as follows:

First pose

- Press the **s** key to set a key on the character at this new position.

7 Grabbing pose

- Go to frame **20**.
- Place the character as follows:

The grabbing pose

8 **Anticipation pose**

- Go to frame **25**.
- Place the character so he lowers his head and hips, anticipating the heavy rock:

The anticipation pose

Tip: *Anticipation usually goes in the opposite direction of the actual motion.*

- Press the **s** key to set a key on the character at this new position.
- **Keyframe** the *rock*'s **Translate** and **Rotate** attributes through the **Channel Box**.

9 Constrain the right hand

Before you can make the character lift the object, you must first constrain the hands to the rock.

- Select the *rock*, then **Shift-select** the *rHandManip*.
- Select **Constrain → Parent**.

The hand is now constrained to the rock for the entire animation range.

Since the hand manipulator had animation on it, notice a new attribute in the Channel Box called Blend Parent 1. This attribute controls the blend between the constraint and the original animation.

- **Keyframe** the **Blend Parent 1** attribute to **0** at frame **24**.
- **Keyframe** the **Blend Parent 1** attribute to **1** at frame **25**.

The right hand is now constrained starting only at frame 25.

Tip: *Remember that if you move the timing of the animation, you will also have to move the constraint animation since it is not part of the character set.*

10 Constrain the left hand

- Select the *rock*, then **Shift-select** the *lHandManip*.
- Select **Constrain → Parent**.
- **Keyframe** the **Blend Parent 1** attribute to **1** at frame **25**.
- **Keyframe** the **Blend Parent 1** attribute to **0** at frame **24**.

The left hand is now constrained starting only at frame 25.

11 Lifting pose

- Go to frame **30**.
- Place the character as follows with the rock lifted a little and both arms almost hyper-extended:

The lifting pose

- Press the **s** key to set a key on the character at this new position.
- **Keyframe** the *rock*'s **Translate** and **Rotate** attributes through the **Channel Box**.

12 Rock on his chest

- Go to frame **40**.
- Place the character as follows:

Rock on chest pose

- Press the **s** key to set a key on the character at this new position.
- **Keyframe** the *rock*'s **Translate** and **Rotate** attributes through the **Channel Box**.

13 Turning pose

- Go to frame **50**.
- Place the character's weight on his left foot, while putting the right foot down on the ground.

The turning pose

- Press the **s** key to set a key on the character at this new position.
- **Keyframe** the *rock*'s **Translate** and **Rotate** attributes through the **Channel Box**.

> **Note:** *It is a difficult task to rotate an entire character and you might experience some problems when doing so. For instance, the Set Driven Keys on the feet may no longer work correctly because there are no animation overrides allowing you to use both the Set Driven Keys and the keyframe animation on the reverse foot setup. This is why much care must be taken at the rigging stage.*

14 Loading pose

- Go to frame **60**.
- Place the rock in the catapult.

The loading pose

- Press the **s** key to set a key on the character at this new position.
- **Keyframe** the *rock*'s **Translate** and **Rotate** attributes through the **Channel Box**.

15 Stop constraining the hands

You will now disable the hand constraints so Delgo can step backwards.

- Select the *lHandManip* and the *rHandManip*.
- **Keyframe** the **Blend Parent 1** attribute to **1** at frame **60**.
- **Keyframe** the **Blend Parent 1** attribute to **0** at frame **61**.

The hands are now free to move from frame 61.

> **Note:** *Blending between constraints and animation can be puzzling and require some preemptive planning. In this exercise, you have created the constraints on the hands and for animating the rock, but you could have decided to constrain the rock to one hand, which might have been more difficult.*

16 End pose

- Go to frame **70**.

- Place the character as follows:

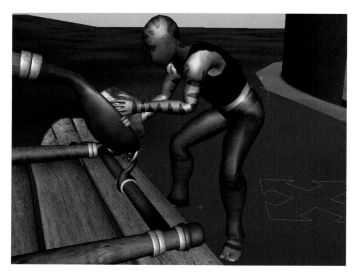

The loading pose

- Press the **s** key to set a key on the character at this new position.

17 Playblast your animation

A playblast is a movie reflecting your scene animation. When making a playblast, Maya software generates the animation by grabbing the image directly from the active viewport, so make sure to display only what you want to see in your playblast.

- Frame the scene in the Perspective view to see it in its entirety.

- From the **Show** menu in the *Perspective* panel, hide object types that you do not want in your playblast such as **Grids**, **NURBS curves**, **Lights**, **Locators,** and **Handles**.

 Tip: *Creating setup display layers allows you to quickly hide the character rig before playblasting your scene.*

- Press **6** if you want the textures to appear in your playblast.

- Select **Window → Playblast**.

  Maya software will render every frame, recording it into the playblast. Once the scene has been entirely played through, the playblast is displayed in your default movie player.

 Note: *For more options on the playblast, select* **Window → Playblast → ❑**.

18 Animation refinement

Once you have seen the playblast and animation at its real speed, you can concentrate on correcting the motion and timing.

- Note areas that appear to be too fast or too slow in the playblast.
- To move a pose to a different frame, hold down **Shift** and click on a keyframe in the **Time Slider**.
- **Click+drag** the keyframe to the left to make the pose faster, and to the right to make the pose more slowly.
- Tweak the poses and tangents to make the motion between them more fluid.

  Make sure you bring everything along when moving the character animation, such as the blend parent and rock animation.

- Add secondary animation to enhance your animation, such as the catapult shaking when dropping the rock.

Note: *You might have to redo your playblast and perform some trial and error before finding the perfect animation speed.*

Tip: *Beginner animators tend to make everything slow motion when animating. Do not be afraid to have only two or three frames between your poses. An entire picking-up motion should take about one or two seconds, which is only 24 to 48 frames.*

19 Save your work

- **Save** this scene to *22-moreAnimation_01.ma*.
- In the current project *images* directory, you can view the playblasts recorded at various stages in the animation.

Create a Trax clip file

The animation is finished, so you will now create another Trax clip file.

1 Open the Trax Editor window

- Make sure that *delgo* is the current character set.
- Select **Window → Animation Editor → Trax Editor**.

2 **Create a clip**

- From the **Trax Editor**, select **Create** → **Animation Clip** → □.

- In the **Create Clip Options** window, select **Edit** → **Reset**.

- Set the following options:

   Name to *pickup*;

   Leave Keys in Timeline to **Off**;

   Clip to **Put Clip in Trax Editor and Visor**;

   Time Range to **Time Slider**;

   Include Subcharacters in Clip to **Off**;

   Create Time Warp Curve to **Off**;

   Include Hierarchy to **On**.

- Click the **Create Clip** button.

- Press **a** in the Trax **Editor** to frame all.

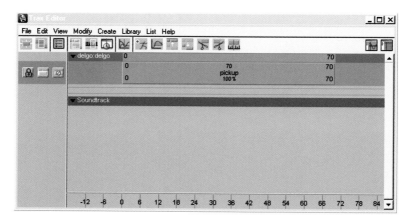

Pickup clip in Trax Editor

3 **Export the clip**

- Select **File** → **Visor...**

- Select the **Character Clips** tab to see the clip source.

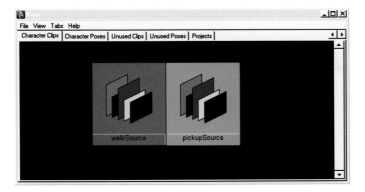

Pickup source clip in Visor

- Select the *pickupSource* clip.
- **RMB** on the clip and select **Export.**
- **Save** the clip as *delgoPickupExport* in the project *data* folder.

Note: *Since you are in a new project, you can either copy the other delgoWalkExport.ma file from the third project or export it again from here.*

- **Close** the Visor.

4 **Save your work**
- **Save** this scene to *22-moreAnimation_02.ma.*

Conclusion

You have now completed a type of animation that requires much more artistic input. As you can see, a lot of practice is required to achieve good animation in an efficient manner, and you might have to correct rigging problems as you work.

In the next lesson you will use non-linear animation techniques to experiment with various ways of creating an animated sequence.

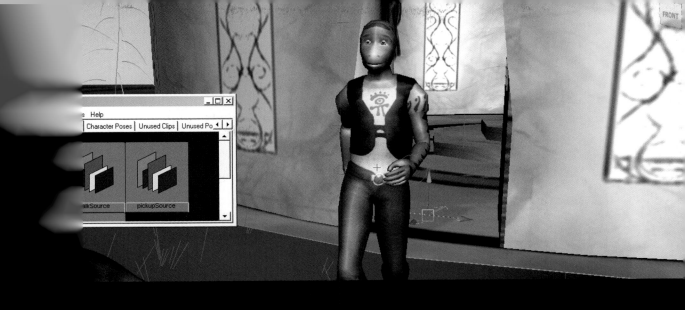

Non Linear Animation

So far in this book, you have animated *Delgo* and created two Trax clips from the animated sequences. In this lesson, you will create a more complex motion by joining the walk clip with the pickup clip in the Trax Editor.

The advantage of working with Trax' non-linear animation lies in the ability to move, edit, connect, and reuse multiple clips freely, without having to edit multiple time curves. You can also add sound files to the scene using Trax.

You will also have a look at animation layers, which allow you to layer refinements on top of your existing animation. This technique can be very useful when modifying dense animation curves or motion capture data, or just to compare two animations easily.

In this lesson, you will learn the following:

- How to work with relative and absolute clips
- How to clip, split, blend, and merge clips
- How to use time warp
- How to redirect animation
- How to use sound in Trax
- How to use animation layers
- How to animate a two node camera

Initial set-up

1 Scene file

- **Open** the file you saved at the end of the last lesson.

  OR

- **Open** the scene file *22-moreAnimation_02.ma*.

2 Set-up the work area

- Set the **Playback Frame Range** to go from **1** to **200**.

- From any panel menu, select **Panels → Saved Layouts → Persp/Trax/Outliner**.

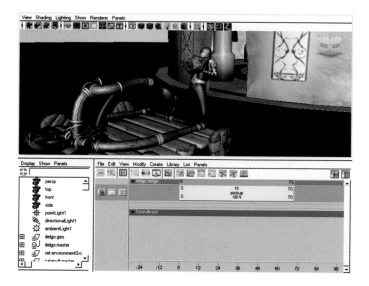

Persp/Trax/Outliner window layout

Generate the animation

The following exercise uses several Trax commands that will establish the new character animation. The animation you want to achieve in the scene goes like this:

Delgo walks up to the catapult looking around. He then picks up a rock and places it in the catapult, getting it ready to fire.

1 Load the first two clips

- Select the *Delgo* character from the **Current Character** menu at the bottom right of the interface.

  The Trax Editor will update, showing the pickup motion from the last lesson.

- From the **Trax Editor**, select **Library** → **Insert Clip** → **walkSource**.

  Both the walk and pickup clips are now in the Trax Editor.

- Press **a** to frame all.

- **Click+drag** each clip in the **Trax Editor** so that the *walk* clip starts at frame **1** and the *pickup* clip starts at frame **121**.

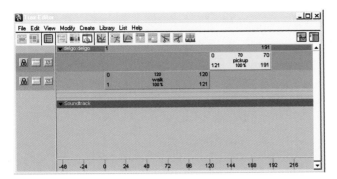

Walk and pickup clips

> **Tip:** If a clip is not in your scene, you can import via the **File** → **Import Animation Clip** menu item in the Trax Editor.

2 Trim the walk clip

- Scrub to frame **41** in the timeline.

  This is a good place to match the pickup clip, since it is a pose similar to the start pose.

- Select the *walk* clip.

- Select the **Trim After** icon from the **Trax** menu to **Trim** the clip after frame **41**.

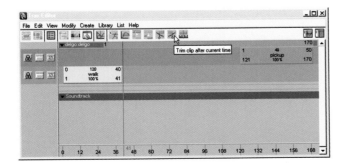

Trim the walk clip after frame 41

- **Move** the *pickup* clip to its new starting position at frame **41**.

3 View the clips with absolute offset

- **Play** the animation by dragging the vertical time indicator in the Trax window.

  As the walk clip switches to the pickup clip during playback, you will see Delgo picks up the rock back at its original keyframed position—or absolute offset.

> **Note:** *You should also notice that the rock animation and constraints need to be offset, which will be seen later in this exercise.*

4 Change the relative/absolute offset

- Select the *pickup* clip, then press **Ctrl+a** to open its **Attribute Editor**.
- Scroll to the **Channel Offsets** section and click the **All Relative** button.
- **Play** the animation.

  Now, as the walk clip switches to the pickup clip during playback, you will see that Delgo does the rock pickup animation from its new position at the end of the walk clip. This is because the clip's animation is relative to the end position of the clip preceding it.

> **Note:** *It is normal at this stage that Delgo walks away from the rock. You will offset the whole animation later in the exercise.*

5 Ease out the walk clip

At this point, you might notice a speed change between the end of the walk clip and the start of the pickup. The following steps will help smooth this.

- Select the *walk* clip.
- **RMB** on the clip and select **Create Time Warp**.

  A time warp is a curve that controls the speed of the clip animation. Using this, you will slow down the walk to have Delgo slow down before picking up the rock.

- Click on the **Open Graph Editor** button located at the top right corner of the **Trax Editor**.
- Scroll down in the **Graph Editor Outliner** and highlight the **Time Warp** attribute.
- Select the first keyframe and set its **Tangent** to **Linear**.
- Select the last keyframe, and then select its left tangent manipulator.
- Press **w** to select the **Move Tool**, and then **MMB+drag** the tangent down a little so it is not perfectly flat.

  If the tangent is perfectly flat, then the animation will gradually slow down in order to be a complete halt on its last frame. Moving the tangent down a little makes the animation slow down, but does not stop completely.

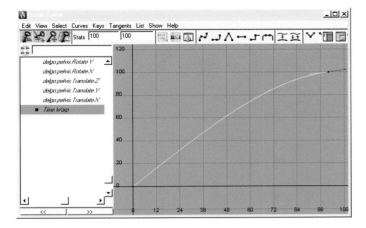

The time warp curve

- Click on the **Open Trax Editor** button located at the top right corner of the **Graph Editor**.

- If you scrub in the animation, you will notice that *Delgo* is now slowing down before picking up the rock.

6 Blend between the two clips

- Select the *walk* clip, then **Shift-select** the *pickup* clip.

- Select **Create → Blend → ❑**.

- In the option window, set **Initial Weight Curve** to **Ease in out**.

- Click the **Create Blend** button.

- Select the *pickup* clip on its own and **drag** it so that it starts at frame **36**.

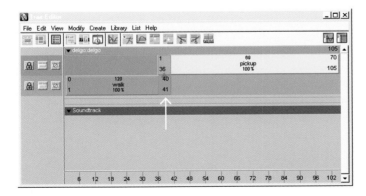

The newly created blend area

- **Playback** the animation. You will notice that the animation is now much more fluid.

Tip: *To frame the animation from the* **Trax Editor** *in the main* **Time Slider**, **RMB** *in the* **Time Slider** *and select* **Set Range To → Enabled Clips**.

7 Merge all the clips

- Select all the clips by **click+dragging** a selection box over the clips in the Trax Editor.
- Select **Edit → Merge → ❑**.
- In the **Merge** option window, set the following:

    Name to *delgoAnim*

    Merged Clip to **Add to Trax**

- Click the **Merge Clip** button.

    The newly merged clip is now in the Trax Editor, and has replaced all the previous clips.

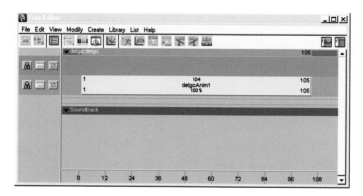

The new merged clip

Redirect the animation

Next, you will change *Delgo's* position so that he walks up to the rock properly.

1 Constraint timing

Since you moved the timing of the picking-up motion, the constraints used to control the rock animation are happening too early.

- Select both *Delgo's handManips*.
- **Shift-select** the *rock*, the catapult's *master*, and the *catapultGrp*.

    You should now have selected everything that was animated outside the actual character.

- In the **Graph Editor**, select all the visible animation curves.
- **Offset** the animation curve by **35** frames, which is the exact length of the walk clip in the **Trax Editor**.

  Doing so fixes the timing of the constraint switch.

2 Change the animation orientation

- Select *Delgo's master* node.
- From the Animate menu set, select **Character** → **Redirect** → ❏.
- Select the **Translation only** option, then click the **Redirect** button.

  Doing so creates an override that allows you to move the animation to the proper place.

The Redirect node

- Go to frame **50**.

  This is where the character picks up the rock.

- With the *OffsetTranslateControl1* still selected, set the following:

      Translate X to **3.3**;

      Translate Y to **1.2**;

      Translate Z to **-50.7**;

  Doing so will change the placement of the entire animation.

The correctly placed animation

3 **Fit the animation to the set**

You will now fit the animation so *Delgo* walks through the door and to the catapult without going through the wall.

- Select both the *OffsetTranslateControl1* node and the catapult *transOverride* node.

- Offset the nodes on their **Translate X** axes by about **-5** units.

- Highlight all **translate** attributes in the **Channel Box**, then **RMB** and select **Key Selected**.

4 **Save your work**

- **Save** the scene as *23-nonlinearAnimation_01.ma*.

Animation layers

You have already experienced the flexibility of working with non-linear animation clips. To further refine the motion, you will add animation layers to the animation. Animation layers allow you to set keyframes on top of the existing animation.

1 **Remove the Trax clip**

For the rest of this lesson, it is unnecessary to leave the clip in the Trax Editor, so you will remove it and keep the existing animation.

- In the Trax Editor, **RMB** on the *delgoAnim1* clip and select **Activate Keys**.

Doing so puts the keyframe found in the clip into the Time Slider.

- With the *delgoAnim1* clip highlighted, press the **Delete** key on your keyboard to delete the clip.

  The clip is now gone, but the animation is still in the scene.

2 Remove the offset control

- Change the active character set to **None**.
- Select the *Delgo master.*
- Highlight the **Translate** attributes in the **Channel Box**.
- Select **Edit → Keys → Bake Simulation → ❑**.
- In the option window, select **Edit → Reset Settings**, then click the **Bake** button.

  The translation animation will be baked at every frame on the master node.

- **Delete** *OffsetTranslateControl1* node.

3 Add an animation layer

- In the **Layer Editor**, select the **Anim** radio button.

  Doing so will display the Animation Layer Editor.

- In the **Animation Layer Editor**, select **Layers → Create Empty Layer.**

  There is now an empty animation layer and a base animation layer visible.

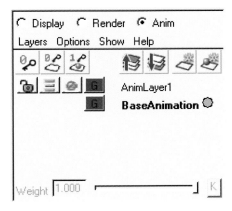

The Animation Layer Editor

4 **Add body parts to the animation layer**

- Click on the *AnimLayer1* to highlight it.
- Select the *neck1*, *head* joints and the *lookAt* locator.
- Select **Layers → Add Selected Objects**.

  Doing so will add all keyable attributes on the objects to the animation layer.

> **Note:** *Notice that when you highlight the BaseAnimation layer, the baked keyframes are visible in the timeline, and when you highlight the AnimLayer1 layer, the timeline is free of all keyframes, allowing you to keyframe layered animation.*

5 **Add keys to modify the head position**

- Highlight the *AnimLayer1* layer.
- Select the *neck1* and *head* joint.
- Go to frame **10** and press the **s** hotkey to keyframe the joints position.

  You will notice a new key has been placed in the timeline.

- Go to frame **20** and rotate the joints so *Delgo* looks to his right.
- Press **s** to keyframe the joints.
- Go to frame **35** and rotate the joints so *Delgo* keeps looking to his right.
- Press **s** to keyframe the joints.

> **Note:** *If Auto Key is on, you don't have to manually key the rotation after you have set a key once.*

- **Playback** the results.

  Now Delgo's head is deviating from his original animation, but notice how the animation is now changed for the rest of the animation. This is because the last offset put on the joints remains beyond frame 35.

6 **Set zero keys**

When setting layered keyframes, you need to set default keys before and after the region where you want to alter the animation. If you don't set those keys, the offset you keyframe will remain throughout the animation.

- Go to frame **45**.
- Select the *neck1* and *head* joints.
- Click the **Zero Key Layer** button in the **Animation Layer Editor**.

  Notice how the animation goes back to its original position.

- Select all the keyframes at frames **10**, **20**, **35** and **45** in the timeline, then **RMB** and select **Tangents** → **Flat** to set the tangents of the selected keyframe.

- **Playback** the results.

Now the character goes back to his original animation past frame 45.

7   **Modify the lookAt**

- **Repeat** the last steps in order to correctly animate where *Delgo* is looking throughout the animation.

Delgo now looks at the rock

> **Note:** *These keys are not altering the original animation in any way. In fact, these keys can be deleted or moved around and the base animation will remain intact.*

8   **Changing the weight of a layer**

If you would like to see what the animation would look like with only a fraction of the added animation, you can keyframe the weight of an animation layer.

- With the *AnimLayer1* layer highlighted, change the **Weight** slider at the bottom of the Animation Layer Editor.

- Press the **K** button to the right to keyframe the value.

9 Merging the animation layers

If you would like to merge the layered animation together with the base animation, simply do the following:

- Highlight all the animation layers using the **Ctrl** key.

- Select **Layers** → **Merge Layers**.

10 Save your work

- **Save** the scene as *23-nonlinearAnimation_02.ma*.

Adding sound to Trax

The Trax Editor offers you the ability to import and easily sync sound files to your animation.

You can import **.wav** or **.aiff** sound files into Trax to synchronize motion and audio. More than one audio clip can be imported into the soundtrack, but you will be able to hear only one file at a time upon playback. The audio file at the top of the soundtrack display will take precedence over those below.

You will now import an existing sound file into your scene.

1 Set playback preferences

- Select **Window** → **Settings/ Preferences** → **Preferences**.

- In the **Timeline** category under the **Playback** section, make sure **Playback speed** is set to **Real-time [24 fps]**.

  If this option is not set to realtime, the sound might not be played.

2 Add a sound file

- From the **Trax Editor**, select **File** → **Import Audio...**

- From the *sound* directory, select *hop.wav*.

3 See and hear the sound file

- **RMB** in the **Time Slider**.

- From the pop-up menu, select **Sound** → **Use Trax Sounds**.

  A green indicator bar will appear on the global timeline and the clips will display an audio waveform.

4 Sync the sound to the animation

- **Play** the animation with the sound.

- **Click+drag** the sound clip so that it syncs up to when *Delgo* picks up the rock.

  The sound clip should be somewhere around frame **43**.

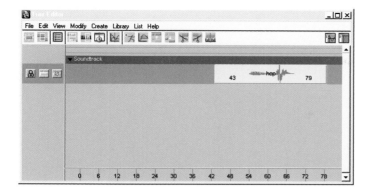

Sound clip in Trax

Note: *When you will playblast your animation, the sound will be added to your movie.*

Animating a camera

You will now add a new camera to the scene and animate it so that you can follow *Delgo* as he walks.

A camera can be created on its own or with additional nodes that provide control over the *aim point* and *up direction*. Most cameras only need one node that lets you key the camera's position and rotation. You will create a camera to control both the *camera point* and the *view point*. Both of these nodes can be keyed individually.

1   **Set-up your panel display**

   • Select a **Two Panes Stacked** view layout.

   • In the *Perspective* view, make sure **Show → Cameras and Show → Pivots** are **On**.

      You will need to see these in order to work with the camera.

2   **Create a two-node camera**

   • Select **Create → Cameras → Camera and Aim**.

   • In the bottom pane, select **Panels → Perspective → camera1**.

   • Press **6** to view the textures in the *camera1* view.

   • In the *camera1* view, select **View → Camera Settings → Resolution Gate**.

   • Still in the *camera1* view, select **View → Camera Attribute Editor...**

   • Change **Fit Resolution Gate** to **Vertical**.

3 Frame the character

- Go to frame **1**.
- Select the **Show Manipulator Tool** by pressing the **t** hotkey.
- In the *Perspective* view, position the *camera* and *camera1_aim* handles as follows:

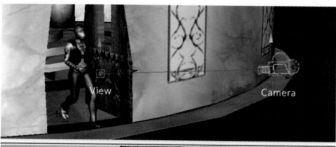

Camera manipulator handles

Note: *You can position the camera using the usual viewport hotkey if wanted.*

4 Follow the action

You will now set keys on the camera point to follow the character from frames 1 to 60.

- Go to frame **1**.
- Select the *camera1* and *camera1_aim* nodes.
- Press **Shift+w** to keyframe the current position.

  Doing so sets a keyframe for the current camera position.

- Go to frame **45**.
- Move the *camera1_aim* node so that it is again looking at the character, framing both characters and the rock.

- Select the *camera1* and *camera1_aim* nodes.
- Press Shift+w to keyframe the new view position.

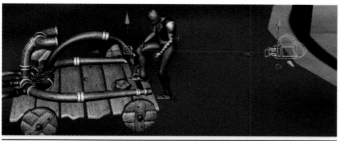

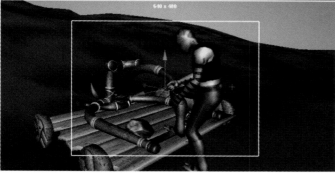

View at frame 45

5 **Dolly around the rock**

The camera animation now frames the first portion of the animation correctly, but the second part of the animation could be better. You can set keys on the viewpoint node to fix this.

- Go to frame **85**.
- Move the *camera1* node from the *Perspective* view to the left of the scene.
- Select the *camera1* and *camera1_aim* nodes.
- Press **Shift+w** to keyframe the new view position.

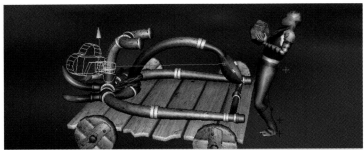

View at frame 85

- If you don't like the framing in the in-between frames, you can reposition the camera and set new keys. **Repeat** this until you get the camera movement you want.

6 Playblast the animation

You can now playblast the scene to test the motion. This will give you the chance to confirm the camera animation.

> **Tip:** *Make sure you maximize the camera view by tapping the spacebar and displaying only NURBS surfaces and polygons. You can also set Delgo's **smooth** attribute found on the master to be high resolution, and set any NURBS smoothness to its finest setting.*

7 Save your work

- **Save** the scene as *23-nonlinearAnimation_03.ma.*

Conclusion

In this lesson, you completed your first non-linear animation using both Trax and the animation layers. You have also used some features available to you in the Trax Editor.

In the next lesson, you will learn about rigid bodies, which will allow you to create realistic animation using dynamics.

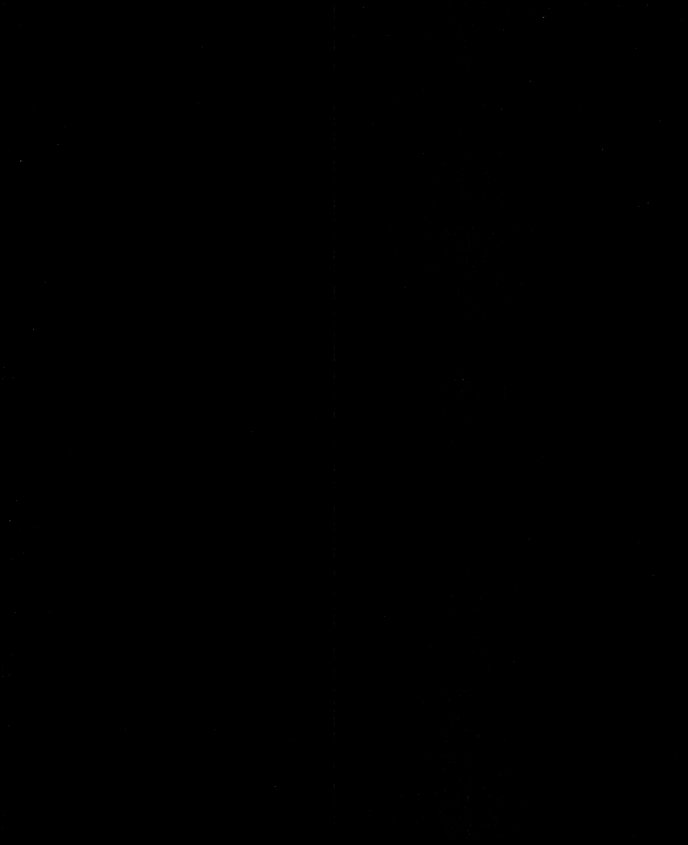

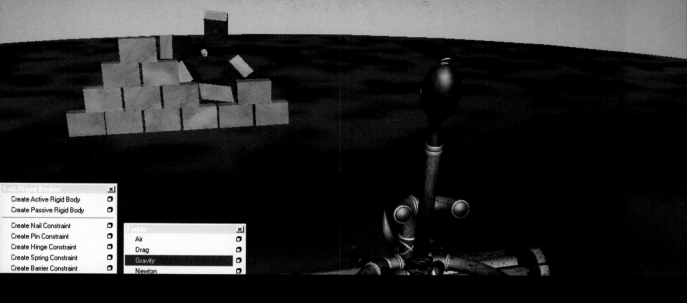

Rigid Bodies

In animation, sometimes there are scenarios that just are not worth spending the time to keyframe. Collisions between objects, for example, would be too complex to animate by hand. For this, it is better to use dynamic simulations.

In this lesson, you will experiment with the basics of rigid bodies, an example of dynamic simulations. Rigid bodies are polygonal or NURBS surfaces converted to unyielding shapes. Unlike conventional 3D surfaces, rigid bodies collide rather than pass through each other during animation. To animate rigid body motion, you use fields, keys, expressions, rigid body constraints, or collisions with other rigid bodies or particles. In this example, the catapult will shoot the rock in the air, which will be colliding with the room and ground plane, all affected by a gravity field.

In this lesson, you will learn the following:

- How to create a passive rigid body

- How to create an active rigid body

- How to use stand-in geometry with dynamics

- How to add a gravity field to rigid bodies

- How to simulate your dynamics

- How to set rigid body keyframes

- How to set rigid body attributes

- How to cache a dynamic simulation

Active and passive

Maya software has two kinds of rigid bodies—active and passive. An active rigid body reacts to dynamics—fields, collisions, and springs—not to keys. A passive rigid body can have active rigid bodies collide with it. You can key its translation and rotation attributes, but dynamics has no effect on it.

1   **Test scene**

• Select **File → New**.

• **Create** one polygonal cube and **scale** it so that it looks like a floor.

• **Rename** the cube to *floor*.

• **Create** a polygonal sphere and another polygonal cube and place them side-by-side above the floor.

The test scene

2   **Active rigid body**

• Select the *sphere*.

• Press **F5** to display the **Dynamics** menu set.

• Select **Soft/Rigid Bodies → Create Active Rigid Body**.

• **Playback** the animation.

Nothing is happening because there are no forces in the scene.

3   **Playback the simulation**

• Click the **Animation preferences** button found at the right side of the **Range Slider**.

• In the **Timeline** section, set the following:

   Playback Speed to **Play every frame**.

> **Note:** *When working with rigid bodies or particles, it is **very important** that the playback speed is set to play every frame. Otherwise, your simulations may act unpredictably.*

• Click the **Save** button.

4 **Gravity field**

- Select the *sphere*.

- Select **Fields → Gravity**.

- In the Attribute Editor, make sure the **Magnitude** is set to **9.8**.

  A magnitude of 9.8 mimics the Earth's gravity.

- **Playback** the animation.

  The sphere falls straight down.

> **Note:** *You may want to increase your playback range in the Time Slider.*

5 **Passive rigid body**

- Select the *floor*.

- Select **Soft/Rigid Bodies → Create Passive Rigid Body**.

- **Playback** the animation.

  The sphere falls and collides with the floor.

6 **Rotate the floor**

- Select the *floor* and **rotate** it sideways.

- **Playback** the animation.

  The sphere collides and rolls off the floor.

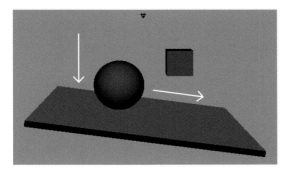

Rotate the floor

> **Note:** *It is very important to rewind to frame 1 before playing a dynamic simulation to see accurate results. Also, you should not scrub in the timeline.*

7 **Set the cube as active**

- Select the *cube*.

- Select **Soft/Rigid Bodies → Create Active Rigid Body**.

- **Playback** the animation.

    The cube does not fall since it was not connected to the gravity field. Instead, the cube slowly spins and flies off.

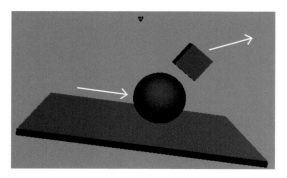

The cube collides without gravity

8 **Assign gravity**

- Select the *cube* and **Shift-select** the gravity field.

- Select **Fields → Affect Selected Object(s)**.

- **Playback** the animation.

    The cube falls on the floor like the sphere.

9 **Change dynamic attributes**

- Select the *cube*.

- In the **Channel Box**, highlight the *rigidBody* input connection.

- Set the following:

    Mass to **2**;

    Bounciness to **0.1**;

    Static Friction to **0.5**;

    Dynamic Friction to **0.5**.

    Setting those attributes specifies that the cube is heavier and will react differently against other rigid bodies, that it doesn't bounce much, and that it has more friction against other rigid bodies.

- **Playback** the animation.

    The cube falls and stops on the floor. This is because you have reduced attributes like bounciness and increased friction.

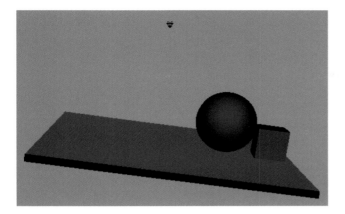

The cube stops the sphere

10 Center of mass

If you look closely at the rigid bodies, you will notice a small **x** that defines the rigid bodies' center of mass.

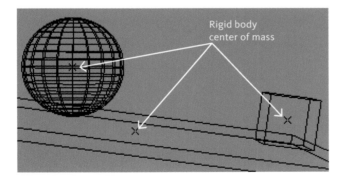

The center of mass

Objects don't usually have their center of mass exactly at their centers. For example, a clown's inflatable boxing bag stays straight even when it is pushed over because its center of mass is very low.

- Select the *sphere* to change its center of mass.

- In the **Channel Box**, highlight the *rigidBody* input connection.

- Set the **Center Of Mass Y** to **-1**.

  The center of mass icon moved to the bottom of the sphere.

The new center of mass

- **Playback** the animation.

The sphere falls and stops on the floor, bobbing from side-to-side.

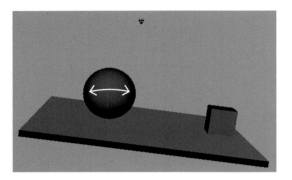

The sphere is bobbing in place

Simulation

With your knowledge, you can now add a rigid body simulation to your animated scene. You will first set the active and passive rigid bodies. You will then keyframe the rigid bodies from passive to active, which will allow them to maintain their positions until they get hit by another object. Once the objects become active rigid bodies, they will crash onto the ground plane with gravity.

1   Scene file

- **Open** the file *24-rigidBodies_01.ma*.

This scene contains the loaded catapult with a brick wall ready to be destroyed.

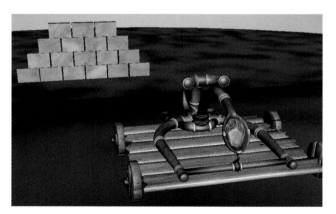

The test scene

In this example scene, the catapult arm was animated to throw the rock between frames 1 and 9.

2   Prepare the scene

Before adding dynamics to your scene, you will need to tweak the different objects to be involved in this lesson.

- Make sure that none of the *bricks* interpenetrate with each other or the ground plane. If this happens, translate them to produce a small gap between the bricks.

3   Arm stand-in

Rigid body geometry should be relatively simple so the dynamic solver can calculate dynamics in a reasonable amount of time. A straightforward way to simplify geometry is to place polygonal stand-in geometry over the complex objects, and use that stand-in geometry as a passive rigid body. Doing so will also speed up dynamic calculations since the model will be very simple.

> **Note:**   *Rigid bodies cannot be deformed. If you deform a surface intended to be a rigid body, the original object will be used, thus generating an incorrect simulation.*

- **Unhide** the *armStandIn* object from the Outliner.

  Since the deforming arm cannot be used as a rigid body, a simplified mesh was generated by converting the arm to polygons and set-up to follow the catapult basket.

> **Tip:**   *When creating rigid bodies, always make sure that the normals are pointing outwards, otherwise the dynamic solver might generate an incorrect simulation.*

- Check the *armStandIn* normals by selecting **Display → Polygons → Face Normals**.
- If the object has inverted normals, select **Normals → Reverse**.

Catapult stand-in geometry

Tip: *A good hint to know if your object should be reversed is to look in the Script Editor and note warnings saying: "The surface of rigid body may be reversed. Reversing the surface may avoid interpenetration errors." It is also preferable to close any holes in your objects to prevent simulation errors.*

- Make sure the *rock* is in the basket but does not interpenetrate with the stand-in object.

4 Arm rigid body

- Go to frame **1**.

  It is important to be at frame 1 when creating an active rigid body on an animated object, or the dynamics might not simulate as expected.

- Select the *armStandIn* object.
- Press **F5** to select the **Dynamics** menu set.
- Select **Soft/Rigid Bodies** → **Create Passive Rigid Body**.
- Press **Ctrl+h** to **hide** the *armStandIn*.

Note: *When creating a rigid body, all translate and rotate attributes must be unlocked.*

5 Create ground rigid body

- Select the *ground* surface.
- Select **Soft/Rigid Bodies** → **Create Passive Rigid Body**.

6 Create the rock rigid body

- Select the *rock*.
- Select **Soft/Rigid Bodies** → **Create Active Rigid Body**.

7 Create the brick rigid bodies

- Go to frame **1**.
- Select all the *bricks*.
- Select **Soft/Rigid Bodies** → **Create Active Rigid Body**.

8 Active key

When you playback the animation, you will notice that the bricks react immediately to the dynamics, thus making your dynamics slow to simulate. What you really want here is for the dynamics to only start evaluating when the rock almost comes into contact with them. The following will show you how to set active/passive keyframes on the rigid bodies.

- Select the *bricks* geometry.

- Select **Soft/Rigid Bodies** → **Set Passive Key**.

  The objects are no longer affected by dynamics.

- Go to frame **65**, or anywhere else before the rock comes into contact with the bricks.

- With the geometry still selected, select **Soft/Rigid Bodies** → **Set Active Key**.

  The bricks will now start being dynamic only when the rock is closer to them.

> **Note:** *You can also set a dynamic initial state for the objects. An initial state tells Maya the position of the dynamics on the first animation frame. In order to set an initial state, playback your scene until you like the current position, then select* **Solvers** → **Initial State** → **Set for All Dynamic**.

9 **Test your scene**

- Set the playback range to go from **1** to **500**.

- **Playback** the animation.

The rock flying off

> **Note:** *During a dynamic simulation, if two objects intersect, a warning is displayed in the Command Feedback line and the objects are automatically selected.*

10 Correcting the rock trajectory

At this time, when you play the animation, the rock might be flying off in the wrong direction. To correct this, you can tweak the shape of the stand-in object so the rock doesn't slip out of the basket early.

• Select the *armStandIn* object.

• **Tweak** its vertices so the tip of the basket is higher as follows:

The modified stand-in object

> **Note:** *Being able to tweak the dynamic geometry is something you could not have done if the real geometry was directly used for the dynamics, thus give you more control over your simulation.*

• Go back into **Object mode**.

• Make sure the *rock* doesn't interpenetrate with the stand-in geometry.

• If you move the *rock*, you need to select **Solvers → Initial State → Set for Selected**.

• With the *armStandIn* still selected, select **Edit → Delete by Type → Rigid Bodies**.

Since you have changed the shape of the surface, the rigid body needs to be recreated.

• Select **Soft/Rigid Bodies → Create Passive Rigid Body**.

11 Assign gravity

• Select **Edit → Select All by Type → Rigid Bodies**.

• Select **Fields → Gravity**.

A new gravity field with the default earth gravity appears at the origin.

12 Rock velocity

The rock is getting its speed from the catapult arm animation. If the rock does not get to its target or overshoots it, simply change the speed of the catapult animation or adjust its tangents.

13 Rock rigid body attributes

When creating a rigid body, default dynamic values are used for such attributes as mass, friction, and bounciness. You must tweak these attributes to best reflect your scenario.

- Select the *rock*, then highlight the *rigidBody* node in the **Channel Box**.
- Set the following:

  Mass to **25**;

  Bounciness to **0.2**;

  Damping to **0.2**;

  Static Friction to **0.8**;

  Dynamic Friction to **0.8**.

  These settings reflect a heavy object that does not bounce much, and has lots of friction against other objects.

- **Playback** the animation.

14 Fine-tune the simulation

For a better simulation, the rigid bodies' attributes should be tweaked to give more realism to the scene. The following are some general steps that you should try, but the results may vary from scene to scene.

- For the *bricks*, change the following:

  Change the **Mass** attribute to between **5** and **20**.

  Lower the **Bounciness** attribute to **0.2**.

  Increase their **Static Friction** and **Dynamic Friction** attributes to **0.8**.

  Values above the rock's mass will have the rock bounce off the wall rather than destroy it. A high friction will cause all the bricks surrounding the impact to also be dragged into falling.

- For the *ground*, change the following:

  Lower the **Bounciness** attribute to **0.1**.

  Increase the **Static Friction** and **Dynamic Friction** attributes to **0.8**.

  Since the ground is made of dirt, the rock should be greatly stopped by it and not bounce.

- For the *armStandIn*, change the following:

  Lower its **Bounciness** attribute to **0.2**.

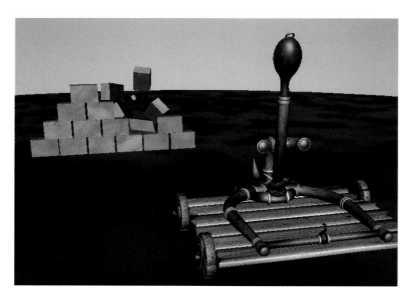

The final simulation

15 Save your work

- **Save** your scene as *26-rigidBodies_02.ma*.

Simulation cache

When you simulate rigid body dynamics, the rigid body solver recalculates the simulation every time you play through the Time Slider. You can speed up the playback of your scene by saving a rigid body cache in memory. A cache stores the positions of all the rigid bodies at every frame, letting you quickly preview the results without having to create a playblast. This offers many benefits, including the ability to scrub back and forth in the Time Slider.

If you want to tweak the objects' attributes to alter the simulation, you will not see the results until you delete the cache so that the solver can recalculate a new simulation.

1 Enable the cache

- Select **Solvers** → **Rigid Body Solver Attributes**.

  This will open the Attribute Editor for the rigid body solver in the scene.

 Note: *It is possible to have multiple rigid body solvers in a scene. This is useful when you have distinct systems that do not interact together.*

- Scroll to the **Rigid Solver States** section in the **Attribute Editor**.

- Turn **On** the **Cache Data** checkbox.
- **Rewind** and **playback** the entire scene so that the solver can create the cache.

  When it finishes playing the scene and writing the cache to memory, you should see a difference in the playback speed since it does not recalculate the simulation.

Note: *The rigid body cache is saved in the software's memory and is not written to disk.*

2 Tweak the simulation
- Select the planks and change some of their rigid body attributes.

  You should not see any difference when you playback your scene since no recalculation is done.
- Select **Solvers → Rigid Body Solver Attributes**.
- In the **Rigid Solver States** section, click the **Delete Cache** button.

  This will force the solver to recalculate the cache.
- **Rewind** your scene and **play** it so that the solver can create a new cache.
- If you want to disable the solver's cache, simply turn **Off** the **Cache Data** checkbox.

Conclusion

You have experienced the basics of the powerful dynamics tools found in Maya. You learned how to create active and passive rigid bodies, as well as gravity fields. You also tweaked their attributes to add realism to your simulation.

In the next lesson, you will change scenes and animate *Delgo* riding the catapult down a hill using a motion path.

Motion Path

In this lesson, you will animate *Delgo* riding the catapult down the hill. To do so, you will use a motion path to determine the trajectory of the catapult, then keyframe some secondary animation to refine the motion.

In this lesson you will learn the following:

- How to constrain the character to the catapult
- How to make a surface live
- How to define a motion path
- How to shape the path to edit the animation
- How to update the path markers
- How to constrain about the normals of a surface
- How to keyframe secondary animation

Path animation

Path animations are created by assigning an object or series of objects to a path. This creates a special *motionPath* node that allows you to key its motion along the path.

1 Scene file

- **Open** the scene file *20-lightsEffects_03.ma* from the last project.
- Set the frame range to go from **1** to **300**.
- **Save** your scene as *25-motionPath_01.ma*.

2 Make live

- Select the *ground* surface.
- Press **3** to display the smooth preview surface.
- Select **Modify → Make Live**.

  When making a surface live, it is displayed in green wireframe. You can then draw a curve directly on the surface, which will create a curve that follows the shape of the hill.

3 Draw a path animation curve

- Go to frame **1**.
- Select **Create → EP Curve Tool → ❏.**
- Make sure to reset the options of the tool.
- **Draw** a curve starting at the top of the hill, as follows:

Path curve

Tip: *Try to keep the curve points evenly spaced.*

- When you have finished, hit **Enter** to complete the curve.
- Select **Modify** → **Make Not Live** again to remove the live state of the hill surface.

> **Note:** *If the hill surface was made of NURBS, the curve would be projected on the surface. You could thus change the position of the curve following perfectly the surface's shape, but since the hill is made of polygons, the curve is only approximating the hill surface.*

4 Constrain *Delgo*

Before you go on with animating the catapult, you must set up *Delgo* to be perfectly synchronized with the catapult. The easiest way of doing this is to constrain *Delgo's* master node to the catapult node.

- Set the *delgo* character to be the active character set.
- Open the **Trax Editor** and **delete** the *walk* clip.
- **Pose** *Delgo* on the catapult and **keyframe** the *delgo* character set.

Delgo moved into position

- Select any plank from the catapult geometry, then **Shift-select** *Delgo's master* node.

  You are constraining to a plank because you need Delgo to perfectly follow the catapult, regardless of how you animate the master or its overrides.

- Select **Constrain** → **Parent** → ❏.
- In the options, make sure that **Maintain Offset** is set to **On**.
- Click the **Add** button.
- Test the constraint by moving the catapult's master.

  Delgo should follow the catapult perfectly.

5 Remove attributes from character set

In order to attach an object to a motion path, you need the translation and rotation attributes to be freed. At this time, the catapult master's attributes are part of the catapult character set. Here you will remove these attributes from the character set.

- Make sure the *catapult* character set is active.
- Select the catapult *master* and highlight the **Translate** and **Rotate** attributes in the **Channel Box**.
- Select **Character → Remove from Character Set**.

The attributes should now be free for the Motion Path node.

Note: *The Channel Box attributes are color coded to let you know the various states of an attribute.*
> *Locked : Grey*
> *Nonkeyable : Light grey*
> *Muted : Brown*
> *Blended : Green*
> *Keyed : Light Orange*
> *Expression : Purple*
> *Constrained : Blue*
> *Connected : Yellow*

6 Catapult pivot

When an object is attached to a motion path, the pivot of the object will follow the curve perfectly. In this example, the pivot of the catapult should be located at the base of the catapult.

- **Move** the pivot of the catapult *master* to ground level, in line with the base of the wheels.

7 Attach the catapult to the path

- Make sure the **Time Slider** range goes from **1** to **300** frames.
- Select the catapult's *master* node using the **Outliner**, then **Shift-select** the path curve.
- Go to the **Animation** menu set.
- Select **Animate → Motion Paths → Attach to Motion Path**.
- **Playback** the results.

Note: *For simplicity reasons, this lesson will not cover wheel animation.*

8 Edit the Motion Path Input node

The catapult is moving down the path, but it is not aimed in the correct direction. You can change this using the *motionPath* Input node.

- With the catapult *master* selected, open the **Attribute Editor**.
- Click the tab for *motionPath1* and set the following:

  Follow to **On**;

  Front Axis to **Z**;

  Up Axis to **Y**.

> **Tip:** *If the catapult does not face the right direction while moving down the path, change the **Front Axis** or turn **On** the **Inverse Front** checkbox.*

- **Playback** the results and notice how the catapult now points in the direction it is traveling.

Catapult attached to path

> **Note:** *You can also use the Bank option to have the object automatically roll when following the path. In this example, you will use another technique involving constraints to have the catapult follow the surface's angle.*

9 **Edit the path's shape**

Edit the shape of the path using the curve's control vertices and the object will follow the path.

- Select the path curve.
- **RMB** on the path curve and select **Control Vertices** from the context menu.
- **Move** the CVs in order to tweak how the catapult follows the hill.
- **Playback** the results.

10 **Path timing**

Notice the start and end markers on the path. They tell you the start and end frame of the animation along the path. You can insert new time keyframes and decide where the character should be on a certain frame.

- Go to frame **100**.
- Ensure that the **Auto Key** button is turned **On**.
- Select the path curve.
- In the **Channel Box**, click on the *motionPath1* Input node.
- Still in the Channel Box, click on the **U Value** channel name to highlight it.

   Notice the two keyframes in the Time Slider at the first and last frame. Those keyframes are defining the animation of the motion path from start to end.

- Hold down **Ctrl** and **click+drag** the **MMB** to change the path value at the current frame.

   This specifies a new location where the catapult should be on the path at that frame.

- Use the virtual slider to move the catapult back on the path.

   *You have just set a key on the motionPath's **U** value. Moving the value lower basically slows down the animation before that frame.*

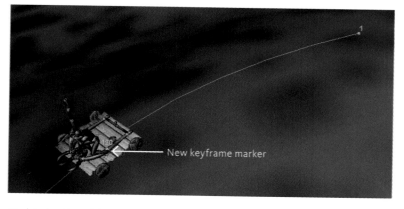

Updated path position

11 Manipulator

Instead of using the virtual slider, you can use the motion path manipulator.

- Go to frame **260**.

- With the *motionPath* still highlighted in the **Channel Box**, select the **Show Manipulator Tool** by pressing **t**.

   A manipulator appears with handles for positioning the object along the path. You will use the handle on the path to move the catapult forward, so that it speeds up as it goes down the hill.

- **Click+drag** on the center marker of the path manipulator handle to move the catapult down the hill.

   Another path marker is placed on the curve and a new key is set.

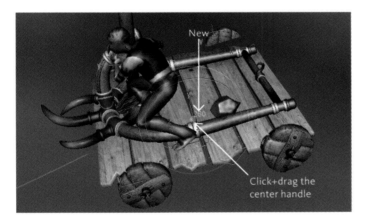

New path marker

> **Tip:** It is always good to remember that Input nodes may have manipulators that you can access using the Show Manipulator Tool.

12 Edit the path marker's position

The position of the markers can be moved to edit the animation of the catapult.

- Click on the **Auto Key** button to turn it **Off**.

- Select the **Move Tool**.

- To select the path marker that is labeled as **260**, click on the number without touching other objects or the curve.

   This will select the marker on its own.

- **Click+drag** the marker to change the position of the catapult.

   The marker is constrained to the curve as you move it.

13 Edit the timing

Since the marker points are simply keys set on the U Value of the *motionPath* node, you can edit the timing of the keys in the Graph Editor.

- Select the catapult *master* using its selection handle, and then click on the *motionPath* Input node in the **Channel Box**.

- Highlight the **U Value** in the **Channel Box**, then **RMB** and select **Editors → Graph Editor**.

- Press **a** to frame all in the **Graph Editor** window.

  The position of the attached object in the U direction of the curve is mapped against time. You can see that a key has been set for each of the path markers.

- Select the key at frame **260**.

- In the Graph Editor's **Stats** area, change the time from **260** to **190**.

- In the **Graph Editor**, select **Tangents → Spline**.

  You can edit the effect of the path keys' in-between frames using the same techniques as for normal keyframes.

- Select the keyframe at frame **100**, then **Tangents → Spline**.

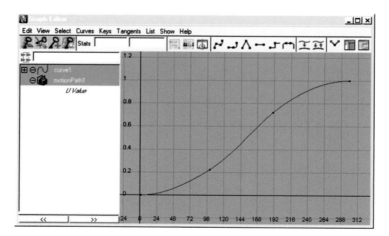

Edited path curve

You can see that the path marker is now labeled as **150** in the view panel.

Secondary animation

Now that you have a basic animation for your catapult, you can keyframe secondary animation on top of what you already have. Secondary animation usually adds life to an animation, making the scene more natural. For the catapult, you will create a normal constraint so it follows the hill, and then keyframe some drifting.

1   Normal constraint

The normal constraint is a constraint that takes the normal from a surface and applies the associated rotation to a constrained object. Here, you will constrain the normal of the hill to one of the catapult's animation override groups.

- Open the Outliner.
- Select the *ground*, then **Ctrl-select** the catapult *transOverride*, which is child of the catapult's *master* node.
- Select **Constrain → Normal → ❑**.
- **Set the options as follows:**

    Aim Vector to **0, 1, 0;**

    Up Vector to **1, 0, 0;**

    World Up Type to **Object Up;**

    World Up Object to *catapult:master.*

    You are setting the up object to be the catapult master since it already defines proper path rotation.

- Click the **Add** button.
- **Playback** the animation.

    Notice how the catapult rolls sideways when on a slope.

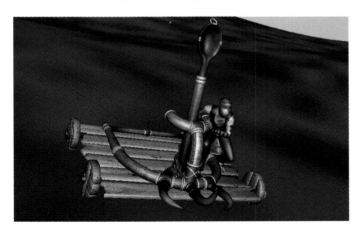

The normal constraint effect

2 **Catapult animation**

- Make sure **Auto Key** is turned **On**.
- Go to frame **1**.
- With the catapult *rotOverride* node selected, press **Shift+w** and **Shift+e** to set a keyframe on translation and rotation.
- **Rotate** the catapult so all four wheels are on the ground.
- Go to frame **100**.
- **Rotate** the catapult so all four wheels are on the ground.
- Scrub in the timeline to a place where you would like the catapult to drift.
- **Translate** the catapult towards the outside of the curve and **rotate** it towards the path.
  Doing so creates a drifting effect.
- **Move** and **rotate** the catapult so it appears on two wheels.

Drifting on two wheels position

- Scrub in the timeline to a place where the catapult should be back in control.
- Set the translation and rotation of the catapult back to **0** in all directions.

3 **Other animation**

- Spend some time animating *Delgo's* reaction to the catapult animation.
  Doing so will add lots of realism, rather than having just a stiff character following the catapult.

4 **Save your work**

- **Save** your scene as *27-motionPath_02.ma*.

5   Playblast or render the animation

Rendered scene

Conclusion

You are now more familiar with animating using motion paths, constraining, and keyframing secondary animation. As a result of your work, *Delgo* is now going downhill while riding a catapult.

You are now ready to delve into more advanced topics. In the next lesson, you will use dynamics along with particles.

Particles

Particles are small object types that can be animated using dynamic forces in place of traditional keyframes. These effects are, in essence, simulations of physical effects such as water, smoke, and dust.

To experiment with particle effects, you will add mud and dust particles to your scene. The dust will be generated using a modified version of the Maya default particle smoke effect. You will then create mud that will collide against the catapult and ground.

In this lesson, you will learn the following:

- How to add a smoke effect to an object
- How to change particle type and shading
- How to set the particles' initial state
- How to add an emitter
- How to define a particle attribute using a ramp
- How to collide particles against geometry
- How to add dynamic fields
- How to software render a particle animation
- How to hardware render a particle animation

Dust

Using one of the Maya software's preset particle effects, you will add dust to your scene. The smoke preset will create everything needed to make the particles look and act like dust.

1 **Scene file**

- **Open** the scene file *28-particles_01.ma* from the support files.

    This scene contains the same content from the last lesson, but with a simplified animation.

2 **Create an emitter object**

In order to have dust coming out from a good location on the board, you will create a curve to be used as an emitter.

- Go to frame **1**.

- Make the *ground* surface **live**.

- Use the **EP Curve Tool** to draw the following curve:

The emitter curve

> *Notice how the curve outlines the area of the catapult that will emit dust. The curve was drawn to go around the wheels in order to emit more particles from there.*

- **Parent** the curve to one of the catapult *planks* and **rename** it to *dustCurve*.

3 Adding smoke

- Press **F5** or hold down **h,** and click in the viewport to select the **Dynamics** menu set.

- Select the *dustCurve.*

- Select **Effects** → **Create Smoke** → ❑.

- Set the following:

  Sprite image name to *Smoke.0;*

  Start and **End Image** to **0**.

  The texture Smoke.0 can be found in the current project's sourceimages.

- Click the **Create** button.

  The smoke effect is the result of a particle object that is controlled by dynamic fields—in this case, turbulence. The smoke preset adds these elements to your scene and lets you easily control them.

- **Rewind** and **play** a few frames of the simulation.

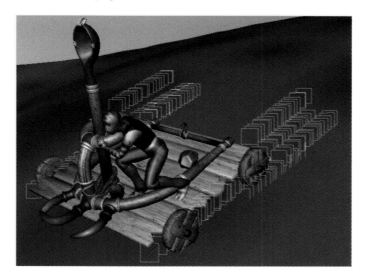

Default smoke particles

> **Note:** *When working with dynamics, it is important that you always use the rewind button to move to the beginning of your simulation and ensure that the scene playback is set to **Play every frame** in the general preferences. Never scrub through a scene that has dynamics in it unless you cache the particles to disk. Otherwise, you might get unpredictable results.*

4   Changing the emitter type

At this time, the particles are only emitting from the curve CVs. You will change this behavior so the particles emit from the entire curve length.

- In the **Outliner**, select the *SmokeEmitter*, which is the child of the *dustCurve*.
- In the **Channel Box**, set the following:

  Emitter Type to **Curve**;

  Rate to **25**.

- **Rewind** and **playback** the simulation to see the difference.

5   Smoke transparency

- Select the *SmokeParticles*.
- In the **Hypershade**, graph the material on the selected particles.
- **MMB+drag** the *file1* texture onto the *lambert2* shader, and select **Transparency**.

  Doing so will map the file texture alpha channel to the transparency of the lambert.

6   Editing the smoke attributes

You will now tweak the smoke effect to create dust-like particles.

- Select the *SmokeParticles*.
- In the **Attribute Editor**, make sure that the *SmokeParticleShape1* tab is selected.

  This is where you can change the particle's general behavior.

- Scroll to the **Lifespan Attributes** section.

  *The **Lifespan** attribute lets you determine how long the particle will remain in the scene before it disappears or dies. You will add a slight randomness to the lifespan of the particles.*

- Set the following attributes:

  Lifespan to **0.5**;

  Lifespan Random to **0.4**.

  This changes the number of seconds the smoke lives before disappearing, with a little bit of randomized values.

- Scroll down to the **Render Attributes** section.

  *Notice that the **Particle Render Type** is set to **Sprites**. This kind of particle is renderable only with the hardware renderer. This means that later, you will have to composite the final hardware rendered particles with software rendered scenes.*

- Click the **Current Render Type** button for more attributes related to this type of particle if not already displayed.

7 Animate the particle's scale

The Particle node has the ability to have new attributes added to it as needed. This lets you add complexity to a Particle node when necessary.

In this step, you will animate the particle scale using a ramp texture. Doing so will have the particles grow in size as they are emitted and scale down as they die.

- Scroll down to the **Per Particle (Array) Attributes** section in the **Attribute Editor**.
- Click on the **General** button.
- In the **Add Attribute** window, select the **Particle** tab.
- Highlight both the **spriteScaleXPP** and **spriteScaleYPP** attributes.
- Click the **OK** button.

  Doing so will add two per particle attributes in the Attribute Editor, which control the scaling of each particle.

- Still in the Attribute Editor, **RMB** in the **Sprite Scale Y PP** field and select **Create Ramp**.
- **RMB** in the **Sprite Scale Y PP** field again and select **<- arrayMapper.outValuePP → Edit Ramp**.
- **Edit** the *ramp* so it goes from **black** at the top, to **white** at about three-quarters down, to **black** at the bottom.
- **Repeat** for the **Sprite Scale X PP** attribute.
- **Rewind** and **playback** the simulation to see the difference.

The effect of the ramps

8   **Increase the scaling**

- **RMB** in the **Sprite Scale Y PP** field again and select **<- arrayMapper.outValuePP** → **Edit Array Mapper.**

- Change the **Max Value** to **5.0**.

  Doing so tells the particles to scale up to 5 when the ramp is white, which increases the particle scale.

- **Repeat** for the **Sprite Scale X PP** attribute.

- **Rewind** and **playback** the simulation to see the difference.

9   **Add color per particle**

You will now add color to the particles individually (per particle or PP), instead of as an entire group.

- In the **Add Dynamic Attributes** section of the **Attribute Editor**, click on the **Color** button.

- From the **Particle color** window, select **Add Per Particle Attribute**, then click the **Add Attribute** button.

  This adds an rgbPP line to the **Per Particle (Array) Attributes** *section.*

- Click on the **rgbPP** field with your **RMB** and select **Create Ramp**.

- Click again on the **rgbPP** field with your **RMB** and select **<-arrayMapper.outColorPP** → **Edit Ramp**.

- Set the bottom of the ramp to be **brown**.

- **Delete** the center marker, then set the top marker to be a **light grey**.

- Press **6** to go into hardware texturing mode.

10 **Setting the initial state**

One thing you may notice with the simulation is that there are no particles when the animation starts. If you want the dust to be visible right from the beginning, you must set the particles' initial state.

- Set the **Playback Range Start Time** to **-30**.

- Select the particles.

- In the **Channel Box**, set the **Start Frame** attribute to **-30**.

  Doing so tells the particles to start emitting at frame **-30**.

- **Rewind** and **playback** the scene up to frame **1**.

  Particles are emitted correctly.

- With the particles still selected, select **Solvers** → **Initial State** → **Set for Selected**.

- Set the **Playback Range Start Time** back to **1**.

- In the **Channel Box**, set the **Start Frame** attribute back to **1**.

- **Rewind** and **playback** the simulation.

  By setting the initial state for the particles, you can see that by frame 1, the particles are already created.

Final dust effect

> **Note:** *If you are to render these particles, they will not be visible using the renderers. You will see later in the lesson how to render and composite hardware particles.*

11 Save your work

- **Save** your scene as *26-particles_02.ma*.

Mud

As an added effect, you will set-up more particles that will represent the mud tracks of the wheels. To create particles that look like mud, you need to adjust various particle attributes. In this case, you will create blobby surface particles that will never die after being emitted. You will also set-up the mud to collide with the surrounding geometry.

1 Add an emitter

In order to have new particles in your scene, you must first create a particle emitter.

- Select the dust particles and press **Ctrl+h** to hide them.

- Select all four wheels.

- Press **F5** to go back to the **Dynamics** menu set, then select **Particles → Emit from Object → ❑**.

- In the option window, set the following:

    Emitter name to *mudEmitter*;

    Emitter type to **Surface**;

    Rate to **150**;

- Click the **Create** button.

    An emitter will be created for each wheel.

- **Playback** your scene to see the new default particles being emitted.

Default particles

2 **Change render type to blobby surface**

Particles can have their render type set from a list of possible looks. You can switch between the different types so you get one that suits your needs.

- Select the new particles.
- **Rename** them to *mud*.
- In the **Attribute Editor**, go to the **Render Attributes** section of the *mudShape* node.
- Set **Particle Render Type** to **Blobby Surface**.

    This render type is designed to work with software rendering. This means that you can render them directly in your scene with the software renderer.

3   **Add and edit render attributes**

   • Click on the **Current Render Type** button.

   • Set the **Render Attributes** as follows:

      Radius to **0.8**;

      Threshold to **1.0**.

   These set the blobby surface particles to blend together at render time, similar to mud.

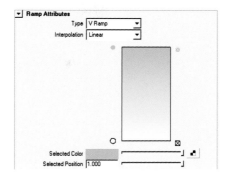

4   **Test render**

   • **Playback** your scene.

   • Select **Render → Render Current Frame**.

The rendered blobby particles

Fine-tuning the mud

The current particles don't quite move like real mud. They should react to gravity and collide with the surrounding surfaces. They should also stay stiff into position as they land on the ground, otherwise, the mud would drip down the hill.

1   **Add gravity to the particles**

   • Select *mud*.

   • From the **Fields** menu, select **Gravity**.

   A gravity field appears at the origin.

   • **Playback** the simulation.

   Now the particles drop with gravity and pass through the ground surface.

2   **Set-up particle collisions**

   To make the particles collide with the ground to create a splash, you must define them as colliding objects.

   • Select the *mud* particles.

   • Press the **Shift** key and **select** the *ground*.

   Note: *The ground should be selected last.*

- From the **Particles** menu, select **Make Collide**.
- Playback your scene.

  The particles now bounce off the ground surface.

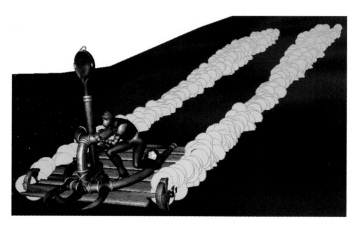

Particle collision

3 Adding friction

As you playback the scene, the mud seems to bounce off the ground. To fix this, you must change the resilience and friction attributes for the *geoConnector* node.

- Select the *mud* particles.
- At the top of the **Attribute Editor**, click on the *geoConnector* tab.

  The geoConnector object has been created for the collision object and specifies how it should affect the dynamics.

- Set the following attributes:

  Resilience to **0.5**;

  Friction to **1**.

- **Playback** the simulation.

  Now the mud reacts more realistically when colliding with the ground. Resilience is used to calculate the bounciness of a surface and friction is used to slow down the particles when they touch a surface.

4 Change the particle settings

The particles should splash out of the wheels and rise in the air before falling to the ground. The following changes some attributes on the particle to do that.

- Select the *mud* particles.

- In the **Channel Box**, set the following:

   Inherit Factor to **0.5**;

   Conserve to **0.95**.

   Doing so sets the particles to inherit velocity from their emitting surface speed, in this case, the wheels. The conserve attribute simply makes the particle lose speed as the simulation plays.

- **Playback** the simulation.

The particles splashing up

5 **Create a particle event**

   You can use the **Collision Event Tool** to emit new particles upon collision for a splash effect.

- Type *particle* in the command line at the bottom of the interface and press **Enter**.

- **Rename** the new particle object to *splash*.

   These new particles will be emitted when the first mud particle collides.

Tip:	*If you do not do this, new particles will duplicate every frame as they collide and slide on the ground.*

- Set the *splash* particles to have the same render attributes as the *mud* particles.

- Select *mud*.

- From the **Particles** menu, select **Particle Collision Event Editor**.

- At the top of the window, make sure *mud* is selected from the **Objects** list.

- In the **Particle Collision Event Editor**, go to the **Event Type** section and set the following:

> **Type** to **Emit** enabled;
>
> **Num particles** to 3;
>
> **Spread** to 1;
>
> **Target particles** to *splash*;
>
> **Inherit velocity** to 1;
>
> **Original particle dies** to **On**.

- Click **Create Event** and close the window.

The options used tell the solver to emit five smoke particles per collision with inherited velocity, and kills the original particles after the collision.

6 Fine-tune the splash particles

- Select the *splash* particles **Inherit Factor** to **1.0** and **Conserve** to **1.0.**

- Set the *splash* particles to collide with the *ground*.

- Select the *splash* particles and the *gravityField*, and select **Fields → Affect Selected Object(s)**.

- **Playback** the simulation.

Several splash particles are emitted after the mud collides with the ground.

7 Assign a shader to the mud

- In the **Hypershade**, create a new **blinn** material.

- **Rename** the blinn to *mudM*.

- **Map** a **Brownian** 3D texture to the **color** and set it to be **brown**.

 Tip: *Software particles look good when using 3D textures.*

- **Connect** the same 3D texture to the **bump map** of the Blinn shader and set its **Bump Depth** to be **0.5**.

- **Assign** the material to the *splash* and *mud* particles.

- Test render your scene.

Rendered mud

> **Tip:** *For a faster rendering, lower the anti-aliasing setting in the* **Preview quality** *preset in the* **Render Settings**.

8 Finalize the scene

- **Unhide** the *SmokeParticles*.
- Use what you have learned earlier to set the initial state for both the mud and splash particles.

9 Save your work

- **Save** the scene as *26-particles_03.ma*.

Rendering particles

It was mentioned earlier that the dust used a particle type that can only be rendered using hardware rendering, while the mud and splash used software rendering. The question, therefore, is: how do you bring hardware rendered particles together with a software rendered scene?

The answer is to render them separately, and then bring them together using a compositing package such as the *Autodesk® Toxik®* software.

To composite the smoke particles with the rest of the scene, you will need to render the top layer (in this case, the smoke) with a matte, or *mask*.

The mask is a grayscale channel that defines which areas of the color image are going to be transparent when brought into a compositing package. In this scene, the background contains all the scene's geometry.

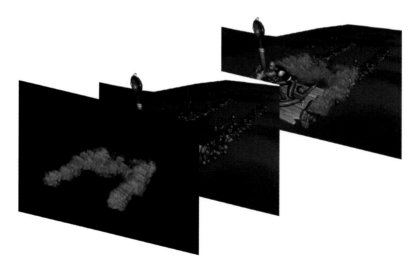

Diagram of compositing layers

Software rendering

The mud can be rendered using software rendering. This will represent the first render pass that can be later composited together with the dust.

1   **Turn Off motion blur**

    Since blobby surface particles do not render motion blur, you will turn this option off.

    - Select **Window → Rendering Editors → Render Settings.**
    - Open the **Motion Blur** section and set the **Motion blur** to **Off**.

2 Raytraced shadows

Raytraced shadows are more accurate than depth map shadows since they are calculated using rays coming from the light source. These shadows take longer to render, but can achieve a much better look.

- Select the directional light that is casting shadows in the scene.

Tip: *Make sure the sky dome surface does not cast shadows; otherwise, your entire scene will be in shadow.*

- In the **Attribute Editor**, open the **Shadows** section, scroll down to **Raytrace Shadow Attributes** and set **Use Ray Trace Shadows** to **On**.
- Set the following:

> **Light Angle** to **2**;
>
> **Shadow Rays** to **3**;
>
> **Ray Depth Limit** to **2**.

This sets up the light to use raytraced shadows, but you will need to turn on raytracing itself in the Render Settings.

- Open the **Render Settings**.
- Open the **Raytracing Quality** section and turn **Raytracing** to **On**.

Note: *Maya software uses a selective raytracer and only objects that require reflections, refractions, or raytraced shadows will use this technique. You can set this in the Attribute Editor per object under the **Render Stats** section.*

3 Limiting the reflections

When raytracing is turned on, any shader that has a reflectivity value will render with reflections. If the object is not required to be reflective, it is a good idea to turn Reflectivity off.

- Go into the *Material* node and set its **Reflectivity** to **0**.
- **Repeat** for each material in the scene that has a shader with unwanted **Reflectivity**.

  OR
- Select the geometry that you do not want to be involved in raytracing.
- Under its **Render Stats** section, turn **Visible in Reflections Off**.

When you do this, the object will not reflect and won't be calculated in the raytrace.

- **Repeat** for each object in the scene that has a shader with the **Reflectivity** attribute.

Note: *Lambert shaders do not have a reflectivity attribute.*

4 Render settings

- Open the **Render Settings**.
- Change the **Common** attributes so you can render from frames **1** to **30**.
- Change the **File name prefix** to *background*.
- Change the **Quality** preset to **Production quality**.

5 Finalize the scene

- Make sure every required display layer is visible, such as the *pfxLayer*.
- Frame the action using the camera **Resolution Gate**.
- **Save** your work.

6 Batch render the scene

- Select **File → Save Scene as...**
- Enter the file name *26-particles_background_03.ma* and click **Save**.
- Press **F6** to change to the **Rendering** menu set and select **Render → Batch Render**.

  This will render a series of images that includes the geometry, Paint Effects, and software particles.

The software render

Hardware rendering

You have been using hardware rendering in the Perspective view panel to help preview the scene. You can also use hardware rendering to render the smoke particles so that they match the rendered scene.

1   Set the hardware render attributes

- Select **Window → Rendering Editors → Render Settings**.
- Select **Render using** the **Maya Hardware** renderer.
- Change the **File name prefix** to *dust*.
- Under the **Maya Hardware** tab, change the **Enable Geometry Mask** to **On**.

   This will use the geometry as mask objects to hide particles falling behind them. An alpha channel, also known as a matte channel, is important for layering images in a compositing package.

- Change the **Motion blur** to **On**.
- Change the **Number of exposure** to **7**.

   The hardware motion blur does not work like the software motion blur. It works by rendering a certain amount of frames and blends them together to create a fake motion blur.

2   Batch render the scene

You can now render an entire animation. Compared to software rendering, the Maya Hardware renderer lets you use the speed of hardware rendering to generate animations quickly.

- Select **File → Save Scene as...**
- Enter the file name *26-particles_dust_03.ma* and click **Save**.
- Press **F6** to change to the **Rendering** menu set and select **Render → Batch Render**.

   This will create a render pass that includes only the hardware particles.

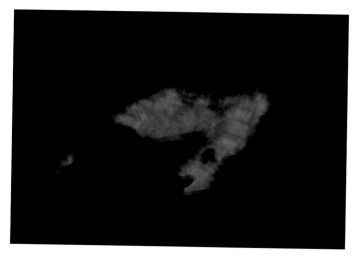

The hardware render

3 **Preview the resulting animation**

Once the rendering is finished, you can use the fcheck utility to play the rendered animation.

4 **Composite rendered animations**

You currently have a software rendered animation of mud, and a hardware rendered sequence of smoke with an embedded alpha channel. You can now use your compositing software to layer these elements together.

Final composite

There are several advantages to compositing your layers instead of rendering all of them into one scene:

- By separating background and foreground elements and rendering them individually, rendering times can be greatly reduced.

- By rendering different elements on different layers, it is easier to make revisions to one layer later without having to re-render the whole scene.

- By compositing hardware and software rendered particles, you can achieve interesting effects.

- By using different layers, your compositing software can adjust the color for one particular layer without affecting other layers.

Conclusion

You now have a better understanding of Maya hardware and software particles. You created and modified the preset smoke effect and added your own effect by customizing the emitter and particle attributes. The lesson also covered some of the most important aspects of particle simulations, including per particle attributes, gravity, collisions, and collision events.

In the next lesson you will experiment with MEL scripting.

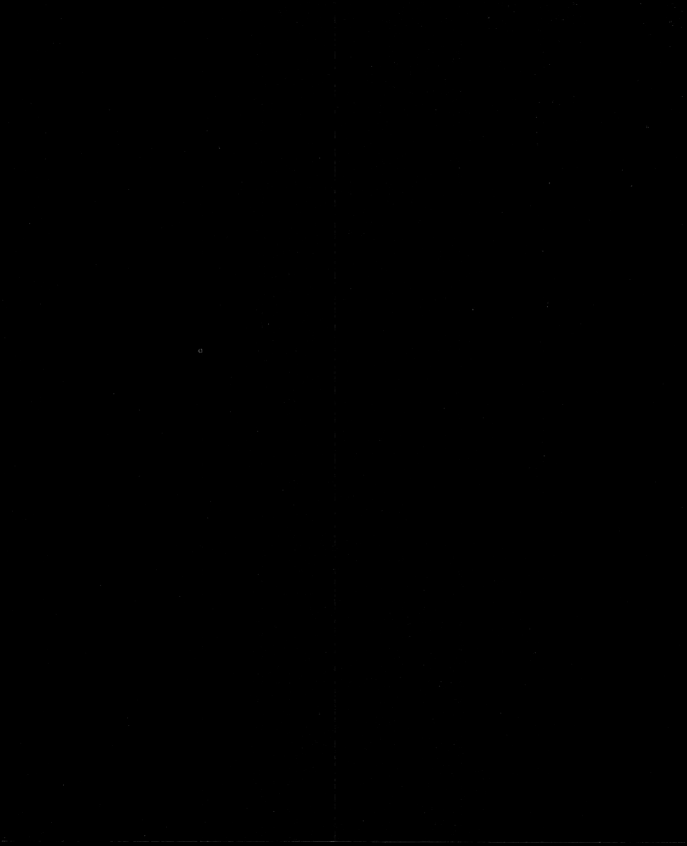

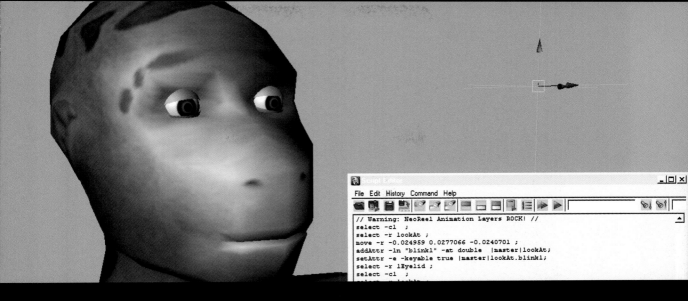

MEL Scripting

In this lesson, you will set keys on the blink attribute that you created on the lookAt node in the character rig from the second project. To help with this task, you will create a MEL (Maya Embedded Language) script that will help you animate the blink.

MEL is a powerful scripting language that can be used by both technical directors and animators to add to Maya software's capability. Animators can take advantage of simple macro-like scripts to enhance their workflows, while technical directors can use more advanced MEL commands to rig up characters, add special visual effects, or set-up customized controls.

If you know nothing about programming and scripts, this lesson will, at first, seem foreign to your world of graphics and animation. While you can certainly be successful with Maya software without relying on the use of MEL, this lesson offers a good chance to get your feet wet and see the possibilities. If you do learn how to use MEL, you might be quite surprised how a simple script can be used to enhance your work.

In this lesson, you will learn the following:

- How to recognize and enter MEL commands
- How to create a MEL script procedure
- How to use this procedure within the existing Maya UI
- How to build a custom UI element for the procedure
- How to animate the creature's blinking using the procedure

New scene

Rather than working in the character scene file, you will practice using MEL in a new scene. Once your scripts have been written and saved, you will return to the character scene and use the custom UI tools in context.

1 Start a new file

- Select **File** → **New Scene**.

- Set-up a single *Perspective* view panel.

- Make sure the Command line, the Help line, and the Channel Box are all visible. If not, you can make them visible in the **Display** → **UI Elements** menu.

What is MEL?

MEL stands for Maya Embedded Language. It is built on top of Maya software's base architecture and is used to execute commands for building scenes and creating user interface elements. In fact, every time you click on a tool, you are executing one or more MEL commands.

 Note: *This book will not cover Python™ scripting.*

A MEL command is a text string that tells the software to complete a particular action. As a user, it is possible to ignore the graphical user interface and use these commands directly. Generally, animators will choose the user interface instead, but it is still a good idea to know what MEL can do at a command level.

The Command line

You will now use the Command line to create and edit some primitive objects. The goal at this point is to explore how simple commands work.

1 Create a cone using the Command line

- Click in the Command line to make it active.

  The Command line can be found at the bottom left of the interface, just above the Help line.

- Make sure the Command line is set to accept **MEL** commands by clicking on the button on the left of the Command line until **MEL** is shown.

- Enter the following:

1.00	1.00	
MEL	cone	
Select Tool: select an object		

Entering a MEL command

- After you finish, press the **Enter** key on the numeric keypad section of your keyboard.

Tip: *The keyboard has two **Enter** keys that each work a little differently with the Command line. The **Enter** key associated with the numeric keypad keeps your focus on the Command line, while the **Enter** key associated with the alpha-numeric keyboard switches your focus back to the view panels.*

2 Rotate and move the cone with commands

The next step is to transform the cone using MEL commands.

- Enter the following:

      rotate 0 0 90 < **Enter** >

      move 5 0 0 < **Enter** >

You now have a cone sitting on the ground surface, five units along the X-axis. You first entered the command, then you added the desired values.

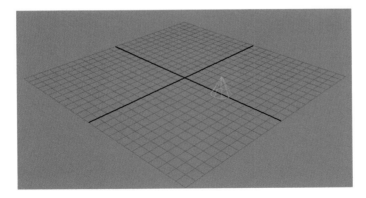

Perspective view of cone

3 Rename the cone

You can also rename objects from the Command line.

- Enter the following:

```
rename nurbsCone1 myCone
< Enter >
```

Look in the Channel Box to confirm that the object has been renamed.

Channels Edit Object Show

myCone
Translate X	5
Translate Y	0
Translate Z	0

Channel Box with cone's name

4 Execute three commands at once

If you want to quickly enter more than one command without pressing the Enter key along the way, you can place a semicolon between the commands.

- Enter the following:

```
sphere; move 0 0 6; scale 4 1 1 < Enter >
```

Using the semicolon(;), you executed three commands in a row. First, you created a sphere, then you moved it, then you scaled it. The semicolon will become more important later when you write scripts.

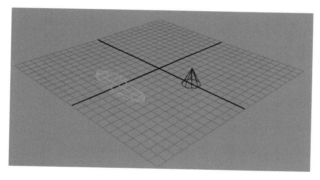

Perspective view of new sphere

5 Execute a command on an unselected object

If you want to execute a command on an object that is not selected, you simply add the name of the node that you want to affect. The node will follow the command without requiring the object to be selected.

- Enter the following:

```
move -5 0 0 mycone < Enter >
```

Oops! You got an error message saying that it cannot find the **mycone** *object. This is because the object name has a capital C for the word "Cone." MEL is case sensitive, which means you should be especially aware of how you spell and capitalize any names or commands.*

- Enter the following:

```
move -5 0 0 myCone < Enter >
scale 5 1 1 myCone < Enter >
```

Always remember the importance of spelling the commands correctly. Just like the semicolon, correct spelling will be essential later when you write scripts.

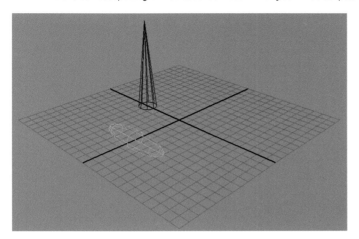

Perspective view of edited cone

6 Use command flags

Another important MEL capability is the command flag. You can use these flags to be more specific about how you want the commands to be executed. The command flags can have short or long names. Flags are indicated with a hyphen in your script. Shown below are examples of both kinds of flags.

- Enter the following using long names for flags:

```
cylinder -name bar -axis 0 1 0 -pivot 0 0 -3 < Enter >
```

- Enter the following using short names for flags:

```
cylinder -n bar2 -ax 0 1 0 -p 0 0 -6 -hr 10 < Enter >
```

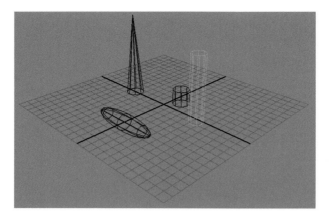

Perspective view of cylinders

The short flag names represent the following:

-n	name
-ax	axis
-p	pivot
-hr	height ratio

> **Tip:** *You will notice that long flag names can create a command that is easy to read, but hard to type in. Short names are harder to decipher, but easy to type. Generally, the Command line is a good place for entering short flags, while long flags should be used in scripts to aid in readability.*

7 Delete all objects

• Enter the following:

```
select -all; delete < Enter >
```

The Script Editor window

You may have noticed that the Command line is a small space to work in and only has one line of feedback. The Script Editor is a special user interface element that will make entering commands easier.

Up until now, you have been entering random commands in order to learn about their syntax and how they work. You will now use the Script Editor to build a sphere and a locator that will mimic the *eyeballs/lookAt* relationship that you created in the character rig from this book. The ultimate goal is to set-up a blink attribute that will control the blinking of your character's eyes.

1 Open the Script Editor window

- Click on the Script Editor button in the lower right of the workspace, or select **Window → General Editors → Script Editor**.

  The window opens to show all of the commands you just entered.

  The upper part of this window contains the commands already executed (the history), while the bottom portion is the input section where you enter commands.

- From the Script Editor, select **Edit → Clear History**.

2 Create a primitive sphere

- Select **Create → Polygon Primitives → Sphere**.

  In the Script Editor, you can see the MEL command that was used to create the sphere. Also included are the flags, with default settings presented in their short form.

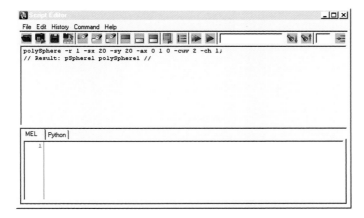

Script Editor

- In the lower portion of the Script Editor, type the following:

  ```
  delete;
  ```

- Press the numeric keypad's **Enter** key to execute the command.

> **Tip:** *In the Script Editor, the numeric keypad's **Enter** key executes an action while the alpha-numeric keypad's **Enter** key returns to the next line.*

3 Copy and edit the sphere commands

Now that the sphere command is in the Script Editor's history, you can use this command as a starting point for writing your own command.

- In the Script Editor, select the part of the command with the **-r 1** flag.

- **Copy** the text into the lower portion of the Script Editor.

  You can do this by highlighting the text and selecting **Edit** → **Copy** *from the Script Editor window, or by pressing* **Ctrl+c**. *Then, click in the input section and select* **Edit** → **Paste** *or press* **Ctrl+v**. *You could also use your* **MMB** *(***LMB** *on Macintosh), to drag and drop the script in the input section.*

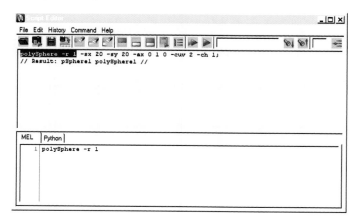

Copied script in the Script Editor

- Edit the first part of the command to read as follows:

      polySphere -r 2 -ax 1 0 0 -name eyeball

- Press the **Enter** key on your numeric keypad.

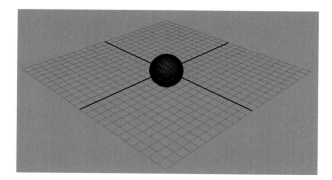

The eyeball

4 Create a locator

- Select **Create** → **Locator**.

  In the Script Editor, you will see a corresponding MEL command.

- Enter **undo** to go back one step.

5 Echo all commands

- In the Script Editor, select **History → Echo All Commands**.

- Select **Create → Locator**.

  In the Script Editor, you can now see a MEL command that you can use to create a locator:

  ```
  createPrimitive nullObject;
  ```

> **Note:** *This command is surrounded by other commands that belong to the Maya software. You only need to focus on the locator command.*

- In the Script Editor, select **History → Echo All Commands** to turn this option **Off**.

6 Rename and move the locator

You will now name the locator as *lookAt*. This object will be used as a substitute for the control node you built earlier in the character scene.

- Enter the following:

  ```
  rename locator1 lookAt;

  move 10 0 0 lookAt < Enter >
  ```

7 Add an attribute to the locator

You will now add a Blink attribute. This command is the same as using **Modify → Add Attribute** from the UI.

- Enter the following:

  ```
  addAttr -ln blink -at "float" -min 0.1 -max 1 -dv 1 lookAt < Enter >
  ```

  The short flag names represent the following;

-ln	long name of the new attribute
-at	attribute type
-min/max	minimum/maximum values for the attribute
-dv	default value for the attribute

8 Make the attribute keyable on the Blink attribute

At this time, the attribute has been added to the node, but is visible only in the Attribute Editor and not in the Channel Box until you set it to keyable. The following will solve this issue.

- Enter the following:

  ```
  setAttr -keyable true lookAt.blink < Enter >
  ```

9 **Set up your Perspective view panel**

- Set-up your view panel to see the eyeball object and locator.
- Press **5** to turn on hardware shading.
- Select **Display** → **Grid** to turn **Off** the grid.
- Select **Shading** → **Wireframe on Shaded**.

Eyeball and locator

Learning more about commands

You now know how to use a few of the many Maya software commands. To learn more about the commands, refer to the online documentation where you will find a complete list of all the commands available in MEL. Each command is listed with descriptions of the various flags.

Expressions

When you write an expression in the Expression Editor, it can be written as a MEL script. You can also use MEL to create the expressions from within the Script Editor.

You will create an expression to control the *scale Y* of the *Eyeball* node. In your character rigs, you used a different setup involving connections, but for the sake of this lesson, it will be simpler to mimic the blink by animating the scaling of the sphere. You can thus compare the use of expressions and connections.

1 **Add an expression to the eyeball**

This expression will ensure that the Blink attribute scales the eyeball on the Y-axis.

- Enter the following:

```
expression -n blinkExpression -s "eyeball.sy = lookAt.blink"
< Enter >
```

2 **Test the Blink attribute**

- Enter the following:

```
setAttr "lookAt.blink" 0.1 < Enter >
```

3 Set keys on the Blink attribute

- Enter the following:

```
setKeyframe -at blink -t 1 -v 1 lookAt;

setKeyframe -at blink -t 5 -v 0.1 lookAt;

setKeyframe -at blink -t 10 -v 1 lookAt <Enter>
```

The short flag names represent the following:

-at	attribute that is being keyed
-t	time at which you want the key set
-v	value of the attribute you want to key

- **Playback** the results.

Keys have been set on three frames so the eye is closing and opening.

Building a blink procedure

You are now going to create a blink procedure that you will save as a MEL script. The next few steps outline every part of the MEL script, with some tips on how to enter and execute it. At the end of this lesson, you will find the script without descriptive text. You can enter the script later, in case you want to read over this section first.

Writing the script

You will write the blink procedure, not in the Script Editor, but in a Text Editor. A Text Editor is an application that lets you work quickly with text and then save in a generic text format.

1 Open a Text Editor

- Open a Text Editor such as *WordPad* or *TextEdit*.

> **Tip:** *The output document needs to be a simple text file without any formatting.*

2 Type comments to create header information

Every script should start with a header that contains important information for other people who might read your script later. Below is an example header. The // placed in front of these lines indicates that they are comments and, therefore, will be ignored when you later execute the script.

• Type the following:

```
//
//      Creation Date:                          Today's date
//      Author:                                 Your name here
//
//      Description:

//                      Learning Maya tutorial script
//                      This script builds a procedure for animating
//                      the character's lookAt.blink attribute
//
```

Tip: *Do not underestimate the importance of commenting on your scripts. Down the line, someone will need to read what you have done and the comments are much easier to follow than the actual script.*

3 Declare the procedure

The first thing you enter is designed to declare the procedure. This line loads the procedure into the Maya software's memory so that it can be executed later.

• Type the following:

```
global proc blink (float $blinkDelay){
```

This line defines a procedure named *blink*. The required argument resides within the parentheses. This tells the Maya software what the script requires to execute. In this case, the length of the blink action is required. This is defined as a floating value called **$blinkDelay**. Because this value is not yet determined, it is known as a variable. The $ sign defines it as a variable. The open bracket—the { symbol—is added to the end of the declaration to let you start inputting MEL statements.

4 Set-up variables

Within your script, you will use variables to represent values that may need to change later. At the beginning of the script, you need to set-up the variables and set their value. In some cases, you may set their value with an actual number. But, for this script, you will use attribute names and values instead.

• Type the following:

```
//      Set up variables that will be used in the script

        string $blink = "lookAt.blink";
        float $time = `currentTime -query`;
        float $blinkCurrent = `getAttr $blink`;
```

The first variable set defines *$blink* as the *blink* attribute found on the *lookAt* node. The second variable queries the Maya software for the current time. The third attribute gets the actual value of the *lookAt.blink* at the queried time.

> **Note:** *To generate the quotation marks for the float $time and float $blinkCurrent in the above lines, use the ` quotation mark located to the left of the number 1 key on most keyboards.*

5   Set keys on the blinking

Next, you want to set keys on the Blink attribute at the beginning, middle, and end of the blink. The length of the blink will be defined by the *blinkDelay* variable that was set as the main argument of the procedure. Notice that while other variables were set at the beginning of the script, the *blinkDelay* is used as an argument so that you can set it when the script is executed later. As you enter the keyframe commands, notice how you use the normal set-up of command/flag/node name.

- Type the following:

```
//      set key for the blink attribute at the current time
        setKeyframe     -value $blinkCurrent
                                        -time $time
                                        -attribute $blink
                                        $blink;

//      set key for a blink of 0 half way through the blink
setKeyframe     -value 0
                                        -time ($time +
$blinkDelay/2)
                                        -attribute $blink
                                        $blink;

//      set key for the original blink value at the end of the
blink
        setKeyframe     -value $blinkCurrent
                                        -time ($time +
$blinkDelay)
                                        -attribute $blink
                                        $blink;

}
```

In this part of the script, you have set keys using the *setKeyframe* command. The keys set at the beginning and end of the blink use the queried value of the Blink attribute, while the key set in the middle uses a value of zero. At the end, a closed bracket—the } symbol—is used to declare the statement complete.

6 Save your script

You can now save your script into your Maya scripts directory. This will ensure that the procedure is easily available any time you need it.

- In your Text Editor, save the script using the following path:

```
\[user profile]\maya\scripts\blink.mel
```

> **Note:** *Because the procedure is named blink, you should save the file as "blink.mel." Though this is not required, Maya software will automatically source the script when MEL calls "blink."*

7 Loading the script

Because you named the file *blink.mel* and placed it in your *maya/scripts* directory, the script will be loaded automatically the next time you launch the Maya software. For now, you need to load the script manually.

- In the Script Editor, select **File → Source Script**...
- **Browse** for the script you saved in the last step.

  The script is loaded and you now have access to it.

8 Testing the script

If you enter `blink` with a value for the blink delay, Maya software will look in the scripts directory for a procedure called *blink.mel*.

- Set the Time Slider to frame **40**.
- Enter the following:

```
blink 10 ‹Enter›
```

- Scrub in the Time Slider to test the results.

  If this works, you can congratulate yourself on completing your first MEL script and move on to the next section.

  If it doesn't, you must have typed something incorrectly. Open the Script Editor to review its feedback to find your mistake.

9 Debugging your script

To debug your script, you need to find out which line is causing the error, and then go back and check your spelling and syntax. Did you use the correct symbols? Did you name your nodes correctly? Is your capitalization correct?

- To display line numbers in the Script Editor, enable **History → Line numbers in errors**.

Adding the function to the UI

Now that you have created your own function, you will want to have easy access to it. Below are three methods for adding your function to the default UI, which you can easily set-up using interactive methods.

1 Creating a shelf button

- In the Script Editor, select the text `blink 10`.
- Click on the selected text with the **MMB** (**LMB** on Macintosh), and drag it up to the shelf.
- Select MEL when you are asked if your script is MEL or Python.

  It is placed on the shelf with a MEL icon. You can now move the Time Slider to a new position and test it. You could also drag up different blinkDelay settings to offer different blink options. Or, you could set-up a marking menu as outlined below.

2 Creating a blink marking menu set

- Select **Window** → **Settings/Preferences** → **Marking Menu Editor**.
- Click on the **Create Marking Menu** button.
- Click on the top middle square with your **RMB** and select **Edit Menu item...** from the pop-up menu.
- In the Edit North window, type *Blink 10* in the **Label** field.
- In the **Command(s)**: field, type `blink 10`.
- Click **Save** and **Close**.
- **Repeat** for the other quadrants to set-up blink commands that use a *blinkDelay* of **20**, **30**, and **40**.
- In the **Menu name** field, enter: `blinking`.
- Click the **Save** button, then **Close**.

3 Prepare the blink marking menu for a hotkey

The blink marking menu now needs to be set-up.

- In the Marking Menus window, set the following:

  Use marking menu in to **Hotkey Editor**.

  Now the marking menu can be set-up in the Hotkey Editor so that it can be accessed using a hotkey.

- Click the **Apply Settings** button, then **Close**.

4   **Assign the blink marking menu to a hotkey**

- Select **Window** → **Settings/Preferences** → **Hotkey Editor**.

- Scroll to the bottom of the **Categories** list and click on the **User Marking Menus** category.

- In the **Commands** window, click on the **blinking_Press** listing.

- In the **Assign New HotKey** section, set the following;

    Key to **9**;

    Direction to **Press**.

A message will appear stating whether or not a particular key has been assigned or not. In this case, 9 is not assigned.

- Press the **Assign** key.

A message should appear stating that the hotkey will not work properly unless the release is also set. The Maya software will ask if you want the release key set for you.

- Click **Yes**.

- Click on **Save** in the Hotkey Editor window and then **Close**.

5   **Use the new marking menu**

- Go to frame **80**.

- Press and hold the **9** hotkey, **LMB+click**, then pick one of the blinking options from the marking menu.

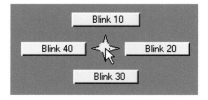

Blink marking menu

Building a custom UI script

In the next section, you will write a second script that will build a custom user interface window that includes a slider for the *blinkDelay* variable and a button that executes the blink procedure you scripted earlier. In the Maya software, you have the ability to use MEL to build custom user interface elements.

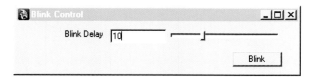

Custom user interface window

1 Start a new text file

2 Adding the opening comments

Start the script with a commented header that helps others read your work. While this was mentioned earlier, it should be emphasized again.

- Type the following:

```
//
//      Creation Date:                          Today's date
//      Author:                                 Your name here
//
//      Description:
//                      Learning Maya tutorial script
//                      This script builds a custom user interface
//                      for executing the blink procedure
//                      and for setting the blink delay
//
```

3 Declare a get info procedure

You are now going to create a procedure called *blinkGetInfo* that will be used to get the *blinkDelay* value from a slider, which you will build later in the script. Since the value set in the slider is meant to be the chosen value for the blink, this procedure queries the slider to set the *blinkDelay*, and then adds that value next to the blink command.

- Type the following:

```
global proc blinkGetInfo() {

        // get necessary information from the Maya software

        float $blinkDelay = `intSliderGrp
        -query -value blinkWindow|columnLayout|delaySlider`;

        blink $blinkDelay;
}
```

4 Declare a second user interface procedure

You are now going to declare a procedure that will build a floating window. This window will look and act like any other window in the Maya software, but will be designed to help you keyframe a blink to any of your character rigs.

- Type the following:

```
global proc blinkWindow() {
```

5 Remove any existing blink windows

As you start a user interface script, it is a good idea to check if the same UI element already exists in the scene and, if so, to delete it. This ensures that your new element is the only one recognized by the Maya software at any one time.

- Type the following:

```
// clean up any existing blinkWindows
if ( (`window -ex blinkWindow`) == true ) deleteUI
blinkWindow;
```

6 Build the window called blinkWindow

The next part of the script is designed to build a window that is 400 pixels wide and 75 pixels tall. You will call it Blink Control in its title bar, but the software will know it as *blinkWindow*.

- Type the following:

```
window
        -width 400
        -height 100
        -title "Blink Control"
blinkWindow;
```

7 Form a column layout

Within the window, you need to organize your user interface elements. One method of organization is a *columnLayout*. This sets up a column with a particular spacing in relation to the window.

- Type the following:

```
columnLayout
        -columnAttach "right" 5
        -rowSpacing 10
        -columnWidth 375
columnLayout;
```

8 Create a slider group

Within the layout, you want to build a slider that lets you set the *blinkDelay* value. MEL offers you preset *kits* using special group commands that build several UI types in one go. The *intSliderGrp* builds a slider along with a field for seeing the resulting value and for entering the value yourself. This slider is set to integer values, since frames are generally set in whole numbers. The flags let you set the various values for the minimum and maximum settings of the slider.

- Type the following:

```
intSliderGrp
        -label "Blink Delay"
        -field true
        -minValue 2
        -maxValue 30
        -fieldMinValue 0
        -fieldMaxValue 100
        -value 10
delaySlider;
```

9 Create a button

The next part of the script builds a button that you will be using to execute the *blinkGetInfo* procedure, which in turn uses the *blinkDelay* value from the slider to execute the *blink* command. At the end, you will enter *setparent* to link the button to the *columnlayout*.

- Type the following:

```
button
        -label "Blink"
        -width 70
        -command "blinkGetInfo"
button;
        setParent ..;
```

10 Show the window

You are almost finished! Now you must tell the Maya software to show the window.

- Type the following:

```
showWindow blinkWindow;
```

11 Finish the script

Finally, you must complete the procedure and make one final declaration of the *blinkWindow* procedure name.

- Type the following:

```
}
blinkWindow;
```

12 Saving the script

You can now save your script into your Maya scripts directory.

- In your Text Editor, save the script using the following path:

```
\[user profile]\maya\scripts\blinkWindow.mel
```

13 Test your script

- In the Script Editor, select **File → Source Script** and browse to the script you just saved.
- In the Command line or the Script Editor, type the following:

    `blinkWindow < Enter >`

    The window should open. You can now set the Time Slider to a new time, and then set the blink delay using the slider. Pressing the button will key the blink.

Keyframing the blink

Congratulations! You now have your own custom user interface element built and ready to go. You can open your character file, such as *13-bigzRig_05.ma,* and use this script to make the character blink.

This will only work if you named your *lookAt* node correctly and created a **Blink** attribute as outlined.

> **Note:** *If your character has been referenced, chances are that it has been prefixed with a certain string. You might have to change your scripts to reflect this name in order to have your script work.*

The scripts

Here are the two scripts listed in their entirety for you to review:

> **Tip:** *These scripts can be found in the MEL folder of the project4 support files.*

```
blink.mel
//
//       Creation Date: Today's date
//       Author:        Your name here
//
//       Description:

//                      Learning Maya tutorial script
//                      This script builds a procedure for animating
//                      the character's lookAt.blink attribute
//
global proc blink (float $blinkDelay){
//       Set up variables that will be used in the script
```

```
            string $blink = "lookAt.blink";
            float $time = `currentTime -query`;
            float $blinkCurrent = `getAttr $blink`;


//      set key for the blink attribute at the current time
        setKeyframe      -value $blinkCurrent
                         -time $time
                         -attribute $blink
                         $blink;


//      set key for a blink of 0 halfway through the blink
        setKeyframe      -value 0
                         -time ($time + $blinkDelay/2)
                         -attribute $blink
                         $blink;


//      set key for the original blink value at the end of the blink
        setKeyframe      -value $blinkCurrent
                         -time ($time + $blinkDelay)
                         -attribute $blink
                         $blink;


        }
blinkWindow.mel
//
//      Creation Date: Today's date
//      Author:        Your name here
//
//      Description:
//                     Learning Maya tutorial script
//                     This script builds a custom user interface
//                     for executing the blink procedure
//                     and for setting the blink delay
//
```

```
global proc blinkGetInfo() {

        // get necessary information from Maya

        float $blinkDelay = `intSliderGrp -query -value blinkWin
dow|columnLayout|delaySlider`;

        blink $blinkDelay;
}

global proc blinkWindow() {
        // clean up any existing blinkWindows
        if ( (`window -ex blinkWindow`) == true ) deleteUI
blinkWindow;
        window
                -width 400
                -height 100
                -title "Blink Control"
        blinkWindow;

        columnLayout
                -columnAttach "right" 5
                -rowSpacing 10
                -columnWidth 375
        columnLayout;

        intSliderGrp
                -label "Blink Delay"
                -field true
                -minValue 2
                -maxValue 30
                -fieldMinValue 0
                -fieldMaxValue 100
                -value 10
        delaySlider;
```

```
button
        -label "Blink"
        -width 70
        -command "blinkGetInfo"
button;


        setParent ..;


showWindow blinkWindow;


    }


blinkWindow;
```

Conclusion

By setting keys on the Blink attribute and using MEL to animate the blink, you took the next step toward advancing your workflow. Understanding MEL scripts and commands and how they fit into your current user interface will allow you to build custom UI elements.

In the next project, you will work with Autodesk® Toxik® software to learn more about rendering and compositing.

Project 05

In this project, you will use Autodesk® Toxik® software for compositing. You will first learn how to render using render layers and Maya's new render passes. Once that is completed, you will learn the basics of the Toxik software interface. After this project, you should feel comfortable rendering and compositing your creations.

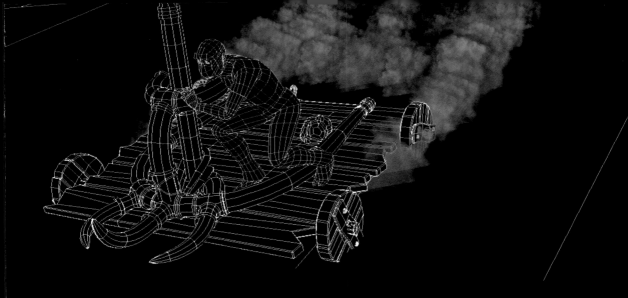

Render Layers and Render Passes

Compositing is the process of merging layers of image information into one image to create a final look. In order to create layers to composite together, you can use render layers, which allows you to separate different objects, assign different shaders, and use different Render Settings within the same scene. In this lesson, you will learn about render layers and render passes.

In this lesson, you will learn the following:

- About different rendering considerations
- How to create render layers
- How to create render passes
- How to specify Render Settings on a layer
- How to test render a layer
- How to check render passes in the preview renderer
- How to use surface shaders for compositing
- How to batch render your scene

Rendering considerations

Before rendering, you should consider which is the best renderer for your needs, as well as setting attributes on the surfaces themselves and in the Render Settings. Listed below is a checklist of some of the considerations you should keep in mind when rendering.

Object issues

Some render attributes need to be set for your objects' *Shape* nodes. You can set these attributes in the Rendering Flags window, in the *Shape* node's Render section in the Attribute Editor, or in the Attribute Spread Sheet window. Below are some of the attributes you should consider when you render.

Surface tessellation

Tessellation (called approximation in mental ray) is the process the renderer uses to convert NURBS surfaces to triangles. Triangles determine how smooth an object looks at close distance to the camera. When poorly tessellated objects are close to the camera, they appear faceted; when they are further away, they don't.

Set a NURBS surface tessellation that is appropriate to the scene. Larger and more prominent objects will require a larger tessellation than background elements.

It is important that you do not over-tessellate, otherwise you will slow down your renders.

You can also use the default tessellation settings, or choose **Explicit Tessellation** and refine even further.

Motion blur

When you turn on motion blur in the Render Settings, you can decide which objects will or will not use motion blur. If you have objects that are motionless or barely moving, turn motion blur off to speed up rendering.

You must also choose between 2D and 3D motion blur. The 2D motion blur is faster.

With the new Maya Render Passes, you are now able to render out motion vectors that can be used in a compositor such as Toxik where blur can be applied in post. The advantage of doing this is a decrease in render time as motion blur does not need to be turned on in Maya with this workflow.

Note: *If you are rendering out motion vectors, the file format must support 32bit framebuffers. At present, only the OpenEXR file format can be used to output such a file.*

Lights and shadows

Limit the number of lights casting shadows in your scene. If possible, use depth map shadows, which are a little faster. If you want to add a lot of lights to a scene, consider linking some of the lights to only those objects that need the illumination.

Render issues

Frame range

If you want to render an animation, you must choose a **Frame/Animation Ext.** in the **Render Settings** that supports animation. It is very easy to forget this and send off what you think is a long night of rendering frames, only to come in the next day to see just a single frame.

Renderable camera

Do you have the right camera set-up for rendering? By default, only the Perspective camera will be used when rendering. Do not leave the default *persp* camera as *renderable* when you want to render another camera.

Masks and depth masks

If you plan to composite your renderings later, you may want to use these settings to create a matte layer (mask) or a Z-depth layer (depth mask) to assist in the compositing process.

Render resolution

What is the render size that you want? Be sure that if you change the pixel size, you use the *resolution gate* in your view panel to make sure that the framing of your scene is preserved.

Raytracing

Do you want to raytrace some of your objects? Remember that the Autodesk® Maya® software has a selective raytracer and only objects that require reflections, refractions, or raytraced shadows will be raytraced.

Therefore, if you limit your reflective and refractive materials to key objects, you can raytrace them knowing that other objects in the scene are using the A-buffer.

If you are raytracing, try to limit the number of reflections set in the Render Settings. A setting of 1 will look good in most animations unless, for example, you have a chrome character looking into a mirror.

Render quality

You may want the *Anti-aliasing Quality presets* dropdown menu to suggest render quality options until you are familiar with the individual settings.

Other rendering considerations

Test render, test render, test render

Do not start a major rendering unless you have test rendered at various levels. You should consider rendering the entire animation at a low resolution with low quality settings and frame steps to test your scene. Render random full-size single frames to confirm that materials, lights, and objects are rendering properly.

The more you test render, the less time you spend redoing renderings that did not work out the way you wanted.

Command line rendering

You have learned how to batch render from within the Maya software. You can also render from a command prompt. Here is the basic workflow for a Maya Command line render for Windows:

- Set-up your Render Settings.

- Save your scene file.

- **Open** a command prompt.

  Windows users: Select **Start** → **Run**. In the Run prompt, type *cmd* and press **Enter**.

  Macintosh users: **Open** the **Terminal** utility. At the prompt type *cd /Applications/ Autodesk/[maya version]/Maya.app/Contents/bin/ and press **Enter**.

Note: *[maya version] corresponds to the folder of your current Maya software installation.*

- Type **Render -help** for a list of all the Command line options.

- Type **chdir** or **cd** into the directory with your file.

- Enter the **Render** command along with any flags, such as the start and end frames for the rendering, followed by the file name as shown in the following:

  ```
  Render -s 1 -e 150 -b 1 walkTest.mb
  ```

Compositing advantages

A common misconception is that compositing is for large productions with many artists. However, smaller production facilities and individual artists can also benefit from the opportunities and advantages offered by compositing. For example, with compositing you can:

- Have the flexibility to re-render or color correct individual elements without having to re-render the whole scene.

- Increase creative potential and achieve effects with a 2D compositing package that are not possible with the renderer.

- Take advantage of effects that are faster and more flexible in 2D, such as depth of field and glow, rather than rendering them in 3D.
- Combine different looks from different renderers, such as hardware and software particle effects.
- Combine 3D rendered elements with 2D live action footage.
- Save time when rendering scenes where the camera does not move—you only need to render one frame of the background to be used behind the whole animation sequence.
- Successfully render large complex scenes in layers so that you don't exceed your hardware and software memory capabilities.

Render for compositing

Rendering in layers/passes refers to the process of separating scene elements so that different objects or sets of objects can be rendered as separate images. For render layers, the first step is to determine how to divide the scene into layers. This may be very simple or incredibly complex, depending entirely on your needs for any given project. Once you have decided how you want to separate your scene elements, you can set-up render layers to suit your needs. For render passes, you determine how those layers should be outputted; whether a layer requires a reflection pass, a shadow pass, an occlusion pass, etc.

Render layers

A typical approach to separating your scene elements is to use *render layers*. You can assign objects to render layers using the same workflow as you would when working with display layers.

Render layers allow you to organize the objects in your scene specifically to meet your rendering needs. The most basic approach would be to separate objects into foreground, mid-ground, and background layers. Or, you may decide to divide the scene elements by specific objects or sets of objects.

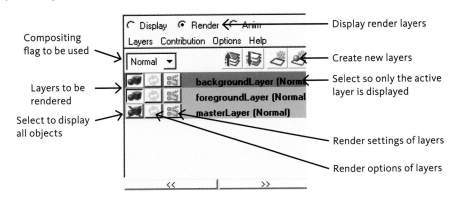

Render Layer Editor

587

Render passes

You can further breakdown your scene by rendering separate passes within any render layer. The term render passes generally refers to the process of rendering various attributes separately, such as beauty, shadow, specular, color, and diffuse. New to Maya 2009 is a functionality to facilitate the use of render passes. These can be found in the Render Settings under a new tab called **Passes**.

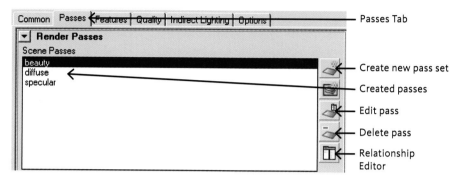

Render Settings Passes tab

> **Note:** *While the new Render Passes workflow is renderer agnostic, only mental ray can output using this method. The software renderer can use the old method of render passes but that will not be covered in this book.*

The following image shows Delgo rendered with two different render passes—specular highlights and diffuse. The image to the right shows the resulting composite image.

Diffuse and specular render passes along with composite image

Scene example

In order to experiment with render layers and render passes, you will render out an entire sequence consisting of Delgo riding a catapult down a hill.

Setting up the Render Layers

There are many elements in the scene so the first thing to do is to separate the appropriate elements into render layers. The first layer will be for most of the elements in the scene, including Delgo, the catapult, the mud, and the background. Because the Paint Effects elements only render with the software renderer, the second layer will contain all the Paint Effects elements. Lastly, the third layer will contain the dust layer. This is a user's choice as this could have been added to the passes layer. However, knowing that the dynamics type sprites are not supported by the volume pass, it might be better to have this on a separate layer.

1   **Scene file**
   - Set your current project to the *project5* folder.
   - **Open** the scene file *28-renderLayers_01.ma*.
   - Locate the correct files that this scene requires.

2   **Render layers**
   - In the **Layer Editor** located at the bottom of the **Channel Box**, select the **Render** radio button.
   - Select **Layers → Create Empty Layer**.
   - Click on the new *layer1* to highlight it.

     Notice that all objects in your scene disappear. This is because this render layer is empty.
   - Click on the *masterLayer* to highlight it.

     The masterLayer contains all the objects in your scene, so everything in the scene is displayed.

3   **Assign objects**
   - **Double-click** on the *layer1* and **rename** it to *delgoCatMudLayer*.
   - Select the *masterLayer* in order to see the content of your scene.
   - Select **Edit → Select All by Type → Polygon Geometry**.
   - **RMB** on the *delgoCatMudLayer* and select **Add Selected Objects**.
   - **Repeat** the last two steps to add all **NURBS Surfaces** to the *delgoCatMudLayer*.
   - Lastly, add the mud and splash particles to the *delgoCatMudLayer*. Open the **Outliner, Window → Outliner** and select the mud and splash nodes. **RMB** on the *delgoCatMudLayer* and select **Add Selected Objects**.

4 Assign lights

By default, the renderer will render a scene that has no lights using default lighting. The same occurs when rendering render layers. In order to get your scene to render properly, you must add your lights to the render layer.

- Select **Edit** → **Select All by Type** → **Lights**.
- **RMB** on the *delgoCatMudLayer* and select **Add Selected Objects**.

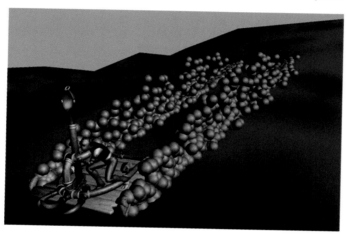

Contents of Render Layer delgoCatMudLayer

Note: *By clicking the Render button at the top of the Maya interface, or when selecting* **Render** → **Render Current Frame**, *only the selected render layer will be rendered.*

5 Render layer settings

By default, all layers use the same Render Settings, so if you change something in the Render Settings window, all the layers will be updated accordingly. Fortunately, you can create layer overrides that are layer dependent. Each render layer can then have its own Render Settings. You will now specify specific Render Settings for the geometry layer.

- Click on the **Render Settings** button located to the right in the *delgoCatMudLayer* item in the **Layer Editor**.

  Doing so brings up the Render Settings specific to this render layer.

- Set **Render Using** to **mental ray**.
- **RMB** on the **Render Using** attribute's name in the **Render Settings** window to pop up a contextual menu.
- Select **Create Layer Override** to override this attribute for the selected layer.

  Notice the overridden attribute's name is now displayed in orange.

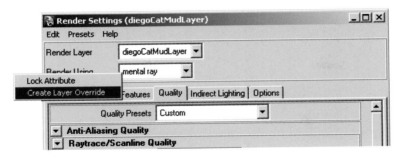

Overridden attributes in the Render Settings

Tip: Make sure to first create the layer override, and then set the attribute's value.

Tip: Macintosh users may have to **Ctrl+RMB on the File name prefix** in order to create a layer override.

6 **Setting Tokens for your File Name prefix**

Since there are going to be quite a bit of render passes for this example, it might be prudent to setup File Name prefixes with what are called tokens. Tokens are preset file structures that allow for outputs in a user defined naming convention.

- Open the **Render Settings**.

- In the **Common** tab, **RMB** select the File name prefix naming area.

  A list of preset naming conventions is displayed.

- Select **Insert Scene Name** <Scene>. The File name prefix now contains <Scene>. This indicates that when you render the scene, the output will be 28-renderLayers followed by the file type you have chosen.

- Next, let's make the naming a bit clearer. Follow the <Scene> with a '/'. Then **RMB** select the File name prefix naming area again and choose Insert layer name <RenderLayer>.

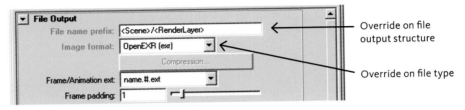

File name and image format override

Now that you've set the File name prefix token, your file output for this particular layer will be *28-renderLayers/delgoCatMudLayer.[15-60].exr.*

7 Paint Effects render layer

- Select the *masterLayer*.

- Select the *pfxGroup*.

- To create the new render layer, click on the **Create new layer and assign selected objects** button in the **Layer Editor**.

- **Rename** the layer to *pfxLayer*.

- **RMB** on the *delgoCatMudLayer* and select **Select Objects**.

- **RMB** on the *pfxLayer* and select **Add Selected Objects**.

- With the *pfxLayer* highlighted and the geometry objects still selected, go to the **Rendering** menu set and select **Lighting/Shading → Assign New Material → Surface Shader**.

  This assigns a black surface shader material to the selected objects only for the selected render layer. The Attribute Editor is shown to let you customize the new material.

- Set the **Out Matte Opacity** of the *surfaceShader* to be completely **black**.

  Doing so ensures that the surface objects render with a black alpha channel, leaving only the front particles with a proper alpha channel to be composited later on.

- **Create** a layer override on the **File name prefix** from the **Common** tab and set it to *pfx*.

- Set the proper rendering attributes to your liking for this layer.

The Paint Effects layer content

8 Dust render layer

The dust layer will be using the metal ray renderer.

- Highlight the *delgoCatMudLayer.*
- From the Layer Editor, select **Layers → Copy Layer → ❏**.
- In the option window, make sure to select the **Copy layer mode: With membership and overrides**.
- Click the **Apply and Close** button.
- **Rename** the new layer to *dustLayer.*
- Select the *mud* and *splash* particles, then **RMB** on the *dustLayer* and select **Remove Selected Objects**.
- Select the *SmokeParticle* and then **add** them to the *dustLayer*.

  You now have a layer similar to the delgoCatMudLayer, but with only the dust visible.
- Click the **Render Settings** button for the *dustLayer.*
- **Create** a layer override on the **Render Using** attribute.
- Change **Render Using** to **mental ray**.
- Set the **File name prefix** from the **Common** tab and set it to *dust.*
- Set the proper rendering attributes to your liking for this layer.

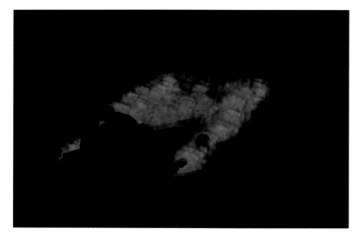

The dust layer content

Setting up the Render Passes

Now that the render layers have been set up, it's time to organize what outputs you want from each layer. In other words, setting up the render passes. In this example, only the delgoCatMudLayer will output passes while the other two layers will render as is.

Setting up render layers takes a certain amount of planning. Basically, you should know which passes you want to bring into your compositor that will best enhance your image. For the passes layer, this can be a number of things.

1 **Particles**

The first pass you might want is one that will separate out the particles from the rest of the scene. Since particles falls under the category of a volume effects, this is the pass we will use.

- Open the **Render Settings** and choose the **Passes** tab.
- Select the **Create New Render Pass** icon.

   A new window pops up called the Create Render Passes window. Here you will choose which passes to create for a given layer.

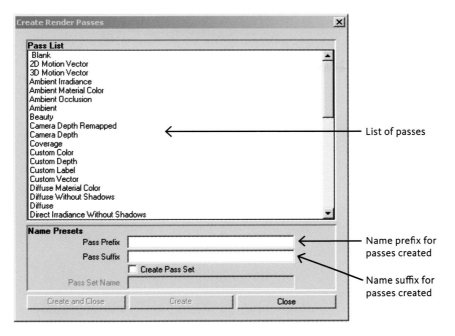

List of passes

Name prefix for passes created

Name suffix for passes created

Create Render passes window

- Scroll down the list of passes and choose the **Object Volume** pass. Then click the **Create** and **Close** button.

  Notice that a volumeObject pass has been created in the Scene Passes box in the Render Settings. The Scene Passes box contains all the passes you will have in your scene. It does not, however, have any connection to the desired render layer you want to output with.

- First, rename your pass so that it is more specific to the scene. Double click on the volumeObject pass or select the **Edit Selected Render Pass** icon.

- Change the render pass name to *mudSplashVolumeObject*. At this stage, leave all the pass options and parameters at default.

  Now we can assign the pass to a layer.

- Make sure you are on the *diegoCatapultMudSplash* layer.

- Select the *mudSplashVolumeObject*.

- Select the **Associate Selected Passes with Current Render** layer icon.

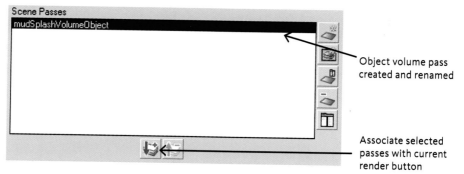

Object volume pass
created and renamed

Associate selected
passes with current
render button

Associating a pass to a layer

The pass is now connected to the *delgoCatMudLayer*. Notice that the *mudSplashVolumeObject* pass now resides in the Associated Passes box in the Render Settings. This indicates that for the *delgoCatMudLayer*, a volume pass will be rendered.

At this point, it seems that the layer needs to be separated even further; between the character (Delgo and the catapult) and the background. This can certainly be done with render layers but the new render passes workflow allows us to do this in the same layer.

Pass Contribution Maps

Pass Contribution Maps allow a user to create a subset of objects within one render layer. These subsets can contain their own set of passes. One of the advantages of using pass contribution maps is that while the objects contained in these maps render out separately, there is still an association with the rest of the objects in the layer that it is in. In other words, no additional render cycles is needed to render out these maps as there would be if you were to separate these elements into individual layers.

1   **Creating Pass Contribution Maps**

   • **RMB** on the *delgoCatMudLayer*.

   • Choose **Pass Contribution Maps → Create Empty Pass Contribution Map**.

   • An arrow is created beside the *delgoCatMudLayer*. Click on that arrow. The layer expands and will contain a *passContributionMap1* subset. It's a good idea to rename this subset right away. Double click on the name *passContributionMap1*. The name now becomes editable. Name this *catapult_diego* to indicate what is in this pass contribution map.

   • Open the **Outliner** (**Window → Outliner**) and select the *catapult:master* node.

   • **RMB** on the *catapult_delgo* pass contribution map and choose **Add Selected Objects**. The catapult is now associated with the *catapult_delgo* pass contribution map.

   • Repeat the last two steps with the *delgo:geo* node. This will add the character, *Delgo*, into the *catapult_delgo* pass contribution map.

- Create a similar pass contribution map called *'background'* where you will add the *set:environmentGroup*.

Assigning passes to pass contribution maps

Now that your pass contribution maps have been created, it's time to assign passes to them. For both the background and the *catapult_delgo* pass contribution map, we are going to create an ambient occlusion, a diffuse, an indirect light, a matte and a shadow pass. An additional couple of passes will be created for the *catapult_delgo* pass contribution map. They are the motion vector and specular pass.

1   Creating passes

- Open the **Render Settings** and go to the **Passes** tab.
- Select the **Create new render pass** icon to open the **Create Render Passes** window.
- Multi select passes by holding down the **Ctrl** key and selecting individual passes. Choose Ambient Occlusion, Diffuse Without Shadows, Indirect, Matte, and Raw Shadow.
- Instead of creating these passes and closing this window, differentiate these passes as either a *background* or a *catapult_delgo* pass. In this case, assign these passes to the background pass.
- In the **Name Presets** section of the **Create Render Passes** window, there is a **Pass Prefix** name box. Select this box and type *'background_'*.
- Select the **Create** button in the **Create Render Passes** window.
- While in the **Create Render Passes** window, create the passes for the *catapult_delgo* pass contribution map. The above passes should still be selected (if they are not, reselect them). Hold down the **Ctrl** key and add the **2D Motion Vector** and **Specular Without Shadows** passes.
- In the **Pass Prefix**, change the name from *background_* to *catapultDelgo_*.
- Now select the **Create and Close** button in the **Create Render Passes** window

    Notice that the passes have been created in the Scene Passes box in the Render Settings. Each pass though is now prefixed with either the word background_. or catapultDelgo_.

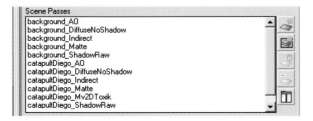

Passes created with correct prefix names

2 **Creating render pass sets**

Now that you have created all your passes, you can simply associate them with their appropriate pass contribution map. However, for organizational purposes, create a pass set for each of the *background* and the *catapult_delgo* pass contribution maps and assign the appropriate pass to them.

- While in the **Passes** tab of the **Render Settings**, click on the **Create new render pass set** icon. A new set is created in the **Scene Passes** box called *(Set) renderPassSet1*.

- Edit the name of the render pass set by selecting it and clicking the **Edit selected render pass** icon.

- Rename the set '*passSetBackground*'.

Created pass set

3 **Assigning passes to render pass sets**

- Select the **Open Relationship Editor to manage pass set membership** icon in the **Passes** tab of the **Render Settings** to open the **Relationship Editor**.

- In the **Render Pass Sets** column, choose the *passSetBackground*.

- In the *RenderPasses* column, choose all the passes you want to associate with the pass set. In this case, all the passes with the prefix *background_*.

Relationship editor

> You've now created a pass set for the background passes. Do the same for the catapultDelgo passes by creating a passSetCatapultDiego pass set.

4 **Assigning pass sets to pass contribution maps**

Now that you have your pass sets created and setup, it's time to assign them to the correct pass contribution map so that you can get the correct render outputs.

- While in the **Passes** tab of the **Render Settings**, choose the *(Set)passSetBackground* from the **Scene Passes** box.

- Make sure you are in the *delgoCatMudLayer* and select the **Associate selected passes with current render layer** icon. The *(Set)passSetBackground* is moved to the **Associated Passes** box.

- Choose background from the **Associated Pass Contribution Map** drop down menu.

  This selects the pass contribution map you want to assign the pass set to.

- Select the **Associate selected passes with current pass contribution map** icon to associate the pass set to the background subset.

- Repeat the above steps and associate your *(Set)passSetCatapultDelgo* pass set with your *catapultDelgo* pass contribution map.

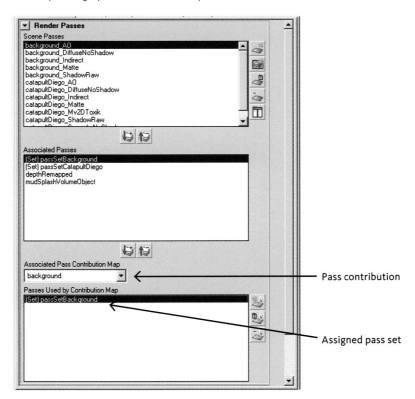

Pass contribution

Assigned pass set

Assigning a pass set to a pass contribution map

The following flow chart illustrates which passes are assigned to which layer or pass contribution map.

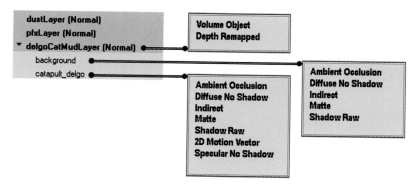

Passes associated with each layer flow chart

 Note: *Notice that an additional pass was created for the delgoCatMudLayer called the Depth Remapped pass. This will allow for additional compositing techniques.*

 Note: *Due to some limitations in Render Passes another render layer was created to output shadows from the mud particles in scene file 28-renderLayers_02.ma.*

Batch render

You now have three render layers in place ready to be rendered. You will now launch the renders with a single command once the final touches are brought to the scene.

1 Renderable camera

It is important to define the proper camera to render your scene from. By default, only the Perspective camera's **Renderable** option is turned **on**. If you keep more than one camera renderable, Maya software will be rendering all of them when batch rendering.

- Open the **Hypershade** and select the **Cameras** tab.
- In the **Attribute Editor** for each camera, make sure only the desired camera, such as the Perspective, is made **Renderable** under the **Output Settings** section.

2 Object attribute override

Just as in the Render Settings, it is possible to add render layer overrides to an object's attributes. Here you will set the sky as blue for the *delgoCatMudLayer*, but black for the other particle layers.

- With the *perspShape* camera displayed in the Attribute Editor, open the **Environment** section.

- With the *geometryLayer* highlighted, **RMB** on the **Background Color** attribute and select **Create Layer Override**.

- Set the **Background Color** to a **light blue.**

- **Repeat** the previous steps to set the **Background Color** to **black** for the *pfx* and *dust* layers.

Note: *You are doing this in case you ever see an empty area in the scene, which would be rendered with the default color.*

3 Place the camera properly

- Make sure to frame the scene properly.

Tip: *Display the camera's* **Resolution Gate** *if you want to clearly see what will be rendered.*

4 Common Render Settings

It is also very important to set the proper frames to render in the **Common** tab of the Render Settings.

- Select the *masterLayer* in the **Render Editor**.

- Click on the **Render Settings** button at the top of the Maya interface.

Notice the tabs at the top of the Render Settings window, showing all the renderers used by the layers.

- Under the **Common** tab, make sure to set the following:

  Frame/Animation ext to **name.#.ext**;

  Start Frame to **15**;

  End Frame to **60**;

  By Frame to **1**;

  Image format to **Tiff [tif].**

Note: *For render layer delgoCatMudLayer, set a layer override on the Image format and set the output for this layer to be OpenEXR.*

Tip: *For testing purposes, you might want to set a much smaller frame range.*

5 Test render the layers

- In the Layer Editor, select **Options → Render All Layers → ❑.**

  *When **Render All Layers** is enabled, this option window allows you to choose from three basic options for previewing your composite image in the Render view. The first one, **Composite layers**, will render all the layers and then composite the frames together. The second option, **Composite and keep layers**, will allow you to display all layers plus the composite images in the Render view. The third option, **Keep layers**, will only show you the individual layers.*

> **Note:** *The order of the layers will determine the order of compositing. The bottom layer is furthest from the camera and the top layer is closest to the camera.*

*When **Render All Layers** is disabled, only the current layer will be previewed in the Render view.*

> **Tip:** *You can specify for each render layer how you would like to blend the layers together by selecting a Blend Mode from the dropdown menu at the top of the* **Layer Editor.**

- Set the **Keep Layers** option, and then click the **Apply and Close** button.
- In the Layer Editor, select **Options → Render All Layers** to enable it.
- If you do not want to render a specific layer, simply toggle the **R** located on the left of the render layer item in the Layer Editor.

6 Check render passes

You'll notice that when you render in the Render View, all of render passes are combined and a final image is shown. You may want to check each of your passes before rendering out an entire sequence to make sure the outputs are correct.

- Make sure you are on the *delgoCatMudLayer* and perform a preview render.
- In the Render View window, select **File → Load Render Pass**. You should see the list of render passes that have been rendered for that particular render layer.
- Choose any of the passes you want to view. Another image viewer called *imf_disp* opens with the image of the chosen render pass.

7 Save your work

- **Save** your scene as *28-renderLayers_02.ma*.

8 Batch render

The time has come to launch a batch render and take a well-earned coffee break. The following shows how to launch a batch render.

- From the **Rendering** menu set, select **Render** → **Batch Render** → ❑.
- If your computer has multiple processors, you may profit from the use all available processors option.

The batch render options

- **Click the Batch render and close button**.

  The batch render will launch and you can read the feedback messages in the Command Feedback line at the bottom of the interface.

Tip: *If you don't want to see the batch render messages in the Command Feedback line or in the Script Editor, you can disable* **History** → **Batch Render Messages** *in the Script Editor.*

Note: *Once the batch render has started, you can close the software and the batch render will still be executed.*

9 **Look at rendered images**

- You can look in the current project's *images* folder for the output images that are placed in a folder named after each render layer.

  The rendered images will be composited together in the bonus Lesson 30.

Conclusion

In this lesson, you have learned the basics of render layers. You should now have several rendered images ready to be composited together.

In the next lesson, you will learn about the Toxik® compositing software. With your knowledge of Toxik techniques, you will be able to finalize your scene render and even implement additional effects.

Lesson 29

Toxik

This lesson is intended to provide a basic understanding of how to operate Toxik software, Autodesk's powerful desktop solution for creating stunning visual effects. It is a resolution-independent, vector paint, animation, editing, and 2D/3D compositing software application for multi-platform work—from the Web to video and HDTV to feature film.

Whether you are a motion graphics designer, animator, visual effects artist, or Web designer, Toxik software empowers you with the tools you need to create outstanding visual effects for your projects. You will now learn the basics of this compositing package.

In this lesson, you will learn the following:

- About Toxik terminology
- How to create a project
- How to use tools
- How to navigate a composition
- How to publish a composition
- About the Toxik interface

Terminology

With Autodesk® Toxik® software, you create projects that contain compositions with any number of media, effects, or compositing operations, and then the software conveniently allows you to render an output sequence.

Interface

The interface is defined by multiple viewports that allow you to simultaneously see the results of different tools. The project can be saved as presets to suit your needs depending on the work to be done.

Project

A project is simply a container for a job in a facility. The scope of a project depends on your facility's needs or individual projects. It may be a complete film, a special effects shot, an image sequence, or any other collection of shots/images. From an administrative point of view, a project is a set of folders and a set of preferences.

Media

Media is a sequence of one or more images that you import. All media are represented as RGBA images. When you import media, Toxik uses the information in the media file to determine whether the media is RGB, RGBA, or A. When you create a composition, Toxik applies the project preferences to create compositions as RGB, RGBA, or A. When you import media into Toxik, it becomes a composition that you can open or use to insert or link to/from another composition.

Composition

Once you have imported media and created a project, you will want to create a composition, set the preferences for that particular composition, and start working. The composition settings you decide upon are used for any subsequent compositions you create in the project. You can open, view, link, or insert a composition, depending on what your work requires.

Schematic

When a node is applied to the output of another node, it creates a flow of image data. A schematic is a set of connected nodes, consisting of one or more inputs, an output, and any number of effects or compositing operations.

Tools

Tools define the different actions taken in your compositing tasks in order to get to the final composition image.

 Tip: *At any time, you can select* **Help → Toxik Help** *to learn more about the software components.*

Create a project

Next, you will learn how to build a project in Toxik software. Since this is only intended to allow you to experience the various features of the software, you will open single images and manipulate them throughout this lesson.

1   Install Toxik software

A link to a trial version of Toxik can be found on the accompanying DVD. Before continuing with this project, you will need to install this package.

2   Launch Toxik software

Toxik interface without a project

3   New project

The first step to take is to create a project.

- In the Project browser, select the **New** tab.
- **Browse** to the location of the fifth project *images* folder.
- Enter a name for your project, such as *DelgoProject*.
- Click the **New** button.

  You are now presented with an empty project interface. The Toxik interface is displayed with the following views: Schematic, Player, and Details area.

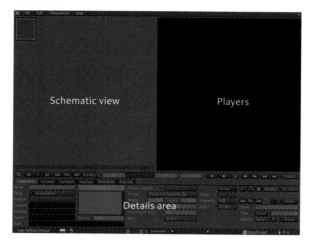

The project interface

4 Import media

As you can see, when you launch the project, the interface is empty because a composition has not been created and no media has been imported.

- Select **File → Import** or press **Ctrl+i**.

  Doing so brings up the Import browser in which you can select the media you want to import.

- You can see the files as **Proxy View** or **List View** by clicking on the **View** button. You can also choose to collapse image sequences with consecutive frame numbers.

- Select the *KylaDelgoHoldingHands.jpg* image from the *project5/image* directory of the support files.

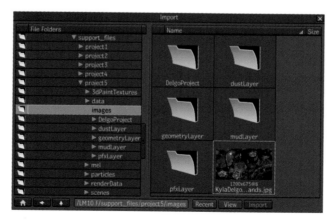

Import browser

- Click the **Import** button.

  The media files are imported into the default Footage folder.

- **Close** the import browser.

5 Create a new composition

- Select **Composition → New or press Ctrl+n**.

- Rename the new composition to your liking, such as *testComposition*.

  A composition output icon is created and appears in the Schematic view. The name of your composition is displayed at the bottom of the interface. You can now begin adding media and tools to create your new composition.

The composition output

6 Bring in your media

You can now bring in the previously imported media and connect it to the output.

- Select **Composition → Open or press Ctrl+o**.

  Doing so opens a library browser, which lists the current project structure.

- **Double-click** on the *Footage* folder.

- **Double-click** on the image imported earlier.

  Doing so automatically links the image to the Output node.

- Select the *Output* node to see the results in the player.

- Hold down **Ctrl+spacebar** to zoom in and out in the view.

- Hold down the **spacebar** to pan in the view.

- Press **Ctrl+Home** to fit the image in the view.

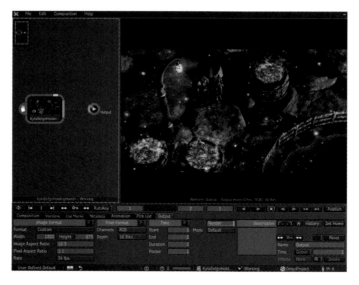

The composition interface

> **Tip:** *Click+drag on the view separator to change the sizing of the different interface sections.*

7 Open the Gate UI

The Gate UI lets you access any of the four hidden panels of the workspace. Each panel runs along one edge of the workspace. The Gate UI resembles a compass, and presents up to four gates, each referred to by one of the four cardinal directions.

- Press the **tilde** [~] hotkey located at the upper left corner of your keyboard.

  OR

- Click your **MMB**.

  This opens the Gate UI.

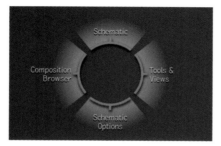

The Gate UI

8 Adding a tool

- Drag your mouse to the right over the **Tools & Views** section.

  Doing so opens the right hidden panel, which contains all the different Toxik tools and views.

- At the top of the panel, select the **Tools & View** tab.

- Select the **Effects** folder, and then pick the **Glow Tool** in the lower section of the panel.

- **Click+drag** the **Glow Tool** into the Schematic view, and **drop** it on the connection between the image media and the Output node.

  Doing so will create a Glow node in the Schematic view, and automatically connects it to your current network.

  If you drag the tool in an empty area of the Schematic view, you will have to manually connect it to your network. You can do so by dragging the connection handles, located on the outer borders of a node, to another handle on another node.

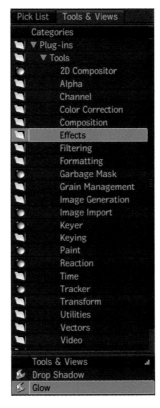

The Glow Tool selected

The new connected Glow node

Note: *Moving the mouse out of a hidden panel automatically closes it.*

9   Tweak the Glow node

- Make sure the *Glow* node is highlighted in the Schematic view.

- In the **Details** area, make sure the **Glow** tab is selected.

  The glow settings are displayed, allowing you to change them to your needs.

- Using the color tracking ball, drag the **Threshold** toward an orange, so the **RGBL** fields show **0.5**, **0.0**, **0.0**, and **0.1**.

  Doing so tells the Glow node to affect only the orange in the image.

- Drag the **Gain** toward a red, so the **RGBL** fields show **3.0**, **0.0**, **0.0**, and **0.6**.

  Doing so tells the Glow node to make the glow red.

- Change the **Master X** and **Y** option to **10**.

Note: *By default, the attributes of a duplicate vector are linked and will change all at once. You can disable this behavior by toggling off the link button at the right of an attribute.*

The Glow settings

10   Node options

In order to better see the results of a node, you can toggle its mute status.

- In the lower right section of the Details area, toggle the **Mute** button, identified by a defense icon.

The Mute button

- If you want to reset the node's settings, click the **Reset** button.
- If you want to rename the node, enter a name in the **Name** field.
- If you want to delete the node, click the **Delete** button, or press the **Delete** key on your keyboard with the node selected in the Schematic view.

11 Publish a composition

In order to save your composition, you need to publish it. By default, a composition is published as a snapshot, which means that it is not yet rendered.

- Click the **Publish** button, located at the top right corner of the Details area.
- Enter a valid name and click **OK**.

12 Render a composition

Once you are ready to render a composition follow these steps:

- Click the **Composition** tab of the Details area.
- Set the **Publish** mode to **Render**.
- Click the **Publish** button to render the composition on disk.

  The composition will be rendered in DelgoProject/publish, under the current composition version. The default output file format is set to OpenEXR.

13 Change the output file format

If required, you can change the output file format to your liking. These preferences are set for the project, which dictates the settings for all the compositions. The following will change the output format from *OpenEXR* to *Tiff*.

- Select **Edit → Preferences → Project**.

  Doing so opens a window that allows you to set the preferences for the project.

- Select the **Render** tab.
- Set the **Format** to **Tiff**.
- Close the preferences window.

14 Re-render the composition

- Select the **Versions** tab in the Details area.

  All the different published versions of the composition are listed.

- Highlight the bottom one, which should be the last rendered composition.
- Click the **Render** button located at the bottom of the list.
- In the Render dialog, choose the **Background** option, which will allow you to keep on working while the output is generated.

  When the rendering is done, a new Tiff image will be in DelgoProject/publish, under the current composition version.

15 Save the project

In order to be able to close the program and later come back to the project you just created, you will need to save your work.

- Select **File → Save Project**.

Interface overview

You are now going to review the Toxik interface. Once you have gone through this, you should be able to customize the interface and locate the various key components.

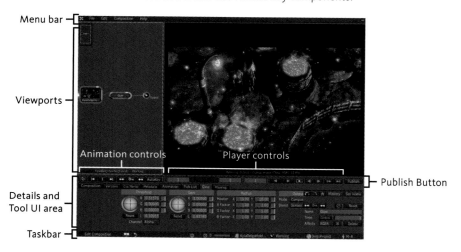

Toxik project

Task Presets

Toxik provides a flexible workspace environment that lets you work within the context of the current task at hand. You can choose from the available task presets to populate the user interface with the views you need to begin working immediately, or you can create your own presets, as well as customize existing presets according to your facility's workflow.

- Click the **Presets** menu located at the left of the taskbar.

- Try the different presets available to you by either selecting one from the list or by pressing its corresponding key on the keypad.

The preset list

Viewports

Next to the Presets item in the taskbar is the Viewport Layout menu. This menu allows you to choose the way to display the Details area and different viewports.

A viewport is simply a container where you drop a view. Like most graphical applications containing viewports or windows, you can place the cursor over a viewport border and drag to change its size.

Views

A view can be a view where you work on or view your compositions, or a browser where you work with files. You can access all available views from the Tools & Views tab using the Gate UI and then dragging a view into a viewport.

The Viewport Layout list

- Press the **Tilde** key to bring up the Gate UI, and select **Tools & Views**.
- Under the **Tools & Views** tab, scroll down to the **Views** folder.
- **Click+drag** any view to any viewport.

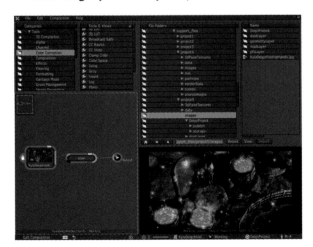

A different view layout

The following views are available:

Player

Lets you play a composition. The options for the Player determine what appears in the Player.

Schematic

Lets you build the process tree for the composition.

Pick List

Lets you store frequently used tools, views, and compositions.

Curve Editor

Lets you work with animation curves for the composition or with individual tools in the process tree for the composition.

Composition

Lets you view and work with all the tools and parameters in a composition in a browser format.

Desktop

Lets you work with a set of compositions drawn from one or more places in the project hierarchy.

Library

Lets you browse the folders in the Library folder.

Layer Editor

Lets you add, edit, and reorder layers associated with one or more Reaction Compositing nodes.

System

For administering your Toxik creative environment. Typically used to add new users and projects, and also lets you view the contents of your Library and Plug-in folders.

Track Editor

For viewing and editing animation tracks.

Import

Lets you create compositions by importing media.

Tool & Views

Lets you add a Tools and Views browser to any viewport.

Tip: *If you like to frequently add or remove a specific view to your workspace, you can add it to the Pick List for even faster access.*

Tools

The Tools & Views tab displays all the available tools you can add to your compositions, as well as the views you can display in the UI. Tools are stored in their respective category folders. When you click on a tool category folder, the tools are displayed in the lower portion of the panel.

A tool is an operation that modifies a branch or a composition. It can be as simple as a blur or as complex as painted tracked animation. Tools are processed one after another in the process tree as seen in the Schematic view. The result of one tool serves as the input for the next. You can apply a tool to a single branch or to an entire schematic, depending where you are connecting the tool.

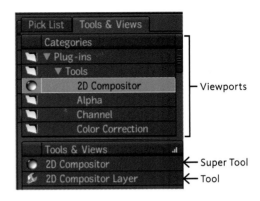

Tools and Super Tools

A Super Tool is a tool that is composed of a set of tools. Super Tools include Reaction, Garbage Mask, 2D Compositor, Image Import, Keyer, Tracker, and Paint. A sphere icon on the left of a tool indicates the tool is a Super Tool.

Pick List

The Pick List is a convenient way to access frequently used tools and other elements. You can add tools, views, and compositions to the Pick List. For example, if you add a Schematic view to the Pick List, then drag and drop it into a viewport, a Schematic view opens in that viewport. This is the same behavior that occurs when you drag the Schematic view from the Tools & Views tab into a viewport.

The Pick List is located as an independent tab in the tool UI and can also be accessed through the east gate where it resides as a tab next to the Tools and Views tab.

The Pick List

You can add and remove items in your Pick List, create a new Pick List group, delete Pick List groups you no longer use, and reorder Pick List groups. You can color code Pick List groups for easier recognition, as well as rename them. You can also set a Pick List as a default, reset a layout to that default, and restore the Pick List to the factory default group layout.

- To add an item to the Pick List, **click+drag** it to the **Pick List** tab and drop it into a group.

  OR

- **RMB** on an item and select **Add to Pick List**.

  The Pick List group which is currently highlighted in the Pick List tab will be the destination Pick List group.

- To create a new Pick List group, **RMB** anywhere in the Pick List tab and select **New Group**.

Schematic

The Schematic is the view in which you build the process tree for a composition, which is a set of connected nodes. You can set the direction in which processing proceeds in the **Edit → Preferences → User**, under the **Creative** tab. You can choose to build the process tree in a left-to-right, top-down, or bottom-top direction.

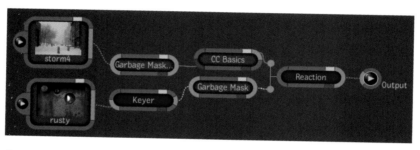

At process tree

When you create a new composition, the only node in the tree is the Output node (every composition has only one primary Output node). When you create a composition by importing media, the composition contains one Input node (which points to the media you imported) and one Output node. You then build the process tree by adding Tool nodes.

 Note: *Nodes do not necessarily have to be connected. For example, you can create branches that you connect or disconnect to experiment with different scenarios.*

Nodes

There are a number of different types of nodes, each represented by a distinct icon.

An Input node for footage is identified by a small film icon on the left of the proxy. The Link Image tab opens when a Footage Input Node is selected in the Schematic.

A Footage node

An Input node for a composition created during a media import is identified by a small sheet icon on the left of the proxy. When you select an Imported Media Input node, the tool UI displays the Import Image tab. The Input node displays a proxy of the media it references.

An Input node for a linked composition is identified by a small composition icon on the left of the proxy. When you select a Linked Composition Input node, the tool UI displays the Link Image tab. The Input node displays a proxy of the rendered output it references.

A Media Input node

A Composition node

A Tool node is created when you add it to the schematic via the Pick List or the Tools & Views panel.

A Super Tool node can have its own icon. The Reaction Super Tool icon is shown here. A Super Tool node behaves as a group node in that you can enter the node to work with the tools it contains.

A Tool node

A Super Tool node

A Group node can be created by selecting two or more nodes and grouping them together. You can right-click on a group and select Edit Group to work only with the nodes in that group.

A Group node

A process tree always has exactly one primary Output node for a composition. You cannot delete this node, but you can add secondary Output nodes to the composition. The Output node represents the result of the composition. When you select this node, the tool UI displays the Output tab. The Output node does not display a proxy of the result.

A composition can support multiple Output nodes, which provide simultaneous renders from different points in the process tree. This characteristic of the composition lets you link to a composition at different points in the process tree. A secondary Output node for a composition varies slightly in appearance from the primary Input node.

The Output node

A secondary Output node

Player controls

The player controls are shared by all player views.

The start frame, end frame, and current frame numbers in the player controls reflect those of the currently selected player.

The player controls

 Tip: *Press the **f** hotkey to toggle between regular and fullscreen display mode.*

Animation controls

The animation controls let you insert cue marks and keyframes. They also allow you to automatically set keyframes on modified attributes.

Repeat mode button

The animation controls

In order to keyframe an attribute, you must first mark it as keyframable. To do so, do the following:

- **RMB** on an attribute field to display the animation menu.

- Select **Mark Tool** to mark all the attributes of the tool for keyframing.

- Select **Mark** to mark only the current attribute for keyframing.

- Select **Set Key** to manually set a keyframe for that attribute.

The animation menu

You can set keyframes for just about anything that has a value, including an object transform, visual attribute, or any tool attribute. When you set a keyframe to animate a particular parameter, a function curve is created. The curve is a graph that represents the animation of that parameter over time. You can edit the animation by editing its curve in the Curve Editor or by modifying the attribute values in the tool UI.

Animation

If you switch to the Animation tab in the Details area, you will see the Composition Browser to the left, and the Curve Editor to the right. The Composition Browser lets you see all the attributes in your composition. Selecting animated attributes in the Composition Browser will display the keyframes and curves in the Curve Editor.

- Switch to the **Animation** tab in the **Details** area.

- In the Composition Browser, **RMB** and select **Expand All**.

- Highlight an animated attribute to see its curve in the Curve Editor.

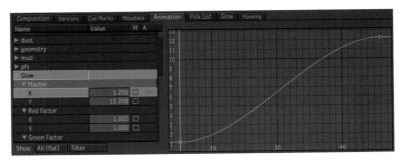

The Composition Browser and Curve Editor

Tip:	You can also switch to the Animate preset to see the Composition Browser and Curve Editor in full view.

Tool examples

Now that you know how to insert a tool in a schematic, you can experiment with any type of tool to see its effect. The following are some tools that you might use in your work.

Blur

Use the Blur Tool to finish shots that require directional, radial, modulated, and vector blurs. This includes shots that require some amount of depth of field or motion blurs. In modulated blurs, you can vary the amount of blur from pixel to pixel. The ability to vary the amount of blur applied at each pixel is sometimes useful for modeling specific physical processes or for purely artistic goals.

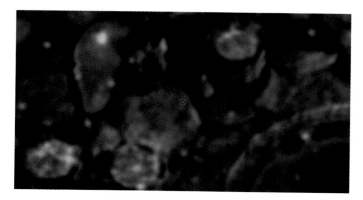

The result of a Blur Tool

Sharpen

The Sharpen Tool lets you increase the clarity and focus of an image. The Sharpen Tool applies a sharpening filter to a number of adjacent pixels in the input image and increases the pixels contrast.

The result of a Sharpen Tool

CC Basics

Use the CC Basics Tool when you need control and precision over the color adjustment of your images.

The result of a CC Basics Tool

Photo Lab

With the Photo Lab Tool, you can set the exposure, gamma, pivot, and lift of each color channel independently and in a variety of units, such as F-stops or printer lights, for exposure.

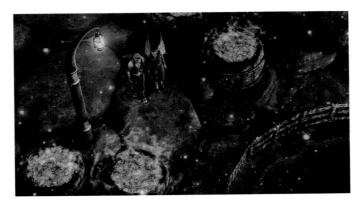

The result of a Photo Lab Tool

Lens Distort

The Lens Distort Tool lets you create or correct lens distortion that may be present in image sequences. Barrel distortion is associated with wide angle (or minimal zoom) lenses. It causes the images to appear slightly curved outward like a barrel. You can notice this when you have straight features close to the image's peripheral sides.

The result of a Lens Distort Tool

Flip

The Flip Tool lets you take an image and flip the pixels left-to-right, top-to-bottom, or both.

The result of a Flip Tool

Motio

The Motio Tool lets you generate forward and backward motion vectors, given an image source. Motion vectors can then be used as inputs for a wide variety of image transformation, analysis, or restoration tools.

The Motio Tool uses the assumption of brightness consistency of an image to generate motion vectors from one frame to the next; that is, the luminance values remain constant over time, though their 2D position in the image may change.

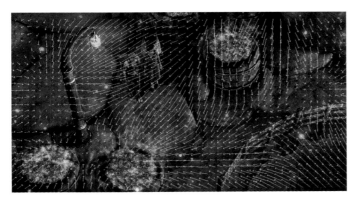

The result of a Motio Tool

Noise

The Noise Generating Tool lets you add realism to computer generated images, or to simulate or match film grain. The generator creates an image of random pixels. The Noise Generating Tool is comprised of three sets of color channel value fields that let you generate a multi-color image based on RGBA values. One set of values is for generating the fill color, and two sets are for generating start and end color values. You can also adjust the level and seed (a method used to generate the noise).

The result of a Noise Tool

Paint

The Paint Super Tool allows you to draw strokes on layers to modify your images. It also allows you to use a Clone Tool to clone different sections of the image or clone another image.

The result of a Paint Super Tool

> **Note:** You should experiment with the tools mentioned above to familiarize yourself with their different settings. Try tweaking the properties of the different tools to obtain different results. You can also enable multiple tools at the same time and change their order.

The result of combined tools

Conclusion

You have now learned the basics of Toxik software! You first learned the terminology and the interface of the software, and then you experimented with different tools to create a composition image to your liking.

Using what you have learned so far, you can now experiment on your own rendered sequences.

> **Note:** *As an added feature to this book, we have included a bonus lesson on a workflow feature that is new to Autodesk Maya 2009 and Autodesk Toxik 2009. This new workflow feature introduces interoperability that will allow users unparalleled, out-of-the-box connectivity between these two software programs.*
>
> *Once you have completed this lesson, you will be able to use Toxik to composite all of your passes, create a connection to Maya which ensures that changes made to renders are reflected in Toxik and finally you'll be able to output a final image from Toxik.*
>
> *To download this bonus lesson, please visit:*
> ***www.autodesk.com/learningtools-updates***

Index

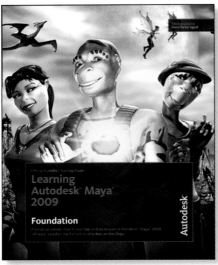

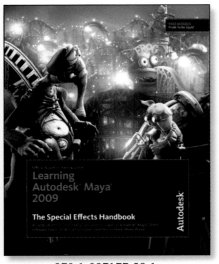
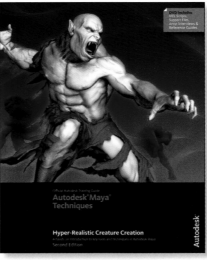

Optimize your investment in Autodesk® software.

Maximize the classroom experience with the latest product downloads, one-on-one support, and access to training and the technical knowledge base when you add Autodesk® Subscription to your Autodesk® Maya® software purchase.

With Autodesk Subscription, educational institutions can extend the value of their educational offerings with the followings benefits:

Product Downloads - Access all Maya software upgrades and bonus tools released during the subscription term – at no additional charge.

Training—Give your students access to a complete library of high-quality, self-paced interactive tutorials developed by Maya software experts.

Support*—Get direct, one-on-one communication with Maya product support specialists – minimize classroom downtime.

Knowledge Base—Easily access a searchable database of Maya solutions - a valuable classroom resource.

And receive many more premium benefits. Access all of these membership benefits quickly and easily via the Subscription Center – the exclusive online membership portal.

No Worries. No Hassles. No Waiting.

Visit **www.autodesk.com/subscription** for a complete overview and online tour. Or contact your local Autodesk authorized education reseller **www.autodesk.com/resellers**

Available for Maya Unlimited + Subscription with Gold Support only

A FREE SUBSCRIPTION LETS YOU
DISCOVER MANY WAYS TO DEVELOP
YOUR SKILLS—AND IT PUTS YOU
IN TOUCH WITH THE EXCITING AUTODESK[R]
3D ANIMATION COMMUNITY.

TUTORIALS & TIPS

DOWNLOADS

ARTISTS' SHOWCASE

COMMUNITY NETWORK

AREA

WWW.THE-AREA.COM < GO